Barron's Regents Exams and Answers

Spanish

CHRISTOPHER KENDRIS, Ph.D.
Former Chairman, Department of Foreign Languages
Farmingdale High School, Farmingdale, New York

Barron's Educational Series, Inc.

All inquiries should be addressed to:
Barron's Educational Series, Inc.
250 Wireless Boulevard
Hauppauge, New York 11788
http://www.barronseduc.com

ISBN 0-8120-3193-8
ISSN 0191-3409

PRINTED IN THE UNITED STATES OF AMERICA
9 8 7 6 5 4 3 2 1

Contents

Introduction

This book is divided into four parts.

Part One contains fifteen short warm-up tests intended for classroom use or homework to prepare for the next Spanish Regents examination. The tests cover essential points in grammar, vocabulary, and idiomatic expressions. The answers to these tests begin on page 33, right after Test 15.

Part Two contains Tests 16 to 20. They consist of five pictures to study and about which to write brief compositions. Instructions as to what to write in Spanish are found at the beginning of Part Two. This feature has been added in order to place emphasis on composition because students are expected to write in Spanish on the Regents examinations. I have, therefore, included more practice in writing Spanish, not only through picture studies in Part Two, but also in many of the short tests in Part One.

Part Three contains a thorough review of basic vocabulary and idioms, including verbal, idiomatic, common, and useful expressions. The content of this part meets the standards set by the Foreign Language Section of the Bureau of Secondary Curriculum Development of the New York State Education Department. At the beginning of Part Three there are tips on how to study and how to take the Regents exam and score high. At the end of Part Three there is a section on definitions of basic grammatical terms with examples in English and Spanish. The purpose of that new feature is to prepare you to become aware of the different parts of a sentence and the grammatical terms used when you analyze the structure of a sentence in Spanish. If you study that section thoroughly and the examples in Spanish and English, you will train yourself to analyze sentences on the next Spanish Regents test that you take. Take a minute to flip the pages to that section now to become familiar with it.

Part Four contains past and current Spanish Regents examinations and answers.

The purpose of this book—in particular, Parts One, Two, and Three— is to help the students review intensively either in the classroom or at home. I believe that the best way to review for final examinations in Spanish is to take a battery of short tests about two or three weeks before examination time.

The Listening Comprehension test in PART TWO of the Regents exam is worth 30 credits, which is a lot. You can get much needed practice and score higher by using the audiocassette that is available with this Barron's Spanish Regents book. It contains 40 selections for listening comprehension on a variety of topics and 40 multiple-choice questions based on the selections. Also included is a complete tapescript of the 60-minute cassette, with answers to questions.

If I have inadvertently omitted any points in Spanish grammar, vocabulary, and idiomatic expressions you think are important, and if you have any suggestions as to the improvement of Parts One, Two, and Three in this book, please write to me, care of the publisher so that I may include them in the next edition.

Christopher Kendris, Ph.D.

Part One

Tests 1 to 15

Short warm-up tests to practice for the next Spanish Regents Exam with answers after the last test in this part.

Test 1

A. Escriba tres oraciones en español. Dé su nombre, su edad y su nacionalidad. ______________________________

____

____

____

____

B. Escriba un antónimo.

1. a la derecha ______________________________
2. ligera ______________________________
3. arriba ______________________________
4. agradecido ______________________________
5. ausente ______________________________

C. Escriba un sinónimo.

1. divertirse ______________________________
2. regresar ______________________________
3. quizá ______________________________
4. célebre ______________________________
5. cruzar ______________________________

D. Escriba las siguientes palabras en el plural.

1. el mes ______________________
2. la lección ______________________
3. el jardín ______________________
4. el joven ______________________
5. la luz ______________________

E. Escriba el participio pasado de cada verbo.

1. hacer ______________________
2. hablar ______________________
3. aprender ______________________
4. vivir ______________________
5. abrir ______________________

F. Escriba un párrafo en español. Diga que usted quiere hacer un viaje a México, que usted no tiene dinero, que usted va a pedirle dinero a su padre, y que al regresar del viaje usted trabajará para ganar el dinero.

____

____

____

____

____

____

____

Test 2

A. Escriba la preposición si es necesario.

1. Pablo vino ______________ verme.
2. Vuelve ______________ hacerlo.
3. Mi amigo consintió ________ acompañarme al cine.
4. Los estudiantes empiezan ______________ escribir.
5. No podemos ______________ partir.

B. Escriba un párrafo en español. Diga que usted fue al teatro la semana pasada, que usted vio una comedia excelente, y que usted se divirtió muchísimo. ________

____

____

____

____

C. Traduzca al español.

1. without saying anything ______________
2. as soon as possible ______________
3. upon arriving ______________
4. to enjoy ______________
5. I like ice cream. ______________

D. Escriba tres oraciones en español. Diga a que hora usted se levantó esta mañana, que usted se duchó, y que usted se vistió. ______________________________

____

____

____

____

____

E. Escriba un antónimo.

1. bello ______________________________
2. último ______________________________
3. la llegada ______________________________
4. la guerra ______________________________
5. costoso ______________________________

F. Traduzca al inglés.

1. hacerse médico ______________________________
2. darse cuenta de ______________________________
3. un billete de ida y vuelta ______________________________
4. desempeñar el papel ______________________________
5. Si yo tuviera dinero, iría a México. ______________________________

Test 3

A. Complete las siguientes oraciones usando el verbo *hacer* en el tiempo que convenga.

1. ¿Cuánto tiempo ______ que usted vive en esta casa?
2. ¿Cuánto tiempo ___ que usted vivía en aquella casa?
3. ______________ dos semanas que no he ido al cine.
4. Si pudiera, yo lo ______________________________ .
5. Yo lo ______________________ mañana por la mañana.

B. Escriba tres oraciones en español. Diga que usted no fue al cine anoche con sus amigos, que usted se quedó en casa para leer un libro, y que usted escribió una carta a un amigo (una amiga) en España. __________

____

____

____

____

____

C. Escriba un sinónimo.

1. elegir ______________________________________
2. conquistar __________________________________
3. el lugar ____________________________________
4. enfadarse ___________________________________
5. una broma ___________________________________

D. Escriba el participio presente (gerundio) de cada verbo.

1. ganar ______
2. tener ______
3. escribir ______
4. pedir ______
5. ir ______

E. Escriba el artículo determinado o el artículo indeterminado, si es necesario.

1. Me gusta ______ leche.
2. Pablo es ______ abogado.
3. ______ Señor Robles está ausente hoy.
4. ¿Habla Vd. ______ español?
5. Vamos a la playa todos ______ veranos.

F. Escriba un antónimo.

1. nacer ______
2. disminuir ______
3. reír ______
4. la luz ______
5. la derrota ______

Test 4

A. Cambie al pretérito.

1. estoy ______________________
2. soy ______________________
3. pide ______________________
4. nos sentamos ______________________
5. dice ______________________

B. Escriba los verbos que corresponden a los siguientes sustantivos. Modelo: la bebida → beber.

1. la comida ______________________
2. la llegada ______________________
3. la salida ______________________
4. la bendición ______________________
5. la conducta ______________________

C. Traduzca al español.

1. I'm sorry but I can't. ______________________
____
2. I have to go shopping now. ______________________
____
3. At what time are we leaving? ______________________
____

D. Escriba el infinitivo de las siguientes formas, según el modelo: hizo ___hacer___

1. vuelo ____________
2. hubo ____________
3. exijo ____________
4. dio ____________
5. comiera ____________

E. Escriba tres oraciones en español. Diga que usted fue al aeropuerto ayer, que usted encontró a su amigo Miguel que es mexicano, y que su amigo pasará las vacaciones de verano en su casa. ____________

____

____

____

____

F. Traduzca las siguientes oraciones al español.

1. Good. I will be ready at six o'clock sharp. ____________
   ____
2. Michael will be ready at seven thirty in the evening.
   ____
3. We want to go to a good Spanish restaurant. ____________
   ____

Test 5

A. Escriba tres oraciones en español. Diga que usted acaba de escribir una carta, que usted escribió una carta a un amigo (una amiga) suyo (suya), y que ahora usted necesita un sello para echar la carta al correo. ________

____

____

____

____

B. Traduzca las siguientes oraciones al español.

1. I would like very much to go to the movies with you. ________
2. I can't go to the movies tonight because I have a date. ________

   ____
3. I thank you very much. ________

C. Cambie al pretérito.

1. he pedido ________
2. hemos visto ________
3. ha cubierto ________
4. nos hemos acordado ________
5. has escrito ________

D. Complete las siguientes oraciones, escogiendo la expresión que convenga.

mientras	más que
con tal que	en donde

1. La casa ______________ vivimos es grande.
2. Elena trabaja ______________ Ana.
3. Roberto vendrá a mi casa esta noche ________ no tenga mucho trabajo.
4. María cantaba ____________ Elena tocaba el piano.

E. De las palabras que se encuentran a la derecha, elija una para llenar las rayas a la izquierda. Son sinónimos.

____ semejante	1. dejar de
____ rezar	2. comida
____ luchar	3. orar
____ cesar de	4. pelear
____ alimento	5. parecido

F. Complete las siguientes oraciones usando *por o para*, según convenga.

1. El señor Fuentes habla inglés muy bien ________ un extranjero.
2. Pagué cinco dólares ______________ este libro.
3. Mi padre fue ______________ el médico.
4. Esta tarea es ______________ el lunes.
5. Juan estaba ____________ salir cuando llegó su amigo.

Test 6

A. Escriba tres oraciones en español. Diga que su padre ha comprado un automóvil, que toda la familia irá al campo este fin de semana, y que ustedes van a divertirse. ____

____

____

____

____

B. Traduzca las siguientes oraciones al español.

1. I think so. ____________
2. I am busy now. ____________
3. I am going to meet my friend at the station. ____

____

C. Complete las siguientes oraciones con la forma correcta del verbo *ir*.

1. Anoche yo ____________ al cine.
2. Mañana nosotros ____________ al parque.
3. Si tuvieran dinero, ____________ a España.
4. Todos los veranos mi familia y yo ______ a la playa.
5. ¿Quiere Vd. ____________ conmigo?

D. Cambie el orden de las palabras para hacer cada frase coherente, según el modelo:

Está no aquí María.

María no está aquí.

1. Que lleve le digo al camarero la lista de platos.

____

2. ¿Le pasó qué a María?

____

3. Cansados de viaje este estamos.

____

E. De las palabras que se encuentran a la derecha, elija una para llenar las rayas a la izquierda. Son sinónimos.

____ permiso	1. llevar
____ conducir	2. licencia
____ alzar	3. fingir
____ disimular	4. dependiente
____ empleado	5. levantar

F. **Aquí el profesor (o la profesora) hará tres preguntas. Conteste en español con frases completas.**

1. ______________________________
2. ______________________________
3. ______________________________

Test 7

A. Complete las siguientes oraciones, escogiendo la expresión que convenga.

cuyo	que
espero que	de quién

1. ¿ ________ es este cuaderno?
2. El señor Robles, ________ hijo es médico, es muy inteligente.
3. ________ mis profesores me den buenas notas.
4. Deseaba ________ no vinieran.

B. Escriba un antónimo.

1. odiar ________
2. fatigado ________
3. limpio ________
4. útil ________
5. la vuelta ________

C. Traduzca al español.

1. You know, I'm very hungry, too. ________

____

2. Don't you like this restaurant? ________

____

3. No, I don't like this restaurant. Let's go to another one. ________

____

D. Traduzca al español.

1. not even ______
2. to pay attention to ______
3. suddenly ______
4. at dawn ______
5. safe and sound ______

E

1. This restaurant is famous. ______
2. What is the specialty in this restaurant? ______
3. I think it's rice with chicken. ______

F. Escriba un párrafo en español. Diga que ciudad Ud. ha visitado recientemente, diga su nombre, diga en donde está situada la ciudad, y diga dos cosas que Ud. hizo en aquella ciudad. ______

Test 8

A. Traduzca al español.

1. from time to time ______
2. however rich he may be ______
3. nor I either ______
4. It is getting late. ______
5. They need money. ______

B. Traduzca al español.

1. What is your favorite sport? ______
2. My favorite sport is swimming. ______
3. During the summer I go to the swimming pool every day in the park. ______

C. Escriba el participio presente (gerundio) de cada verbo.

1. **abrir** ______
2. **atraer** ______
3. **seguir** ______
4. **sentir** ______
5. **hablar** ______

D. Escriba un párrafo en español. Diga que Ud. leyó un libro recientemente, diga el título, el nombre del autor, diga de que se trata, y si el libro le gustó a usted. ____________________
____
____
____

E. Escriba un antónimo.

1. fuerte ____________________
2. la mentira ____________________
3. aburrirse ____________________
4. ahorrar ____________________
5. olvidar ____________________

F. Traduzca al español.

1. Of the four seasons of the year, I prefer summer.
____
____
2. I like this season because there are no classes in July and August. ____________________
____
3. Generally, the weather is very pleasant in summer.
____
____

Test 9

A. Escriba un párrafo en español. Diga adonde Ud. irá para pasar las vacaciones de verano, las personas que estarán con usted, y diga dos cosas que Ud. hará. ____

____

____

____

____

B. Traduzca al español.

1. I prefer to stay home. ______________
2. I will arrive tomorrow. ______________
3. I'm eating right now. ______________
4. I like to read books. ______________
5. I like to walk in the rain. ______________

C. Seleccione la respuesta correcta, según convenga.

1. ¿Por qué no quiere Ud. _____ ? (a) parte (b) parta (c) partir (d) partirá
2. Aquí tiene Ud. dos naranjas. ¿ ______ prefiere Ud.? (a) Qué (b) Cuál (c) La cuál (d) La qué
3. Al __________ en la sala de clase, saludé a mi profesor de español. (a) entrando (b) entrar (c) entré (d) entró

D. Complete las siguientes oraciones con la forma correcta del verbo entre paréntesis.

1. Yo le (dar) ___ los libros a mi hermano cuando vino.
2. No conozco a nadie que (saber) ________ decírmelo.
3. Mi padre me dio dinero para que (comprar) __________ zapatos.
4. Mi madre está dándome dinero para que (comprar) ________________________________ libros.
5. Vamos a partir antes que (llegar) ______ el profesor.

E. Complete las siguientes oraciones, escogiendo la expresión que convenga.

Ojalá	para que	fuera
Si tuviera	quien	

1. Este hombre me habla como si _________ mi padre.
2. El padre le da libros a su hijo ____________ los lea.
3. La señora con _________ usted hablaba es profesora.
4. ¡ _______________ que Enrique estuviera aquí!
5. _____________________________ tiempo iría al cine.

F. Cambie a la forma negativa.

1. Démelo ______________________________
2. Dígaselo _____________________________
3. Dime ________________________________
4. Levántese ____________________________
5. Tómalo, amigo mío. ___________________

Test 10

A. Traduzca al español.

1. **Next Saturday I plan to go shopping.**

2. **I have a lot to do.**

3. **For example, I would like to buy something for my best friend.**

4. **I shall leave the house at about ten o'clock.**

5. **I shall be back around three in the afternoon.**

B. Escriba un párrafo en español sobre el tema *Mi primer día en la escuela este año.* ______________________________

____

____

____

____

C. Traduzca al inglés.

1. atreverse a + inf. ______________________________
2. tirar ______________________________
3. aprovecharse de algo ______________________________
4. despedirse de ______________________________
5. cambiarse de ropa ______________________________

D. Cambie al futuro.

1. pasé ______________________________
2. dije ______________________________
3. harían ______________________________
4. fueron ______________________________
5. vino ______________________________

E. Complete las siguientes oraciones con la forma correcta de *ser* o *estar*, según convenga.

1. Ahora María ______________________________ cansada.
2. Hoy ______________________________ el primero de junio.
3. Nosotros ______________________________ norteamericanos.
4. ______________________________ las nueve cuando salió.
5. Paco nos lo diría si ______________________________ aquí.

Test 11

A. Traduzca al español.

1. to take a nap ______
2. to make fun of ______
3. without saying good-bye ______
4. tonight ______
5. Sunday night ______

B. Traduzca al inglés.

1. poner la mesa ______
2. ponerse a + inf. ______
3. Hace un mes que estoy aquí. ______
4. equivocarse ______
5. casi ______

C. Escriba un párrafo en español sobre el tema *Mi deporte predilecto.* ______

______

______

______

D. Traduzca al español.

1. Tomorrow I'm going to take a trip with some friends of mine. ______________________________
____
____
2. I have to make preparations for the trip. ____________
____
3. I have to pack a suitcase. ______________
____
4. I have to go to bed early. ______________
____
5. I have to get up at daybreak. ____________
____

E. De las palabras que se encuentran a la derecha, elija una para llenar las rayas a la izquierda. Son sinónimos.

____ predilecto	1. el mandato
____ la orden	2. feliz
____ el enfado	3. la lengua
____ el idioma	4. favorito
____ dichoso	5. el enojo

Test 12

A. De las palabras que se encuentran a la derecha elija una para llenar las rayas a la izquierda.

____ uva	1. walnut
____ cerveza	2. grape
____ toronja	3. grapefruit
____ nuez	4. beer
____ gaseosa	5. soda pop

B. Traduzca al español.

1. unfortunately ____________________
2. to take a step ____________________
3. to take a walk ____________________
4. upon arriving ____________________
5. I am very hungry. ____________________

C. Escriba un párrafo en español. Diga que Ud. hizo un viaje recientemente, diga adonde Ud. fue, y diga cuanto tiempo Ud. se quedó allí. ____________________

____

____

____

____

D. Traduzca al inglés.

1. la muerte ____________________
2. robar ____________________
3. la sangre ____________________
4. la esperanza ____________________
5. mezclar ____________________
6. el metro ____________________
7. aborrecer ____________________
8. ciego ____________________
9. la esquina ____________________
10. mas ____________________

E. Escriba un párrafo en español sobre el tema *Como pasé el sábado pasado.* ____________________

Test 13

A. Escriba un antónimo en español.

1. modesto ______
2. lejano ______
3. la verdad ______
4. alegre ______
5. la pobreza ______

B. Escriba un párrafo en español. Diga que Ud. recibió una carta. Diga quien la escribió, si la carta es larga o corta, diga dos cosas que la carta contiene, y diga si Ud. contestó la carta. ______

C. Complete las siguientes oraciones, escogiendo la expresión que convenga.

de lo que	lo cual	qué
lo que	cuál	

1. Carlos mintió, ________ me sorprendió.
2. Este trabajo es más fácil ________ yo pensaba.
3. No comprendo ________ dice el profesor.
4. ¿ ________ es la diferencia entre éste y ése?
5. ¿ ________ quiere Ud. decir?

D. De las palabras que se encuentran a la derecha, elija una para llenar las rayas a la izquierda.

____ el pescado	1. heavy
____ pesado	2. fish
____ predilecto	3. fact
____ peor	4. worse
____ el hecho	5. favorite

E. Traduzca al español.

1. to do harm ________
2. before showing it to me ________
3. after writing it to her ________
4. to dream of ________
5. to think of ________

Test 14

A. Write a short paragraph in Spanish about a trip that you would like to take. Tell where you would go if you had enough money, what you would do and what you would see, with whom you would go, how long you would stay there, and how you would return home. ________________

B. Cambie al potencial (*conditional*).

1. iba ________________
2. pude ________________
3. puso ________________
4. saqué ________________
5. huelo ________________

C. Complete las siguientes oraciones usando la forma correcta del verbo entre paréntesis, según convenga.

1. Teresa (venir) ________ a verme la semana que viene.
2. Carlos quiso hacerlo, pero no (poder) ______________.
3. ¿Qué hora (ser) ____________ cuando vino su amigo?
4. Esta casa (ser) __________ construida por mis abuelos.
5. El chico que Ud. (ver) __________ conmigo ayer es mi hermano.

D. Aquí el profesor (o la profesora) hará tres preguntas. Conteste en español con frases completas.

1. ____
   ____
2. ____
   ____
3. ____
   ____

Test 15

A. De las palabras que se encuentran a la derecha, elija una para llenar las rayas a la izquierda.

____ fuera (de)	1. to smell
____ ganar	2. dawn
____ el miedo	3. outside
____ oler	4. to nail
____ preciso	5. earn
____ tonto	6. necessary
____ el ala	7. fear
____ el alba	8. bird
____ clavar	9. stupid, foolish
____ el ave	10. wing

B. Traduzca al inglés.

1. inquieto ______________________________
2. así como ______________________________
3. la prisa ______________________________
4. acercarse a ______________________________
5. la puesta del sol ______________________________

C. Write three or four sentences in Spanish about last Christmas. Tell where and how you spent Christmas vacation, how many cards you sent to friends, if you gave any presents, and if you received any. ______________________________
____
____
____
____
____
____
____

D. Traduzca al español.

1. before returning home ______________________
2. on Friday ______________________
3. two years ago ______________________
4. last summer ______________________
5. tomorrow night ______________________

ANSWERS TO SHORT WARM-UP TESTS 1 TO 15

Note: In the short guided composition questions, for example in A and F in Test 1, what you write may not always be phrased exactly in the same order as the sample answers given here. However, you must pay special attention to the spelling of the words, the proper verb forms, masculine or feminine agreements in the singular or plural in nouns, pronouns, adjectives, and other grammatical structures as given in these answers. All Spanish words in these tests are used in the Regents exams. If you don't know your verb forms in the various tenses, consult Barron's book, *501 Spanish Verbs*. It contains verbs fully conjugated in all the tenses in a new easy to learn format alphabetically arranged with an in-depth analysis.

Test 1

A. Mi nombre es Juan (*or* Me llamo Juan). Tengo dieciséis años. Soy norteamericano (*or, if a woman*, norteamericana).

B.
1. a la izquierda
2. pesada
3. bajo
4. desagradecido (*or* ingrato)
5. presente

C.
1. pasar un buen rato
2. volver
3. tal vez (*or* acaso)
4. famoso (*or* ilustre)
5. atravesar

D.
1. los meses
2. las lecciones
3. los jardines
4. los jóvenes
5. las luces

E.
1. hecho
2. hablado
3. aprendido
4. vivido
5. abierto

F. Quiero hacer un viaje a México pero no tengo dinero. Voy a pedirle dinero a mi padre. Al regresar del viaje trabajaré (*or* voy a trabajar) para ganar dinero.

Test 2

A. 1. a
2. a
3. en
4. por
5. no preposition needed

B. La semana pasada (yo) fui al teatro. (Yo) vi una comedia excelente. (Yo) me divertí muchísimo.

C. 1. sin decir nada
2. cuanto antes
3. al llegar
4. gozar, gustar de
5. Me gusta el helado.

D. Esta mañana me levanté a las seis y media. Me duché. Me vestí.

E. 1. feo
2. primero
3. la partida
4. la paz
5. barato

F. 1. to become a doctor
2. to realize
3. round-trip ticket
4. to play the role (part)
5. If I had money, I would go to Mexico.

Test 3

A. 1. hace
2. hacía
3. Hace
4. haría
5. haré

B. (Yo) no fui al cine anoche con mis amigos. (Yo) me quedé en casa para leer un libro. (Yo) escribí una carta a un amigo (una amiga) en España.

C. 1. escoger
2. vencer
3. el sitio
4. enojarse
5. un chiste

D. 1. ganando
2. teniendo
3. escribiendo
4. pidiendo
5. yendo

E. 1. la
2. —
3. El
4. —
5. los

F. 1. morir
2. aumentar
3. llorar
4. la sombra
5. la victoria (el triunfo)

Test 4

A. 1. estuve
2. fui
3. pidió
4. nos sentamos
5. dijo

B. 1. comer
2. llegar
3. salir
4. bendecir
5. conducir

C. 1. Lo siento pero no puedo.
2. Tengo que ir de compras ahora.
3. ¿A qué hora vamos a partir?

D. 1. volar
2. haber
3. exigir
4. dar
5. comer

E. Ayer fui al aeropuerto. Encontré a mi amigo Miguel que es mexicano. Mi amigo pasará las vacaciones de verano en mi casa.

F. 1. Bueno. Estaré listo (lista) a las seis en punto.
2. Miguel estará listo a las siete y media de la noche.
3. Queremos ir a un buen restaurante español.

Test 5

A. Acabo de escribir una carta. Escribí la carta a un amigo mío (a una amiga mía). Ahora necesito un sello para echar la carta al correo.

B. 1. Me gustaría muchísimo ir al cine contigo (*or* con usted).
2. No puedo ir al cine esta noche porque tengo cita.
3. Te (*or* Le) agradezco muchísimo.

C. 1. (Yo) pedí
2. (Nosotros) vimos
3. (Ud., él, ella) cubrió
4. (Nosotros) nos acordamos
5. (Tú) escribiste (**Note:** These verb forms are probably not easy for you to come up with. You need to know verb forms, especially for the two required compositions on the Regents exam. They are discussed in Part Three in the front part of this book where there is a section on tips about how to study and how to take the Regents exam. If you don't know your verb forms in the various tenses, consult Barron's book, *501 Spanish Verbs*.)

D. 1. en donde
2. más que
3. con tal que
4. mientras (**Note:** Study Part Three in the first half of this book where there is a lengthy section of basic vocabulary and idioms, including verbal, idiomatic, common and useful phrases and expressions.)

E. 5, 3, 4, 1, 2

F. 1. para
2. por
3. por
4. para
5. para

Test 6

A. Mi padre ha comprado un automóvil. Toda la familia irá al campo este fin de semana. Nosotros vamos a divertirnos.

B. 1. Creo que sí.
2. Estoy ocupado (ocupada) ahora.
3. Voy a encontrar a mi amigo (amiga) en la estación.

C. 1. fui
2. iremos
3. irían
4. vamos
5. ir

D. 1. Le digo al camarero que lleve la lista de platos.
2. ¿Qué le pasó a María?
3. Estamos cansados de este viaje.

E. 2, 1, 5, 3, 4

F. 1. ¿Qué dice Ud. cuando alguien llama a la puerta? (Contestación: Cuando alguien llama a la puerta, digo, "¡Adelante!").
2. ¿En qué estación del año hace frío, por lo general? (Contestación: Por lo general, hace frío en el invierno.)
3. ¿Adónde fuiste ayer? (Contestación: Fui de compras.)

Test 7

A. 1. De quién
2. cuyo
3. Espero que
4. que

B. 1. amar
2. descansado
3. sucio
4. inútil
5. la ida

C. 1. Sabes (*or* Sabe), yo también tengo mucha hambre.
2. ¿No te (*or* le) gusta este restaurante?
3. No. No me gusta este restaurante. Vamos a otro.

D. 1. ni siquiera
2. prestar atención a (*or* hacer caso de)
3. de repente (*or* repentinamente)
4. al amanecer (*or* de madrugada)
5. sano y salvo

E. 1. Este restaurante es famoso.
2. ¿Cuál es la especialidad de este restaurante?
3. Creo que es el arroz con pollo.

F. Recientemente, he visitado (visité) Madrid. Es la capital de España. La ciudad está situada aproximadamente en el centro del país. Cuando visité aquella ciudad, fui a la ópera y al Museo del Prado para ver las pinturas y las esculturas. También, vi muchas películas españolas. Hablé en español con muchas personas y ahora tengo muchos amigos madrileños.

Test 8

A. 1. de vez en cuando
2. por rico que sea
3. ni yo tampoco
4. Se hace tarde.
5. Les hace falta dinero (*or* Necesitan dinero.)

B. 1. ¿Cuál es su deporte favorito?
2. Mi deporte favorito es la natación.
3. Durante el verano, voy a la piscina en el parque todos los días.

C. 1. abriendo
2. atrayendo
3. siguiendo
4. sintiendo
5. hablando

D. Leí un libro recientemente. Es *Don Quijote de la Mancha*. El autor de esta novela es Cervantes. Se trata de las aventuras de Don Quijote y su escudero Sancho Panza. Los dos hombres son inseparables.

E. 1. débil
2. la verdad
3. divertirse (*or* pasar un buen rato)
4. gastar
5. acordarse de (*or* recordar)

F. 1. De las cuatro estaciones del año, (yo) prefiero el verano.
2. Me gusta esta estación porque no hay clases en julio y agosto.
3. Por lo general, hace buen tiempo en el verano.

Test 9

A. Iré (*or* Voy) a pasar las vacaciones de verano en la playa. Mi familia y uno de mis amigos (*or* una de mis amigas) estarán conmigo. Vamos a nadar en el mar. También, voy a tomar el sol y jugar en la arena con mi amigo (amiga).

B. 1. Prefiero quedarme en casa.
2. Llegaré (*or* Voy a llegar) mañana.
3. Estoy comiendo ahora.
4. Me gusta leer libros.
5. Me gusta pasearme en la lluvia.

C. 1. (c) 2. (b) 3. (b)

D. 1. di
2. sepa
3. comprara (*or* comprase)
4. compre
5. llegue

E. 1. fuera
2. para que
3. quien
4. Ojalá
5. Si tuviera

F. 1. No me lo dé.
2. No se lo diga.
3. No me digas.
4. No se levante.
5. No lo tomes, amigo mío.

Test 10

A. 1. El sábado que viene pienso ir de compras.
2. Tengo mucho que hacer.
3. Por ejemplo, quisiera comprar algo para mi mejor amigo (amiga).
4. Saldré de casa a eso de las diez.
5. Estaré de vuelta a eso de las tres de la tarde.

B. Mi primer día en la escuela este año era estupendo. Conocí a muchos alumnos y ahora tengo muchos amigos. Hablé en español con la profesora (el profesor) y leí en español delante de la clase. Me gusta la lectura.

C. 1. to dare
2. to pull
3. to take advantage of something
4. to take leave of, to say good-bye
5. to change one's clothing

D. 1. (Yo) pasaré
2. (Yo) diré
3. (Uds., ellos, ellas) harán
4. (Uds. ellos, ellas) irán (*or* serán)
5. (Ud., él, ella) vendrá (**Note:** If you had difficulty with these verb forms, consult Barron's book, *501 Spanish Verbs*.)

E. 1. está
2. es
3. somos
4. Eran
5. estuviera

Test 11

A. 1. dormir la siesta
2. burlarse de
3. sin despedirse (sin decir adiós)
4. esta noche
5. el domingo por la noche

B. 1. to set the table
2. to begin
3. I have been here for one month.
4. to be mistaken
5. almost, nearly

C. Mi deporte predilecto es la natación. Todos los veranos voy a la playa con mis amigos para nadar en el mar. Me gusta, también, nadar en el lago que está cerca de mi casa. Cuando no hace buen tiempo, voy a la piscina de la escuela.

D. 1. Mañana voy a hacer un viaje con unos amigos míos.
2. Tengo que hacer los preparativos para el viaje.
3. Tengo que hacer la maleta.
4. Tengo que acostarme temprano.
5. Tengo que levantarme de madrugada (al amanecer).

E. 4, 1, 5, 3, 2 (**Note:** In Part Three in the first half of this book, study the lists of antonyms (words of opposite meaning) and synonyms (words of similar meaning), following the tips on how to study and how to take a Spanish Regents exam which is in the same section.)

Test 12

A. 2, 4, 3, 1, 5

B. 1. por desgracia (desgraciadamente)
2. dar un paso
3. dar un paseo (dar una vuelta, pasearse)
4. al llegar
5. Tengo mucha hambre.

C. (Yo) hice un viaje recientemente. Fui a Puerto Rico. Me quedé allí dos semanas.

D. 1. death
2. to steal
3. blood
4. hope
5. to mix
6. subway (*or* meter)
7. to hate, to abhor
8. blind
9. outside corner
10. but

E. (Yo) pasé el sábado pasado en el parque. Jugué al tenis con mi hermano (hermana) y entonces fuimos a nadar en la piscina. Después, fuimos al cine para ver una película española. Nos divertimos mucho. Al fin del día estábamos muy cansados.

Test 13

A. 1. orgullloso
2. cercano
3. la mentira
4. triste
5. la riqueza

B. (Yo) recibí una carta. Mi amigo Paco la escribió. La carta es larga. En su carta Paco me dijo que está enfermo y no puede ir a la escuela. Tiene que quedarse en casa dos semanas. Por supuesto, contesté la carta.

C. 1. lo cual
2. de lo que
3. lo que
4. Cuál
5. Qué

D. 2, 1, 5, 4, 3

E. 1. hacer daño
2. antes de mostrármelo
3. después de escribírselo
4. soñar con
5. pensar en

Test 14

A. Si (yo) tuviera bastante dinero, me gustaría hacer un viaje al Canadá. Iría a la provincia de Quebec para ver las montañas y los lagos magníficos. Allí, me gustaría ir de camping con mi familia. Me quedaré en el Canadá dos semanas. Regresaré en el coche de mis padres.

B. 1. iría
2. podría
3. pondría
4. sacaría
5. olería

C. 1. vendrá
2. pudo
3. era
4. fue
5. vio

D. 1. ¿A qué hora se acostó usted anoche? (Anoche me acosté a las diez.)
2. ¿A qué hora se levantó? (Me levanté a las seis.)
3. ¿Cuántas horas durmió? (Dormí ocho horas.)

Test 15

A. 3, 5, 7, 1, 6, 9, 10, 2, 4, 8

B.
1. restless, uneasy, worried
2. as well as, just as
3. haste, rush
4. to approach, to draw near
5. sunset

C. El año pasado fui a casa de mis abuelos para pasar las vacaciones de Navidad con ellos. Su árbol de Navidad era muy bonito. La víspera de Navidad fuimos a la iglesia y cantamos villancicos. Di regalos a mis abuelos y me dieron dinero para comprar lo que necesito.

D.
1. antes de volver a casa
2. el viernes
3. hace dos años
4. el verano pasado
5. mañana por la noche

Part Two

Tests 16 to 20

PICTURE STUDY

INSTRUCTIONS: Study each of the five pictures in the five tests that follow.

Write a composition in Spanish telling a STORY suggested by the picture. You may include what you think happened before and after the scene.

Each composition must contain at least ten clauses. To qualify for credit, a clause must contain a verb, a stated or implied subject, and additional words necessary to convey meaning. The ten clauses may be contained in fewer than ten sentences if some of the sentences have more than one clause.

Examples:

One clause: Ayer fui al cine con mis amigos.

Two clauses: Ayer fui al cine con mis amigos para ver una película en español.

Three clauses: Ayer fui al cine con mis amigos para ver una película en español que era excelente.

Test 16

For instructions as to what to write in Spanish, see the beginning of Part Two.

Test 17

For instructions as to what to write in Spanish, see the beginning of Part Two.

Test 18

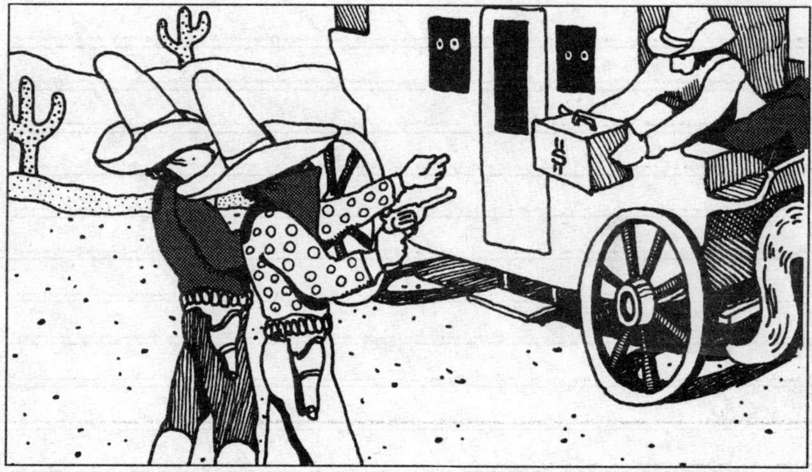

For instructions as to what to write in Spanish, see the beginning of Part Two.

Test 19

For instructions as to what to write in Spanish, see the beginning of Part Two.

Test 20

For instructions as to what to write in Spanish, see the beginning of Part Two.

Part Three

Tips on How to Study and How to Take the Regents Exam

Review of Vocabulary

Definitions of Basic Grammatical Terms with Examples in English and Spanish

Tips on How to Study and How to Take the Regents Exam

STEP 1

Let's examine carefully the most recent Regents exam and answers in the back pages of this book. Let's analyze how a perfect score of 100 percent is distributed.

PART ONE—Skill in Speaking Spanish (24 credits). Your teacher has evaluated your skill, fluency, and progress in speaking Spanish in class. Now it's the end of the school year and you're about to take the Regents examination. You ought to ask your teacher how many credits you earned of the twenty-four. If it's below half, that's not good news! This means that you have a lot of review and studying to do so you can do better than usual in the remaining parts of the Regents examination. The most important thing you need to know is vocabulary. What do all those Spanish words in the exam mean?! Tips on how to increase your vocabulary are given on page 60.

MORE TIPS

Be confident, be prepared.

SUGGESTIONS

- Review previous classroom tests and learn from your mistakes. Did you save your old tests or did you toss them out?
- At home, do the Regents exams in this book, using a clock or watch. Do one a day until you have done them all. Pretend it's Spanish Regents day. After you have finished, compare your answers with the answers in this book.
- After you have done all the Regents exams in this book, do them all again—one a day—and compare your answers with those in this book. Did you do better the second time? If not, do them again.

PART TWO—Listening Comprehension (30 credits). Twenty-four credits in Part One and thirty credits in this part add up to fifty-four! Already that's a little over half of 100 percent! How you do in this part depends on how well you understand spoken Spanish. If you feel you did not have enough practice in listening comprehension during the school year for whatever reasons, ask your teacher to spend about ten minutes near the end of each class period to read aloud one or two of the listening comprehension passages and questions that are found in the Answers section at the end of the latest exam in this book. Why not practice listening to *all* the selections in this part of the Regents exam? Part Four of this book contains many past Regents exams.

Also, ask a classmate to meet with you so you can listen to the selections and questions. You can take turns. Your friend can read aloud to you so you can listen and you can read aloud to your friend. Reading aloud and listening will tune your ear to understanding spoken Spanish and this practice will help you do better in this part of the Regents exam. There are usually fifteen passages with one question based on each. Two credits for each correct answer adds up to thirty credits. That's quite a chunk! There are four multiple-choice answers for each question. To select the correct answer, you must listen carefully to the passage that is read to you, paying careful attention to key words that you can associate with the question and the correct answer. To help yourself do your best in the listening comprehension test, do not attempt to translate silently into English what you hear in Spanish. If you do, you will fall behind the speaker and you won't hear everything spoken. Just listen to the Spanish attentively and try to get an idea of what's happening.

Also, repeat silently to yourself the Spanish words that the examiner reads to you and try to see a picture of the situation. If you don't catch all the words, don't stop to figure out what that last word meant; just keep listening and repeat all the Spanish that you hear. Some of it (maybe all of it) will stick with you so you can recognize the correct answer when you read it in the multiple-choice answers.

You can get much needed practice and score higher by using the audiocassette that comes with this Regents review book. It contains 40 selections for listening comprehension on a variety of topics and 40 multiple-choice questions based on the selections. Also included is a complete tapescript of the 60-minute cassette, with answers to questions.

MORE TIPS

Read exam instructions and questions carefully.
Budget your exam time.

SUGGESTIONS

- Be familiar with the expectations of the examination ahead of time.
- Read carefully the instructions on the exam and if you don't understand them clearly, ask the examiner to explain them.
- Where there is a choice of questions, read them all carefully. When you make a decision, practice writing the answer in Spanish on the blank practice sheet of paper.
- Remember that there is a lot of Spanish printed in the examination booklet. Therefore, look for Spanish words that you can use in your compositions in another part of the exam.
- Underline important words and phrases. They may help you to decide on the right answer; maybe you can use them somewhere else in the exam.
- Answer the easy questions first. Then go back and think about the difficult questions.

STEP 2

Now, let's examine the reading comprehension part of the most current exam in the back pages of this book.

PART THREE—Reading Comprehension (30 credits). This part is divided into three sections (a), (b), and (c). There is no choice. You have to do all three. Each section is worth ten credits. Traditionally, (a) contains a very long selection to read, almost a full page, sometimes longer. It is followed by five multiple-choice questions.

Read the passage from start to finish just to get an idea of what it's all about. Don't look at the five questions or the answer choices yet! While reading the passage, don't waste any time translating it silently into English because you are not being asked to translate it. All you have to do is read it in Spanish because you are being tested in reading comprehension, not in the art of translating from Spanish into beautiful, perfect English. Besides, there are only five questions based on the lengthy passage and they test your reading comprehension on only certain parts of the selection.

Read all five questions and their answer choices. Read them again. At this point, read the selection a second time, maybe even a third time if there is enough time. Now you are ready to read the questions again to select the correct answers. In doing so, certain key words in the reading selection and in the questions with answer choices will stand out. Usually, the correct answers to the questions are in sequence according to what you read in the passage. In other words, the answer to the first of the five questions is usually in the beginning part of the reading selection, the answer to the second question is in an area after that part, and so on. Sometimes they are not in any sequence.

You must be aware of the fact that synonyms (words of similar meaning) and antonyms (words of opposite meaning) are frequently used. Don't expect the correct answer among the choices to contain the same words and be phrased exactly in the same way as in the reading selection. That would make it too easy to spot the correct answer. At times, you have to interpret what is in the selection to associate it with the thought in the correct answer. For example, in a selection it may state that Mr. and Mrs. X cannot go somewhere because they have a lot of work to do. The question might ask why they are not going to go to that place. The correct answer will surely not say that they can't go because they have a lot of work to do. The correct answer might be worded something like this: They don't have the time. You can figure that out because you know that in the selection it says they have a lot of work to do; therefore, they don't have the time.

If your knowledge of Spanish vocabulary is not so great, you must study (and even memorize) frequently used antonyms and synonyms with their English meanings because they are used abundantly in the Regents exams. There are lists of essential Regents vocabulary, idioms, phrases, and expressions in the pages that follow these tips. Pay special attention to those that contain verbs.

Do you know how to study vocabulary? Take a 3 × 5 card and cover the Spanish words. Look at the English and give the Spanish equivalent. If you don't know it, move the card to see the Spanish, then read it aloud. Repeat this procedure until you know the words from Spanish to English and from English to Spanish.

Another good way to study vocabulary so you can remember it is to write the Spanish words while saying them aloud. Follow this procedure not only with the lists of antonyms and synonyms but with *all* the vocabulary, idioms, including verbal, idiomatic, common, and useful phrases and expressions with verbs that are given in this part of the book. They have all been used frequently in past Regents exams. I compiled them for you. Don't just look at them. Study them methodically as I have suggested above. The best way to remember a new word or expression is to use it in a sentence. That way you get to think about it.

MORE TIPS

Read for comprehension. Look for key words.

SUGGESTIONS

- Turn to the June 1997 exam in this book and do the reading comprehension selection (a) in PART THREE. (It's the one about Costa Rica.)
- Read the long selection in Spanish from beginning to end. Underline key words.
- Read it again. Don't translate it into English—you will understand the Spanish better as you read it a second time. Underline more key words that you missed during the first reading.
- Now read all the questions (numbers 16–20) and the multiple-choice answers 1, 2, 3, 4. As you read, underline key words in the questions and in the answer choices.
- Look at question number 16. The answer to the first question is usually found in the beginning of the selection, the answer to the second question is usually farther down, and so on. When you underlined key words in the first paragraph, did you select the following? **"Allí, se pueden encontrar parques nacionales, ríos, montañas, una fauna increíble, bosques y hasta volcanes"**/There, one can find national parks, rivers, mountains, and so on. In question number 16, Costa Rica offers the visitor the opportunity to enjoy oneself in a variety of places. The key words are in answer no. 1: **divertirse en una variedad de sitios.** That is the correct answer. Answer no. 2 is wrong because the paragraph doesn't say anything about **"disfrutar de las estaciones del año"**/to enjoy the seasons of the year. Note that **disfrutar** and **gozar** are synonyms of **divertirse.** Answer no. 3 is wrong because in the paragraph nothing is said about earning enough money. And answer no. 4 is wrong because nothing is said about participating in an international project. The word "international" appears in the second line but it's about

international tourism, not an international project. If you need to expand and improve your knowledge of Spanish vocabulary, study all the Spanish/English words in this Regents review book.

STEP 3

Now, let's examine sections (b) and (c) of the Reading Comprehension test in PART THREE of the latest Regents exam in the back pages of this book.

There are five short selections to read in section (b). Each is followed by one question or incomplete statement. Read each selection at least two times to get an idea of what it's all about. Some people may not read very fast. In that case, read the selection the first time to get an idea of what it's about, then read the questions to figure out the point that each question is getting at. Then read the selection again, looking for these points. Always think about the answer you choose. Does it make sense?

In section (c), there is one very long selection to read. In different parts of the selection there are blank spaces that represent missing words or expressions with four answers from which to choose the correct one. Here, too, before selecting an answer, you ought to read the selection at least two times to understand the general meaning. Then, after you have become well acquainted with the selection, read it again and pause during the blank space to read the selection of answers. At that point, you will be ready to select the correct answer. Then, you should go back to the beginning of the selection. Read it again, but this time insert the Spanish word or expression you selected as the correct answer and see if it makes any sense.

If your knowledge of Spanish vocabulary, synonyms, antonyms, verb forms, idiomatic expressions and phrases is not as extensive as it ought to be, you must follow the tips on studying given above in **Step 2.** If you really want to do your best to build your vocabulary, you must also do the fifteen short warm-up tests in Part One of this book because the verbs, words, expressions and phrases they contain have been used in past Regents examinations. You ought to compare your answers in those warm-up tests with the correct answers given in the Answers section at the end of Part One in this book.

MORE TIPS

Look for clues when reading.

SUGGESTIONS

- Now, let's continue in the June 1997 exam, PART THREE, question no. 24 in part (b). It's the selection about Mario Vargas Llosa. Follow the same kind of analysis used in **More Tips** at the end of **Step 2,** page 63.
- The clues to the correct answer are in the first sentence of the paragraph: "The Miguel de Cervantes Literary Award was given to the Peruvian writer Mario Vargas Llosa in recognition of his extensive literary work." In answer no. 3, "his numerous literary publications" are words associated with **"su extensa obra literaria"** in the first sentence.
- Answer no. 1 is wrong because the only mention of dogs is in one of the titles.
- Answers no. 2 and 4 are wrong because there is nothing in the paragraph about Latin American research or dedication to the study of Cervantes. Clearly, you will do well in the Spanish Regents exam if you have an extensive, strong vocabulary and if you train yourself to analyze and look for clues—like a detective!

STEP 4

Now, let's examine carefully the composition part of the most current Regents exam in the back pages of this book.

PART FOUR—Compositions (16 credits). This part is divided into two sections, (a) and (b). Each section contains a choice of one out of two topics. That means you must write two compositions, one for (a) and one for (b).

In (a), you are required to write a composition containing at least six clauses on the chosen topic, which is worth six credits. The form of the composition is usually a note to someone about something.

In (b), you are required to write at least ten clauses in your composition on the chosen topic, which is worth ten credits. The form of the composition is usually a narrative, based either on a story about a picture that is given or a letter to someone about something. A clause must contain a verb, a stated or implied subject, and additional words necessary to convey meaning. The six clauses for the topic you choose in (a) and the ten clauses for the topic you choose in (b) may be contained in fewer than six or ten sentences if some of the sentences you write include more than one clause.

Examples:

One clause in one sentence:	Ayer **fui** al cine con mis amigos.
Two clauses in one sentence:	Ayer **fui** al cine con mis amigos para **ver** una película española.
Three clauses in one sentence:	Ayer **fui** al cine con mis amigos para **ver** una película española que **era** excelente.

As you can see, the most important word in each clause is the required use of a verb either in a tense (for example, in the *presente, pretérito,* or any of the other tenses) or in the infinitive form, for example: para **ver** una película española, as in the above examples. At the beginning of the Regents exam, the teacher usually hands out to the students a blank sheet of paper to use as a work sheet. Here is what you should do: On that sheet of paper list the words that come to mind as you study the topic you have chosen, making sure that you jot down at least six verbs you plan to use for the topic worth six credits and at least ten verbs you plan to use for the ten-credit topic. Make sure you understand clearly in your mind what the two topics are that you have chosen so that the verbs you plan to use are appropriate. On your work sheet, write short sentences containing those verbs related to the topic you have chosen. Remember that each sentence may contain one or more clauses. If you write a sentence that contains more than one clause, make sure that you use a verb in each clause, as in the examples given above. More than one clause in the same sentence is usually separated by conjunctions, such as **y, pero, que, porque, como, cuando.** The prepositions **a, de, para,** and others, can frequently be used plus a verb in the infinitive form, for example: **a escribir, de ir, para ver,** as in the above examples. As long as you are using a verb in a tense or in the infinitive form, you are complying with the minimum requirement of what you are expected to do.

If you want to use the future tense of a verb you have in mind but you don't remember the correct verb form, you can usually get around it by using the verb **ir** in the present tense plus the infinitive form of the verb to express a future action; for example, if you don't remember the future of

estar, as in **(Yo) estaré en casa a las seis** (I will be at home at six o'clock), you can write: **(Yo) voy a estar en casa a las seis** (I am going to be at home at six o'clock). Or, if you don't remember or don't know how to say, **(Nosotros) nadaremos en la piscina** (We will swim in the pool), you can write: **(Nosotros) vamos a nadar en la piscina** (We are going to swim in the pool).

Commonly used Spanish verbs that a student frequently needs to write on any topic in a Regents exam are **ser, estar, ir, hacer, haber, tener, llegar, venir, divertirse, entrar, salir, partir, llamar, llamarse, esperar, necesitar, jugar, volver, querer, invitar, pensar.** You definitely must know these verbs in the three persons of the singular and the three persons of the plural in the present tense and in the *pretérito.* There are many others, of course, but you must be aware of these at least. As was mentioned earlier in this section of tips on how to study and how to take the Regents exam, you ought to make sure you know all the review material that begins at the end of this section.

To help you do your best in the two compositions you have to write, you must also do the fifteen short warm-up tests in Part One in the beginning pages of this book. They contain a lot of practice in writing sentences and short paragraphs. After you do those short tests, check the Answers section that begins right after Test 15.

Consult the table of contents in the preliminary pages of this book to find the page number of PART TWO. It contains five pictures for you to examine and about which to write a composition containing at least ten clauses. Do them, following the procedure outlined above about how to use the work sheet for the composition you selected to do in (a) and the one in (b). Then, ask your teacher to correct what you have written.

You can use more practice in writing compositions based on pictures. There is a picture in every Regents exam given in the past. The exams begin in PART FOUR of this book. Sample compositions are given in the Answers section at the end of each exam.

After you work methodically on the work sheet for the topic you selected in (a) that must contain at least six clauses, use the same side to write your composition. Then, read it at least two times and pretend you are correcting somebody else's work. You are bound to find a few mistakes! Then, write your final composition in the booklet that will be collected. But, wait! Don't make any mistakes when you transfer your composition from the work sheet to the booklet that the examiner will collect. You must check your work!

Then, turn the work sheet to the other side and follow the same suggested procedure for your second composition in (b) where you must write at least ten clauses.

Here's another tip: You probably will not be able to recall the Spanish for some words you would like to use in your two compositions. Just remember that the entire examination booklet contains a lot of Spanish in it, for example, in the multiple-choice questions where there is a choice to make among four answers containing words, phrases, expressions, or sentences. Consult the reading selections in PART THREE—Reading Comprehension. If you don't remember the present tense, or the *pretérito*, or some other tense of a verb, or a particular word you want to use in your compositions, take a careful look at all the Spanish printed in your exam booklet. It is natural for someone to recognize the meaning of a printed Spanish word but difficult to recall it and to write it. The word you can't recall to use in your two compositions may very well be somewhere in there waiting for you to recognize it and use it. Or, another appropriate word may be there. Seek and you shall find!

STEP 5

When you take the latest exam in the back pages of this book for practice, follow the suggested procedures given in Steps 1 through 4. Set your watch or clock and time yourself to complete it within the three hours allowed. But don't stop after you do only the latest exam! There are at least eleven complete exams with answers beginning in PART FOUR of this book. Do one a day or every other day until you have completed them all. And don't forget to do the fifteen short warm-up tests in the front half of this book. The answers begin right after Test 15. All the material I put together for you in one place by topics in PART THREE of this book is basic Regents stuff. Study them until you know them cold, following the suggestions and tips given above.

¡Comience en seguida!/Start immediately!
¡No pierda su tiempo!/Don't waste your time!
¡Buena suerte!/Good luck!

Review of Vocabulary

ANTONYMS

aburrirse / to be bored; **divertirse** / to have a good time
aceptar / to accept; **ofrecer** / to offer
acordarse de / to remember; **olvidar, olvidarse de** / to forget (Does **acordarse de** remind you of **recordar**, which means *to remember, to remind*? When you remember something or someone, don't you *record* it in your mind? As for **olvidar** and **olvidarse de,** you might think of the English words *oblivion, oblivious*.)
admitir / to admit; **negar** / to deny
agradecido, agradecida / thankful; **ingrato, ingrata** / thankless (You might think of *grateful* and associate it with **agradecido.** As for **ingrato,** you might think of *ungrateful* or *ungracious*; there is also the word *ingrate* in English.)
alejarse de / to go away from; **acercarse a** / to approach (In **acercarse a,** do you see the word **cerca** / near, close by? In **alejarse de,** do you see the word **lejos** / far? See a picture of a person coming close to you (**acercarse a**) and then that person goes away from you (**alejarse de.**)
amar / to love; **odiar** / to hate
ancho, ancha / wide; **estrecho, estrecha** / narrow
antipático, antipática / unpleasant; **simpático, simpática** / nice (people)
aplicado, aplicada / industrious; **flojo, floja** / lazy
apresurarse a / to hasten, to hurry; **tardar en** / to delay (Here, you have the cognate *tardy* and as for **apresurarse a,** you can picture a person who is hurrying because he or she is *pressed* for time.)
atrevido, atrevida / bold, daring; **tímido, tímida** / timid, shy
aumentar / to augment, to increase; **disminuir** / to diminish, to decrease
ausente / absent; **presente** / present
claro, clara / light; **oscuro, oscura** / dark
cobarde / cowardly; **valiente** / valiant, brave
cómico, cómica / comic, funny; **trágico, trágica** / tragic
costoso, costosa / costly, expensive; **barato, barata** / cheap, inexpensive
culpable / guilty, culpable; **inocente** / innocent
dar / to give; **recibir** / to receive
débil / weak, debilitated; **fuerte** / strong
delgado, delgada / thin; **gordo, gorda** / stout, fat
derrota / defeat; **victoria** / victory
descansar / to rest; **cansar** / to tire, **cansarse** / to get tired

descubrir / to uncover; **cubrir** / to cover (Here is another word with the prefix **des**, which usually makes the word opposite in meaning.)
descuido / carelessness; **esmero** / meticulousness
desgraciado, desgraciada / unfortunate; **afortunado, afortunada** / fortunate
destruir / to destroy; **crear** / to create
desvanecerse / to disappear; **aparecer** / to appear (Here, you might think of *vanish* to remind you of the meaning of **desvanecerse;** for the meaning of **aparecer,** isn't it an obvious cognate?)
distinto, distinta / different; **semejante** / similar
elogiar / to praise; **censurar** / to criticize (Here, you might see a picture of a clergyman reading a eulogy in praise of someone; do I need to suggest to you what word to think of in English for the Spanish **censurar**?)
este / east; **oeste** / west
fatigado, fatigada / tired; **descansado, descansada** / rested (Here, in **descansado,** do you see the Spanish word **cansar** within that word? See the entry **descansar** above.)
feo, fea / ugly; **bello, bella** / beautiful
gastar / to spend (money); **ahorrar** / to save (money) (You might see a picture of a person *hoarding* money for **ahorrar**; you might see an opposite picture of a person *wasting* money to remind you of **gastar.**)
gigante / giant; **enano** / dwarf
hablador, habladora / talkative; **taciturno, taciturna** / silent, taciturn
hembra / female; **macho** / male
ida / going; **vuelta** / return
ignorar / not to know; **saber** / to know
interesante / interesting; **aburrido, aburrida** / boring
inútil / useless; **útil** / useful
juntar / to join; **separar** / to separate
lejano / distant; **cercano** / nearby (Do these two words remind you of **alejarse de** and **acercarse a** given above?)
lentitud / slowness; **rapidez** / speed
libertad / liberty; **esclavitud** / slavery
luz / light; **sombra** / shadow
llegada / arrival; **partida** / departure
llenar / to fill; **vaciar** / to empty (Think of *vacate.*)
maldecir / to curse; **bendecir** / to bless (Think of *malediction* and *benediction.*)
menor / younger; **mayor** / older (Think of *minor* and *major.*)
mentira / lie, falsehood; **verdad** / truth (Think of *veracity.*)
meridional / southern; **septentrional** / northern
negar / to deny; **otorgar** / to grant
orgulloso / proud; **humilde** / humble

oriental / eastern; **occidental** / western
peligro / danger; **seguridad** / safety
perder / to lose; **ganar** / to win
porvenir / future; **pasado** / past
puesta del sol / sunset; **salida del sol** / sunrise
recto / straight; **tortuoso** / winding
riqueza / wealth; **pobreza** / poverty
romper / to break; **componer** / to repair (Here, in *romper*, you can see a picture in your mind of something *ruptured* in the sense that it is broken. In *componer*, you can see something that is put (*poner*) together in the sense that it is repaired.)
seco / dry; **mojado** / wet
separar / to separate; **juntar** / to join
sucio / dirty; **limpio** / clean
tonto / foolish; **listo** / clever
tranquilo / tranquil, peaceful; **turbulento** / restless, turbulent

MORE ANTONYMS

You ought to know the following antonyms to prepare yourself for the next Spanish Regents exam:

alegre / happy; **triste** / sad
algo / something; **nada** / nothing
alguien / someone; **nadie** / no one
alguno (algún) / some; **ninguno (ningún)** / none
amigo, amiga / friend; **enemigo, enemiga** / enemy
antes (de) / before; **después (de)** / after
antiguo, antigua / ancient, old; **moderno, moderna** / modern
aparecer / to appear; **desaparecer** / to disappear
aprisa / quickly; **despacio** / slowly
aquí / here; **allí** / there
arriba / above, upstairs; **abajo** / below, downstairs
bajo, baja / low, short; **alto, alta** / high, tall
bien / well; **mal** / badly, poorly
blanco, blanca / white; **negro, negra** / black
bueno (buen), buena / good; **malo (mal)** / bad
caballero / gentleman; **dama** / lady
caliente / hot; **frío** / cold
caro, cara / expensive; **barato, barata** / cheap
cerca (de) / near; **lejos (de)** / far

cerrar / to close; **abrir** / to open
cielo / sky; **tierra** / earth, ground
comprar / to buy; **vender** / to sell
común / common; **raro, rara** / rare
con / with; **sin** / without
contra / against; **con** / with
corto, corta / short; **largo, larga** / long
chico / boy; **chica** / girl
dar / to give; **recibir** / to receive
dejar caer / to drop; **recoger** / to pick up
delante de / in front of; **detrás de** / in back of
dentro / inside; **fuera** / outside
despertarse / to wake up; **dormirse** / to fall asleep
dulce / sweet; **amargo** / bitter
duro, dura / hard; **suave, blando, blanda** / soft
empezar / to begin, to start; **terminar, acabar** / to end
encender / to light; **apagar** / to extinguish
encima (de) / on top; **debajo (de)** / under
entrada / entrance; **salida** / exit
esta noche / tonight, this evening; **anoche** / last night, yesterday evening
este / east; **oeste** / west
estúpido, estúpida / stupid; **inteligente** / intelligent
éxito / success; **fracaso** / failure
fácil / easy; **difícil** / difficult
feliz / happy; **triste** / sad
feo, fea / ugly; **hermoso, hermosa** / beautiful
fin / end; **principio** / beginning
flaco, flaca / thin; **gordo, gorda** / fat
grande (gran) / large, big; **pequeño, pequeña** / small, little
guerra / war; **paz** / peace
hablar / to talk, to speak; **callarse** / to keep silent
hombre / man; **mujer** / woman
ida / departure; **vuelta** / return (**ida y vuelta** / round trip)
ir / to go; **venir** / to come
joven / young; **viejo, vieja** / old
jugar / to play; **trabajar** / to work
juventud / youth; **vejez** / old age
levantarse / to get up; **sentarse** / to sit down
limpio, limpia / clean; **sucio, sucia** / dirty
lleno, llena / full; **vacío, vacía** / empty

llorar / to cry, to weep; **reír** / to laugh
madre / mother; **padre** / father
mañana / tomorrow; **ayer** / yesterday
marido / husband; **esposa** / wife
más / more; **menos** / less
mejor / better; **peor** / worse
menor / younger; **mayor** / older
mentir / to lie; **decir la verdad** / to tell the truth
meter / to put in; **sacar** / to take out
mismo, misma / same; **diferente** / different
morir / to die; **vivir** / to live
muchacho / boy; **muchacha** / girl
mucho, mucha / much; **poco, poca** / little
nacer / to be born; **morir** / to die
natural / natural; **innatural** / unnatural
necesario / necessary; **innecesario** / unnecessary
noche / night; **día** / day
obeso, obesa / obese, fat; **delgado, delgada** / thin
obscuro, obscura / dark; **claro, clara** / light
odio / hate, hatred; **amor** / love
perder / to lose; **hallar** / to find
perezoso, perezosa / lazy; **diligente** / diligent
permitir / to permit; **prohibir** / to prohibit
pesado, pesada / heavy; **ligero, ligera** / light
ponerse / to put on (clothing); **quitarse** / to take off (clothing)
posible / possible; **imposible** / impossible
pregunta / question; **respuesta, contestación** / answer
preguntar / to ask; **contestar** / to answer
presente / present; **ausente** / absent
prestar / to lend; **pedir prestado** / to borrow
primero (primer), primera / first; **último, última** / last
princesa / princess; **príncipe** / prince
quedarse / to remain; **irse** / to leave, to go away
quizá(s) / maybe, perhaps; **seguro, cierto** / sure, certain
rey / king; **reina** / queen
rico, rica / rich; **pobre** / poor
rubio, rubia / blond; **moreno, morena** / brunette
ruido / noise; **silencio** / silence
sabio, sabia / wise; **tonto, tonta** / foolish
salir (de) / to leave (from); **entrar (en)** / to enter (in, into)
sí / yes; **no** / no

siempre / always; **nunca** / never
sobrino / nephew; **sobrina** / niece
subir / to go up; **bajar** / to go down
sur / south; **norte** / north
temprano / early; **tarde** / late
tío / uncle; **tía** / aunt
tomar / to take; **dar** / to give
unir / to unite; **desunir** / to disunite
usual / usual; **extraño, raro** / unusual
verano / summer; **invierno** / winter
vida / life; **muerte** / death
virtud / virtue; **vicio** / vice
y / and, plus; **menos** / minus, less
zorro / fox; **zorra** / vixen, she-fox

CONJUNCTIONS, CONJUNCTIVE LOCUTIONS, AND CORRELATIVE CONJUNCTIONS

Definition: A conjunction is a word that connects words, phrases, clauses or sentences, *e.g.*, and, but, or, because / **y, pero, o, porque.**

Here are some conjunctions that you certainly ought to know before you take the next Regents test in Spanish.

(a) **a fin de que** / so that, in order that
a menos que / unless
antes (de) que / before
apenas . . . cuando / hardly, scarcely . . . when
asi que / as soon as, after
aun / even, still
aunque / although
como / as, since, how
como si / as if
con tal (de) que / provided that
cuando / when
de manera que / so that
de modo que / so that, in such a way that
después (de) que / after
e / and
en cuanto / as soon as
hasta que / until

como quiera que / although, since
con la condición de que / on condition that
con que / so then, and so, then
conque / and so, well then, so then, now then
dado caso que / supposing that
dado que / supposing that
de condición que / so as to
de suerte que / so that, in such a manner as
del mismo modo que / in the same way that
desde que / since
empero / yet, however, notwithstanding
en caso de que / in case, in case that
en razón de que / for the reason that, because of
entretanto que / meanwhile, while
lo mismo que / as well as, the same as
lo mismo . . . que . . . / both . . . and . . . *or* as well . . . as
más bien que / rather than
mientras tanto / meanwhile, in the meantime
no bien . . . cuando / no sooner . . . than
no obstante / in spite of the fact that (notwithstanding)
por más que / no matter how, however much
por razón de que / because of, for the reason that
salvo que / unless
siempre que / whenever, provided that
supuesto que / since, allowing that, granting that
tan luego como / therefore
tanto . . . como / both . . . and *or* as well . . . as

TRICKY WORDS

NOTE well the English meanings of the following Spanish words. They often appear in the reading comprehension passages on Regents exams in Spanish.

actual *adj.* present, of the present time, of the present day
el anciano, la anciana old (man or woman)
antiguo, antigua *adj.* former, old, ancient
la apología eulogy, defense
la arena sand
asistir a *v.* to attend, to be present at
atender *v.* to attend to, to take care of

el auditorio audience
el bachiller, la bachillera graduate of a secondary school; *also means* babbler
el bagaje beast of burden, military equipment
la bala bullet, shot, bale, ball
bizarro, bizarra *adj.* brave, gallant, generous
el campo field, country(side), military camp
el carbón coal, charcoal, carbon
el cargo duty, post, responsibility, burden, load
la carta letter (to mail)
el collar necklace
colorado, colorada *adj.* red, ruddy
la complexión temperament, constitution
la conferencia lecture
la confianza confidence, trust
la confidencia secret, trust
constipado, constipada *adj.* sick with a head cold or common cold
la consulta conference
convenir *v.* to agree, to fit, to suit, to be suitable
la chanza joke, fun
de *prep.* from, of
dé *irreg. v. form: imper., 3rd pers., s. and 1st & 3rd pers. s.,* pres. subj. of **dar**
la decepción disappointment
el delito crime
la desgracia misfortune
el desmayo fainting
diario, diaria *adj.* daily; **el diario** diary, journal, daily newspaper
disfrutar *v.* to enjoy
divisar *v.* to perceive indistinctly
el dormitorio bedroom, dormitory
el editor publisher
embarazada *adj.* pregnant
emocionante *adj.* touching (causing an emotion)
esperar *v.* to hope, to expect, to wait for
el éxito success, outcome
la fábrica factory
hay *idiomatic form* there is, there are
el idioma language
ignorar *v.* not to know, to be unaware
intoxicar *v.* to poison, to intoxicate

el labrador farmer
largo, larga *adj.* long
la lectura reading
la librería bookstore
la maleta valise, suitcase
el mantel tablecloth
mayor *adj.* greater, older
la mesura moderation
la pala shovel
el palo stick, pole
el pan bread
pasar *v.* to happen, to pass
el pastel pie; **la pintura al pastel** pastel painting
pinchar *v.* to puncture, to prick, to pierce
realizar *v.* to achieve (to realize, in the sense of achieving something: He realized his dreams, *i.e.*, his dreams came true)
recordar *v.* to remember
el resfriado common cold (illness)
restar *v.* to deduct, to subtract
sano, sana *adj.* healthy
soportar *v.* to tolerate, to bear, to endure, to support
suceder *v.* to happen, to come about, to succeed (follow)
el suceso event, happening
la tabla board, plank, table of contents
la tinta ink, tint
la trampa trap, snare, cheat, trick
tu *poss. adj., 2nd pers. s., fam.* your
tú *persl. subj. pron., 2nd pers. s., fam.* you
el vaso drinking glass

IDIOMS, INCLUDING VERBAL, IDIOMATIC, COMMON, AND USEFUL EXPRESSIONS (ARRANGED ALPHABETICALLY BY KEY WORD)

With A

a beneficio de / for the benefit of
a bordo / on board
a caballo / on horseback
a cada instante / at every moment, at every turn

a casa / home (Use with a verb of motion; use **a casa** if you are going *to* the house; use **en casa** if you are *in* the house: **Salgo de la escuela y voy a casa** / I'm leaving school and I'm going home; **Me quedo en casa esta noche** / I'm staying home tonight.)
a causa de / because of, on account of
a derecha / to (on, at) the right
a eso de / about, around (**Llegaremos a Madrid a eso de las tres de la tarde** / We will arrive in Madrid at about 3 o'clock in the afternoon.)
a fines de / about the end of, around the end of (**Estaremos en Madrid a fines de la semana** / We will be in Madrid around the end of the week.)
a fondo / thoroughly
a fuerza de / by dint of (**A fuerza de trabajar, tuvo éxito** / By dint of working, he was successful.)
a mano / by hand
a mediados de / around the middle of (**Estaremos en Málaga a mediados de julio** / We will be in Málaga around the middle of July.)
a menudo / often, frequently
a mi parecer / in my opinion
a pesar de / in spite of
a pie / on foot
a pierna suelta / without a care
a principios de / around the beginning of (**Estaremos en México a principios de la semana que viene** / We will be in Mexico around the beginning of next week.)
a saltos / by leaps and bounds
a solas / alone
a su parecer / in your (his, her, their) opinion
a tiempo / on time
a toda brida / at top speed
a través de / across, through
a veces / at times, sometimes
conforme a / in accordance with
cuesta a diez dólares / It costs about ten dollars.
estar a punto de / to be about to (**Estoy a punto de salir** / I am about to leave.)
frente a / in front of
junto a / beside, next to
poco a poco / little by little
ser aficionado a / to be a fan of
uno a uno / one by one

With A LA

a la derecha / to (on, at) the right
a la española / in the Spanish style
a la francesa / in the French style
a la italiana / in the Italian style
a la izquierda / to (on, at) the left
a la larga / in the long run
a la madrugada / at an early hour, at daybreak
a la semana / a week, per week
a la vez / at the same time

With AL

al + inf. / on, upon + pres. part. (**Al entrar en la cocina, comenzó a comer** / Upon entering into the kitchen, he began to eat.)
al aire libre / outdoors, in the open air
al amanecer / at daybreak, at dawn
al anochecer / at nightfall, at dusk
al cabo / finally, at last
al cabo de / at the end of
al contrario / on the contrary
al día / current, up to date
al día siguiente / on the following day, on the next day
al fin / at last, finally
al lado de / next to, beside
al menos / at least
al mes / a month, per month
al parecer / apparently
al por mayor / wholesale
al por menor / retail (sales)
al pronto / at first
al través de / across, through
echar al correo / to mail, to post a letter

With CON

con anterioridad / beforehand
con anterioridad a / prior to
con arreglo a / in accordance with
con frecuencia / frequently
con los brazos abiertos / with open arms
con motivo de / on the occasion of
con mucho gusto / gladly, willingly, with much pleasure
con permiso / excuse me, with your permission

con rumbo a / in the direction of
con voz sorda / in a low (muffled) voice
ser amable con / to be kind to

With CUANTO, CUANTA, CUANTOS, CUANTAS

cuanto antes / as soon as possible
¿Cuánto cuesta? / How much is it? How much does it cost?
cuanto más . . . tanto más . . . / the more . . . the more . . . (**Cuanto más estudio tanto más aprendo** / The more I study the more I learn.)
¿Cuántos años tiene Ud.? / How old are you?
unos cuantos libros / a few books
unas cuantas flores / a few flowers

With DAR and DARSE

dar a / to face (**El comedor da al jardín** / The dining room faces the garden.)
dar con algo / to find something, to come upon something (**Esta mañana di con dinero en la calle** / This morning I found money in the street.)
dar con alguien / to meet someone, to run into someone, to come across someone, to find someone (**Anoche, di con mi amiga Elena en el cine** / Last night I met my friend Helen at the movies.)
dar contra / to hit against
dar cuerda al reloj / to wind a watch
dar de beber a / to give something to drink to
dar de comer a / to feed, to give something to eat to (**Me gusta dar de comer a los pájaros en el parque** / I like to feed the birds in the park.)
dar en / to hit against, to strike against
dar en el blanco / to hit the target, to hit it right
dar gritos / to shout
dar la bienvenida / to welcome
dar la hora / to strike the hour
dar la mano a alguien / to shake hands with someone
dar las buenas noches a alguien / to say good evening (good night) to someone
dar las gracias a alguien / to thank someone
dar los buenos días a alguien / to say good morning (hello) to someone
dar por + past part. / to consider (**Lo doy por perdido** / I consider it lost.)
dar recuerdos a / to give one's regards (best wishes) to

dar un abrazo / to embrace
dar un paseo / to take a walk
dar un paseo a caballo / to go horseback riding
dar un paseo en automóvil (en coche) / to go for a drive
dar un paseo en bicicleta / to ride a bicycle
dar una vuelta / to go for a short walk, to go for a stroll
dar unas palmadas / to clap one's hands
dar voces / to shout
darse cuenta de / to realize, to be aware of, to take into account
darse la mano / to shake hands with each other
darse por + past part. / to consider oneself (**Me doy por insultado** / I consider myself insulted.)
darse prisa / to hurry

With DE

abrir de par en par / to open wide
acabar de + inf. / to have just + past part. (**María acaba de llegar** / Mary has just arrived; **María acababa de llegar** / Mary had just arrived.)
acerca de / about, concerning
alrededor de / around (**alrededor de la casa** / around the house)
antes de / before
aparte de / aside from
billete de ida y vuelta / round-trip ticket
cerca de / near, close to
de abajo / down, below
de acuerdo / in agreement, in accord
de ahora en adelante / from now on
de algún modo / someway
de alguna manera / someway
de antemano / ahead of time
de aquí en adelante / from now on
de arriba / upstairs
de arriba bajo / from top to bottom
de ayer en ocho días / a week from yesterday
de balde / free, gratis
de broma / jokingly
de buena gana / willingly
de común acuerdo / by mutual accord, by mutual agreement
de cuando en cuando / from time to time
de día / by day, in the daytime

de día en día / from day to day
de esa manera / in that way
de ese modo / in that way
de esta manera / in this way
de este modo / in this way
de hoy en adelante / from today on, from now on
de hoy en ocho días / a week from today
de la mañana / in the morning (Use this when a specific time is mentioned: **Tomo el desayuno a las ocho de la mañana** / I have breakfast at 8 o'clock in the morning.)
de la noche / in the evening (Use this when a specific time is mentioned: **Mi amigo llega a las nueve de la noche** / My friend is arriving at 9 o'clock in the evening.)
de la tarde / in the afternoon (Use this when a specific time is mentioned: **Regreso a casa a las cuatro de la tarde** / I am returning home at 4 o'clock in the afternoon.)
de madrugada / at dawn, at daybreak
de mal humor / in bad humor, in a bad mood
de mala gana / unwillingly
de memoria / by heart (memorized)
de moda / in fashion
de nada / you're welcome
de ningún modo / no way, in no way, by no means
de ninguna manera / no way, in no way, by no means
de noche / by night, at night, during the night
de nuevo / again
de otra manera / in another way
de otro modo / otherwise
de pie / standing
de prisa / in a hurry
de pronto / suddenly
de repente / all of a sudden
de rodillas / kneeling, on one's knees
de todos modos / anyway, in any case, at any rate
de uno en uno / one by one
de veras / really, truly
de vez en cuando / from time to time
dentro de poco / soon, shortly, within a short time
echar de menos / to miss
en lo alto de / at the top of
en lugar de / in place of, instead of

enfrente de / opposite
estar de acuerdo / to agree
fuera de sí / beside oneself, aghast
ir de compras / to go shopping
la mayor parte de / the greater part of, the majority of
no hay de qué / you're welcome, don't mention it
un billete de ida y vuelta / round-trip ticket
un poco de / a little (of): **un poco de sucre** / a little sugar

With DECIR

decirle al oído / to whisper in one's ears
dicho y hecho / no sooner said than done
Es decir / That is to say . . .
querer decir / to mean **¿Qué quiere decir este muchacho?** / What does this boy mean?

With DÍA, DÍAS

al día / current, up to date
al romper el día / at daybreak
algún día / someday
de dĭa en dia / day by day
dia por día / day by day
estar al día / to be up to date
hoy día / nowadays
ocho días / a week
poner al día / to bring up to date
por día / by the day, per day
quince dias / two weeks
un día de éstos / one of these days

With EN

abrir de par en par / to open wide
de ayer en ocho días / a week from yesterday
de casa en casa / from house to house
de cuando en cuando / from time to time
de día en día / from day to day
de hoy en adelante / from today on
de hoy en ocho días / a week from today
de uno en uno / one by one
de vez en cuando / from time to time
en alto / high, high up, up high, on high

en balde / in vain
en bicicleta / by bicycle
en broma / jokingly, in fun
en cambio / on the other hand
en casa / at home (Use **en casa** if you are *in* the house; use **a casa** with a verb of motion, if you are going *to* the house: **Me quedo en casa esta noche** / I am staying home tonight; **Salgo de la escuela y voy a casa** / I'm leaving school and I'm going home.)
en casa de / at the house of (**María está en casa de Elena** / Mary is at Helen's house.)
en caso de / in case of
en coche / by car
en contra de / against
en cuanto / as soon as
en cuanto a / as for, with regard to, in regard to
en efecto / as a matter of fact, in fact
en el mes próximo pasado / in the month just past, this past month
en este momento / at this moment
en lo alto de / on top of it, at the top of, up
en lugar de / in place of, instead of
en marcha / under way, on the way
en medio de / in the middle of
en ninguna parte / nowhere
en punto / sharp, exactly (telling time: **Son las dos en punto** / It is two o'clock sharp.)
en seguida / immediately, at once
en suma / in short, in a word
en todas partes / everywhere
en vano / in vain
en vez de / instead of
en voz alta / in a loud voice
en voz baja / in a low voice

With ESTAR

está bien / all right, okay
estar a punto de + inf. / to be about + inf. (**Estoy a punto de salir** / I am about to go out.)
estar a sus anchas / to be comfortable
estar conforme con / to be in agreement with
estar de acuerdo / to agree
estar de acuerdo con / to be in agreement with

estar de boga / to be in fashion, to be fashionable
estar de buenas / to be in a good mood
estar de pie / to be standing
estar de vuelta / to be back
estar en boga / to be in fashion, to be fashionable
estar para + inf. / to be about to (**Estoy para salir** / I am about to go out.)
estar por / to be in favor of
no estar para bromas / not to be in the mood for jokes

With HABER

ha habido . . . / there has been . . . , there have been . . .
había . . / there was . . . , there were . . .
habrá . . . / there will be . . .
habría . . . / there would be . . .
hubo . . . / there was . . . , there were . . .

With HACER and HACERSE

hace poco / a little while ago
hace un año / a year ago
Hace un mes que partió el señor Molina / Mr. Molina left one month ago.
hace una hora / an hour ago
hacer caso de / to pay attention to
hacer daño a algo / to harm something
hacer daño a alguien / to harm someone
hacer de / to act as (**El señor González siempre hace de jefe** / Mr. González always acts as a boss.)
hacer el baúl / to pack one's trunk
hacer el favor de + inf. / please (**Haga Ud. el favor de entrar** / Please come in.)
hacer el papel de / to play the role of
hacer falta / to be wanting, lacking, needed
hacer la maleta / to pack one's suitcase
hacer pedazos / to smash, to break, to tear into pieces
hacer un viaje / to take a trip
hacer una broma / to play a joke
hacer una pregunta / to ask a question
hacer una visita / to pay a visit
hacerle falta / to need (**A Juan le hace falta un lápiz** / John needs a pencil.)

hacerse / to become (**Elena se hizo dentista** / Helen became a dentist.)
hacerse daño / to hurt oneself, to harm oneself
hacerse tarde / to be getting late (**Vámonos; se hace tarde** / Let's leave; it's getting late.)

With HASTA

hasta ahora / until now
hasta aquí / until now, up to here
hasta después / see you later, until later
hasta entonces / see you then, see you later, up to that time, until that time
hasta la vista / see you again
hasta luego / see you later, until later
hasta mañana / see you tomorrow, until tomorrow
hasta más no poder / to the utmost
hasta no más / to the utmost

With LO

a lo largo de / along
a lo lejos / in the distance
a lo más / at most
a lo mejor / probably
a lo menos / at least
en lo alto / on top of, at the top of, up
lo bueno / what is good, the good part; **¡Lo bueno que es!** / How good it is! **¡Lo bien que está escrito!** / How well it is written!
lo de + inf., adv., or noun / "that matter of . . .," "that business of . . ."
lo escrito / what is written
lo malo / what is bad, the bad part
lo más pronto posible / as soon as possible
lo mejor / what is best, the best part
lo primero que decir / the first thing to say
lo simpático / whatever is kind
por lo común / generally, commonly, usually
por lo contrario / on the contrary
por lo general / generally, usually
por lo menos / at least
por lo pronto / in the meantime, for the time being
por lo tanto / consequently
por lo visto / apparently

¡Ya lo creo! / I should certainly think so!

With LUEGO

desde luego / naturally, of course, immediately
hasta luego / see you later, so long
luego luego / right away
luego que / as soon as, after

With MAÑANA

ayer por la mañana / yesterday morning
de la mañana / in the morning (Use this when a specific time is mentioned: **Voy a tomar el tren a las seis de la mañana** / I am going to take the train at six o'clock in the morning.)
mañana por la mañana / tomorrow morning
mañana por la noche / tomorrow night
mañana por la tarde / tomorrow afternoon
pasado mañana / the day after tomorrow
por la mañana / in the morning (Use this when no exact time is mentioned: **El señor Pardo llega por la mañana** / Mr. Pardo is arriving in the morning.)
por la mañana temprano / early in the morning

With MISMO

ahora mismo / right now
al mismo tiempo / at the same time
allá mismo / right there
aqui mismo / right here
asi mismo / the same, the same thing
el mismo de siempre / the same old thing
eso mismo / that very thing
hoy mismo / this very day
lo mismo / the same, the same thing
lo mismo da / it makes no difference, it amounts to the same thing
lo mismo de siempre / the same old story
lo mismo que / the same as, as well as
por lo mismo / for the same reason

With NO

Creo que no / I don't think so; I think not
No cabe duda / No doubt about it
No es verdad / It isn't so, It isn't true; **¿No es verdad?** / Isn't that so?

No hay de qué / You're welcome
No hay remedio / There's no way, It cannot be helped
No importa / It doesn't matter
No + verb + más que + amount of money (**No tengo más que un dólar** / I have only one dollar.)
no obstante / notwithstanding (in spite of), nevertheless
todavía no / not yet
ya no / no longer

With PARA

estar para / to be about to, to be at the point of (**El autobús está para salir** / The bus is about to leave.)
no estar para bromas / not to be in the mood for jokes
no ser para tanto / not to be so important
para eso / for that matter
para mí / for my part
para que / in order that, so that
para ser / in spite of being (**Para ser tan viejo, él es muy ágil** / In spite of being so old, he is very agile.)
para siempre / forever
un vaso para agua / a water glass; **una taza para café** / a coffee cup; **una taza para té** / a tea cup

With POCO

a poco / in a short while, presently
dentro de poco / in a short while, in a little while
en pocos días / in a few days
poco a poco / little by little
poco antes / shortly before
poco después / shortly after
por poco / nearly, almost
tener poco que hacer / to have little to do
un poco de / a little (of); **Quisiera un poco de azúcar** / I would like a little sugar.
y por si eso fuera poco / and as if that were not enough

With POR

acabar por + inf. / to end up by + pres. part. (**Mi padre acabó por comprarlo** / My father finally ended up by buying it.)
al por mayor / wholesale
al por menor / retail (sales)

ayer por la mañana / yesterday morning
ayer por la noche / yesterday evening
ayer por la tarde / yesterday afternoon
estar por / to be in favor of
mañana por la mañana / tomorrow morning
mañana por la noche / tomorrow night, tomorrow evening
mañana por la tarde / tomorrow afternoon
por ahí / over there
por ahora / for just now, for the present
por allá / over there
por aquí / this way, around here
por avión / by air mail
por consiguiente / consequently
por desgracia / unfortunately
por Dios / for God's sake
por ejemplo / for example
por el contrario / on the contrary; or, **por lo contrario**
por escrito / in writing
por eso / for that reason, therefore
por favor / please (**Entre, por favor** / Come in, please.)
por fin / at last, finally
por hora / by the hour, per hour
por la mañana / in the morning (Use this when no exact time is mentioned: **Me quedo en casa por la mañana** / I'm staying home in the morning.)
por la mañana temprano / early in the morning
por la noche / in the evening (Use this when no exact time is mentioned: **Me gusta mirar la televisión por la noche** / I like to watch television in the evening.)
por la noche temprano / early in the evening
por la tarde / in the afternoon (Use this when no exact time is mentioned: **Tengo tres clases por la tarde** / I have three classes in the afternoon.)
por la tarde temprano / early in the afternoon
por lo común / commonly, generally, usually
por lo contrario / on the contrary; or, **por el contrario**
por lo general / generally, usually
por lo menos / at least
por lo pronto / in the meantime, for the time being
por lo tanto / consequently, therefore
por lo visto / apparently
por mi cuenta / in my way of thinking

por mi parte / as for me, as far as I am concerned
por nada / you're welcome
por poco / nearly, almost
por regla general / as a general rule
por semana / by the week, per week
por si acaso / in case
por supuesto / of course
por teléfono / by phone
por todas partes / everywhere
por valor de / worth

With PRONTO

al pronto / at first
de pronto / suddenly
lo más pronto posible / as soon as possible
por de pronto / for the time being
por el pronto or **por lo pronto** / in the meantime, for the time being
tan pronto como / as soon as

With QUE

Creo que no / I don't think so, I think not.
Creo que sí / I think so.
el año que viene / next year
la semana que viene / next week
¡Qué le vaya bien! / Good luck!
¡Qué lo pase Ud. bien! / Good luck! (I wish you a good outcome!)

With SER

Debe de ser . . . / It is probably . . .
Debe ser . . . / It ought to be . . .
Es de lamentar / It's too bad.
Es de mi agrado / It's to my liking.
Es hora de . . . / It is time to . . .
Es lástima or **Es una lástima** / It's a pity; It's too bad.
Es que . . . / The fact is . . .
para ser / in spite of being (**Para ser tan viejo, él es muy ágil** / In spite of being so old, he is very nimble.)
sea lo que sea / whatever it may be
ser aficionado a / to be a fan of (**Soy aficionado al béisbol** / I'm a baseball fan.)
ser amable con / to be kind to (**Mi profesora de español es amable conmigo** / My Spanish teacher is kind to me.)

ser todo oídos / to be all ears (**Te escucho; soy todo oídos** / I'm listening to you; I'm all ears.)
si no fuera por . . . / if it were not for . . .

With SIN

sin aliento / out of breath
sin cuento / endless
sin cuidado / carelessly
sin duda / without a doubt, undoubtedly
sin ejemplo / unparalleled, nothing like it
sin embargo / nevertheless, however
sin falta / without fail
sin fondo / bottomless
sin novedad / nothing new, same as usual

With TENER

¿Cuántos años tienes? ¿Cuántos años tiene Ud.? / How old are you? **Tengo dieciséis años** / I am sixteen years old.
¿Qué tienes? ¿Qué tiene Ud.? / What's the matter? What's the matter with you? **No tengo nada** / There's nothing wrong; There's nothing the matter (with me).
tener algo que hacer / to have something to do
tener calor / to feel (to be) warm (persons)
tener cuidado / to be careful
tener dolor de cabeza / to have a headache
tener dolor de estómago / to have a stomachache
tener éxito / to be successful
tener frío / to feel (to be) cold (persons)
tener ganas de + inf. / to feel like + pres. part. (**Tengo ganas de tomar un helado** / I feel like having an ice cream.)
tener gusto en + inf. / to be glad + inf. (**Tengo mucho gusto en conocerle** / I am very glad to meet you.)
tener hambre / to feel (to be) hungry
tener la bondad de / please, please be good enough to . . . (**Tenga la bondad de cerrar la puerta** / Please close the door.)
tener la culpa de algo / to take the blame for something, to be to blame for something (**Tengo la culpa de eso** / I am to blame for that.)
tener lugar / to take place (**El accidente tuvo lugar anoche** / The accident took place last night.)
tener miedo de / to be afraid of

tener mucha sed / to feel (to be) very thirsty (persons)
tener mucho calor / to feel (to be) very warm (persons)
tener mucho frío / to feel (to be) very cold (persons)
tener mucho que hacer / to have a lot to do
tener poco que hacer / to have little to do
tener prisa / to be in a hurry
tener que + inf. / to have + inf. (**Tengo que estudiar** / I have to study.)
tener que ver con / to have to do with (**No tengo nada que ver con él** / I have nothing to do with him.)
tener razón / to be right (**Usted tiene razón** / You are right.); **no tener razón** / to be wrong (**Usted no tiene razón** / You are wrong.)
tener sed / to feel (to be) thirsty (persons)
tener sueño / to feel (to be) sleepy
tener suerte / to be lucky
tener vergüenza de / to be ashamed of

With TODO, TODA, TODOS, TODAS

a todo / at most
a todo correr / at full speed
ante todo / first of all, in the first place
asi y todo / in spite of everything
con todo / all in all, still, however, nevertheless
de todos modos / anyway, in any case, at any rate
del todo / completely, entirely
en un todo / in all its parts
en todo y por todo / in each and every way
ir a todo correr / to run by leaps and bounds
jugar el todo por todo / to risk everything
por todo / throughout
sobre todo / above all, especially
toda la familia / the whole family
todas las noches / every night
todas las semanas / every week
todo aquel que / whoever
todo aquello que / whatever
todo el mundo / everybody
todo el que / everybody who
todos cuantos / all those that
todos los años / every year
todos los días / every day
todos los que / all who, all those who

With VEZ and VECES

a la vez / at the same time (**Carlos come y habla a la vez** / Charles eats and talks at the same time.)
a veces / sometimes, at times
alguna vez / sometime
algunas veces / sometimes
cada vez / each time
cada vez más / more and more (each time)
de vez en cuando / from time to time
dos veces / twice, two times
en vez de / instead of
las más veces / most of the time
muchas veces / many times
otra vez / again, another time, once more
raras veces / few times, rarely
repetidas veces / repeatedly, over and over again
tal vez / perhaps
una vez / once, one time
una vez más / once more, one more time
unas veces / sometimes
varias veces / several times

With Y

dicho y hecho / no sooner said than done
mañana y pasado / tomorrow and the following day
sano y salvo / safe and sound
un billete de ida y vuelta / round-trip ticket
¿y bien? / and then? and so? so what?
y eso que / even though
y por si eso fuera poco . . . / and as if that were not enough . . .

With YA

¡Hazlo ya! Hágalo ya! / Do it now!
no ya . . . sino / not only . . . but also
¡pues ya! / of course! certainly!
si ya . . / if only . . .
ya . . . ya . . . / now . . . now . . .
ya . . . ya / whether . . . or; as well . . . as
¡Ya lo creo! / I should certainly think so! Of course!
Ya lo veré / I'll see to it.
ya no / no longer

Ya pasó / It's all over now.
ya que / since, as long as, seeing that . . .
¡Ya se ve! / Yes, indeed!
¡Ya voy! / I'm coming! I'll be there in a second!

TELLING TIME

¿Qué hora es? / What time is it?

Es la una / It is one o'clock. Note that the 3rd pers. sing. of **ser** is used because the time is one (o'clock), which is singular.

Son las dos / It is two o'clock. Note that the 3rd pers. pl. of **ser** is used because the time is two (o'clock), which is more than one.

Son las tres, son las cuatro, *etc.* / It is three o'clock, it is four o'clock, *etc.*

When the time is a certain number of minutes after the hour, the hour is stated first (**Es la una**) **+ y +** the number of minutes:

Es la una y cinco / It is five minutes after one o'clock / It is 1:05.
Son las dos y diez / It is ten minutes after two o'clock / It is 2:10.

When the hour is a quarter after, you can express it by using either **y cuarto** or **y quince (minutos):**

Son las dos y cuarto or **Son las dos y quince (minutos)** / It is 2:15.

When it is half past the hour, you can express it by using either **y media** or **y treinta (minutos):**

Son las dos y media or **Son las dos y treinta** / It is 2:30.

When telling time, the verb **ser** is used in the 3rd pers. sing. if the time is one and in the 3rd pers. plural if the time is more than one.

When the time is of (to, toward, before) the hour, state the hour that it will be + **menos** + the number of minutes or **menos cuarto** (a quarter of):

Son las cuatro menos cuarto / It is a quarter of (to) four *or* It is 3:45.
Son las cinco menos veinte / It is twenty minutes to five *or* It is 4:40.

When you are not telling what time it is and you want only to say *at* a certain time, merely say: **a la una, a las dos, a las tres** / at one o'clock, at two o'clock, at three o'clock; **a la una y cuarto** / at 1:15; **a las cuatro y media** / at 4:30, *etc.*

¿A qué hora va Ud. a la clase de español? / At what time do you go to Spanish class? **Voy a la clase a las dos y veinte** / I go to class at 2:20.

¿A qué hora toma Ud. el almuerzo? / At what time do you have lunch? **Tomo el almuerzo a las doce en punto** / I have lunch at exactly twelve o'clock.

¿A qué hora toma Ud. el autobús para ir a la escuela? / At what time do you take the bus to go to school? **Tomo el autobús a las ocho en punto** / I take the bus at eight o'clock sharp.

¿Llega Ud. a la escuela a tiempo? / Do you arrive at school on time? **Llego a la escuela a eso de las ocho y media** / I arrive at school at about 8:30.

When you state what time it is or at what time you are going to do something, sometimes you have to make it clear whether it is in the morning (A.M.), in the afternoon (P.M.), or in the evening (P.M.):

Tomo el tren a las ocho de la noche / I am taking the train at 8:00 P.M. (at eight o'clock in the evening).

Tomo el tren a las ocho de la mañana / I am taking the train at 8:00 A.M. (at eight o'clock in the morning).

Tomo el tren a las cuatro de la tarde / I am taking the train at 4:00 P.M. (at four o'clock in the afternoon).

Tomo el tren a las tres de la madrugada / I am taking the train at 3:00 A.M. (at three o'clock in the morning). Note that in Spanish we say **de la madrugada** (before daylight hours) instead of **de la noche** if the time is between midnight and the break of dawn.

¿Qué hora es? / What time is it? **Es mediodía** / It is noon.

¿Qué hora es? / What time is it? **Es medianoche** / It is midnight.

¿A qué hora toma Ud. el almuerzo? / At what time do you have lunch? **Tomo el almuerzo a mediodía** (or **al mediodía**).

¿A qué hora se acuesta Ud. por lo general? / At what time do you generally get to bed? **Generalmente, me acuesto a medianoche** (or **a la medianoche**).

When telling time in the past, use the imperfect indicative tense of the verb **ser:** It was two o'clock when I had lunch today / **Eran las dos cuando tomé el almuerzo hoy;** It was one o'clock when I saw them / **Era la una cuando los vi; ¿Qué hora era cuando sus padres llegaron a casa?** / What time was it when your parents arrived home? **Eran las dos de la madrugada** / It was two in the morning.

The future tense is used when telling time in the future or when you wonder what time it is at present or when you want to state what time it probably is:

En algunos minutos serán las tres / In a few minutes it will be three o'clock.

¿Qué hora será? / I wonder what time it is: **Serán las seis** / It is probably six o'clock.

When wondering what time it was in the past or when stating what time it probably was in the past, use the conditional: **¿Qué hora sería?** / I wonder what time it was; **Serían las seis cuando llegaron** / It was probably six o'clock when they arrived.

When no specific time is stated and you merely want to say *in the morning, in the afternoon, in the evening,* use the prep. **por** instead of **de: Los sábados estudio mis lecciones por la mañana, juego por la tarde, y salgo por la noche** / On Saturdays I study my lessons in the morning, I play in the afternoon, and I go out in the evening.

To express *a little after the hour,* state the hour + **y pico: Cuando salí eran las seis y pico** / When I went out it was a little after six o'clock.

To say *about* or *around* a particular time, say **a eso de** + the hour: **Te veré a eso de la una** / I will see you about one o'clock; **Te veré a eso de las tres** / I will see you around three o'clock.

Instead of using **menos** (of, to, toward, before the hour), you may use the verb **faltar,** which means *to be lacking:* **Faltan cinco minutos para les tres** / It's five minutes to three (In other words, five minutes are lacking before it is three o'clock). In this construction, which is idiomatic, note the use of the prep. **para.**

Finally, note another way to tell time, which is used on radio and TV, in railroad and bus stations, at airports, and at other places where many people gather:

It is the 24 hour system around the clock.

When using the 24 hours around the clock, the stated time is perfectly clear and there is no need to say **de la madrugada, de la mañana, de la tarde,** or **de la noche.**

When using the 24 hour system around the clock, there is no need to use **cuarto, media, menos** or **y** (except when **y** is required in the cardinal number, *e.g.*, diez y seis).

When you hear or see the stated time using this system, subtract 12 from the number that you hear or see. If the number is less than 12, it is A.M. time. Midnight is **veinticuatro horas.** This system uses the cardinal numbers. Examples:

trece horas / 1 P.M.	**quince horas treinta** or 15.30 / 3:30 P.M.
catorce horas / 2 P.M.	**veinte horas cuarenta y dos** or 20.42 / 8:42 P.M.
veinte horas / 8 P.M.	**nueve horas diez** or 09.10 / 9:10 A.M.

WEATHER EXPRESSIONS

With HACER

¿Qué tiempo hace? / What is the weather like?
Hace buen tiempo / The weather is good.
Hace calor / It is warm (hot).
Hace fresco hoy / It is cool today.
Hace frío / It is cold.
Hace mal tiempo / The weather is bad.
Hace sol / It is sunny.
Hace viento / It is windy.
¿Qué tiempo hacía cuando usted salió esta mañana? / What was the weather like when you went out this morning?

Hacía mucho frío ayer por la noche / It was very cold yesterday evening.
Hacía mucho viento / It is very windy.
¿Qué tiempo hará mañana? / What will the weather be like tomorrow?
Se dice que hará mucho calor / They say it will be very hot.

With HABER

Hay lodo / It is muddy; **Había lodo** / It was muddy.
Hay luna / The moon is shining *or* There is moonlight; **Había luna ayer por la noche** / There was moonlight yesterday evening.
Hay mucha nieve aquí en el invierno? / Is there much snow here in winter?
Hay neblina / It is foggy; **Había mucha neblina** / It was very foggy.
Hay polvo / It is dusty; **Había mucho polvo** / It was very dusty.

Other weather expressions

Está lloviendo ahora / It is raining now.
Está nevando / It is snowing.
Está mañana llovía cuando tomé al autobús / This morning it was raining when I took the bus.
Estaba lloviendo cuando tomé el autobús / It was raining when I took the bus.
Estaba nevando cuando me desperté / It was snowing when I woke up.
¿Nieva mucho aquí en el invierno? / Does it snow much here in winter?
Las estrellas brillan / The stars are shining.
¿Le gusta a usted la lluvia? / Do you like rain?
¿Le gusta a usted la nieve? / Do you like snow?

SYNONYMS

Another very good way to increase your Spanish vocabulary in preparation for a Regents exam in Spanish is to think of a synonym (similar meaning) for every word in Spanish that you already know. Of course, there is no synonym for all words in the Spanish language—nor in English. If you hope to achieve a high score on standardized tests, you must try now to increase your vocabulary. Study the following synonyms. You can be sure that a good number of them will be on standardized tests. They are standard words of high frequency.

acercarse (a), aproximarse (a) / to approach, to come near
acordarse (de), recordar / to remember
alabar, elogiar / to praise, to glorify, to eulogize
alimento, comida / food, nourishment
alumno (alumna), estudiante / pupil, student
andar, caminar / to walk
anillo, sortija / ring (finger)
antiguo (antigua), viejo (vieja) / ancient, old
así que, luego que, tan pronto como / as soon as
asustar, espantar / to frighten, to terrify, to scare
atreverse (a), osar / to dare, to venture
aún, todavía / still, yet, even
ayuda, socorro, auxilio / aid, succor, help, assistance
barco, buque, vapor / boat, ship
bastante, suficiente / enough, sufficient
batalla, combate, lucha / battle, combat, struggle, fight
bonito (bonita), lindo (linda) / pretty
breve, corto (corta) / brief, short
burlarse de, mofarse de / to make fun of, to mock
camarero, mozo / waiter
campesino, rústico, labrador / farmer, peasant
cara, rostro, semblante / face
cariño, amor / affection, love
cocinar, cocer, guisar / to cook
comenzar, empezar, principiar / to begin, to start, to commence
comprender, entender / to understand, to comprehend
conquistar, vencer / to conquer, to vanquish
contento (contenta), feliz, alegre / content, happy, glad
contestar, responder / to answer, to reply
continuar, seguir / to continue
cruzar, atravesar / to cross
cuarto, habitación / room
cura, sacerdote / priest
chiste, chanza, broma / jest, joke, fun
dar un paseo, pasearse / to take a walk, to go for a walk
dar voces, gritar / to shout, to cry out
de manera que, de modo que / so that
dejar de + inf., cesar de + inf. / to cease + pres. part., to stop + pres. part.
delgado, esbelto, flaco / thin, slender, slim, svelte
desafortunado, desgraciado / unfortunate

desaparecer, desvanecerse / to disappear, to vanish
desear, querer / to desire, to want, to wish
desprecio, desdén / scorn, disdain, contempt
diablo, demonio / devil, demon
diferente, distinto (distinta) / different, distinct
diligente, trabajador (trabajadora), aplicado (aplicada) / diligent, hard-working, industrious
diversión, pasatiempo / diversion, pastime
dueño (dueña), propietario (propietaria), amo (ama) / owner, master, boss
echar, lanzar, tirar, arrojar / to throw, to lance, to hurl
elevar, levantar, alzar / to elevate, to raise, to lift
empleado (empleada), dependiente / employee, clerk
enojarse, enfadarse / to become angry, to become annoyed
enviar, mandar / to send
error, falta / error, mistake, fault
escoger, elegir / to choose, to select, to elect
esperar, aguardar / to wait for
esposa, mujer / wife, spouse
estrecho (estrecha), angosto (angosta) / narrow
famoso (famosa), célebre, ilustre / famous, celebrated, renowned, illustrious
fatigado (fatigada), cansado (cansada), rendido (rendida) / tired, exhausted, worn out
fiebre, calentura / fever
grave, serio (seria) / serious, grave
habilidad, destreza / ability, skill, dexterity
hablador (habladora), locuaz / talkative, loquacious
halagar, lisonjear, adular / to flatter
hallar, encontrar / to find
hermoso (hermosa), bello (bella) / beautiful, handsome
igual, semejante / equal, alike, similar
invitar, convidar / to invite
irse, marcharse / to leave, to go away
joya, alhaja / jewel, gem
lanzar, tirar, echar / to throw, to lance, to hurl
lengua, idioma / language, idiom
lentamente, despacio / slowly
luchar, combatir, pelear, pugnar / to fight, to battle, to combat, to struggle
lugar, sitio / place, site

llevar, conducir / to take, to lead
maestro (maestra), profesor (profesora) / teacher, professor
marido, esposo / husband, spouse
mendigo (mendiga), pordiosero (pordiosera), limosnero (limosnera) / beggar
miedo, temor / fear, dread
morir, fallecer, fenecer / to die, to expire
mostrar, enseñar / to show
nobleza, hidalguez, hidalguía / nobility
nunca, jamás / never
obtener, conseguir / to obtain, to get
ocurrir, suceder, acontecer, acaecer / to occur, to happen, to come about, to come to pass
odiar, aborrecer / to hate, to abhor
onda, ola / wave
país, nación / country, nation
pájaro, ave / bird
pararse, detenerse / to stop (oneself)
parecido, semejante / like, similar
pasar un buen rato, divertirse / to have a good time
pena, dolor / pain, grief
perezoso (perezosa), flojo (floja) / lazy
periódico, diario / newspaper
permiso, licencia / permission, leave
permitir, dejar / to permit, to allow, to let
poner, colocar / to put, to place
porfiado (porfiada), terco (terca), testarudo (testaruda) / obstinate, stubborn
posponer, diferir, aplazar / to postpone, to defer, to put off, to delay
premio, galardón / prize, reward
quedarse, permanecer / to remain, to stay
rapidez, prisa, velocidad / rapidity, haste, speed, velocity
regresar, volver / to return (to a place)
rezar, orar / to pray
rogar, suplicar / to beg, to implore, to entreat
romper, quebrar / to break
sin embargo, no obstante / nevertheless, however
solamente, sólo / only
sorprender, asombrar / to surprise, to astonish
suceso, acontecimiento / happening, event
sufrir, padecer / to suffer, to endure

susto, espanto / fright, scare, dread
tal vez, acaso, quizá, quizás / maybe, perhaps
terminar, acabar, concluir / to terminate, to finish, to end
tonto (tonta), necio (necia) / foolish, stupid, idiotic
trabajo, tarea, obra / work, task
tratar de, intentar / to try to, to attempt
ya que, puesto que / since, inasmuch as

NUMBERS

Cardinal numbers: zero to one hundred million

0 cero
1 uno, una
2 dos
3 tres
4 cuatro
5 cinco
6 seis
7 siete
8 ocho
9 nueve
10 diez
11 once
12 doce
13 trece
14 catorce
15 quince
16 diez y seis or dieciséis
17 diez y siete or diecisiete
18 diez y ocho or dieciocho
19 diez y nueve or diecinueve
20 veinte
21 veinte y uno or veintiuno
22 veinte y dos or veintidós
23 veinte y tres or veintitrés
24 veinte y cuatro or veinticuatro
25 veinte y cinco or veinticinco
26 veinte y seis or veintiséis
27 veinte y siete or veintisiete
28 veinte y ocho or veintiocho
29 veinte y nueve or veintinueve
30 treinta
31 treinta y uno, treinta y una
32 treinta y dos, *etc.*
40 cuarenta
41 cuarenta y uno, cuarenta y una
42 cuarenta y dos, *etc.*
50 cincuenta
51 cincuenta y uno, cincuenta y una
52 cincuenta y dos, *etc.*
60 sesenta
61 sesenta y uno, sesenta y una
62 sesenta y dos, *etc.*
70 setenta
71 setenta y uno, setenta y una
72 setenta y dos, *etc.*
80 ochenta
81 ochenta y uno, ochenta y una
82 ochenta y dos, *etc.*

90	**noventa**	**1,000**	**mil**
91	noventa y uno, noventa y una	2,000	dos mil
92	noventa y dos, *etc.*	3,000	tres mil, *etc.*
100	**ciento (cien)**	100,000	cien mil
101	ciento uno, ciento una	200,000	doscientos mil, doscientas mil
102	ciento dos, *etc.*	300,000	trescientos mil, trescientas mil, *etc.*
200	**doscientos, doscientas**	**1,000,000**	**un millón (de + noun)**
300	trescientos, trescientas	2,000,000	dos millones (de + noun)
400	cuatrocientos, cuatrocientas	3,000,000	tres millones (de + noun), *etc.*
500	quinientos, quinientas	100,000,000	cien millones (de + noun)
600	seiscientos, seiscientas		
700	setecientos, setecientas		Approximate numbers
800	ochocientos, ochocientas		**unos veinte libros** / about (some) twenty books
900	novecientos, novecientas		**unas treinta personas** / about (some) thirty persons

Simple arithmetical expressions

dos **y** dos son cuatro	$2 + 2 = 4$
diez **menos** cinco son cinco	$10 - 5 = 5$
tres **por** cinco son quince	$3 \times 5 = 15$
diez **dividido por** dos son cinco	$10 \div 2 = 5$

Ordinal numbers: first to tenth

primero, primer, primera	first	1st
segundo, segunda	second	2nd
tercero, tercer, tercera	third	3rd
cuarto, cuarta	fourth	4th
quinto, quinta	fifth	5th
sexto, sexta	sixth	6th
séptimo, séptima	seventh	7th

octavo, octava	eighth	8th
noveno, novena	ninth	9th
décimo, décima	tenth	10th

NOTE that beyond 10th the cardinal numbers are used instead of the ordinal numbers, but when there is a noun involved, the cardinal number is placed after the noun: **el día 15** (**el día quince** / the fifteenth day).

NOTE also that in titles of monarchs, *etc.* the definite article is not used between the person's name and the number, but it is in English: **Alfonso XIII** (**Alfonso Trece** / Alfonso the Thirteenth).

AND NOTE that **noveno** (9th) changes to **nono** in such titles: **Luis IX** (**Luis Nono** / Louis the Ninth).

PARTICIPLES

Present participle: A present participle is a verb form which, in English, ends in *-ing*; for example, *singing, eating, receiving.* In Spanish, a present participle is regularly formed as follows:

drop the **ar** of an **-ar** ending verb, like **cantar,** and add **-ando: cantando** / singing

drop the **er** of an **-er** ending verb, like **comer,** and add **-iendo: comiendo** / eating

drop the **ir** of an **-ir** ending verb, like **recibir,** and add **-iendo: recibiendo** / receiving

In English, a gerund also ends in *-ing* but there is a distinct difference in use between a gerund and a present participle in English. In brief, it is this: In English, when a present participle is used as a noun it is called a gerund; for example: *Reading is good.* As a present participle in English: The boy fell asleep *while reading.*

In the first example (*Reading is good*), *reading* is a gerund because it is the subject of the verb *is.* In Spanish, however, we must not use the present participle form as a noun to serve as a subject; we must use the infinitive form of the verb in Spanish: **Leer es bueno.**

Common irregular present participles are as follows. You ought to know them so that you may be able to recognize them if they are on the next Spanish Regents exam that you take.

Infinitive	Present Participle
caer / to fall	**cayendo** / falling
conseguir / to attain, to achieve	**consiguiendo** / attaining, achieving
construir / to construct	**construyendo** / constructing
corregir / to correct	**corrigiendo** / correcting
creer / to believe	**creyendo** / believing
decir / to say, to tell	**diciendo** / saying, telling
despedirse / to say good-bye	**despidiéndose** / saying good-bye
destruir / to destroy	**destruyendo** / destroying
divertirse / to enjoy oneself	**divirtiéndose** / enjoying oneself
dormir / to sleep	**durmiendo** / sleeping
huir / to flee	**huyendo** / fleeing
ir / to go	**yendo** / going
leer / to read	**leyendo** / reading
mentir / to lie (tell a falsehood)	**mintiendo** / lying
morir / to die	**muriendo** / dying
oír / to hear	**oyendo** / hearing
pedir / to ask (for), to request	**pidiendo** / asking (for), requesting
poder / to be able	**pudiendo** / being able
reír / to laugh	**riendo** / laughing
repetir / to repeat	**repitiendo** / repeating
seguir / to follow	**siguiendo** / following
sentir / to feel	**sintiendo** / feeling
servir / to serve	**sirviendo** / serving
traer / to bring	**trayendo** / bringing
venir / to come	**viniendo** / coming
vestir / to dress	**vistiendo** / dressing

Uses of the present participle

To form the progressive tenses:

The Progressive Present is formed by using **estar** in the present tense plus the present participle of the main verb you are using; *e.g.*, **Estoy hablando** (*I am talking*), *i.e.*, *I am* (in the act of) *talking* (right now).

The Progressive Past is formed by using **estar** in the imperfect indicative plus the present participle of the main verb you are using;

e.g., **Estaba hablando** (*I was talking*), *i.e.*, *I was* (in the act of) *talking* (then, at some point in the past).

The progressive forms are generally used when you want to emphasize what you are saying; if you don't want to do that, then just use the simple present or the imperfect, *e.g.*, say **Hablo,** rather than **Estoy hablando;** or **Hablaba,** rather than **Estaba hablando.**

In brief, the Progressive Present is used to describe with intensification what is happening or going on at present. The Progressive Past is used to describe with intensification what was happening, what was going on at some point in the past.

Instead of using **estar,** as noted above, to form these two progressive tenses, sometimes **ir** is used: **Va hablando** / *He (she) keeps right on talking;* **Iba hablando** / *He (she) kept right on talking.* NOTE that they do not have the exact same meaning as **Está hablando** and **Estaba hablando,** as explained above.

Also, at time **andar, continuar, seguir** and **venir** are used as helping verbs in the present or imperfect indicative tenses plus the present participle to express the progressive forms: **Los muchachos andaban cantando** / The boys were walking along singing; **La maestra seguía leyendo a la clase** / The teacher kept right on reading to the class.

To express vividly an action that occurred (preterit + present participle): **El niño entró llorando en la casa** / The little boy came crying into the house.

To express the English use of *by* + present participle in Spanish, we use the gerund form, which has the same ending as a present participle explained above: **Trabajando, se gana dinero** / By working, one earns (a person earns) money; **Estudiando mucho, Pepe recibió buenas notas** / By studying hard, Joe received good grades.

NOTE here that no preposition is used in front of the present participle (the Spanish gerund) even though it is expressed in English as *by + present participle*.

NOTE, too, that in Spanish we use **al + infinitive** (not + present participle) to express *on* or *upon* + *present participle* in English: **Al entrar en la casa, el niño comenzó a llorar** / Upon entering the house, the little boy began to cry.

To form the Perfect Participle: habiendo hablado / having talked.

Finally, note that the only preposition that may be used in front of the Spanish gerund (English present participle) is **en** which gives the meaning of *after* + present participle in English: **En corriendo rápidamente, el viejo cayó y murió** / After running rapidly, the old man fell and died.

Past participle: A past participle is a verb form which, in English, usually ends in *-ed*; for example, *worked, talked, arrived,* as in *I have worked, I have talked, I have arrived.* There are many irregular past participles in English; for example: *gone, sung,* as in *She has gone, We have sung.* In Spanish, a past participle is regularly formed as follows:

drop the **ar** of an **-ar** ending verb, like **trabajar,** and add **-ado: trabajado** / worked
drop the **er** of an **-er** ending verb, like **comer,** and add **-ido: comido** / eaten
drop the **ir** of an **-ir** ending verb, like **recibir,** and add **-ido: recibido** / received

Common irregular past participles are as follows. You ought to know them so that you may be able to recognize them when you see them on the next Spanish Regents exam that you take.

Infinitive	Past Participle
abrir / to open	**abierto** / opened
caer / to fall	**caído** / fallen
creer / to believe	**creído** / believed
cubrir / to cover	**cubierto** / covered
decir / to say, to tell	**dicho** / said, told
descubrir / to discover	**descubierto** / discovered
deshacer / to undo	**deshecho** / undone
devolver / to return (something)	**devuelto** / returned (something)
escribir / to write	**escrito** / written

hacer / to do, to make | **hecho** / done, made
imponer / to impose | **impuesto** / imposed
imprimir / to print | **impreso** / printed
ir / to go | **ido** / gone
leer / to read | **leído** / read
morir / to die | **muerto** / died
oír / to hear | **oído** / heard
poner / to put | **puesto** / put
rehacer / to redo, to remake | **rehecho** / redone, remade
reír / to laugh | **reído** / laughed
resolver / to resolve, to solve | **resuelto** / resolved, solved
romper / to break | **roto** / broken
traer / to bring | **traído** / brought
ver / to see | **visto** / seen
volver / to return | **vuelto** / returned

SPANISH VERB FORMS YOU SHOULD KNOW

Common irregular Spanish verb forms and uncommon Spanish verb forms identified by infinitive.

A

abierto **abrir**
acierto, *etc.* **acertar**
acuerdo, *etc.* **acordar**
acuesto, *etc.* **acostarse**
alce, *etc.* **alzar**
ase, *etc.* **asir**
asgo, *etc.* **asir**
ate, *etc.* **atar**

C

caí, *etc.* **caer**
caía, *etc.* **caer**
caigo, *etc.* **caer**
cayera, *etc.* **caer**
cierro, *etc.* **cerrar**
cojo, *etc.* **coger**
cuece, *etc.* **cocer**
cuelgo, *etc.* **colgar**
cuento, *etc.* **contar**
cuesta, *etc.* **costar**
cuezo, *etc.* **cocer**
cupiera, *etc.* **caber**

D

da, *etc.* **dar**
dad **dar**
dé **dar**
demos **dar**
den **dar**
des **dar**
di, *etc.* **dar, decir**
dice, *etc.* **decir**
diciendo **decir**
dicho **decir**
diera *etc.* **dar**
diese, *etc.* **dar**
digo, *etc.* **decir**
dije, *etc.* **decir**
dimos, *etc.* **dar**

dio **dar**
diré, *etc.* **decir**
diría, *etc.* **decir**
doy **dar**
duelo, *etc.* **doler**
duermo, *etc.* **dormir**
durmamos **dormir**
durmiendo **dormir**

E

eliges, *etc.* **elegir**
eligiendo **elegir**
eligiera, *etc.* **elegir**
elijo, *etc.* **elegir**
era, *etc.* **ser**
eres **ser**
es **ser**

F

fíe, *etc.* **fiar**
fío, *etc.* **fiar**
freindo, *etc.* **freír**
friera, *etc.* **freír**
frío, *etc.* **freír**
frito **freír**
fue, *etc.* **ir, ser**
fuera, *etc.* **ir, ser**
fuese, *etc.* **ir, ser**
fui, *etc.* **ir, ser**

G

gima, *etc.* **gemir**
gimiendo **gemir**
gimiera, *etc.* **gemir**
gimiese, *etc.* **gemir**
gimo, *etc.* **gemir**
goce, *etc.* **gozar**
gocé **gozar**

H

ha **haber**
habré, *etc.* **haber**
haga, *etc.* **hacer**
hago, *etc.* **hacer**
han **haber**
haría, *etc.* **hacer**
has **haber**
haya, *etc.* **haber**
haz **hacer**
he **haber**
hecho **hacer**
hemos **haber**
hice, *etc.* **hacer**
hiciera, *etc.* **hacer**
hiciese, *etc.* **hacer**
hiela **helar**
hiele **helar**
hiera, *etc.* **herir**
hiero, *etc.* **herir**
hiramos **herir**
hiriendo **herir**
hiriera, *etc.* **herir**
hiriese, *etc.* **herir**
hizo **hacer**
hube, *etc.* **haber**
hubiera, *etc.* **haber**
hubiese, *etc.* **haber**
huela, *etc.* **oler**
huelo, *etc.* **oler**
huya *etc.* **huir**
huyendo **huir**
huyera, *etc.* **huir**
huyese, *etc.* **huir**
huyo, *etc.* **huir**

I

iba, *etc.* **ir**
id **ir**
ido **ir**

idos **irse**
irgo, *etc.* **erguir**
irguiendo **erguir**
irguiera, *etc.* **erguir**
irguiese, *etc.* **erguir**

J

juego, *etc.* **jugar**
juegue, *etc.* **jugar**

L

lea, *etc.* **leer**
leído **leer**
leo, *etc.* **leer**
leyendo **leer**
leyera, *etc.* **leer**
leyese, *etc.* **leer**

LL

llueva **llover**
llueve **llover**

M

mida, *etc.* **medir**
midiendo **medir**
midiera, *etc.* **medir**
midiese, *etc.* **medir**
mido, *etc.* **medir**
mienta, *etc.* **mentir**
miento, *etc.* **mentir**
mintiendo **mentir**
mintiera, *etc.* **mentir**
mintiese, *etc.* **mentir**
muerda, *etc.* **morder**
muerdo, *etc.* **morder**
muero, *etc.* **morir**
muerto **morir**
muestre, *etc.* **mostrar**
muestro, *etc.* **mostrar**
mueva, *etc.* **mover**
muevo, *etc.* **mover**
muramos **morir**
muriendo **morir**
muriera, *etc.* **morir**
muriese, *etc.* **morir**

N

nazca, *etc.* **nacer**
nazco **nacer**
niego, *etc.* **negar**
niegue, *etc.* **negar**
nieva **nevar**
nieve **nevar**

O

oíd **oír**
oiga, *etc.* **oír**
oigo, *etc.* **oír**
oliendo **oler**
oliera, *etc.* **oler**
oliese, *etc.* **oler**
oye, *etc.* **oír**
oyendo **oír**
oyera, *etc.* **oír**
oyese, *etc.* **oír**

P

pida, *etc.* **pedir**
pidamos **pedir**
pidiendo **pedir**
pidiera, *etc.* **pedir**
pidiese, *etc.* **pedir**
pido, *etc.* **pedir**
pienso, *etc.* **pensar**
pierda, *etc.* **perder**
pierdo, *etc.* **perder**
plegue **placer**
plugo **placer**

pluguiera **placer**
pluguieron **placer**
pluguiese **placer**
ponga, *etc.* **poner**
pongámonos **ponerse**
ponte **ponerse**
pruebe, *etc.* **probar**
pruebo, *etc.* **probar**
pude, *etc.* **poder**
pudiendo **poder**
pudiera, *etc.* **poder**
pudiese, *etc.* **poder**
puedo, *etc.* **poder**
puesto **poner**
puse, *etc.* **poner**
pusiera, *etc.* **poner**
pusiese, *etc.* **poner**

Q

quepo, *etc.* **caber**
quiebro **quebrar**
quiero, *etc.* **querer**
quise, *etc.* **querer**
quisiera, *etc.* **querer**
quisiese, *etc.* **querer**

R

raí, *etc.* **raer**
raía, *etc.* **raer**
raiga, *etc.* **raer**
raigo, *etc.* **raer**
rayendo **raer**
rayera, *etc.* **raer**
rayese, *etc.* **raer**
ría, *etc.* **reír**
riamos **reír**
riendo **reír**
riera, *etc.* **reír**
riese, *etc.* **reír**
riña, *etc.* **reñir**
riñendo **reñir**
reñera, *etc.* **reñir**
riñese, *etc.* **reñir**
riño, *etc.* **reñir**
río, *etc.* **reír**
roto **romper**
ruego, *etc.* **rogar**
ruegue, *etc.* **rogar**

S

saque, *etc.* **sacar**
sé **saber, ser**
sea, *etc.* **ser**
sed **ser**
sepa, *etc.* **saber**
seque, *etc.* **secar**
sido **ser**
siendo **ser**
siento, *etc.* **sentar, sentir**
sigo, *etc.* **seguir**
siguiendo **seguir**
siguiera, *etc.* **seguir**
siguiese, *etc.* **seguir**
sintiendo **sentir**
sintiera, *etc.* **sentir**
sintiese, *etc.* **sentir**
sintió **sentir**
sirviendo **servir**
sirvo, *etc.* **servir**
sois **ser**
somos **ser**
son **ser**
soy **ser**
suela, *etc.* **soler**
suelo, *etc.* **soler**
suelto, *etc.* **soltar**
sueno, *etc.* **sonar**
sueño, *etc.* **soñar**
supe, *etc.* **saber**
supiera, *etc.* **saber**
supiese, *etc.* **saber**

T

tiemblo, *etc.* **temblar**
tiendo, *etc.* **tender**
tienes, *etc.* **tener**
tiento, *etc.* **tentar**
toque, *etc.* **tocar**
tuesto, *etc.* **tostar**
tuve *etc.* **tener**

U

uno, *etc.* **unir**

V

va **ir**
vais **ir**
vámonos **irse**
vamos **ir**
van **ir**
vas **ir**
vaya, *etc.* **ir**
ve **ir, ver**
vea, *etc.* **ver**
ved **ver**
vendré, *etc.* **venir**
venga, vengo **venir**
veo, *etc.* **ver**
ves **ver**
vete **irse**
vi **ver**
viendo **ver**
viene **venir**
viera, *etc.* **ver**
viese, *etc.* **ver**
vimos, *etc.* **ver**
vine, vino, *etc.* **venir**
vio **ver**
viste **ver, vestir**
vistiendo **vestir**
vistiéndose **vestirse**
vistiese, *etc.* **vestir(se)**
visto **ver, vestir**
voy **ir**
vuelo, *etc.* **volar**
vuelto **volver**
vuelvo, *etc.* **volver**

Y

yaz **yacer**
yazco, *etc.* **yacer**
yendo **ir**
yergo, *etc.* **erguir**
yerro, *etc.* **errar**

SEQUENCE OF TENSES WHEN THE SUBJUNCTIVE IS REQUIRED: A SUMMARY

When the verb in the main clause is in the:	The verb in the following clause (the dependent clause) most likely will be in the:
1. Present Indicative or Future or Present Perfect Indicative or Imperative (Command)	1. Present Subjunctive or Present Perfect Subjunctive
2. Conditional or a past tense (Imperfect Indicative or Preterit or Pluperfect Indicative)	2. Imperfect Subjunctive or Pluperfect Subjunctive

EXAMPLES:

Deseo que Ana cante / I want Anna to sing.

Le diré a Ana que baile / I will tell Anna to dance.

Le he dicho a Ana que cante y baile / I have said to Anna to sing and dance.

Dígale a Ana que cante y baile / Tell Anna to sing and dance.

Dudo que mi madre tome el tren / I doubt that my mother is taking (*or* will take) the train.

Dudo que mi madre haya tomado el tren / I doubt that my mother has taken the train.

Le gustaría al profesor que los alumnos hicieran los ejercicios / The professor would like the pupils to do the exercises.

Sentía que su madre estuviera enferma / I felt sorry that your mother was ill.

Dudé que mi madre hubiera tomado el tren / I doubted that my mother had taken the train.

SI CLAUSE: A SUMMARY OF CONTRARY-TO-FACT CONDITIONS

When the verb in the Si clause is:	The verb in the main or result clause is:
1. Present Indicative	1. Future

Example: **Si tengo bastante tiempo, vendré a verle** / If I have enough time, I will come to see you.

Note that the present subjunctive form of a verb is never used in a clause beginning with the conjunction *si*.

2. Imperfect Subjunctive (**-se** form or **-ra** form)	2. Conditional or Imperfect Subjunctive (**-ra** form)

Example: **Si yo tuviese** (*or* **tuviera**) **bastante tiempo, vendría a verle** / If I had enough time, I would come to see you.

OR: **Si yo tuviese** (*or* **tuviera**) **bastante tiempo, viniera a verle** / If I had enough time, I would come to see you.

3. Pluperfect Subjunctive (**-se** form or **-ra** form)	3. Conditional Perfect or Pluperfect Subjunctive (**-ra** form)

Example: **Si yo hubiese tenido** (*or* **hubiera tenido**) **bastante tiempo, habría venido a verle** / If I had had enough time, I would have come to see you.

OR: **Si yo hubiese tenido** (*or* **hubiera tenido**) **bastante tiempo, hubiera venido a verle** / If I had had enough time, I would have come to see you.

VERBS USED IN IDIOMATIC EXPRESSIONS

* Acabar de + inf.

The Spanish idiomatic expression **acabar de + inf.** is expressed in English as *to have just* + past participle.

In the present indicative:

María acaba de llegar. Mary has just arrived.

Acabo de comer. I have just eaten.

Acabamos de terminar la lección. We have just finished the lesson.

In the imperfect indicative:

María acababa de llegar. Mary had just arrived.

Acababa de comer. I had just eaten.

Acabábamos de terminar la lección. We had just finished the lesson.

Note:

(a) When you use **acabar** in the present tense, it indicates that the action of the main verb (+ inf.) has just occurred now in the present. In English, we express this by using *have just* + the past participle of the main verb: *Acabo de llegar* / I have just arrived. (See the other examples above under present indicative.)

(b) When you use **acabar** in the imperfect indicative, it indicates that the action of the main verb (+ inf.) had occurred at some time in the past when another action occurred in the past. In English, we express this by using *had just* + the past participle of the main verb: *Acabábamos de entrar en la casa cuando el teléfono sonó* / We had just entered the house when the telephone rang. (See the other examples above under imperfect indicative.)

Note also that when **acabar** is used in the imperfect indicative + the inf. of the main verb being expressed, the verb in the other clause is usually in the preterit.

Conocer and saber

These two verbs mean *to know* but they are each used in a distinct sense:

(a) Generally speaking, **conocer** means to know in the sense of *being acquainted* with a person, a place, or a thing: *¿Conoce Ud. a María?* / Do you know Mary? *¿Conoce Ud. bien los Estados Unidos?* / Do you know the United States well? *¿Conoce Ud. este libro?* / Do you know (Are you acquainted with) this book?

In the preterit tense, **conocer** means *met* in the sense of *first met, first became acquainted with someone: ¿Conoce Ud. a Elena?* / Do you know Helen? *Sí, (yo) la conocí anoche en casa de un amigo mío* / Yes, I met her (for the first time) last night at the home of one my friends.

(b) Generally speaking, **saber** means to know a fact, to know something thoroughly: *¿Sabe Ud. qué hora es?* / Do you know what time it is? *¿Sabe Ud. la lección?* / Do you know the lesson?

When you use **saber + inf.**, it means *to know how: ¿Sabe Ud. nadar?* / Do you know how to swim? *Sí, (yo) sé nadar* / Yes, I know how to swim.

In the preterit tense, **saber** means *found out: ¿Lo sabe Ud.?* / Do you know it? *Sí, lo supe ayer* / Yes, I found it out yesterday.

Dar and darse

dar a to face (*El comedor da al jardín*/The dining room faces the garden.)

dar con algo to find something, to come upon something (*Esta mañana di con dinero en la calle*/This morning I found money in the street.)

dar con alguien to meet someone, to run into someone, to come across someone, to find someone (*Anoche, di con mi amiga Elena en el cine*/Last night I met my friend Helen at the movies.)

dar cuerda al reloj to wind a watch

dar de beber a to give something to drink to

dar de comer a to feed, to give something to eat to (*Me gusta dar de comer a los pájaros en el parque*/I like to feed the birds in the park.)

dar en to hit against, to strike against

dar en el blanco to hit the target, to hit it right

dar gritos to shout

dar la bienvenida to welcome

dar la hora to strike the hour

dar la mano a alguien to shake hands with someone

dar las buenas noches a alguien to say good evening (good night) to someone

dar las gracias a alguien to thank someone

dar los buenos días a alguien to say good morning (hello) to someone

dar por + past part. to consider (*Lo doy por perdido*/I consider it lost.)

dar recuerdos a to given one's regards (best wishes) to

dar un abrazo to embrace

dar un paseo to take a walk

dar un paseo a caballo to go horseback riding

dar un paseo en automóvil to go for a drive

dar una vuelta to go for a short walk, to go for a stroll

dar unas palmadas to clap one's hands

dar voces to shout

darse cuenta de to realize, to be aware of, to take into account

dar la mano to shake hands with each other

darse por + past part. to consider oneself (*Me doy por insultado*/I consider myself insulted.)

darse prisa to hurry

Deber, deber de, and tener que

Generally speaking, use **deber** when you want to express a moral obligation, something you ought to do but that you may or may not actually do: *Debo estudiar esta noche pero estoy cansado y no me siento bien*/I ought to study tonight but I am tired and I do not feel well.

Generally speaking, **deber de + inf.** is used to express a supposition, something that is probable: *La señora Gómez debe de estar enferma porque sale de casa raramente*/Mrs. Gómez must be sick (is probably sick) because she goes out of the house rarely.

Generally speaking, use **tener que** when you want to say that you *have to* do something: *No puedo salir esta noche porque tengo que estudiar*/I cannot go out tonight because I have to study.

Decir

decirle al oído to whisper in one's ear

dicho y hecho no sooner said than done

Es decir That is to say . . .

querer decir to mean (*¿Qué quiere decir este muchacho?*/What does this boy mean?)

Dejar, salir, and salir de

These verbs mean *to leave,* but notice the difference in use:

Use **dejar** when you leave someone or when you leave something behind you: *El alumno dejó sus libros en la sala de clase*/The pupil left his books in the classroom.

Dejar also means *to let* or *to allow* or *to let go: Déjelo!*/Let it! (Leave it!)

Use **salir de** when you mean *to leave* in the sense of *to go out of* (a place): *El alumno salió de la sala de clase*/The pupil left the classroom: *¿Dónde está su madre? Mi madre salió*/Where is your mother? My mother went out.

Dejar de + inf. and dejar caer

Use **dejar de + inf.** when you mean *to stop* or *to fail to: Los alumnos dejaron de hablar cuando la profesora entró en la sala de clase*/The students stopped talking when the teacher came into the classroom; *¡No deje Ud. de llamarme!*/Don't fail to call me!

Dejar caer means *to drop: Luis dejó caer sus libros*/Louis dropped his books.

Estar

está bien all right, okay

estar a punto de + inf. to be about + inf. (*Estoy a punto de salir*/I am about to go out.)

estar a sus anchas to be comfortable

estar aburrido (aburrida) to be bored

estar al día to be up to date

estar bien to be well

estar conforme con to be in agreement with

estar de acuerdo to agree

estar de acuerdo con to be in agreement with

estar de boga to be in fashion, to be fashionable

estar de buenas to be in a good mood

estar de más to be unnecessary

estar de pie to be standing

estar de vuelta to be back

estar en boga to be in fashion, to be fashionable

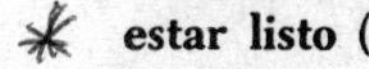

estar listo (lista) to be ready

estar mal to be ill

estar para + inf. to be about to (*Estoy para salir*/I am about to go out.)

estar por to be in favor of

no estar para bromas not to be in the mood for jokes

Gastar and pasar

These two verbs mean *to spend,* but notice the difference in use:

Use **gastar** when you spend money: *No me gusta gastar mucho dinero*/I do not like to spend much money.

Use **pasar** when you spend time: *Me gustaría pasar un año en España*/I would like to spend a year in Spain.

Gustar

(a) Essentially, the verb **gustar** means *to be pleasing to . . .*

(b) In English, we say, for example, *I like ice cream.* In Spanish, we say *Me gusta el helado;* that is to say, "Ice cream is pleasing to me (To me ice cream is pleasing)."

(c) In English, the thing that you like is the direct object. In Spanish, the thing that you like is the subject. Also, in Spanish, the person who likes the thing is the indirect object: to me, to you, etc.: *A Roberto le gusta el helado*/Robert likes ice cream; in other words, "To Robert, ice cream is pleasing to him."

(d) In Spanish, therefore, the verb **gustar** is used in the third person, either in the singular or plural, when you talk about something that you like—something that is pleasing to you. Therefore, the verb form must agree with the subject; if the thing liked is singular, the verb is third person singular; if the thing liked is plural, the verb **gustar** is third person plural: *Me gusta el café*/I like coffee; *Me gustan el café y la leche*/I like coffee and milk (Coffee and milk are pleasing to me).

(e) When you mention the person or the persons who like something, you must use the preposition **a** in front of the person; you must also use the indirect object pronoun of the noun which is the person: *A los muchachos y a las muchasas les gusta jugar*/Boys and girls like to play; that is to say, "To play is pleasing to them, to boys and girls."

(f) Other examples:

Me gusta leer. I like to read.

Te gusta leer. You *(familiar)* like to read.

A Felipe le gusta el helado. Philip likes ice cream.

Al chico le gusta la leche. The boy likes milk.

A Carlota le gusta bailar. Charlotte likes to dance.

A las chicas les gustó el libro. The girls liked the book.

Nos gustó el cuento. We liked the story.

¿Le gusta a Ud. el español? Do you like Spanish?

A Pedro y a Ana les gustó la película. Peter and Anna liked the film.

A mi amigo le gustaron los chocolates. My friend liked the chocolates; that is to say, "The chocolates were pleasing to (pleased) him (to my friend)."

Haber

ha habido . . . there has been . . ., there have been . . .

había . . . there was . . ., there were . . .

habrá . . . there will be . . .

habría . . . there would be . . .

hubo . . . there was . . ., there were . . .

Haber, haber de + inf., and tener

The verb **haber** (to have) is used as an auxiliary verb (or helping verb) in order to form the seven compound tenses, which are as follows:

Compound Tenses	Example (in the 1st person sing.)
Present Perfect (or Perfect) Indicative	**he hablado** (I have spoken)
Pluperfect (or Past Perfect) Indicative	**había hablado** (I had spoken)
Preterit Perfect (or Past Anterior)	**hube hablado** (I had spoken)
Future Perfect (or Future Anterior)	**habré hablado** (I will have spoken)
Conditional Perfect	**habría hablado** (I would have spoken)
Present Perfect (or Past) Subjunctive	**haya hablado** (I may have spoken)
Pluperfect (or Past Perfect) Subjective	**hubiera hablado** *or* **hubiese hablado** (I might have spoken)

The verb **haber** is also used to form the perfect (or past) infinitive: *haber hablado* (to have spoken). As you can see, this is formed by using the infinitive form of haber + the past participle of the main verb.

The verb **haber** is also used to form the perfect participle: *habiendo hablado* (having spoken). As you can see, this is formed by using the present participle of haber + the past participle of the main verb.

The verb **haber + de + inf.** is equivalent to the English use of "to be supposed to . . ." or "to be to . . .": *María ha de traer un pastel, yo he de traer el helado, y mis amigos han de traer sus discos*/Mary is supposed to bring a pie, I am supposed to bring the ice cream, and my friends are to bring their records.

The verb **tener** is used to mean *to have* in the sense of *to possess* or *to hold: Tengo un perro y un gato*/I have a dog and a cat; *Tengo un lápiz en la mano*/I have (am holding) a pencil in my hand.

In the preterit tense, **tener** can mean *received: Ayer mi padre tuvo un cheque*/Yesterday my father received a check.

Hay and hay que + inf.

The word **hay** is not a verb. You might regard it as an impersonal irregular form of **haber**. Actually, the word is composed of **ha** +

the archaic **y**, meaning *there.* It is generally regarded as an adverbial expression because it points out that something or someone "is there." Its English equivalent is *There is . . .* or *There are . . .*, for example: *Hay muchos libros en la mesa*/There are many books on the table; *Hay una mosca en la sopa*/There is a fly in the soup; *Hay veinte alumnos en esta clase*/There are twenty students in this class.

Hay que + inf. is an impersonal expression that denotes an obligation and it is commonly translated into English as: *One must . . .* or *It is necessary to . . .* Examples: *Hay que estudiar para aprender*/It is necessary to study in order to learn; *Hay que comer para vivir*/One must eat in order to live.

Hacer and hacerse

hace poco a little while ago

hace un año a year ago

Hace un mes que partió el señor Molina. Mr. Molina left one month ago.

hace una hora an hour ago

hacer caso de to pay attention to

hacer daño a algo to harm something

hacer daño a alguien to harm someone

hacer de to act as (*El señor González siempre hace de jefe*/Mr. González always acts as a boss.)

hacer el baúl to pack one's trunk

hacer el favor de + inf. please (*Haga Ud. el favor de entrar*/Please come in.)

hacer el papel de to play the role of

hacer la maleta to pack one's suitcase

hacer pedazos to smash, to break, to tear into pieces

hacer un viaje to take a trip

hacer una broma to play a joke

hacer una pregunta to ask a question

hacer una visita to pay a visit

hacerle falta to need (*A Juan le hace falta un lápiz*/John needs a pencil.)

hacerse to become (*Elena se hizo dentista*/Helen became a dentist.)

hacerse daño to hurt oneself, to harm oneself

hacerse tarde to be getting late (*Vámonos; se hace tarde*/Let's leave; it's getting late.)

¿Cuánto tiempo hace que + present tense . . .?

(a) Use this formula when you want to ask *How long + the present perfect tense* in English:

¿Cuánto tiempo hace que Ud. estudia el español? How long have you been studying Spanish?

¿Cuánto tiempo hace que Ud. espera el autobús? How long have you been waiting for the bus?

(b) When this formula is used, you generally expect the person to tell you how long a time it has been, e.g., one year, two months, a few minutes.

(c) This is used when the action began at some time in the past and continues up to the present moment. That is why you must use the present tense of the verb—the action of studying, waiting, etc. is still going on at the present.

Hace + length of time + que + present tense

(a) This formula is the usual answer to the question **¿Cuánto tiempo hace que + present tense . . .?**

(b) Since the question is asked in terms of *how long*, the usual answer is in terms of time: a year, two years, a few days, months, minutes, ect.:

Hace tres años que estudio el español. I have been studying Spanish for three years.

Hace veinte minutos que espero el autobús. I have been waiting for the bus for twenty minutes.

(c) The same formula is used if you want to ask *how many weeks, how many months, how many minutes*, etc.:

¿Cuántos años hace que Ud. estudia el español? How many years have you been studying Spanish?

¿Cuántas horas hace que Ud. mira la televisión? How many hours have you been watching television?

¿Desde cuándo + present tense . . .?

¿Desde cuándo estudia Ud. el español? How long have you been studying Spanish?

Present tense + desde hace + length of time

Estudio el español desde hace tres años. I have been studying Spanish for three years.

¿Cuánto tiempo hacía que + imperfect tense . . .?

(a) If the action of the verb began in the past and ended in the past, use the imperfect tense.

(b) This formula is equivalent to the English: *How long + past perfect tense: ¿Cuánto tiempo hacía que Ud. hablaba cuando entré en la sala de clase?* How long had you been talking when I entered into the classroom?

(c) Note that the action of talking in this example began in the past and ended in the past when I entered the classroom.

Hacía + length of time + que + imperfect tense

The imperfect tense of the verb is used here because the action began in the past and ended in the past; it is not going on at the present moment.

Hacía una hora que yo hablaba cuando Ud. entró en la sala de clase. I had been talking for one hour when you entered the classroom.

¿Desde cuándo + imperfect tense . . .?

¿Desde cuándo hablaba Ud. cuando yo entré en la sala de clase? How long had you been talking when I entered into the classroom?

Imperfect tense + desde hacía + length of time

(Yo) hablaba desde hacía una hora cuando Ud. entró en la sala de clase. I had been talking for one hour when you entered into the classroom.

Ir, irse

Use **ir** when you simply mean *to go: Voy al cine*/I am going to the movies.

Use **irse** when you mean *to leave* in the sense of *to go away: Mis padres se fueron al campo para visitar a mis abuelos*/My parents left for (went away to) the country to visit my grandparents.

ir a caballo to ride horseback

ir a medias to go halves

ir a pie to walk (to go on foot)

ir bien to get along well

ir con tiento to go quietly, softly

ir delante to go ahead

ir por to go for, to go ahead

irse de prisa to rush away

¡Qué va! Nonsense! Rubbish!

¡Vaya! You don't say!

Vaya con Dios. God be with you.

Jugar and tocar

Both these verbs mean *to play* but they have different uses. **Jugar a** means to play a sport, a game: *¿Juega Ud. al tenis?*/Do you play tennis? *Me gusta jugar a la pelota*/I like to play ball.

The verb **tocar** means to play a musical instrument: *Carmen toca muy bien el piano*/Carmen plays the piano very well.

The verb **tocar** has other meanings, too. It is commonly used as follows: *to be one's turn,* in which case it takes an indirect object: *¿A quién le toca?*/Whose turn is it? *Le toca a Juan*/It is John's turn. *to knock on a door* (tocar a la puerta): *Alguien toca a la puerta*/Someone is knocking on (at) the door.

Essentially, **tocar** means *to touch.*

Llegar a ser, hacerse, and ponerse

These three verbs mean *to become.* Note the difference in use:

Use **llegar a ser + a noun,** e.g., *to become a doctor, to become a teacher;* in other words, the noun indicates the goal that you are striving for: *Quiero llegar a ser doctor*/I want to become a doctor. **Hacerse** is used similarly: *Juan se hizo abogado*/John became a lawyer.

Use **ponerse + adj.,** e.g., *to become pale, to become sick*; in other words, the adj. indicates the state or condition (physical or mental) that you have become: *Cuando vi el accidente, me puse pálido*/When I saw the accident, I became pale; *Mi madre se puso triste al oír la noticia desgraciada*/My mother became sad upon hearing the unfortunate news.

Llevar and tomar

These two verbs mean *to take* but note the difference in use:

Llevar means *to take* in the sense of carry or transport from place to place: *José llevó la silla de la cocina al comedor*/Joseph took the chair from the kitchen to the dining room.

The verb **llevar** is also used when you *take someone somewhere: Pedro llevó a María al baile anoche*/Peter took Mary to the dance last night.

As you probably know, **llevar** also means *to wear: María, ¿por qué llevas la falda nueva?*/Mary, why are you wearing your new skirt?

Tomar means *to take* in the sense of grab or catch: *La profesora tomó el libro y comenzó a leer a la clase*/The teacher took the book and began to read to the class; *Mi amigo tomó el tren esta mañana a las siete*/My friend took the train this morning at seven o'clock.

Pedir and preguntar

Both these verbs mean *to ask* but note the difference:

Pedir means *to ask for something* or *to request: El alumno pidió un lápiz al profesor*/The pupil asked the teacher for a pencil.

Preguntar means *to inquire, to ask a question: La alumna preguntó a la profesora cómo estaba*/The pupil asked the teacher how she was.

Pensar de and pensar en

Both these verbs mean *to think of* but note the difference:

Pensar is used with the prep. **de** when you ask someone what he/

she thinks of someone or something, when you ask for someone's opinion: *¿Qué piensa Ud. de este libro?*/What do you think of this book? *Pienso que es bueno*/I think that it is good.

Pensar is used with the prep. **en** when you ask someone what or whom he/she is thinking about: *Miguel, no hablas mucho; ¿en qué piensas?*/Michael, you are not talking much; of what are you thinking? (what are you thinking of?); *Pienso en las vacaciones de verano*/I'm thinking of summer vacation.

Poder and saber

Both these verbs mean *can* but the difference in use is as follows:

Poder means *can* in the sense of *ability: No puedo ayudarle; lo siento*/I cannot (am unable to) help you; I'm sorry.

Saber means *can* in the sense of *to know how: Este niño no sabe contar*/This child can't (does not know how to) count.

In the preterit tense **poder** has the special meaning of *succeeded: Después de algunos minutos, Juan pudo abrir la puerta*/After a few minutes, John succeeded in opening the door.

In the preterit tense, **saber** has the special meaing of *found out: Lo supe ayer*/I found it out yesterday.

no poder más to be exhausted, to be all in

No puede ser. It's impossible. (It can't be.)

Poner and ponerse

al poner del sol at sunset

poner coto a to put a stop to

poner el dedo en la llaga to hit the nail right on the head

poner en claro to explain simply and clearly

poner en duda to doubt, to question

poner en marcha to set in motion

poner en ridículo to ridicule

poner los puntos sobre las íes to mind one's p's and q's; to mind one's own business; to dot the i's

poner por escrito to put in writing

ponerse de acuerdo to reach an agreement

ponerse cómodo to make oneself at home

ponerse en marcha to start (out)

ponerse mal to get sick

Ser

Debe de ser . . . It is probably . . .

Debe ser . . . It ought to be . . .

Es de lamentar. It's too bad.

Es de mi agrado. It's to my liking.

Es hora de . . . It is time to . . .

Es lástima or **Es una lástima.** It's a pity; It's too bad.

Es que . . . The fact is . . .

para ser in spite of being (*Para ser tan viejo, él es muy ágil*/In spite of being so old, he is very nimble.)

sea lo que sea whatever it may be

ser aficionado a to be a fan of (*Soy aficionado al béisbol*/I'm a baseball fan.)

ser amable con to be kind to (*Mi profesora de español es amable conmigo*/My Spanish teacher is kind to me.)

ser todo oídos to be all ears (*Te escucho; soy todo oídos*/I'm listening to you; I'm all ears.)

si no fuera por . . . if it were not for . . .

Ser and estar

These two verbs mean *to be* but note the differences in use:

Generally speaking, use **ser** when you want to express *to be*.

Use **estar** when *to be* is used in the following ways:

(a) Health:
- (1) *¿Cómo está Ud.?* How are you?
- (2) *Estoy bien.* I am well.
- (3) *Estoy enfermo (enferma).* I am sick.

(b) Location: persons, places, things
- (1) *Estoy en la sala de clase.* I am in the classroom.
- (2) *La escuela está lejos.* The school is far.

(3) *Barcelona está en España.* Barcelona is (located) in Spain.
(4) *Los libros están en la mesa.* The books are on the table.

(c) State or condition: persons
(1) *Estoy contento (contenta).* I am happy.
(2) *Los alumnos están cansados. (Las alumnas están cansadas.)* The students are tired.
(3) *María está triste hoy.* Mary is sad today.
(4) *Estoy listo (lista).* I am ready.
(5) *Estoy pálido (pálida).* I am pale.
(6) *Estoy ocupado (ocupada).* I am busy.
(7) *Estoy seguro (segura).* I am sure.
(8) *Este hombre está vivo.* This man is alive.
(9) *Ese hombre está muerto.* That man is dead.
(10) *Este hombre está borracho.* This man is drunk.

(d) State or condition: things and places
(1) *La ventana está abierta.* The window is open.
(2) *La taza está llena.* The cup is full.
(3) *El té está caliente.* The tea is hot.
(4) *La limonada está fría.* The lemonade is cold.
(5) *La biblioteca está cerrada los domingos.* The library is closed on Sundays.

(e) To form the progressive present of a verb, use the persent tense of **estar** + the present part. of the main verb:
Estoy estudiando en mi cuarto y no puedo salir esta noche.
I am studying in my room and I cannot go out tonight.

(f) To form the progressive past of a verb, use the imperfect tense of **estar** + the present part. of the main verb:
Mi hermano estaba leyendo cuando (yo) entré en el cuarto.
My brother was reading when I entered (came into) the room.

ser aburrido to be boring

ser de to belong to; **Este libros es de María.** This book is Mary's.

ser de rigor to be indispensable

ser de ver to be worth seeing

ser listo (lista) to be clever

estar aburrido (aburrida) to be bored

estar de buenas to be lucky

estar de buen humor to be in good spirits, a good mood

estar listo (lista) to be ready

Tener and tenerse

¿Cuántos años tienes? ?Cuántos años tiene Ud.? How old are you? **Tengo diez y seis años.** I am sixteen years old.

¿Qué tienes? ¿Qué tiene Ud.? What's the matter? What's the matter with you? **No tengo nada.** There's nothing wrong; There's nothing the matter (with me).

tener algo que hacer to have something to do

tener apetito to have an appetite

tener calor to feel (to be) warm (persons)

tener cuidado to be careful

tener dolor de cabeza to have a headache

tener dolor de estómago to have a stomach ache

tener en cuenta to take into account

tener éxito to be successful

tener frío to feel (to be) cold (persons)

tener ganas de + inf. to feel like + pres. part. (*Tengo ganas de tomar un helado*/I feel like having an ice cream.)

tener gusto en + inf. to be glad + inf. (*Tengo mucho gusto en conocerle*/I am very glad to meet you.)

tener hambre to feel (to be) hungry

tener la bondad de please, please be good enough to . . . (*Tenga la bondad de cerrar la puerta*/Please close the door.)

tener la culpa de algo to take the blame for something, to be to blame for something (*Tengo la culpa de eso*/I am to blame for that.)

tener lugar to take place (*El accidente tuvo lugar anoche*/The accident took place last night.)

tener miedo de to be afraid of

tener mucha sed to feel (to be) very thirsty (persons)

tener mucho calor to feel (to be) very warm (persons)

tener mucho frío to feel (to be) very cold (persons)

tener mucho que hacer to have a lot to do

tener poco que hacer to have little to do

tener por to consider as

tener prisa to be in a hurry

tener que + inf. to have + inf. (*Tengo que estudiar*/I have to study.)

tener que ver con to have to do with (*No tengo nada que ver con él*/I have nothing to do with him.)

tener razón to be right (*Usted tiene razón*/You are right.) **no tener razón** to be wrong (*Usted no tiene razón*/You are wrong.)

tener sed to feel (to be) thirsty (persons)

tener sueño to feel (to be) sleepy

tener suerte to be lucky

tener vergüenza de to be ashamed of

tenerse en pie to stand

Volver and devolver

These two verbs mean *to return* but note the difference:

Volver means *to return* in the sense of *to come back: Voy a volver a casa*/I am going to return home. A synonym of **volver** is **regresar:** *Los muchachos regresaron a las ocho de la noche*/The boys came back (returned) at eight o'clock.

Devolver means *to return* in the sense of *to give back: Voy a devolver el libro a la biblioteca*/I am going to return the book to the library.

Definitions of Basic Grammatical Terms with Examples in English and Spanish

The purpose of this section is to prepare you to become aware of the different parts of a sentence and the grammatical terms used when you analyze the structure of a sentence in Spanish. If you study this section thoroughly, it will help you train yourself to analyze sentences on the next Spanish Regents exam that you take. You can acquire this skill through practice. When you read a sentence in Spanish, you must ask yourself, for example:

- What is the subject of this sentence?
- Is there a direct object or indirect object noun or pronoun? If so, where is it?
- Is it in front of the verb or after it?
- Is it attached to the infinitive?
- Do I have to make it agree in gender and number with some other part of the sentence?
- Are there any words in the sentence that indicate the tense of the verb as being in the present, past, or future?
- What is the tense of the verb?
- Is it singular or plural?
- First, second, or third person?
- Do I know my Spanish verb forms in all the tenses?
- Is there a certain type of conjunction in the sentence that requires the subjunctive mood in the verb form that follows it?

There are many more questions you should ask yourself while analyzing a sentence in Spanish so you can score high on the Regents exam.

To prepare yourself for the Spanish Regents exam, you must also know Spanish verb forms in all the tenses. To do this, study the conjugation of verbs and explanations of verb tenses with examples in Barron's book, *501 Spanish Verbs Fully Conjugated in All the Tenses, 4th edition*.

ACTIVE VOICE

When we speak or write in the active voice, the subject of the verb performs the action of the verb. The action falls on the direct object if there is one.

Example:

The robber opened the window/**El ladrón abrió la ventana.**

The subject is *the robber*. The verb is *opened*. The direct object is *the window*.

ADJECTIVE

An adjective is a word that modifies a noun or a pronoun. In grammar, to modify a word means to describe, limit, expand, or make the meaning particular.

Examples:

a beautiful garden/**un jardín hermoso;** she is pretty/**ella es bonita.**

The adjective *beautiful*/***hermoso*** modifies the noun *garden*/***jardín.*** The adjective *pretty*/***bonita*** modifies the pronoun *she*/***ella.*** The adjective agrees in gender (masculine or feminine) and number (singular or plural) with the noun or pronoun it modifies.

ADVERB

An adverb is a word that modifies a verb, an adjective, or another adverb. An adverb says something about how, when, where, to what extent, or in what way.

Examples:

Mary runs swiftly/**María corre rápidamente.** The adverb *swiftly*/***rápidamente*** modifies the verb *runs*/***corre.*** The adverb shows *how* she runs.

John is very handsome/**Juan es muy guapo.** The adverb *very*/***muy*** modifies the adjective *handsome*/***guapo.*** The adverb shows *how handsome* he is.

The boy is talking very fast now/**El muchacho habla muy rápidamente ahora.** The adverb *very*/***muy*** modifies the adverb *fast*/***rápi-***

damente. The adverb shows *to what extent* he is talking *fast*. The adverb *now/**ahora*** tells us *when*.

The post office is there/**La oficina de correos está allá.** The adverb *there/**allá*** modifies the verb *is/**está.*** It tells us *where* the post office is.

Mary writes meticulously/**María escribe meticulosamente.** The adverb *meticulously/**meticulosamente*** modifies the verb *writes/ **escribe.*** It tells us *in what way* she writes.

AFFIRMATIVE STATEMENT, NEGATIVE STATEMENT

A statement in the affirmative is the opposite of a statement in the negative. To negate an affirmative statement is to make it negative.

Example in the affirmative:

I like ice cream/**Me gusta el helado.**

Example in the negative:

I do not like ice cream/**No me gusta el helado.**

AGREEMENT OF ADJECTIVE WITH NOUN

Agreement is made on the adjective with the noun it modifies in gender (masculine or feminine) and number (singular or plural).

Examples:

a white house/**una casa blanca.**

The adjective **blanca** is feminine singular because the noun **una casa** is feminine singular.

many white houses/**muchas casas blancas.**

The adjectives **muchas** and **blancas** are feminine plural because the noun **casas** is feminine plural.

AGREEMENT OF VERB WITH ITS SUBJECT

A verb agrees in person (1st, 2nd, or 3rd) and in number (singular or plural) with its subject.

Examples:

Paul tells the truth/**Pablo dice la verdad.** The verb **dice** (of **decir**) is 3rd person singular because the subject ***Pablo***/*Paul* is 3rd person singular.

Where are the tourists going?/**¿Adónde van los turistas?** The verb **van** (of **ir**) is 3rd person plural because the subject ***los turistas***/*the tourists* is 3rd person plural.

ANTECEDENT

An antecedent is a word to which a relative pronoun refers. It comes *before* the pronoun.

Examples:

The girl who is laughing loudly is my sister/**La muchacha que está riendo a carcajadas es mi hermana.** The antecedent is *girl*/***la muchacha.*** The relative pronoun *who*/***que*** refers to the girl.

The car that I bought is very expensive/**El carro que yo compré es muy costoso.** The antecedent is *car*/**el carro.** The relative pronoun *that*/***que*** refers to the car.

AUXILIARY VERB

An auxiliary verb is a helping verb. In English grammar it is *to have*. In Spanish grammar it is **haber**/*to have*. An auxiliary verb is used to help form the compound tenses.

Example in the present perfect tense:

I *have* eaten/**(Yo) *he* comido.**

CARDINAL NUMBER

A cardinal number is a number that expresses an amount, such as *one*, *two*, *three*, and so on.

CLAUSE

A clause is a group of words that contains a subject and a predicate. A predicate may contain more than one word. A conjugated verb form is revealed in the predicate.

Example:

Mrs. Gómez lives in a large apartment/**La señora Gómez vive en un gran apartamento.**

The subject is *Mrs. Gómez/**la señora Gómez**.* The predicate is *lives in a large apartment/**vive en un gran apartamento**.* The verb is *lives/**vive***.

COMPARATIVE ADJECTIVE

When making a comparison between two persons or things, an adjective is used to express the degree of comparison in the following ways.

Examples:

Of the same degree of comparison:

Helen is *as tall as* Mary/**Elena es *tan alta como* María.**

Of a lesser degree of comparison:

Jane is *less intelligent than* Eva/**Juana es *menos inteligente que* Eva.**

Of a higher degree of comparison:

This apple is *more delicious than* that one/**Esta manzana es *más deliciosa que* ésa.**

COMPARATIVE ADVERB

An adverb is compared in the same way as an adjective is compared. *See* comparative adjective above.

Examples:

Of the same degree of comparison:

Mr. Robles speaks *as well as* Mr. Vega/**El señor Robles habla *tan bien como* el señor Vega.**

Of a lesser degree of comparison:

Alice studies *less diligently than* her sister/**Alicia estudia *menos diligentemente que* su hermana.**

Of a higher degree of comparison:

Albert works *more slowly than* his brother/**Alberto trabaja *más lentamente que* su hermano.**

COMPLEX SENTENCE

A complex sentence contains one independent clause and one or more dependent clauses.

Examples:

One independent clause and one dependent clause:

Joseph works but his brother doesn't/**José trabaja pero su hermano no trabaja.**

The independent clause is *Joseph works*. It makes sense when it stands alone because it expresses a complete thought. The dependent clause is *but his brother doesn't*. The dependent clause, which is introduced by the conjunction *but*/***pero***, does not make complete sense when it stands alone because it *depends* on the thought expressed in the independent clause.

One independent clause and two dependent clauses:

Anna is a good student because she studies but her sister never studies/**Ana es una buena alumna porque estudia pero su hermana nunca estudia.**

The independent clause is *Anna is a good student*. It makes sense when it stands alone because it expresses a complete thought. The first dependent clause is *because she studies*. This dependent clause, which is introduced by the conjunction *because*/***porque*,** does not make complete sense when it stands alone because it *depends* on the thought expressed in the independent clause. The second dependent clause is *but her sister never studies*. That dependent clause, which is introduced by the conjunction *but*/***pero*,** does not make complete sense either when it stands alone because it *depends* on the thought expressed in the independent clause.

COMPOUND SENTENCE

A compound sentence contains two or more independent clauses.

Example:

Mrs. Fuentes went to the supermarket, she bought a few things, and then she went home/**La señora Fuentes fue al supermercado, compró algunas cosas, y entonces fue a casa.**

This compound sentence contains three independent clauses. They are independent because they make sense when they stand alone.

CONJUGATION
The conjugation of a verb is the fixed order of all its forms showing their inflections (changes) in the three persons of the singular and the three persons of the plural in a particular tense.

CONJUNCTION
A conjunction is a word that connects words or groups of words.

Examples:

and/**y**, or/**o**, but/**pero**, because/**porque**

Charles *and* Charlotte/**Carlos *y* Carlota**

You can stay home or you can come with me/**(Tú) puedes quedarte en casa *o* venir conmigo.**

Note that **y** (and) changes to **e** if the word right after **y** begins with **i** or **hi**.

Examples:

María es bonita e inteligente/Mary is pretty and intelligent.

Fernando e Isabel/Fernando and Isabel

padre e hijo/father and son; **madre e hija**/mother and daughter

However, if **y** is followed by a word that begins with **hie,** keep **y: flores y hierba**/flowers and grass.

CONTRARY TO FACT
This term refers to an "if" clause. *See* if **(si)** clause.

DECLARATIVE SENTENCE
A declarative sentence makes a statement.

Example:

I have finished the work/**(Yo) he terminado el trabajo.**

DEFINITE ARTICLE
The definite article in Spanish has four forms and they all mean *the*. They are: **el, la, los, las.**

Examples:

el libro/the book, **la casa**/the house, **los libros**/the books, **las casas**/ the houses.

The definite articles **la, los, las** are also used as direct object pronouns.

DEMONSTRATIVE ADJECTIVE
A demonstrative adjective is an adjective that points out. It is placed in front of a noun.

Examples:

this book/**este libro;** these books/**estos libros;** this cup/**esta taza;** these flowers/**estas flores.**

DEMONSTRATIVE PRONOUN
A demonstrative pronoun is a pronoun that points out. It takes the place of a noun. It agrees in gender and number with the noun it replaces.

Examples:

I have two oranges; do you prefer *this one* or *that one*?/**Tengo dos naranjas; ¿prefiere usted ésta o ésa?**

I prefer *those* [over there]/**Prefiero *aquéllas*.**

DEPENDENT CLAUSE
A dependent clause is a group of words that contains a subject and a predicate. It does not express a complete thought when it stands alone. It is called

dependent because it depends on the independent clause for a complete meaning. Subordinate clause is another term for dependent clause.

Example:

Edward is absent today because he is sick/**Eduardo está ausente hoy porque está enfermo.**

The independent clause is *Edward is absent today*. The dependent clause is *because he is sick*.

DESCRIPTIVE ADJECTIVE

A descriptive adjective is an adjective that describes a person, place, or thing.

Examples:

a pretty girl/**una muchacha bonita;** a big house/**una casa grande;** an expensive car/**un carro costoso.**

DIRECT OBJECT NOUN

A direct object noun receives the action of the verb *directly*. That is why it is called a direct object, as opposed to an indirect object. A direct object noun is normally placed *after* the verb.

Example:

I am writing a letter/**Escribo una carta** or **Estoy escribiendo una carta.**

The direct object is the noun *letter*/**una carta.**

DIRECT OBJECT PRONOUN

A direct object pronoun receives the action of the verb *directly*. It takes the place of a direct object noun. In Spanish a pronoun that is a direct object of a verb is ordinarily placed *in front of* the verb.

Example:

I am writing it [the letter]/**La escribo.**

However, in the *affirmative imperative*, a direct object pronoun is placed *after* the verb and is joined to it, resulting in one word.

Example:

Write it [the letter] now!/**¡Escríbala [Ud.] ahora!**

Note that an accent mark is added on the vowel **i [í]** in order to keep the emphasis on that vowel as it was in **escriba** before the direct object pronoun **la** was added to the verb form.

DISJUNCTIVE PRONOUN

A disjunctive pronoun is a pronoun that is stressed; in other words, emphasis is placed on it. It is usually the object of a preposition. Prepositional pronoun is another term for disjunctive pronoun.

Examples:

for me/**para mí;** for you *(fam.)*/**para ti; con usted**/with you; **con él**/with him; **con ella**/with her

Note the following exceptions with **con:**

conmigo/with me; **contigo**/with you *(fam.)*; **consigo**/with yourself (yourselves, himself, herself, themselves).

ENDING OF A VERB

In Spanish grammar the ending of a verb form changes according to the person (1st, 2nd, or 3rd) and number (singular or plural) of the subject and the tense of the verb.

Example:

To form the present indicative tense of a regular **-ar** type verb like **hablar,** drop **ar** of the infinitive and add the following endings: **-o, -as, -a** for the 1st, 2nd, and 3rd persons of the singular; **-amos, -áis, -an** for the 1st, 2nd, and 3rd persons of the plural.

You then get: **hablo, hablas, habla; hablamos, habláis, hablan**

FEMININE

In Spanish grammar the gender of a noun, pronoun, or adjective is feminine or masculine, not male or female.

Examples:

Masculine			Feminine		
noun	pronoun	adjective	noun	pronoun	adjective
el hombre	**él**	**guapo**	**la mujer**	**ella**	**hermosa**
the man	*he*	*handsome*	*the woman*	*she*	*beautiful*

GENDER

Gender means masculine or feminine.

Examples:

Masculine: the boy/**el muchacho;** the book/**el libro**

Feminine: the girl/**la muchacha;** the house/**la casa**

GERUND

In English grammar, a gerund is a word formed from a verb. It ends in *ing*. Actually, it is the present participle of a verb. However, it is not used as a verb. It is used as a noun.

Example:

Seeing is believing/**Ver es creer** *[to see is to believe]*. It is sometimes stated as **Ver y creer** *[to see and to believe]*.

However, in Spanish grammar, the infinitive form of the verb is used, as in the above example, when the verb is used as a noun.

The Spanish gerund is also a word formed from a verb. It is the present participle of a verb. The Spanish gerund **[el gerundio]** regularly ends in **ando** for **ar** type verbs (of the 1st conjugation), in **iendo** for **er** type verbs (of the 2nd conjugation), and **iendo** for **ir** type verbs (of the 3d conjugation). There are also irregular present participles that end in **yendo.**

Examples of a Spanish gerund:

hablando/talking **comiendo**/eating **viviendo**/living

IF (SI) CLAUSE

Another term for an "if" clause is contrary to fact, as in English, if I were king . . ., if I were rich . . .

Example:

Si yo tuviera bastante dinero, iría a España/If I had enough money, I would go to Spain.

IMPERATIVE

The imperative is a mood, not a tense. It is used to express a command. In Spanish it is used in the 2nd person of the singular **(tú)**, the 3rd person of the singular **(usted)**, the 1st person of the plural **(nosotros, nosotras)**, the 2nd person of the plural **(vosotros, vosotras)**, and in the 3rd person of the plural **(ustedes)**.

Example:

Call me/**Llámame.**

INDEFINITE ARTICLE

In English the indefinite articles are *a, an,* as in *a book, an apple*. They are indefinite because they do not refer to any definite or particular noun.

In Spanish there are two indefinite articles in the singular: one in the masculine form **(un)** and one in the feminine form **(una)**.

Examples:

Masculine singular: **un libro**/a book

Feminine singular: **una manzana**/an apple

In the plural they change to **unos** and **unas.**

Examples:

unos libros/some books; **unas manzanas**/some apples

INDEFINITE PRONOUN

An indefinite pronoun is a pronoun that does not refer to any definite or particular noun.

Examples:

something/**algo;** someone, somebody/**alguien**

INDEPENDENT CLAUSE

An independent clause is a group of words that contains a subject and a predicate. It expresses a complete thought when it stands alone.

Example:

The cat is sleeping on the bed/**El gato está durmiendo sobre la cama.**

INDICATIVE MOOD

The indicative mood is used in sentences that make a statement or ask a question. It is used most of the time when we speak or write in English or Spanish.

Examples:

I am going to the movies now/**Voy al cine ahora.**

Where are you going?/**¿Adónde vas?**

INDIRECT OBJECT NOUN

An indirect object noun receives the action of the verb *indirectly*.

Example:

I am writing a letter to Christine *or* I am writing Christine a letter/ **Estoy escribiendo una carta a Cristina.**

The verb is *am writing*/***estoy escribiendo.*** The direct object noun is a *letter*/ ***una carta.*** The indirect object noun is **Cristina**/Christine.

INDIRECT OBJECT PRONOUN

An indirect object pronoun takes the place of an indirect object noun. It receives the action of the verb *indirectly*.

Example:

I am writing a letter to her or I am writing her a letter/**Le escribo una carta a ella.**

The indirect object pronoun is *(to) her*/**le.** It is clarified by adding **a ella.**

INFINITIVE

An infinitive is a verb form. In English, it is normally stated with the preposition *to*, as in *to talk, to drink, to receive*. In Spanish, the infinitive form of a verb consists of three major types: those of the 1st conjugation that end in **-ar,** the 2nd conjugation that end in **-er,** and the 3rd conjugation that end in **-ir.**

In Spanish grammar, the infinitive **(el infinitivo)** is considered a mood.

Examples:

hablar/*to talk, to speak;* **beber**/*to drink;* **recibir**/*to receive*

INTERJECTION

An interjection is a word that expresses emotion, a feeling of joy, of sadness, an exclamation of surprise, and other exclamations consisting of one or two words.

Examples:

Ah!/**¡Ah!** Ouch!/**¡Ay!** Darn it!/**¡Caramba!** My God!/**¡Dios mío!**

INTERROGATIVE ADJECTIVE

In Spanish, an interrogative adjective is an adjective that is used in a question. As an adjective, it is placed in front of a noun.

Examples:

What book do you want?/**¿Qué libro desea usted?**

What time is it?/**¿Qué hora es?**

INTERROGATIVE ADVERB

In Spanish, an interrogative adverb is an adverb that introduces a question. As an adverb, it modifies the verb.

Examples:

How are you?/**¿*Cómo* está usted?**

How much does this book cost?/**¿*Cuánto* cuesta este libro?**

When will you arrive?/**¿*Cuándo* llegará usted?**

INTERROGATIVE PRONOUN

An interrogative pronoun is a pronoun that asks a question. There are interrogative pronouns that refer to persons and those that refer to things.

Examples:

Who is it?/**¿*Quién* es?**

What are you saying?/**¿*Qué* dice usted?**

INTERROGATIVE SENTENCE

An interrogative sentence asks a question.

Example:

What are you doing?/**¿Qué hace usted?**

INTRANSITIVE VERB

An intransitive verb is a verb that does not take a direct object.

Example:

The professor is talking/**El profesor habla.**

An intransitive verb takes an indirect object.

Example:

The professor is talking to us/**El profesor nos habla.**

IRREGULAR VERB

An irregular verb is a verb that does not follow a fixed pattern in its conjugation in the various verb tenses.

Examples of basic irregular verbs in Spanish:

estar/to be **hacer**/to do, to make **ir**/to go **ser**/to be

For many commonly used irregular verb forms, see pages 106–110.

LIMITING ADJECTIVE

A limiting adjective is an adjective that limits a quantity.

Example:

three lemons/**tres limones;** a few candies/**algunos dulces**

MAIN CLAUSE

Main clause is another term for independent clause. *See* independent clause.

MASCULINE

In Spanish grammar the gender of a noun, pronoun, or adjective is masculine or feminine, not male or female.

MOOD OF VERBS

Some grammarians use the term *the mode* instead of *the mood* of a verb. Either term means *the manner or way* a verb is expressed. In English and Spanish grammar a verb expresses an action or state of being in a particular mood.

In Spanish grammar, we have the following moods **(modos):** the infinitive **(el infinitivo),** the indicative **(el indicativo),** the imperative **(el imperativo),** the conditional **(el potencial),** and the subjunctive **(el subjuntivo).**

In English grammar, there are three moods: the indicative mood, the subjunctive mood, and the imperative mood.

Most of the time, in English and Spanish, we speak and write in the indicative mood.

NEGATIVE STATEMENT, AFFIRMATIVE STATEMENT

See Affirmative Statement, Negative Statement

NEUTER

A word that is neuter is neither masculine nor feminine. Common neuter demonstrative pronouns in Spanish are **esto**/*this,* **eso**/*that,* **aquello**/*that* [farther away].

Examples:

What's this?/**¿Qué es esto?** What's that?/**¿Qué es eso?**

For demonstrative pronouns that are not neuter, *see* demonstrative pronoun.

There is also the neuter pronoun **lo.** It usually refers to an idea or statement. It is not normally translated into English but often the translation is *so*.

Examples:

¿Estás enferma, María?/Are you sick, Mary? **Sí, lo estoy**/Yes, I am.

No lo creo/I don't think so.

Lo parece/It seems so.

NOUN

A noun is a word that names a person, animal, place, thing, condition or state, or quality.

Examples:

the man/**el hombre,** the woman/**la mujer,** the horse/**el caballo,** the house/**la casa,** the pencil/**el lápiz,** happiness/**la felicidad,** excellence/ **la excelencia**

In Spanish the noun **el nombre** is the word for name and noun. Another word for noun in Spanish is **el sustantivo**/*substantive*.

NUMBER

In English and Spanish grammar, number means singular or plural.

Examples:

Masc. sing.: the boy/**el muchacho;** the pencil/**el lápiz;** the eye/**el ojo**

Masc. pl.: the boys/**los muchachos;** the pencils/**los lápices;** the eyes/ **los ojos**

Fem. sing.: the girl/**la muchacha;** the house/**la casa;** the cow/**la vaca**

Fem. pl.: the girls/**las muchachas;** the houses/**las casas;** the cows/ **las vacas**

ORDINAL NUMBER

An ordinal number is a number that expresses position in a series, such as *first*, *second*, *third*, and so on. In English and Spanish grammar we talk about 1st person, 2nd person, 3rd person singular or plural regarding subjects and verbs.

ORTHOGRAPHICAL CHANGES IN VERB FORMS

An orthographical change in a verb form is a change in spelling.

Example:

The verb **conocer**/*to know*, *to be acquainted with* changes in spelling in the 1st person singular of the present indicative. The letter **z** is inserted in front of the second **c**. When formed regularly, the ending **er** of the infinitive drops and **o** is added for the 1st person singular form of the present indicative. That would result in ***conoco,*** a peculiar sound to the Spanish ear for a verb form of **conocer.** The letter **z** is added to keep the sound of **s** as it is in the infinitive **conocer.** Therefore, the spelling changes and the form is **yo conozco.** In the other forms of **conocer** in the present indicative **z** is not inserted because they retain the sound of **s.** There are many verb forms in Spanish that contain orthographical changes.

PASSIVE VOICE

When we speak or write in the active voice and change to the passive voice, the direct object becomes the subject, the subject becomes the object of a preposition, and the verb becomes *to be* plus the past participle of the active verb. The past participle functions as an adjective.

Example:

The window was opened by the robber/**La ventana fue abierta por el ladrón.**

The subject is ***la ventana.*** The verb is ***fue.*** The word ***abierta*** is a feminine adjective agreeing with ***la ventana.*** Actually, it is the past participle of **abrir**/*to open* but here it serves as an adjective. The object of the preposition *by*/**por** is the *robber*/**el ladrón.**

PAST PARTICIPLE

A past participle is derived from a verb. It is used to form the compound tenses. Its auxiliary verb in English is *to have*. In Spanish, the auxiliary verb is **haber**/*to have*. It is part of the verb tense.

Examples:

Infinitive	Present Perfect Indicative
hablar/to speak, to talk	I have *spoken*/**he *hablado***
comer/to eat	I have *eaten*/**he *comido***
recibir/to receive	I have *received*/**he *recibido***

PERSON (1ST, 2ND, 3RD)

Verb forms in a particular tense are learned systematically according to person (1st, 2nd, 3rd) and number (singular, plural).

Example, showing the present indicative tense of the verb **ir**/*to go* in the three persons of the singular and the three persons of the plural with the subject pronouns in parentheses:

Singular	Plural
1st person: **(yo) voy**	1st person: **(nosotros, nosotras) vamos**
2nd person: **(tú) vas**	2nd person: **(vosotros, vosotras) vais**
3rd person: **(Ud., él, ella) va**	3rd person: **(Uds., ellos, ellas) van**

PERSONAL PRONOUN

A personal pronoun is a pronoun that refers to a person. Review the personal subject pronouns above in the entry *person: yo, tú,* and so on.

For examples of other types of pronouns, *see also* demonstrative pronoun, direct object pronoun, disjunctive pronoun, indefinite pronoun, indirect object pronoun, interrogative pronoun, possessive pronoun, reflexive pronoun, relative pronoun.

PLURAL

Plural means more than one. *See also* person (1st, 2nd, 3rd), and singular.

POSSESSIVE ADJECTIVE

A possessive adjective is an adjective that is placed in front of a noun to show possession.

Examples:

my book/**mi libro** my friends/**mis amigos** our school/**nuestra escuela**

POSSESSIVE PRONOUN

A possessive pronoun is a pronoun that shows possession. It takes the place of a possessive adjective with the noun. Its form agrees in gender (masculine or feminine) and number (singular or plural) with what it is replacing.

Examples in English: mine, yours, his, hers, its, ours, theirs

Examples in Spanish:

Possessive adjective	Possessive pronoun
my book/**mi libro**	*mine*/**el mío**
my house/**mi casa**	*mine*/**la mía**
my shoes/**mis zapatos**	*mine*/**los míos**

PREDICATE

The predicate is that part of the sentence that tells us something about the subject. The main word of the predicate is the verb.

Example:

Today the tourists are going to the Prado Museum/**Hoy los turistas van al Museo del Prado.**

The subject is *the tourists*/**los turistas.** The predicate is *are going to the Prado Museum*/***van al Museo del Prado.*** The verb is *are going*/***van.***

PREPOSITION
A preposition is a word that establishes a rapport between words.

Examples: with, without, to, at, between

with her/***con* ella** *without* money/***sin* dinero**

between you and me/***entre* tú y yo** *to* Spain/***a* España**

PREPOSITIONAL PRONOUN
A prepositional pronoun is a pronoun that is the object of a preposition. The term disjunctive pronoun is also used. For examples, *see* disjunctive pronoun.

PRESENT PARTICIPLE
A present participle is derived from a verb form. In English a present participle ends in *ing*. In Spanish a present participle is called **un gerundio.**

Examples:

cantando/singing **comiendo**/eating **yendo**/going

PRONOUN
A pronoun is a word that takes the place of a noun.

Examples:

el hombre/***él***	**la mujer**/***ella***
the man/*he*	the woman/*she*

REFLEXIVE PRONOUN AND REFLEXIVE VERB
In English a reflexive pronoun is a personal pronoun that contains *self* or *selves*. In Spanish and English a reflexive pronoun is used with a verb that is called reflexive because the action of the verb falls on the reflexive pronoun.

In Spanish there is a required set of reflexive pronouns for a reflexive verb.

Examples:

lavarse to wash oneself	**(Yo) me lavo.** I wash myself.
afeitarse to shave oneself	**Pablo se ha afeitdado.** Paul has shaved himself.

REGULAR VERB

A regular verb is a verb that is conjugated in the various tenses according to a fixed pattern. Three examples of regular Spanish verbs are **hablar, aprender, vivir.**

RELATIVE PRONOUN

A relative pronoun is a pronoun that refers to its antecedent.

Example:

> The girl who is talking with John is my sister/**La muchacha que está hablando con Juan es mi hermana.**

The antecedent is *girl*/***la muchacha.*** The relative pronoun *who*/***que*** refers to the girl.

SENTENCE

A sentence is a group of words that contains a subject and a predicate. The verb is contained in the predicate. A sentence expresses a complete thought.

Example:

> The train leaves at two o'clock in the afternoon/**El tren sale a las dos de la tarde.**

The subject is *train*/***el tren.*** The predicate is *leaves at two o'clock in the afternoon*/***sale a las dos de la tarde.*** The verb is *leaves*/***sale.***

SIMPLE SENTENCE

A simple sentence is a sentence that contains one subject and one predicate. The verb is the core of the predicate. The verb is the most important word in a sentence because it tells us what the subject is doing.

Example:

Mary is eating an apple from her garden/**María está comiendo una manzana de su jardín.**

The subject is *Mary*/**María.** The predicate is *is eating an apple from her garden*/***está comiendo una manzana de su jardín.*** The verb is *is eating*/***está comiendo.*** The direct object is *an apple*/***una manzana.*** *From her garden*/***de su jardín*** is an adverbial phrase. It tells you from where the apple came.

SINGULAR

Singular means one. *See also* plural.

STEM OF A VERB

The stem of a verb is what is left after we drop the ending of its infinitive form. It is needed to add to it the required endings of a regular verb in a particular verb tense.

Examples:

Infinitive	Ending of infinitive	Stem
hablar/to talk	**ar**	**habl**
comer/to eat	**er**	**com**
escribir/to write	**ir**	**escrib**

STEM-CHANGING VERB

In Spanish there are many verb forms that change in the stem.

Example:

The verb **dormir**/*to sleep* changes the vowel **o** in the stem to **ue** when the stress (emphasis, accent) falls on that **o;** for example, **(yo) duermo.**

When the stress does not fall on that **o,** it does not change; for example, **(nosotros) dormimos.** Here, the stress is on the vowel **i.**

SUBJECT

A subject is that part of a sentence that is related to its verb. The verb says something about the subject.

Example:

Clara and Isabel are beautiful/**Clara e Isabel son hermosas.**

The subject of this sentence is **Clara e Isabel.** To know when to use **e** instead of **y** for *and*, review the entry *conjunction* in this list.

SUBJUNCTIVE MOOD

The subjunctive mood is the mood of a verb that is used in specific cases, *e.g.*, after certain verbs expressing a wish, doubt, emotion, fear, joy, uncertainty, an indefinite expression, an indefinite antecedent, certain conjunctions, and others. The subjunctive mood is used more frequently in Spanish than in English.

SUBORDINATE CLAUSE

Subordinate clause is another term for dependent clause.

SUPERLATIVE ADJECTIVE

A superlative adjective is an adjective that expresses the highest degree when making a comparison of more than two persons or things.

Examples:

Adjective	Comparative	Superlative
bueno/good	**mejor**/better	**el mejor**/best
alto/tall	**más alto**/taller	**el más alto**/tallest

SUPERLATIVE ADVERB

A superlative adverb is an adverb that expresses the highest degree when making a comparison of more than two persons or things.

Example:

Adverb	Comparative	Superlative
lentamente slowly	**más lentamente** more slowly	**lo más lentamente** most slowly

TENSE OF VERB

In English and Spanish grammar, tense means time. The tense of the verb indicates the time of the action or state of being. The three major segments of time are past, present, and future. In Spanish there are fourteen major verb tenses, of which seven are simple tenses and seven are compound.

TRANSITIVE VERB

A transitive verb is a verb that takes a direct object.

Example:

I am closing the window/**Cierro la ventana.**

The subject is *I*/***(Yo).*** The verb is *am closing*/***cierro.*** The direct object is *the window*/***la ventana.***

VERB

A verb is a word that expresses action or a state of being.

Examples:

Action: **Los pájaros están volando**/The birds are flying.

The verb is ***éstan volando***/*are flying*.

State of being: **La señora López está contenta**/Mrs. López is happy.

The verb is ***está***/*is*.

Part Four

Spanish Regents Exams and Answers

Examination June 1993

Comprehensive Examination in Spanish

PART 1

Your performance on Part 1, Speaking (24 credits), has been evaluated prior to the date of this written examination.

PART 2

Answer all questions in Part 2 according to the directions for *a* and *b*. [30]

a Directions (1–9): For each question, you will hear some background information in English once. Then you will hear a passage in Spanish *twice* and a question in English *once*. After you have heard the question, the teacher will pause while you read the question and the four suggested answers. Choose the best suggested answer and write its *number* in the space provided. Base your answer *on the content of the passage, only*. The passages that the teacher will read aloud to you are found in the ANSWERS section, Part 2, at the end of this examination. [18]

1 What event is being advertised?

1 a book exhibit
2 a new movie
3 an art exhibition
4 a travel show

1___

2 For whom is this recipe most useful?

1 for those who have little time
2 for those who like to prepare rich foods
3 for those who do not have microwave ovens
4 for those who have large families 2___

3 Why did you get this message?

1 The telephone lines were all busy.
2 The telephone number was changed.
3 Your friend was not at home.
4 Your friend's telephone was out of order. 3___

4 What information is offered on this program?

1 how to maintain good dental hygiene
2 how to grow a variety of plants
3 how to install a home security system
4 how to conserve natural resources 4___

5 What does this announcer say about Julio Iglesias?

1 He feels lonely.
2 He is enjoying his success.
3 He wants to get married again.
4 He wants to have more children. 5___

6 According to this survey, which household chore is disliked the most?

1 cooking
2 washing dishes
3 shopping for food
4 cleaning the floors 6 ___

7 What does your friend tell you about this group?

1 They have been playing together for 12 years.
2 They play traditional Japanese instruments.
3 They sing in a language they do not speak.
4 They mix Japanese and Latin rhythms. 7___

8 What is Mario Vargas Llosa doing in London?

1 He is promoting a book about elections in Peru.
2 He is writing for a newspaper.
3 He is writing about the problems of Peru.
4 He is presenting an award. 8___

9 What is the purpose of this announcement?

1 to report a delay
2 to report an arrival
3 to report about new services
4 to report about boarding passes 9___

b Directions (10–15): For each question, you will hear some background information in English *once*. Then you will hear a passage in Spanish *twice* and a question in Spanish *once*. After you have heard the question, the teacher will pause while you read the question and the four suggested answers. Choose the best suggested answer and write its *number* in the space provided. Base your answer *on the content of the passage, only*. The passages that the teacher will read aloud to you are found in the ANSWERS section, Part 2, at the end of this examination. [12]

10 ¿Cuál es un aspecto importante para este gran diseñador?

1 Diseña la ropa a un precio económico.
2 Usa muchos colores vibrantes.
3 Crea líneas deportivas.
4 Diseña vestidos muy cortos. 10___

11 ¿Por qué fue importante este concierto?

1 Se celebró un día de fiesta en Sevilla.
2 Se inauguró un nuevo teatro.
3 Se reunieron los miembros de la familia real de España.
4 Se reunieron los más importantes cantantes españoles. 11___

12 ¿Por qué es especial este programa?

1 Los padres pueden continuar con su propia educación.
2 Los padres pueden ayudar a los maestros a enseñar.
3 La escuela está abierta durante el verano.
4 Los niños pueden ayudar a la gente en la comunidad. 12___

13 ¿Por qué ganó un premio Natalia Figueroa?

1 Publicó un libro para viajeros que van a México.
2 Publicó un diario sobre la vida mexicana.
3 Escribió un artículo sobre México.
4 Dibujó un cuadro con tema mexicano. 13___

14 ¿Qué se escuchó en la radio?

1 un aviso sobre ciertos alimentos contaminados
2 una oferta especial en un supermercado
3 un anuncio sobre un restaurante nuevo
4 una receta de cocina 14___

15 ¿De qué está hablando esta dependiente?

1 de una tienda nueva
2 de un descuento especial
3 de algunos alimentos
4 de unos cosméticos nuevos 15___

PART 3

Answer all questions in Part 3 according to the directions for *a*, *b*, and *c*. [30 credits]

a Directions (16–20): After the following passage, there are five questions or incomplete statements. For *each*, choose the word or expression that best answers the question or completes the statement *according to the meaning of the passage,* and write its *number* in the space provided. [10]

La mayor colección de arte mexicano que se ha logrado reunir y presentar fuera de México en 50 años inició su recorrido por tres ciudades de los Estados Unidos de América, empezando por la ciudad de Nueva York. Esta exposición permanecerá hasta el 4 de agosto en la ciudad de San Antonio, Texas, y terminará en Los Angeles el 29 de diciembre. Durante su estancia en el Museo Metropolitano de Arte en Nueva York, fue visitada por tanta gente que se convirtió en la segunda exposición más popular de artes plásticas mexicanas. Las piezas, de una gran diversidad de tamaños, materiales y funciones, fueron seleccionadas de colecciones privadas y públicas de México, Europa y Estados Unidos. Esta exposición examina en profundidad la historia de las artes plásticas mexicanas.

México tiene una de las herencias más antiguas, continuas e importantes del mundo. La exposición está organizada cronológicamente para reflejar los principales períodos de la historia mexicana. Comienza con el arte precolombino y termina con el arte del siglo XIX y parte del siglo XX.

La sección del siglo XX empieza en los tiempos de la Revolución, mostrando los ideales políticos y redefiniendo la identidad artística mexicana. La representación de esta época está centrada en los muralistas mexicanos como Diego Rivera y José Clemente Orozco, quienes trabajaron en Estados Unidos en algún momento de su vida artística. La exposición continúa con otros artistas mexicanos como Rufino Tamayo y Frida Kahlo.

Desde el principio, expertos mexicanos y estadounidenses trabajaron en este ambicioso proyecto. El catálogo de la exposición, de 728 páginas, está escrito por profesores expertos, y diversas personalidades internacionales coordinaron sus esfuerzos en este proyecto. El ensayo introductorio está escrito por el reconocido poeta mexicano Octavio Paz. La publicación incluye ensayos e ilustraciones a todo color de todas las obras, con 100 fotografías en blanco y negro.

Cuando se exhibió en el Museo Metropolitano, hubo al mismo tiempo una presentación audiovisual. Esta presentación contenía cientos de imágenes de los sitios arqueológicos tal como están hoy día, dando un contexto histórico a las obras de arte. Además, se organizaron programas de educación, incluyendo una serie de conferencias, un simposio de arte precolombino, documentales, y películas.

16 ¿Por qué es tan importante esta exposición?

1 Es la colección más grande de este tipo fuera de México.
2 Incluye muchas obras de artistas de Estados Unidos.
3 Será presentada en trece ciudades americanas.
4 Muestra la vida moderna de México. 16____

17 Durante la exposición en Nueva York, fue notable que

1 se rompieron varias piezas
2 se perdió una obra
3 vino muchísima gente a visitarla
4 decidieron mandar la colección a Europa 17____

18 En general, ¿qué representa esta exposición?

1 las relaciones políticas entre México y Estados Unidos
2 la herencia artística mexicana
3 la guerra de independencia mexicana
4 el arte internacional 18____

19 ¿Qué influyó a los artistas del siglo XX?

1 la Revolución mexicana
2 la mitología antigua
3 los ensayos políticos
4 la cultura española 19____

20 ¿Qué ofreció el Museo Metropolitano a los visitantes?

1 una variedad de programas para entender mejor las obras
2 unas cenas para acompañar las conferencias
3 unos grupos musicales para animarles
4 una foto gratis de la exposición 20____

b Directions (21–25): Below each of the following selections, there is either a question or an incomplete statement. For *each*, choose the word or expression that best answers the question or completes the statement *according to the meaning of the selection*, and write its *number* in the space provided. [10]

21

A los 16 años, muchos estudiantes comienzan a pensar en irse de la escuela. Desafortunadamente, 3.000 estudiantes abandonan la escuela cada día. La epidemia de deserción escolar en Estados Unidos es un terrible desperdicio de potencial humano y fomenta el crimen y las drogas en nuestras escuelas y en la calle. Pero Ud. puede ayudar participando en los programas de prevención de la deserción escolar en su ciudad.

Llame

al 1-800-868-3475 o al 1-800-433-6392.

Quédese en la escuela.

What is this article about?

1 an antidrug program
2 school transportation
3 high school dropouts
4 a driver education program

21____

22

AHORA TU CUOTA TE PROTEGE CON UN SEGURO

AL USAR LAS INSTALACIONES DE CAMINOS Y PUENTES, CUENTAS CON UN SEGURO QUE CUBRE.

A) RESPONSABILIDAD CIVIL
B) GASTOS MEDICOS
C) ULTIMOS GASTOS

EN CASO DE SINIESTRO, INFORMA A LA CASETA MAS CERCANA O A LOS **TELEFONOS 86-49-06 86-14-10**

EXIGE TU BOLETO Y CONSERVALO

What benefit do you get when you pay tolls on these highways?

1 insurance in case of an accident
2 free towing service
3 traffic information
4 discounts on future trips 22____

23

CARTAS A SU SER QUERIDO

Al compás cambiante de estos tiempos, El Diario-La Prensa quiere ofrecerle una forma diferente de saludar a su ser querido este año. El Diario publicará la carta que usted escriba a su ser querido en el Día de Las Madres. Su carta será publicada en su puño y letra y con su firma. Su carta debe contener no más de 2 párrafos de 6 líneas cada uno más el saludo y su firma, a un módico costo de sólo **$25.00** por carta. Debe enviarnos su carta acompañada de un giro postal o número de tarjeta de crédito no más tardar el 6 de mayo, 1993 . Sus cartas serán publicadas el ***Día de Las Madres.***

What is this newspaper offering its readers?

1 a $25 prize for the best letter
2 the opportunity to publish their own letters
3 a gift subscription for Mother's Day
4 free advertisements on Mother's Day 23____

24

PARA ESTUDIANTES

Como estudiante de español he disfrutado mucho con su revista. Me gusta el estilo cotidiano que me ayuda a aprender, no solamente vocabulario, sino también sobre la cultura hispana. Creo que otros estudiantes de español van a beneficiarse de la revista y ya la he recomendado a unas cuantas amigas. En particular me gustó muchísimo el suplemento especial Guía de la Copa Mundial. Leí todos los artículos y aprendí mucho sobre fútbol, de lo que no sabía nada.

Elena Muñoz

What is the purpose of this letter?

1 to complain about the lack of cultural articles
2 to request some information for a friend
3 to ask for more sports articles
4 to express satisfaction with the magazine 24____

25

2 libros por sólo $5.00 cada uno

CIRCULO DE LECTORES
65 Commerce Road, Stamford, CT 06902

SI, deseo hacerme miembro de CIRCULO DE LECTORES. Envíeme los 2 libros que he indicado abajo junto con su factura por $10.00, más gastos de manejo y envío (más impuestos para residentes de Nueva York y Connecticut).

Si decidiera quedarme con los libros, me comprometo a comprar tres libros por año para continuar como miembro. Si decido no quedarme con los libros introductorios, los devolveré (dentro de 10 días), no deberé nada y mi nombre se eliminará de su lista de miembros.

Por favor, envíeme los siguientes libros (indique los códigos solamente). ☐ ☐

Nombre ____________________

Dirección ____________________ Apt. ______

Ciudad ____________________

Estado __________ Zona Postal __________

Teléfono ____________________

Firma ____________________

Oferta válida en los Estados Unidos. Todas las órdenes están sujetas a aprobación de crédito.

How many books must you buy each year to remain a member?

(1) 5
(2) 2
(3) 3
(4) 10 25 ___

c *Directions* (26–30): In the following passage there are five blank spaces numbered 26 through 30. Each blank space represents a missing word or expression. For each blank space, four possible completions are provided. Only one of them makes sense *in the context of the passage*.

First, read the passage in its entirety to determine its general meaning. Then read it a second time. For each blank space, choose the completion that makes the best sense and write its *number* in the space provided. [10]

Una Entrevista con Gabriela Sabatini

Acabo de conocer a Gabriela Sabatini, la famosa jugadora de tenis. En la última media hora me ha contado historias personales acerca de su vida.

La joven tenista ha obtenido muches triunfos en los últimos años. Sabatini descubrió su ___(26)___ a la tierna edad de siete años. Ahora, a la edad de 20 años, ha ganado el U.S. Open y ha firmado numerosos contratos para endorsar productos comerciales.

Ese día, Gaby (así la llaman todos) se encontraba en medio de un frenético torneo de promoción. Yo me encontraba en las canchas del estadio cuando la reconocí: una mujer sumamente bella y radiante vestida con ropa deportiva. Nos presentamos, y creo que me enamoré. Gabriela ___(27)___ mi admiración tan pronto como nos conocimos.

Está tan segura de sí misma que uno puede notar su fuerza. Sabe que puede llegar a ser la número uno en el mundo. Yo suponía que me trataría con distancia como a los otros ___(28)___ que querían entrevistarla. Para mi sorpresa, la belleza argentina conversó conmigo amistosamente.

Con su victoria sobre Steffi Graf en el U.S. Open, Sabatini confirmó su gran habilidad.

Finalmente ha callado a sus críticos, que decían que era una ___(29)___ con cierto talento que decaería en poco tiempo.

Gaby se sonríe y se me acerca, contándome lo mucho que le gustaría tener las cosas más sencillas de la vida como por ejemplo una familia. Debido a sus constantes viajes y su fama, es difícil mantener relaciones sentimentales.

Tiene pocas amigas en el tenis; trata de hacer una vida normal, lo más sencilla posible. Cuando está con sus amigos es otra persona; va al cine o a una discoteca, se ríe, habla, juega, hace chistes y se ___(30)___ mucho. "Lo que me gusta es que la gente me quiera mucho", afirma Gaby. "Me hace sentir bien. No sólo me interesa el tenis; más importante es la personalidad de uno."

(26) 1 debilidad 3 riqueza
2 pasado 4 talento 26 ___

(27) 1 ganó 3 rechazó
2 aruinó 4 cambió 27 ___

(28) 1 árbitros 3 pasajeros
2 cocineros 4 periodistas 28 ___

(29) 1 maestra 3 jugadora
2 actriz 4 escritora 29 ___

(30) 1 duerme 3 enfada
2 divierte 4 enferma 30 ___

PART 4

Write your answers to Part 4 according to the directions for *a* and *b*. [16]

a Directions: Write **one** well-organized note in Spanish as directed below. [6]

Choose **either** question 31 **or** 32. Write a well-organized note, following the specific instructions given in the question you have chosen. Your note must consist of **at least six clauses**. To qualify for credit, a clause must contain a verb, a stated or implied subject, and additional words necessary to convey meaning. The six clauses may be contained in fewer than six sentences if some of the sentences have more than one clause.

31 You are watching the children of your Spanish-speaking neighbors for the afternoon. You decide to take the children out. Write a note in Spanish to your neighbors telling them about your plans.

In the note, you may choose to tell them where you are going, why you are going, and when you will return. **Be sure you accomplish the purpose of the note, which is *to tell your neighbors about your plans*.**

Use the following:

Salutation: Señores
Closing: [your first name]

The salutation and closing will *not* be counted as part of the six required clauses.

32 An exchange student from Costa Rica is spending the year in your school. Next week your Spanish Club is holding a special event. Write a note in Spanish inviting the exchange student to the special event.

In your note, you may wish to identify yourself, describe the club's purpose and activities, give the date, time, and place of the event, and encourage the student to attend. **Be sure you accomplish the purpose of the note, which is *to invite the exchange student to the club's special event.***

Use the following:

Salutation: [the exchange student's name]
Closing: [your first name]

The salutation and closing will *not* be counted as part of the six required clauses.

b Directions: Write **one** well-organized composition in Spanish as directed below. [10]

Choose **either** question 33 **or** 34. Write a well-organized composition, following the specific instructions given in the question you have chosen. Your composition must consist of **at least 10 clauses**. To qualify for credit, a clause must contain a verb, a stated or implied subject, and additional words necessary to convey meaning. The 10 clauses may be contained in fewer than 10 sentences if some of the sentences have more than one clause.

33 In Spanish, write a story about the situation shown in the picture below. It must be a story relating to the picture, **not** a description of the picture. Do *not* write a dialogue.

34 Your friends gave you a present on a special occasion. Write a letter in Spanish to your Spanish pen pal telling about the present.

You <u>must</u> accomplish the purpose of the letter, which is *to tell your pen pal about the present your friends gave you.*

In your letter, you may wish to explain what the present is, who gave it to you, why they gave it to you, who was there when they gave it to you, what people said and what they did, and how you feel about the present.

You may use any or all of the ideas suggested above *or* you may use your own ideas. **Either way, you must tell your pen pal about the present your friends gave you.**

Use the following:

Dateline:	18 de junio de 1993
Salutation:	Querido/Querida
Closing:	Tu amigo/Tu amiga

The dateline, salutation, and closing will *not* be counted as part of the 10 required clauses.

Answers June 1993

Comprehensive Examination in Spanish

PART 1

This part of the examination was evaluated prior to the date of this written examination. [24 credits]

PART 2

The following passages are to be read aloud to the students according to the directions given for this part at the beginning of this examination. The correct answers are given after number 15. [30 credits]

1. You hear this announcement on the radio in Spain:

Organizada por el Museo Picasso de Barcelona, se inauguró el pasado 17 de octubre la exposición *De Pablo a Jacqueline*. En ella hay pinturas, dibujos, esculturas y obras gráficas que representan más de 140 obras del genial malagueño con su esposa Jacqueline como modelo. Algunas de las obras son poco conocidas.

What event is being advertised?

2. You are watching a cooking demonstration on television and hear this introduction:

Este menú ha sido creado para aquellas personas que disponen de poco tiempo pero quieren una alimentación sana, equilibrada, y al mismo tiempo, apetitosa para la vista. Estas recetas son para hornos microondas. La única advertencia al usar un horno microondas es que no todos tienen la misma potencia, por lo que pueden variar ligeramente los minutos y segundos necesarios.

For whom is this recipe most useful?

3. You arrive in México and you telephone a friend. After you dial, you hear this message:

Lo sentimos mucho pero el número que usted acaba de marcar ha sido cambiado a petición del cliente. Lamentamos no poder darle el nuevo número por expreso deseo del cliente. Esperamos que esto no le cause ningún inconveniente. Este es un mensaje grabado.

Why did you get this message?

4. You are watching a special program on television and hear:

Sin duda, el agua es uno de los recursos naturales más valiosos con que contamos, pero que malgastamos. El precioso líquido ha comenzado a escasear de una manera alarmante en numerosas partes del mundo. Con sólo tener el cuidado de cerrar el grifo mientras nos cepillamos los dientes podremos economizar, cada uno, hasta doce litros al día. También podemos ahorrar agua cuando tomamos un baño, fregamos los platos, lavamos la ropa, y regamos el jardín.

What information is offered on this program?

5. You are watching television in Spain and hear this announcement about Julio Iglesias:

Julio Iglesias, que ha llevado sus canciones a los cinco continentes de la tierra y ha sido aplaudido y aclamado con éxito en todas partes por su público, dice que se siente sólo y que su vida está vacía. Según los rumores, el famoso cantante ha dicho que quiere regresar a España, y que solamente quiere tener un hogar y reunirse con sus hijos. ¿Pueden ustedes creer esto de nuestro querido Julio?

What does this announcer say about Julio Iglesias?

6. You are listening to the results of a survey about household chores and hear:

De acuerdo con una encuesta realizada recientemente sobre todos los trabajos domésticos, el más odiado es fregar los platos; le siguen limpiar el baño y barrer el piso. A la inversa, de todas las labores de la casa, lo que más disfrutan es comprar alimentos en el mercado, seguida de limpiar el patio. ¿Cocinar? Curiosamente, ni les gusta ni les disgusta.

According to this survey, which household chore is disliked the most?

7. You are at a friend's home, and he is telling you about a compact disc he bought:

¿Sabes? La música de salsa ha llegado hasta el Japón. Hay un grupo que se llama *La Orquesta de la Luz,* y es una curiosidad. Fue formado hace más de cinco años por una docena de japoneses que cantan en español aunque no lo hablan. Sin embargo, han logrado colocar un disco compacto entre los grandes éxitos del año. Escuchemos una canción de ese disco . . . a ver si te gusta.

What does your friend tell you about this group?

8. You are in an audience listening to a speaker who is talking about Mario Vargas Llosa, a Peruvian writer. The speaker says:

Después de su derrota en las elecciones peruanas, el escritor Mario Vargas Llosa se fue a vivir a Londres donde sigue escribiendo. Los temas de sus libros tratan de los problemas de su país. Ahora está escribiendo una novela sobre los problemas en un pueblecito de los Andes en el Perú. Nunca ha obtenido el Premio Nobel de Literatura aunque evidentemente ha estado muy cerca en varias ocasiones.

What is Mario Vargas Llosa doing in London?

9. You are at the airport in Bogotá waiting for your flight and hear this announcement:

Avianca anuncia a los pasajeros del vuelo 913 con destino a la ciudad de Nueva York que habrá un retraso de tres horas debido a un problema con el tren de aterrizaje. Rogamos a los señores pasajeros que pasen por nuestro mostrador para recibir un vale que podrán usar en el restaurante del aeropuerto. Sentimos mucho las molestias que este retraso les pueda causar. Gracias.

What is the purpose of this announcement?

10. You are at a fashion show and the moderator says:

Los grandes diseñadores de la moda para la temporada otoño-invierno anuncian que se puede vestir con la mayor libertad del mundo. Los diseños del famoso modisto dominicano, Oscar de la Renta, están llenos de color. Este abrigo, por ejemplo, integra diseños con brillantes tonos de rojo, anaranjado y azul, y es ideal tanto para el día como para la noche.

¿Cuál es un aspecto importante para este gran diseñador?

11. You are listening to the news in Spain and hear the following:

España se convirtió anoche en la capital mundial de la música con la actuación en Sevilla de nueve de las más grandes y prestigiosas voces de España. En el Teatro de la Maestranza actuaron entre otras famosas figuras: Plácido Domingo, Montserrat Caballé y José Carreras. La Reina, doña Sofía, les saludó y les felicitó personalmente al final.

¿Por qué fue importante este concierto?

12. You are watching a Spanish cable television station and hear this news item:

Una escuela elemental inicia una campaña contra el analfabetismo. Con una visita a la escuela se puede ver el nuevo programa del instituto que invita a los padres a regresar a la escuela. A las siete de la mañana, todos los martes, miércoles y jueves, los padres van con sus hijos a la escuela y asisten a clases que les permitirán obtener el diploma de Educación General Básica. Este programa puede servir como ejemplo para otras comunidades.

¿Por qué es especial este programa?

13. You are watching the news on television and hear the following:

Natalia Figueroa acaba de recibir en Acapulco, el importante premio literario *Pluma de Plata Mexicana,* que la Secretaría de Turismo de aquel país otorga a un solo escritor de cada país por un artículo publicado sobre México. Carlos González, político de enorme carisma y popularidad, entregó el premio a Natalia. Natalia Figueroa recibió el premio por su artículo titulado "Querido México", que fue publicado en el diario *A B C* hace unos meses.

¿Por qué ganó un premio Natalia Figueroa?

14. You are in Santo Domingo. You turn on the television and hear the following:

En una sartén grande, fría el pollo en el aceite a fuego lento. Tape la sartén y cocine durante quince minutos. En un plato hondo mezcle la cebolla, el pimiento verde, el vinagre, el azúcar y las especias. Vierta la mezcla sobre el pollo y siga cocinando hasta que el pollo esté tierno. ¡Buen provecho!

¿Qué se escuchó en la radio?

15. You are in a Spanish department store and hear the salesclerk say to a group of customers:

En marzo del año pasado nuestra firma lanzó al mercado una nueva fragancia. En vista del gran éxito obtenido, hemos decidido añadir otros productos. Ahora contamos con una línea que incluye el champú, la loción, el talco y la crema...todos con el nuevo aroma. Estos productos tienen como ingrediente principal el aceite de nueces. ¿Les gustaría probar alguno de ellos?

¿De qué está hablando esta dependiente?

PART 2

(1) 3
(2) 1
(3) 2
(4) 4
(5) 1
(6) 2
(7) 3
(8) 3
(9) 1
(10) 2
(11) 4
(12) 1
(13) 3
(14) 4
(15) 4

PART 3

(a) **(16)** 1
(17) 3
(18) 2
(19) 1
(20) 1

(b) **(21)** 3
(22) 1
(23) 2
(24) 4
(25) 3

(c) **(26)** 4
(27) 1
(28) 4
(29) 3
(30) 2

PART 4

(a) Notes in writing

For each note, an example of a response worth six credits follows. The slash marks indicate how each sample note has been divided into clauses.

31. Señores,

Estamos en el parque./$_1$ Los chicos necesitan ejercicio./$_2$ Vamos a jugar al béisbol./$_3$ Después, iremos a comprar unos helados./$_4$ Volveremos a las cuatro./$_5$ No se preocupen./$_6$

Enrique

32. María Luisa,

El sábado próximo, nuestro club de español va a un restaurante mexicano/$_1$ y quisiéramos invitarte a cenar con nosotros./$_2$ Pensamos salir a eso de las seis./$_3$ Nos encontraremos en la casa de Jerry/$_4$ e iremos en su coche./$_5$ Déjame saber lo más pronto posible/$_6$ si puedes venir. Nos divertiremos mucho.

Karen

(b) Narrative based on picture/letter

For each narrative/letter, an example of a response worth 10 credits follows. The slash marks indicate how each sample narrative/letter has been divided into clauses.

33. (Picture)

Paco, Ramón y su hermana Clara están en la cocina./$_1$ Sus padres salieron esta manaña/$_2$ para ir al supermercado./$_3$ Ahora los tres hijos quieren darles una gran sorpresa a mamá y papá:/$_4$ van a preparar la cena y también un delicioso pastel de chocolate./$_5$ ¡Mamá no tendrá que cocinar hoy!/$_6$ Los niños sacan la leche, el azúcar y muchos platos./$_7$ Cuando algunas cosas caen al suelo,/$_8$ el gato y el perro les ayudan a limpiar./$_9$ Clara ve por la ventana/$_{10}$, que papá y mamá ya volvieron a casa. ¡Caramba la cena no está lista todavía!

34. (Letter)

18 de junio de 1993

Querida Luisa,

Ayer recibí un regalo para mi cumpleaños./$_1$ Mis amigos vinieron a mi casa/$_2$ y me dieron una caja muy grande./$_3$ Abrí la caja/$_4$ y dentro había una caja pequeña./$_5$ Puedes imaginar mi sorpresa/$_6$ cuando la abrí./$_7$ Era on reloj de oro,/$_8$ una cosa que quería desde hace mucho tiempo./$_9$ Tengo mucha suerte/$_{10}$ porque mis amigos son tan simpáticos.

Tu amiga,
Paquita

Examination January 1994

Comprehensive Examination in Spanish

PART 1

Your performance on Part 1, Speaking (24 credits), has been evaluated prior to the date of this written examination.

PART 2

Answer all questions in Part 2 according to the directions for *a* and *b*. [30]

a Directions (1–9): For each question, you will hear some background information in English once. Then you will hear a passage in Spanish *twice* and a question in English *once*. After you have heard the question, the teacher will pause while you read the question and the four suggested answers. Choose the best suggested answer and write its *number* in the space provided. Base your answer *on the content of the passage, only*. The passages that the teacher will read aloud to you are found in the ANSWERS section, Part 2, at the end of this examination. [18]

1 What do these women want?

1 a reduction of crime in the cities
2 greater understanding among different peoples
3 the elimination of drugs
4 lower college tuition

1____

2 What is J.C. Penney offering?

1 management-training programs
2 salesclerk positions in various cities
3 opportunities to become models
4 four-year college scholarships 2____

3 What new service will be offered?

1 Mail will arrive at destinations within eight hours.
2 More telephones will be installed.
3 Stamp machines will be available in several locations.
4 Telephone credit cards will be issued. 3____

4 What advice is offered?

1 Invite a local music group to play.
2 Prepare your own musical tapes.
3 Begin with romantic music.
4 Buy the most recent recordings. 4____

5 For what problem would you use this product?

1 wrinkles 3 sunburn
2 hair loss 4 poor vision 5____

6 What is of particular interest about Santo Domingo?

1 The city was recently destroyed by a hurricane.
2 The city has a museum that features early Spanish settlements.
3 The city is building several modern hospitals.
4 The city is restoring buildings to the original Spanish style. 6____

7 What did Emilio Butragueño do?

1 He retired.
2 He got married.
3 He celebrated his birthday.
4 He signed a new professional contract. 7___

8 What was the purpose of this festival?

1 to celebrate a religious holiday
2 to honor a nationally recognized organization
3 to promote tourism in Texas
4 to commemorate a historic event 8___

9 What did William Hernández highlight in the newscast?

1 a sculpture for the community
2 adult-education opportunities
3 the collecting of disposable materials for reuse
4 the retraining of the unemployed for high-technology jobs 9___

b *Directions* (10–15): For each question, you will hear some background information in English *once*. Then you will hear a passage in Spanish *twice* and a question in Spanish *once*. After you have heard the question, the teacher will pause while you read the question and the four suggested answers. Choose the best suggested answer and write its *number* in the space provided. Base your answer *on the content of the passage, only*. The passages that the teacher will read aloud to you are found in the ANSWERS section, Part 2, at the end of this examination. [12]

10 ¿Por qué sería popular esta ropa nueva?

1 Es sencilla y cómoda.
2 Es barata.
3 Es lavable.
4 Es ostentosa y vistosa. 10___

11 ¿Por qué le gusta este juego a tu amigo?

1 porque puede aprender a jugar un deporte
2 porque puede aprender otra lengua
3 porque puede ganar mucho dinero
4 porque puede divertirse con toda la familia 11____

12 ¿Cuál es el problema principal de este auto?

1 No hay ruedas de este tamaño.
2 Necesita una gasolina especial.
3 No es posible manejarlo.
4 Le faltan unos aparatos modernos. 12____

13 ¿Qué quiere saber la delegación puertorriqueña?

1 la nación caribeña donde se efectuarán los juegos
2 el número de participantes en cada delegación
3 el horario de los eventos
4 la posibilidad de participar en más eventos deportivos 13____

14 ¿Por qué le gusta a su amiga este restaurante?

1 Hay un grupo que canta música moderna.
2 El servicio es rápido.
3 Hay un ambiente divertido.
4 El dueño es un pariente suyo 14____

15 ¿De qué se acusó a Julio Iglesias?

1 de copiar una canción
2 de negarse a pagar una multa
3 de responder mal a la Corte Civil
4 de no aparecer en su concierto 15____

PART 3

Answer all questions in Part 3 according to the directions for *a*, *b*, and *c*. [30 credits]

a Directions (16–20): After the following passage, there are five questions or incomplete statements. For *each*, choose the word or expression that best answers the question or completes the statement *according to the meaning of the passage*, and write its *number* in the space provided. [10]

Carlos Fuentes, el novelista más famoso de México, es ahora también narrador en la televisión. Carlos Fuentes, el célebre ensayista, crítico y autor de novelas, ha completado una serie televisiva para la cadena británica BBC, sobre la historia y cultura hispánica. Este programa, *El Espejo Enterrado: Reflexiones sobre España y el Nuevo Mundo*, saldrá al aire en Europa, Estados Unidos y Latinoamérica. El programa ha condensado diez siglos de historia en segmentos de una hora de duración cada uno. La historia comienza con las pinturas en las Cuevas de Altamira y termina con los graffiti del este de Los Angeles.

El primer segmento tiene lugar en la España de 1492, cuando los moros fueron expulsados de España y la Reina Isabel bendijo el primer viaje de Cristóbal Colón al Nuevo Mundo. Otros episodios tratan de las civilizaciones precoloniales, las debilidades políticas y los triunfos artísticos del Imperio español, las Guerras de Independencia de Latinoamérica y la Revolución mexicana. Al final Fuentes analiza el enriquecimiento de las culturas hispanicas de Estados Unidos, Latinoamérica y España, y trata de reflejar sobre el futuro.

Nacido en Panamá y educado en Argentina, Chile, Washington y México, Fuentes ha sido embajador de México en Francia y ha dado conferencias en las universidades de Oxford y Harvard. La capacidad plurilingüe del autor resultó muy útil durante la filmación de los programas: Fuentes asombró al equipo de la BBC con su habilidad para grabar un segmento en inglés y entonces, con apenas una pausa, repetir de nuevo el texto en español para la edición de Latinoamérica.

En cuanto al mensaje presentado, Carlos Fuentes dice: "Los indios de América están pidiéndonos a nosotros, los hombres y mujeres de las ciudades, que respetemos sus valores. Sin condenarlos al olvido, sino salvándolos de las injusticias, diciéndonos que ellos son también parte de nuestra comunidad cultural, advirtiéndonos que si los olvidamos, estarémos olvidándonos a nosotros".

Al final de *El Espejo Enterrado* Fuentes pregunta "¿Quién ganó? ¿Quién perdió?" El contesta que los hispanoamericanos tienen que comprender que su pasado forma parte de su futuro. Aunque la conquista fue un desastre para las poblaciones indias, algo gratificante ha resultado. "Nació algo nuevo. Nacieron los hispanoamericanos".

16 ¿Qué hizo Carlos Fuentes?

1 Decidió no continuar escribiendo.
2 Se convirtió en director.
3 Narró un programa histórico.
4 Escribió su autobiografía. 16___

17 ¿Quién produjo este programa?

1 una universidad española
2 una empresa mexicana
3 una estación americana
4 una compañía inglesa 17___

18 ¿De qué trata esta serie televisiva?

1 de mil años de historia del mundo hispánico
2 de una novela española
3 de un viaje del novelista a España
4 de un sistema educativo europeo 18____

19 ¿Dónde empieza la historia televisiva?

1 en México
2 en España
3 en Panamá
4 en Chile 19____

20 ¿A qué conclusión llegó Fuentes acerca de la historia de la América Latina?

1 Resultó una nueva cultura.
2 Las guerras de independencia fueron necesarias.
3 Se terminaron las injusticias.
4 Los indios olvidaron su pasado. 20____

b Directions (21–25): Below each of the following selections, there is either a question or an incomplete statement. For *each*, choose the word or expression that best answers the question or completes the statement *according to the meaning of the selection*, and write its *number* in the space provided. [10]

21

"No lo cambiaría por nada."

Mi carrera es muy emocionante. ¡Soy enfermera! Gano un buen salario, siempre tomo decisiones importantes y me siento contenta conmigo misma. Eso no lo cambiaría por nada.

¡Me encanta ser enfermera!

Llama al **1-800-962-6877** para recibir más información sobre las oportunidades, buenos salarios, programas de estudio de 2 ó 4 años y las diferentes opciones de trabajo que te ofrece la carrera de enfermera.

Who should call the number listed in this advertisement?

1 people who need personal advice
2 people who need medical treatment
3 people who are looking for a new career
4 people who have trouble making decisions 21____

22

Para este delicioso plato no se necesita ninguna receta de cocina porque las Croquetas Goya están ya preparadas con trocitos de jamón curado mezclado con patatas y especies y finamente empanado. Y de la misma forma están preparadas y totalmente precocinadas las Croquetas Goya de pollo. Se pueden servir solas o con salsa verde Goya y también con arroz y habichuelas para una comida sabrosa y rápida. Se pueden conseguir en los departamentos de productos congelados de los establecimientos de comestibles, al lado de los otros productos congelados Goya: burritos, empanadillas, tamales, yuca, alcapurrias y otros más, todos sabrosos.

Why is this a popular dish?

1 It can be served hot or cold.
2 It requires few ingredients.
3 It is a traditional Puerto Rican specialty.
4 It is already prepared. 22____

23

Visitas a un museo

El Museo de la Reconquista – especializado en la Reconquista de Buenos Aires y la historia de Tigre – atiende al público en su nuevo horario, de miércoles a domingo, de las 14 a las 18. Las instituciones pueden solicitar visitas guiadas en Liniers 818, Tigre, tel. 749-0090.

What is this museum announcing to its visitors?

1 a new location
2 a new time schedule
3 a historical lecture
4 a collection of paintings of animals 23____

24

Si se lesiona en el trabajo, el seguro de compensación de empleados de su empleador paga por sus beneficios semanales, rehabilitación vocacional, y gastos médicos. También puede tener el derecho a recuperar dinero por su dolor y sufrimiento si su lesión es causada por la negligencia de otro. Por ejemplo, si su lesión es causada por una máquina, el diseño de esa máquina puede ser defectuoso, y el fabricante de ella pueda ser responsable a pagar, además de sus beneficios de compensación de empleado. Si usted se ha lesionado en el trabajo, nosotros le podemos ayudar. Nuestras oficinas están localizadas en Salem, Massachusetts, y representamos a los trabajadores en Boston y el North Shore. Consultas gratis. 1-508-745-8948.

What does this announcement offer?

1 housing for people on fixed incomes
2 assistance in finding a job
3 health insurance for retired people
4 help to employees who get hurt on the job 24____

25

Palabras infantiles. Soy Margarita de la Rasilla y tengo 11 años. Normalmente miro por encima EL PAÍS. Cuando hay algo interesante, lo leo; pero hay un vocabulario y no me entero de la mitad. Por eso se me ha venido a la cabeza una idea que yo creo que es buena. Es la siguiente: hay muchos niños a los que les gusta saber cosas sobre nuestro mundo, pero hay palabras muy complicadas. Por eso creo conveniente que todos los domingos saliese un pequeño fascículo destacando sucesos que nos puedan interesar (adecuados a nuestro vocabulario). Así podríamos enterarnos de cosas de las que ahora no podemos.
— **Margarita de la Rasilla**
y 33 firmas más.

What suggestion does this reader make to the editor?

1 to print a special section for young people on Sundays
2 to include more articles on health in the Sunday edition
3 to write more articles about world events
4 to encourage more young people to write 25___

c *Directions* (26–30): In the following passage, there are five blank spaces numbered 26 through 30. Each blank space represents a missing word or expression. For each blank space, four possible completions are provided. Only one of them makes sense *in the context of the passage*.

First, read the passage in its entirety to determine its general meaning. Then read it a second time. For each blank space, choose the completion that makes the best sense and write its *number* in the space provided. [10]

La Infanta Cristina

La infanta Cristina de Borbón — la infanta de la dulce sonrisa—es la hija menor de los Reyes de España. Es una joven de nuestro tiempo, llena de inquietudes . . . una persona sencilla, cordial, timida y excelente deportista.

Siempre buena estudiante, la infanta Cristina asistió en primer lugar al colegio de Los Rosales y posteriormente pasó al de Nuestra Señora del Camino. Decidió estudiar Ciencias Políticas y, hace dos años, se convirtió en la primera mujer que posee un título universitario en la historia de la familia real española. Pero no quiso detener su ___(26)___ ahí y poco después se trasladó a Nueva York donde hizo su maestría en Relaciones Internacionales. En mayo de 1990, a punto de finalizar sus estudios allí, manifestó: "Tengo que completar mi preparación intelectual para

___(27)___ un trabajo u ocupación a la que dedicarme profesionalmente".

Su vida hoy es su trabajo. Trabaja en París para la UNESCO preocupándose de los problemas del mundo. Los derechos de la mujer, las dificultades por las que pasa nuestro planeta, y los problemas de educación son algunos de los temas que captan ahora ___(28)___ de la infanta.

No por ser hija de Reyes tiene el mundo a sus pies. Y aunque en ciertos ambientes así pudiera suceder, ella quiere ganárselo todo por sí misma. El hecho de ser infanta de España es para ella tan sólo una condición que, ante todo, supone modos exquisitos de conducta. Por otra parte, en fondo, la hija menor de los Reyes, que se siente identificada con los jóvenes de su tiempo en cuanto a inquietudes y ganas de mejorar el mundo en que les ha tocado vivir, es una persona con bastante timidez, tal y como ella misma lo afirmó en una entrevista al iniciar sus estudios universitarios. Naturalmente que el tiempo, y sobre todo los viajes y el trato diario con sus compañeros de estudios, han ido convirtiéndola en una joven más abierta, más desenvuelta. Ella habló de este cambio hace ahora casi dos años: "Aunque cuesta superar la timidez, a medida que se va siendo mayor y se va madurando, se tienen mayores recursos para superar las situaciones incómodas que a veces se plantean."

Tiene, sin embargo, tiempo para todo . . . tiempo para el ___(29)___ —la vela es su gran afición y formó parte del equipo olímpico en Seúl; tiempo para salir con amigos y amigas de su edad—le encanta el *rock and roll*, baila muy bien, le apasiona la música; tiempo para la lectura—intercambia muchos libros con su madre, la Reina: y tiempo para llevar a cabo todo su trabajo oficial y profesional. Es una joven de hoy con muchas ___(30)___. Como infanta de España tiene deberes oficiales: viajes y actos benéficos. Hace meses, por ejemplo, visitó a Chile representando España.

Ahora llega a los veintiséis años la infanta de la dulce sonrisa. Es momento para felicitarla por su forma de afrontar su vida, por su sentido de la responsabilidad, por su simpatía y por sus inquietudes.

(26) 1 viaje
2 visita
3 empleo
4 educación
26___

(27) 1 encontrar
2 rechazar
3 financiar
4 recordar
27___

(28) 1 el sueño 3 el interés
2 la felicidad 4 la libertad 28____

(29) 1 estudio 3 deporte
2 teatro 4 arte 29____

(30) 1 obligaciones 3 carreras
2 compañeras 4 preferencias 30____

PART 4

Write your answers to Part 4 according to the directions for *a* and *b*. [16]

a Directions: Write **one** well-organized note in Spanish as directed below. [6]

Choose **either** question 31 **or** 32. Write a well-organized note, following the specific instructions given in the question you have chosen. Your note must consist of **at least six clauses**. To qualify for credit, a clause must contain a verb, a stated or implied subject, and additional words necessary to convey meaning. The six clauses may be contained in fewer than six sentences if some of the sentences have more than one clause.

31 You are an exchange student in Costa Rica. You will not be home for dinner. Write a note in Spanish to your host parents explaining why.

In your note, you may wish to indicate where you will be, what you will be doing, and what time you expect to return. **Be sure you accomplish the purpose of the note, which is *to explain why you will not be home for dinner*.**

Use the following:

Salutation: Hola,
Closing: [your first name]

The salutation and closing will *not* be counted as part of the six required clauses.

32 You have found something that your friend lost. Write a note in Spanish telling your friend that you have found it.

In your note, you may wish to tell what you found, where you found it, and what you are going to do with it. **Be sure you accomplish the purpose of the note, which is *to tell your friend that you have found the object your friend lost.***

Use the following:

Salutation: [the friend's first name]
Closing: [your first name]

The salutation and closing will *not* be counted as part of the six required clauses.

b Directions: Write **one** well-organized composition in Spanish as directed below. [10]

Choose **either** question 33 **or** 34. Write a well-organized composition, following the specific instructions given in the question you have chosen. Your composition must consist of **at least 10 clauses**. To qualify for credit, a clause must contain a verb, a stated or implied subject, and additional words necessary to convey meaning. The 10 clauses may be contained in fewer than 10 sentences if some of the sentences have more than one clause.

33 In Spanish, write a story about the situation shown in the picture below. It must be a story relating to the picture, **not** a description of the picture. Do *not* write a dialogue.

34 Your friends gave you a surprise party. Write a letter in Spanish to your pen pal telling about the party.

You <u>must</u> accomplish the purpose of the letter, which is *to tell your pen pal about the surprise party your friends gave you.*

In your letter, you may wish to explain who gave the party, why they gave it, where it took place, who attended it, what people did at the party, and how you felt about the party.

You may use any or all of the ideas suggested above *or* you may use your own ideas. **Either way, you must tell your pen pal about the surprise party your friends gave you.**

Use the following:

Dateline: el 27 de enero de 1994
Salutation: Querida/Querido
Closing: Tu amiga/Tu amigo

The dateline, salutation, and closing will *not* be counted as part of the 10 required clauses.

Answers January 1994

Comprehensive Examination in Spanish

PART 1

This part of the examination was evaluated prior to the date of this written examination. [24 credits]

PART 2

The following passages are to be read aloud to the students according to the directions given for this part at the beginning of this examination. The correct answers are given after number 15. [30 credits]

1. You are listening to the news in Miami and hear the newscaster say:

Más de 170 mujeres de todos los orígenes, países e idiomas del condado de Dade se reunieron aquí para tratar de romper las barreras de la discriminación y construir los puentes de entendimiento entre los diferentes grupos étnicos de esta ciudad.

La reunión fue convocada por el Comité Hebreo-Americano con el objetivo de entenderse mejor, enfocando la atención de mujeres profesionales, estudiantes y amas de casa.

What do these women want?

2. You are watching a Spanish cable television station and hear this announcement:

Una de las profesiones más atractivas de nuestra época es la del modelaje. Para jóvenes que aspiran a esta profesión, la compañía J.C. Penney patrocina todos los años una búsqueda de modelos hispanos. Los dos ganadores, un hombre y una mujer, recibirán un premio de $1,000 y tendrán la oportunidad de conocer a diseñadores como Adolfo, Carolina Herrera y Oscar de la Renta. Para información sobre el concurso llame al (214) 591-4182.

What is J.C. Penney offering?

3. You hear this announcement on the radio:

Una carta que ahora puede tardar en llegar a su destinatario casi 48 horas, estará en su destino en menos de ocho horas a partir de este año. Será posible gracias al llamado *correo electrónico*, un moderno sistema de transmisión. Se podrá mandar los documentos desde computadoras conectadas a una línea telefónica o desde las oficinas públicas de Correos.

What new service will be offered?

4. You are listening to someone give advice about how to give a successful party. The person says:

¿Piensas dar una fiesta pronto? Prepara con anticipación tus propias cintas de 60 minutes de duración cada una. Selecciona la música que piensas grabar. Lo ideal es que tu primera cinta tenga piezas que sean bien conocidas, aunque no sean propias para bailar. En la siguiente cinta, graba piezas de moda para que se animen a bailar . . . aquí puedes mezclar todo tipo de música. Durante la etapa final de tu fiesta, la música romántica será la más adecuada. Lleva a la práctica esta recomendación y sin duda tendrás una gran fiesta.

What advice is offered?

5. You are listening to the news in Spanish and hear this information:

Un inventor español patentó el primer maquillaje para calvos. Se llama José Fernando Alonso Varea y tiene treinta años de edad. Explicó que el maquillaje se aplica come laca. Sirve para las zonas pequeñas de la cabeza donde una persona ha perdido el pelo. La crema produce el efecto óptico de poseer pelo. Alonso precisó que su crema cosmética se venderá en las farmacias en los próximos meses.

For what problem would you use this product?

6. You are listening to someone from the Dominican Republic talk about her country. She says:

Santo Domingo, capital de la República Dominicana, fue fundada en 1496 por Bartolomé Colón. Un huracán destruyó la ciudad en 1502, pero fue reconstruída. La ciudad conserva la arquitectura de los primeros edificios construídos por los españoles en el Nuevo Mundo. Incluye el primer hospital, la primera catedral y el primer recinto fortificado de América. Ahora en Santo Domingo se llevan a cabo reconstrucciones para conservar estos sitios históricos.

What is of particular interest about Santo Domingo?

7. You are listening to the news in Madrid and hear this report:

El futbolista español Emilio Butragueño, de 27 años, firmó el lunes el contrato más largo de su vida, aquel que incluye la cláusula "hasta que la muerte os separe." Al menos eso fue lo que dijo Vicente Mundina, el sacerdote que ofició la boda entre el futbolista y Sonia González, su novia de siempre, en la iglesia de la Asunción de Nuestra Señora en Torrelodones. El casamiento fue tan secreto que sus familiares desconocieron el lugar y la hora de la ceremonia hasta una hora antes de celebrarse.

What did Emilio Butragueño do?

8. A classmate who has just returned from Texas is telling your Spanish class about a festival he attended. He says:

Hace 100 años se dio la primera fiesta de la ciudad de San Antonio con el desfile de la Batalla de las Flores para honrar a los héroes de Tejas en la batalla de San Jacinto. Este año, la ciudad celebró el centenario de la fiesta con 150 acontecimientos diferentes. La celebración comenzó el viernes, el 29 de abril, con cuatro desfiles diferentes que se juntaron frente a la Plaza Alamo. La celebración final comenzó con un espectáculo de sonido y video que sintetizó los 300 años de la historia de la ciudad y los 100 años de la fiesta.

What was the purpose of this festival?

9. You hear this announcement on a news broadcast:

William Hernández, portavoz de la comunidad hispana, dijo que el punto más importante del programa de reciclaje es el de reeducar la comunidad para que participe diariamente y siga los consejos básicos de este programa. Comenzando esta semana, todos los hogares recibirán dos recipientes: uno verde y otro azul. Se colocarán los periódicos en el verde, y los artículos de plástico, vidrio, aluminio y metal se colocarán en el azul.

What did William Hernández highlight in the newscast?

10. You are at a fashion show in Madrid and hear this commentary:

Hay una forma de sentirse cómoda sin perder elegancia. Les presentamos un nuevo tipo de ropa ligera y natural que se adapta a nuestra figura. Aquí vemos estos dos vestidos de corte piramidal, fáciles de elaborar por su simplicidad. Son fáciles de llevar en esta temporada. La gente prefiere el sentido práctico con colores que permiten accesorios llamativos.

¿Por qué sería popular esta ropa nueva?

11. Your friend is telling you about a new game. Your friend says:

¿Conoces el programa Sábado Gigante? Pues ahora han hecho un juego basado en este programa. En este juego hay que sacar el Gran Premio contestando preguntas curiosas, adivinando las letras escondidas, los precios y los sonidos. Es un juego que podemos jugar con toda la familia. Hasta mi hermanito puede jugar con nosotros. Además, podemos divertirnos jugando en español o en inglés. ¿Quieres venir a mi casa esta noche para jugar?

¿Por qué le gusta este juego a tu amigo?

12. Your friend is telling you about a special car. She says:

El Cadillac más grande del mundo es una limosina de 23 metros de largo que contiene un baño de jacuzzi, espacio para acostarse y tomar el sol o ver la televisión. El auto tiene 18 ruedas y un potente motor. Costó aproximadamente tres millones de dólares. Lo malo es que es demasiado largo y pesado para ser conducido. Sin embargo, el vehículo ha ganado un sitio en el libro de records Guinness.

¿Cuál es el problema principal de este auto?

13. While you are listening to the radio, you hear this announcement:

Puerto Rico estará presente en los Juegos Centro-Americanos y del Caribe que se celebrarán en noviembre en México. La delegación puertorriqueña está casi completa; unos 500 deportistas formarán la delegación. De los 27 deportes en los juegos, ya hay la seguridad de participar en 22 de ellos. El director del Comité Olímpico de Puerto Rico dijo que los puertorriqueños quieren participar en otros dos deportes. Ya han solicitado permiso para esos deportes y ahora esperan la respuesta.

¿Qué quiere saber la delegación puertorriqueña?

14. A friend is telling you about a restaurant in Madrid. Your friend says:

Uno de mis sitios favoritos es La Carreta, un restaurante argentino que lleva abierto siete años en Madrid. Tiene paredes decoradas con grandes banderas argentinas y españolas, y fotos de la Pampa. Se oye la melodiosa música tradicional de la Argentina. Los dueños y camareros, vestidos con los típicos trajes de gaucho, ofrecen un bonito espectáculo acompañando a los platos típicos. La comida es deliciosa, y el servicio es agradable y divertido.

¿Por qué le gusta a su amiga este restaurante?

15. You hear this news item on the radio:

Julio Iglesias estaba en Nueva York para ir a la Corte Civil de Manhattan. Tenía que responder a los cargos de que su canción *Hey* era un plagio. Julio interrumpío su gira por Europa para venir a Nueva York a responder a la demanda del compositor Enrique Chía, que insistió que la canción era suya. Iglesias dijo que grabó la canción en España hace más de doce años. La corte lo exoneró porque no se logró probar que Julio hubiera escuchado la canción de Chía antes de grabar *Hey*.

¿De qué se acusó a Julio Iglesias?

PART 2

(1) 2
(2) 3
(3) 1
(4) 2
(5) 2
(6) 4
(7) 2
(8) 4
(9) 3
(10) 1
(11) 4
(12) 3
(13) 4
(14) 3
(15) 1

PART 3

(a) **(16)** 3
(17) 4
(18) 1
(19) 2
(20) 1

(b) **(21)** 3
(22) 4
(23) 2
(24) 4
(25) 1

(c) **(26)** 4
(27) 1
(28) 3
(29) 3
(30) 1

PART 4

(a) Notes in writing

For each note, an example of a response worth six credits follows. The slash marks indicate how each sample note has been divided into clauses.

31. Hola,

No voy a cenar con Uds. esta noche.$/_1$ Hay un partido de básquetbol.$/_2$ Empieza a las seis.$/_3$ Quiero ir con mis amigos.$/_4$ Vamos a tomar algo después del partido.$/_5$ Vuelvo a casa a las nueve.$/_6$

Carmen

32. Eduardo,

¡Que suerte! Encontré tus llaves esta tarde.$/_1$ Estaban en mi coche.$/_2$ Las llevaré conmigo a la fiesta esta noche.$/_3$ Tú podrás conseguirlas allí.$/_4$ Si las necesitas antes,$/_5$ llámame lo más pronto posible.$/_6$

Diego

(b) Narrative based on picture/letter

For each narrative/letter, an example of a response worth 10 credits follows. The slash marks indicate how each sample narrative/letter has been divided into clauses.

33. (Picture)

Los Gómez son una pareja muy feliz.$/_1$ Hace cuatro años que están casados.$/_2$ Un día el Señor Gómez regresó de su trabajo$/_3$ y le dijo a su esposa$/_4$ que no quería trabajar más.$/_5$ Decidió quedarse en casa$/_6$ y ser el amo de casa.$/_7$ La Señora Gómez estaba contenta$/_8$ porque tiene un buen trabajo$/_9$ que paga suficiente$/_{10}$ para mantener la familia.

34. (Letter)

el 27 de enero de 1994

Querida Dolores,

Tengo que contarte algo estupendo.$/_1$ Para mi cumpleaños en diciembre, mis hermanos prepararon una gran sorpresa.$/_2$ Dieron una fiesta en un restaurante$/_3$ e invitaron a todos mis amigos de la escuela.$/_4$ Nunca dijeron nada.$/_5$ Cuando yo entré en el restaurante$/_6$ todo el mundo gritó "Sorpresa."$/_7$ Comimos mucho$/_8$ y terminamos la comida con un pastel delicioso.$/_9$ También recibí muchos regalos.$/_{10}$ Me divertí mucho. En mi proxima carta te mandaré fotografías.

Tu amiga,
María

Examination June 1994

Comprehensive Examination in Spanish

PART 1

Your performance on Part 1, Speaking (24 credits), has been evaluated prior to the date of this written examination.

PART 2

Answer all questions in Part 2 according to the directions for *a* and *b*. [30]

a *Directions* (1–9): For each question, you will hear some background information in English once. Then you will hear a passage in Spanish *twice* and a question in English *once*. After you have heard the question, the teacher will pause while you read the question and the four suggested answers. Choose the best suggested answer and write its *number* in the space provided. Base your answer *on the content of the passage, only.* The passages that the teacher will read aloud to you are found in the ANSWERS section, Part 2, at the end of this examination. [18]

1 Why are the Mexicans having this festival?

1 to reunite dancers and singers
2 to attract tourists
3 to sell arts and crafts
4 to maintain a cultural tradition

1____

2 Why is Vicente Cánovas mentioned in the Guinness book?

1 He has been driving for many years without an accident.
2 He is the oldest person to pass a driving test.
3 He holds the record for the most automobile accidents in Spain.
4 He has never gotten a ticket while driving a car. 2___

3 What problem does this customer have?

1 There are not enough salesclerks.
2 The style is not what she wanted.
3 She cannot find the merchandise she is looking for.
4 She is too late to take advantage of a sale. 3___

4 What does the exchange student want?

1 He wants the library to offer more reference materials.
2 He wants you to tutor him in English.
3 He wants the school to provide examinations in Spanish.
4 He wants the teacher to present the material more clearly. 4___

5 What should you do next?

1 go to the police station
2 talk to the clerk's friend
3 retrace your steps
4 show proper identification 5___

6 What had Mr. Fonseca requested when he made his reservation?

1 a room with a view of the ocean
2 a room facing the morning sun
3 a room on the first floor
4 a room for his children 6___

7 Who would be most interested in this new program?

1 people who want to learn about regional cooking
2 people who want to watch local festivals
3 people who want to read restaurant reviews
4 people who want to earn some extra money 7___

8 What is special about this restaurant?

1 Mario Tamayo dances the samba.
2 Music is used to complement the food.
3 It imports foods from Latin America.
4 It is famous for its Caribbean desserts. 8___

9 What does the tour guide suggest to the group?

1 that they return to the museum tomorrow afternoon
2 that they purchase a recommended guide book
3 that they have an understanding of Spanish history
4 that they visit only the most famous paintings 9___

b Directions (10–15): For each question, you will hear some background information in English *once*. Then you will hear a passage in Spanish *twice* and a question in Spanish *once*. After you have heard the question, the teacher will pause while you read the question and the four suggested answers. Choose the best suggested answer and write its *number* in the space provided. Base your answer *on the content of the passage, only*. The passages that the teacher will read aloud to you are found in the ANSWERS section, Part 2, at the end of this examination. [12]

10 ¿Qué deben recordar los estudiantes?

1 llevar un mapa de la ciudad
2 estudiar para un examen especial
3 comprar entradas para las funciones
4 prepararse para un viaje 10___

11 ¿Por qué no puede salir Maricarmen?

1 Tiene que visitar a sus padres.
2 Tiene que ir al aeropuerto.
3 Espera una llamada de su familia.
4 Va a ayudar con los quehaceres. 11___

12 ¿Por qué es especial Juan Pedro Galan?

1 porque es muy joven
2 porque tiene muchos años de experiencia
3 porque viene de una familia de toreros famosos
4 porque es el entrenador de muchos toreros famosos 12___

13 ¿Qué premio recibió Mike Dealy?

1 20 millones de pesetas
2 una semana gratis en un sitio interesante
3 una figura de la mascota *Curro*
4 cinco entradas a la Exposición Universal 13___

14 ¿Qué consejo se ofrece aquí?

1 escuchar la música para sentirse mejor
2 tener cuidado al tomar medicinas
3 hacer ejercicio con frecuencia para mantener la salud
4 cantar canciones para divertirse en las fiestas 14____

15 ¿De qué trata este anuncio?

1 de una clase de astrología
2 de un problema médico
3 de una lección de biología
4 de un problema ecológico 15____

PART 3

Answer all questions in Part 3 according to the directions for *a*, *b*, and *c*. [30 credits]

a Directions (16–20): After the following passage, there are five questions or incomplete statements. For *each*, choose the word or expression that best answers the question or completes the statement *according to the meaning of the passage,* and write its *number* in the space provided. [10]

El famoso músico Carlos Santana vuelve a Tijuana, México, después de una ausencia de muchos años. En sus giras de conciertos, Santana ha recorrido el mundo y actuado en diversas partes de Europa, América y Japón, pero nunca en Tijuana, su ciudad natal, porque no había interés.

Ahora quiere tocar allí porque tiene, según dice, mucho que agradecer. *Santana regresa a casa* es el nombre del concierto que tendrá lugar próximamente en la Plaza de Toros Monumental de la ciudad de Tijuana. El latino más importante de la escena del rock hará llorar a su guitarra una vez más, como en los viejos tiempos.

Orgulloso de ser mexicano, espiritual y filosófico, Santana dice, ". . . con mi música llevo un poco de paz al hombre." En los últimos años, ha estado en Tijuana varias veces—en plan nostálgico, sin pulsar la guitarra—y no ha podido evitar ver y sentir lástima de la pobreza extrema de algunos barrios. Por ello, decidió reunirse con la esposa del gobernador, Margarita de Ruffo, que es la coordinadora del Desarrollo Integral de la Familia, y entre ambos diseñaron un plan de acción con el objetivo de concienciar a la gente de estos problemas. Una de las actividades previstas es un concierto de Santana, cuyas entradas se pondrán a la venta dentro de pocas semanas. Parte del dinero de este concierto se destinará a los niños necesitados de la región.

Durante su entrevista con la señora de Ruffo, Carlos Santana también la informó sobre sus muchos proyectos. Uno de los más inmediatos es grabar su LP numero 27 que se llamará *Milagro* y que es un homenaje a los músicos Bill Graham y Miles Davis.

Santana asegura que él no es el tipo de artista que incluye elefantes o plumas en sus conciertos, o que dé muchos saltos en el escenario, porque su música es más bien espiritual y con ella pretende llegar a los sentimientos.

16 Según este artículo, un deseo de Carlos Santana es

1 dar unos conciertos en Europa
2 viajar por el mundo
3 tocar su música en su ciudad natal
4 cambiar su estilo de tocar 16____

17 Santana no ha tocado en Tijuana hasta ahora porque

1 los boletos costaron demasiado dinero
2 su horario ocupado no lo permitió
3 el estadio no tuvo suficiente espacio
4 la gente no tuvo interés en su tipo de música 17____

18 Una cosa que molesta mucho a Santana es

1 la música contemporánea en su país
2 la pobreza en su país
3 la condición ecológica en su país
4 la falta de líderes en su país 18____

19 En el diálogo entre Santana y la coordinadora discutieron

1 unos problemas con sus discos
2 la distribución del dinero
3 el futuro del gobernador
4 una visita a los músicos de su barrio 19___

20 Se sabe que su música refleja

1 sus pensamientos espirituales
2 las esperanzas de tener dinero
3 los suenos de los enamorados
4 sus sentimientos políticos 20___

b Directions (21–25): Below each of the following selections, there is either a question or an incomplete statement. For *each*, choose the word or expression that best answers the question or completes the statement *according to the meaning of the selection*, and write its *number* in the space provided. [10]

21

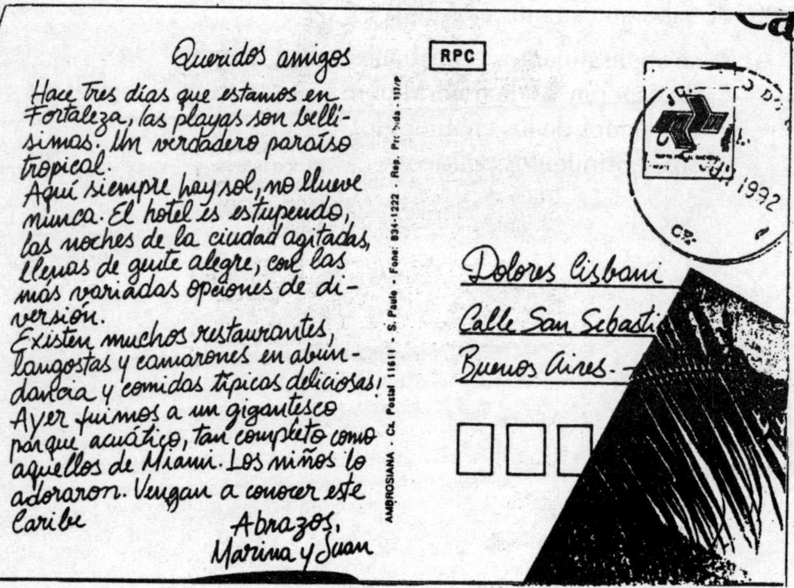

Queridos amigos

Hace tres días que estamos en Fortaleza, las playas son bellísimas. Un verdadero paraíso tropical.

Aquí siempre hay sol, no llueve nunca. El hotel es estupendo, las noches de la ciudad agitadas, llenas de gente alegre, con las más variadas opciones de diversión.

Existen muchos restaurantes, langostas y camarones en abundancia y comidas típicas deliciosas!

Ayer fuimos a un gigantesco parque acuático, tan completo como aquellos de Miami. Los niños lo adoraron. Vengan a conocer este Caribe

Abrazos,
Marina y Juan

RPC

Dolores Lisbani
Calle San Sebasti
Buenos Aires.

AMBROSIANA - Cx. Postal 11611 - S. Paulo - Fone: 834-1222

What did Marina and Juan tell Dolores?

1 Their vacation spot is excellent.
2 They are unable to keep their appointment.
3 Their children are feeling better now.
4 They are staying an extra week. 21___

22

Gane sus vacaciones de Semana Santa desde YA

El diario YA sortea entre sus lectores la estancia en un apartamento, con capacidad para cuatro personas, en los Alpes franceses. El premio incluye además: un seguro de asistencia y accidentes, el desplazamiento y la asistencia de guías.

El sorteo tendrá lugar el jueves 6 de febrero. Los nombres de los ganadores se publicarán en el diario YA el viernes 7 de febrero. Sólo tiene que mandar este cupón con sus datos al diario YA:
Calle Valportillo Primera, número 11. 28100 Alcobendas (Madrid)
(PROMOCIÓN: SEMANA SANTA)

NOMBRE

DOMICILIO

CIUDAD

PROVINCIA

TELÉFONO DNI

Puede mandar más de un cupón en cada carta. Tendrá más oportunidades de ganar.

A person would mail in this form in order to

1 receive discount coupons for use during vacation
2 be considered for a job opportunity during the holiday week
3 contribute to a fund that supports charitable causes
4 enter a drawing for a free trip to France

22____

23

FELICITACIONES Y PETICIONES

¡La NUEVA BUENHOGAR me encanta! Verdaderamente la revista está preciosa, entretenida e interesante. Hasta ahora me leo completos los temas de belleza, porque son muy actuales y prácticos... Con decirles que ya tramité una suscripción, porque en el supermercado donde compro ¡vuela! y a veces tengo que pedirle a mi hermana la suya... Ahora quiero hacerles dos peticiones: que publiquen más minipatrones de ropa para niños (tengo tres y les coso) y decoración sobre cocinas, porque pienso redecorar pronto la mía. A todos, un abrazo de esta fiel lectora.

Mimí Sánchez,
San Juan, Puerto Rico

Ante todo mil gracias por sus palabras de elogio; nos encanta saber que disfruta tanto cada número de BUENHOGAR. Sobre ambas peticiones le diremos que es casi seguro que haya visto los minipatrones en BH # 13. Verdaderas bellezas que se pueden hacer en "batik" o en un lindo algodón estampado similar. En cuanto a la decoración de cocina ¡no se pierda el próximo número, o sea, BH # 17! en él encontrará cientos de ideas.

What does this writer want?

1 She wants to see fewer articles about health and beauty.
2 She wants a list of places where she can buy the magazine.
3 She wants more information written about her special interests.
4 She wants to cancel her subscription to the magazine.

23____

24

PODER COLORISTA

La Fundación Juan March presenta hasta el 14 de junio una exposición del pintor ruso Alexei Jawlensky (1864-1941). La muestra recoge una amplia selección de obras que revelan la intensidad del poder colorista de Jawlensky y la soltura con la que abordó tanto los cuadros expresionistas como sus aproximaciones a la abstracción. Este artista, se relacionó con los principales movimientos y grupos estéticos de su época como Die Blauen Vier (Los Cuadros Azules) y Die Blaue Reiter (El Jinete Azul), y en ellos con artistas como Kandisnky, Klee y Nolde. Su dedicación al arte logró superar durante varios años las limitaciones de una enfermedad que le impedía pintar. Aun así, sus últimos cuadros tienen el doble poder de la voluntad y la sabiduría.

F.J.

FUNDACIÓN JUAN MARCH. Castelló, 77. Tel. 435 42 40. Hasta el 14 de junio

Mujer con abanico (1909), de Alexei Jawlensky.

According to this article, what is noteworthy about the artist Alexei Jawlensky?

1 He painted masterpieces despite a lack of materials.
2 He excelled despite a serious illness.
3 He was forced to paint under an assumed name.
4 He established an extremely wealthy foundation. 24____

25

Querida Amparo,

Pienso viajar durante el verano y necesito tu ayuda. En mi casa dejo un perro, dos gatos, y diez plantas tropicales. ¡Imagínate! Todas estas criaturas necesitan comida y atención de una amiga simpática. No creo que tengas problema. Mi perro Yovi y mis gatos Mimi y Titi son adorables. Las plantas, pobrecitas, no se quejan. Por supuesto por tu ayuda durante dos semanas recibirás un regalito.

Gracias,
Lola

What does Lola want Amparo to do?

1 travel with her
2 help her plant a garden
3 feed her animals
4 help her choose a gift 25___

c *Directions* (26–30): In the following passage, there are five blank spaces numbered 26 through 30. Each blank space represents a missing word or expression. For each blank space, four possible completions are provided. Only one of them makes sense *in the context of the passage.*

First, read the passage in its entirety to determine its general meaning. Then read it a second time. For each blank space, choose the completion that makes the best sense and write its *number* in the space provided. [10]

Lo mejor de "Mountain Bike"

No hace mucho tiempo en España nadie practicaba la *bicicleta de montaña*. Formaba parte de la larga lista de deportes desconocidos. Sin embargo, con el paso de los años ha conseguido tener un impacto en los gustos de los aficionados.

Ahora hay muchos que participan en este deporte y hay un gran interés en las __(26)__ que se ofrecen. Una de ellas se llama *El Gran Premio Coronas Mountain Bike*, que consiste en cinco pruebas. La primera tendrá lugar este fin de semana.

Los participantes deben presentar su licencia federativa. Para que la clasificación de cada equipo sea válida en cada carrera, hay que tener un mínimo de cinco __(27)__ . Cada equipo tendrá un color distinto de camiseta para su mejor identificación. La prueba consiste en dos partes. Una contra-reloj de tres kilómetros, que tendrá lugar el sábado, a la una de la tarde, y un"rally", que se correrá el sábado a las once de la mañana. Los equipos azul y rojo participarán en una ___(28)___ más difícil con una distancia más larga por un terreno más difícil.

Los primeros 20 del "rally" y también los primeros 10 de la contra-reloj obtendrán puntos para la clasificación general del campeonato. El que ___(29)___ el "rally" se llevará 75.000 pesetas de premio.

La bicicleta de cada participante deberá ser sometida a una ___(30)___ antes de la prueba. Las ruedas deben tener 26 pulgadas. No está permitida la ayuda exterior ni tampoco cambiar de bicicletas durante el transcurso de la carrera.

Se ha organizado una carrera de promoción de 12 kilómetros para el domingo a las nueve y media de la mañana.

(26) 1 cartas 3 comidas
2 competiciones 4 motocicletas 26___

(27) 1 personas 3 papeles
2 parientes 4 pelotas 27___

(28) 1 estructura 3 semana
2 cuenta 4 categoría 28___

(29) 1 publique 3 gane
2 camine 4 descubra 29___

(30) 1 inspección 3 cámara
2 práctica 4 llamada 30___

PART 4

Write your answers to Part 4 according to the directions for *a* and *b*. [16]

a Directions: Write **one** well-organized note in Spanish as directed below. [6]

Choose **either** question 31 **or** 32. Write a well-organized note, following the specific instructions given in the question you have chosen. Your note must consist of **at least six clauses.** To qualify for credit, a clause must contain a verb, a stated or implied subject, and additional words necessary to convey meaning. The six clauses may be contained in fewer than six sentences if some of the sentences have more than one clause.

31 While you were on vacation, you had a problem. Write a note in Spanish to your pen pal telling him or her about what happened.

In the note, you may wish to write about where you were, what the problem was, how the problem was solved, who helped you, whether or not money was needed, and what the rest of your vacation was like. **Be sure you accomplish the purpose of the note, which is *to tell your pen pal about the problem you had during your vacation*.**

Use the following:

Salutation: Querido/Querida ________,
Closing: Un abrazo fuerte,

The salutation and closing will *not* be counted as part of the six required clauses.

32 You are an exchange student in a Spanish-speaking country. A teacher in your host school is organizing a field trip. Write a note in Spanish to that teacher expressing your interest in participating in this trip.

In the note, you may want to mention how you heard about the trip, express your interest in the trip and the reasons for your interest, and tell how you would benefit from the trip. You may also wish to express your hope to participate and indicate how the teacher may contact you. **Be sure you accomplish the purpose of the note, which is *to express your interest in participating in the trip*.**

Use the following:

Salutation: Querido/Querida ________,
Closing: Muchas gracias

The salutation and closing will *not* be counted as part of the six required clauses.

b Directions: Write **one** well-organized composition in Spanish as directed below. [10]

Choose **either** question 33 **or** 34. Write a well-organized composition, following the specific instructions given in the question you have chosen. Your composition must consist of **at least 10 clauses**. To qualify for credit, a clause must contain a verb, a stated or implied subject, and additional words necessary to convey meaning. The 10 clauses may be contained in fewer than 10 sentences if some of the sentences have more than one clause.

33 In Spanish, write a story about the situation shown in the picture below. It must be a story relating to the picture, **not** a description of the picture. Do *not* write a dialogue.

34 The school year is almost over. In Spanish, write a letter to your friend in Costa Rica telling him or her about the school year.

You must accomplish the purpose of the letter, which is *to tell your friend about the school year*.

In your letter, you may wish to mention the following: the friends you made, the subjects you studied, the subject you liked best, athletic activities or sports events, after-school clubs, final examinations, and your impressions of the school year in general. You may use any or all of the ideas suggested above *or* you may use your own ideas. **Either way, you must tell your friend about the school year.**

Use the following:

Dateline:	17 de junio de 1994
Salutation:	Querido/Querida ________,
Closing:	Sinceramente,

The dateline, salutation, and closing will *not* be counted as part of the 10 required clauses.

Answers
June 1994
Comprehensive Examination in Spanish

PART 1

This part of the examination was evaluated prior to the date of this written examination. [24 credits]

PART 2

The following passages are to be read aloud to the students according to the directions given for this part at the beginning of this examination. The correct answers are given after number 15. [30 credits]

1. While traveling by car in Mexico, you hear this information on the radio about a festival in Puebla:

Más de mil quinientos músicos y bailarines de once regiones se reunirán el próximo treinta de septiembre con el objeto de celebrar una fiesta indígena dedicada a Quetzalcóatl. El objetivo es continuar esta tradición que pertenece a todos los mexicanos. Se espera que asistan más de treinta mil personas, entre mexicanos y extranjeros a esta fiesta de música, bailes, costumbres y artesanías.

Why are the Mexicans having this festival?

2. You are listening to the radio in Spain and hear the announcer say:

Vicente Cánovas, un hombre español de noventa y seis años de edad, aparece mencionado en el libro de Guinness. Este señor ha manejado coches durante más de setenta y cinco años. El sacó su licencia de conducir cuando tenía veinte años y todavía sigue al volante. Lo más extraordinario de esta noticia es que durante este largo tiempo, él nunca ha tenido un accidente. Sin embargo, el Sr. Cánovas fue multado en una ocasión por no usar su cinturón de seguridad mientras manejaba.

Why is Vicente Cánovas mentioned in the Guinness book?

3. You are in a department store and overhear a customer talking with the manager. The customer says:

Oiga, por favor, estoy buscando una camiseta con unos estampados en la espalda, y no la puedo encontrar por ninguna parte. Me dijeron que estaba en la planta de jóvenes, pero el dependiente que trabaja allí me dijo que no la puede encontrar. Una amiga mía compró la misma camiseta ayer y me dijo que había muchas. ¿Me puede ayudar?

What problem does this customer have?

4. An exchange student at your school is telling you about a problem. The exchange student says:

Tengo un problema en mi clase de historia. Cuando la profesora está hablando, no puedo entender todo lo que dice, así que no puedo tomar apuntes. Me gustaría que hablara un poco más despacio o que escribiera en la pizarra para tener mis propios apuntes.

What does the exchange student want?

5. You are at a train station in Colombia. You have just explained to a clerk that you have lost your wallet. This is what you are told:

Lo siento mucho, pero no tenemos su cartera aquí. Le recomiendo que vaya al departamento de Objetos Perdidos. Cuando llegue, pregunte por el Sr. Sánchez, que trabaja allí. El es amigo mío. Dígale que Ud. va de mi parte. Espero que tenga buena suerte y que encuentre su cartera con sus documentos.

What should you do next?

6. You have just arrived at a hotel in San Juan and overhear this conversation between a guest and the hotel manager:

Sí, señor Fonseca. Recibimos su carta pidiendo alojamiento en nuestro hotel hace dos meses. Sí, claro que hay un cuarto reservado para Ud. y su esposa. Aquí ofrecemos todos los servicios y todas las comodidades posibles, pero siento decirle que no tenemos disponible un cuarto que dé al mar. Sin embargo, tenemos para Uds. un cuarto mirando a la piscina. Espero que les guste.

What had Mr. Fonseca requested when he made his reservation?

7. You are watching a Spanish television broadcast and hear this preview for another show:

¡Ahora, Euskal Telebista promueve el talento culinario del País Vasco! "Menú del Día" se emitirá dos veces al día. Aproveche esta oportunidad para aprender a preparar los platos regionales. Su familia gozará de una alimentación sana sin tener que gastar mucho. Cuente con "Menú del Día" para usar las recetas tradicionales. En muchos casos, estas recetas se relacionarán con fechas y celebraciones especiales. Será una oportunidad única para celebrar la cultura vasca.

Who would be most interested in this new program?

8. You hear this announcement on the radio:

Este año el restaurante de moda en Los Angeles ha sido el Café Mambo donde el menú es mexicano, puertorriqueño, cubano, y un poco californiano. Aquí se pueden degustar platos típicos en porciones grandes mientras se escucha música latina. En este local, mientras se sirve la salsa, se oye la samba. El dueño, Mario Tamayo, dice que no hay nada como la buena música latina para acompañar una buena comida.

What is special about this restaurant?

9. You are with a tour group in Spain. Your tour guide says:

Buenas tardes. Estamos en este momento en el museo del Prado donde se exponen cientos de cuadros de los mejores pintores del mundo. Vamos a visitar todo el museo, pero nos detendremos solamente ante los cuadros más famosos. No nos dará tiempo para ver todos los cuadros que se encuentran en el museo. Necesitaríamos tres días para ello. Bueno, espero que disfruten los cuadros de estos selectos pintores.

What does the tour guide suggest to the group?

10. You are an exchange student in Spain. While you are at school, you hear this announcement for foreign students:

¿Están ya preparadas las mochilas? ¿Y los bocadillos de tortilla y la bota de agua? Por supuesto, nos estamos refiriendo solamente a los viajeros, a los que han decidido ir de excursión a Toledo mañana. Recuerden que el autobús saldrá muy temprano, a las siete y media de la mañana, de la Avenida Mirat, junto a la Puerta de Zamora. Por favor: se ruega puntualidad.

¿Qué deben recordar los estudiantes?

11. You and your friends are discussing plans for Friday night. Maricarmen, an exchange student from Mexico, says:

No puedo salir el viernes. Tengo que quedarme en casa porque mis padres me van a llamar de México para decirme la hora de su vuelo. Ellos vienen a visitarme en quince días.

¿Por qué no puede salir Maricarmen?

12. You are listening to a program on television about bullfighting and hear the following:

Hace poco más de dos años, Juan Pedro Galán era totalmente desconocido por los aficionados a las corridas de toros. Hoy, en cambio, cuando se anuncia su participación en alguna plaza de toros, las entradas se agotan en pocas horas. Juan Pedro Galán es uno de los matadores más populares en estos momentos en España. En primer lugar, Juan Pedro es el torero más joven del mundo. ¡Solamente cuenta con 9 años de edad! Además, se ha destacado por la gran destreza con que se mueve en la plaza de toros.

¿Por qué es especial Juan Pedro Galán?

13. A friend is telling you this story:

¿Sabes que un hombre de los Estados Unidos, Mike Dealy, recibió un premio de una semana en la ciudad de Sevilla con todos los gastos pagados? El ganó este premio porque fue el visitante número 20 millones de la Exposición Universal en 1992. A la entrada de la Exposición, la mascota *Curro* y una banda de música le dieron la bienvenida.

¿Qué premio recibió Mike Dealy?

14. You are listening to the radio and hear this advice:

Escuchar el disco apropiado en el momento oportuno puede ser más efectivo que tomar medicinas. Así que, si te sientes algo melancólico o deprimido, la terapia musical te levantará ese estado de ánimo. Para que puedas poner en práctica esta información, piensa en las melodías y en las canciones que te alegran y estimulan. Escúchalas a diario. Haz los trabajos de la casa con un ritmo estimulante que te haga sentir bien.

¿Qué consejo se ofrece aquí?

15. You are listening to the news on the radio and hear this report:

Los plásticos abandonados en el mar se han convertido en uno de los mayores peligros para los seres marinos que los encuentran. Los leones marinos, focas, tortugas y albatros todos pueden estrangularse o asfixiarse con los plásticos y redes. Dada la gravidad del problema, se está estudiando la implantación de leyes que impedirán el abuso de las redes de plástico y el vertido de basura plástica en el mar.

¿De qué trata este anuncio?

PART 2

(1) 4	**(4)** 4	**(7)** 1	**(10)** 4	**(13)** 2
(2) 1	**(5)** 2	**(8)** 2	**(11)** 3	**(14)** 1
(3) 3	**(6)** 1	**(9)** 4	**(12)** 1	**(15)** 4

PART 3

(a) **(16)** 3
(17) 4
(18) 2
(19) 2
(20) 1

(b) **(21)** 1
(22) 4
(23) 3
(24) 2
(25) 3

(c) **(26)** 2
(27) 1
(28) 4
(29) 3
(30) 1

PART 4

(a) Notes in writing

For each note, an example of a response worth six credits follows. The slash marks indicate how each sample note has been divided into clauses.

31. Querido Diego,

Acabo de regresar de vacaciones/$_1$ y no vas a creer/$_2$ lo que me pasó./$_3$ Una noche, después de asistir a un partido profesional de béisbol,/$_4$ me di cuenta de que/$_5$ dejé mis llaves en el coche/$_6$ y todas las puertas estaban cerradas. Después de un largo rato, un policía bien simpático me ayudó a entrar en el coche. ¡Qué tonto soy!

Un abrazo fuerte,
Roberto

32. Querida señora Molinas,

He oído/$_1$ que usted está haciendo planes para una visita al museo el viernes./$_2$ Nunca he visitado este museo,/$_3$ pero estoy muy interesada./$_4$ Conozco a algunos de los pintores españoles famosos/$_5$ y quiero aprender más./$_6$ Yo puedo hablar con usted hoy por la tarde. Ojalá que pueda ir. Muchas gracias.

Lola Santiago

(b) Narrative based on picture/letter

For each narrative/letter, an example of a response worth 10 credits follows. The slash marks indicate how each sample narrative/letter has been divided into clauses.

33. (Picture)

El señor y la señora Martínez le dieron una fiesta de cumpleaños a su hija Anita./$_1$ Anita cumplió hoy día tres años de edad./$_2$ Después de comer torta de cumpleaños/$_3$ y de abrir los regalos,/$_4$ todos los niños salieron a jugar./$_5$ Mientras los niños jugaban,/$_6$ empezó a llover fuertemente./$_7$ Los niños se divertían mucho/$_8$ y por eso los padres decidieron dejarlos jugar por más tiempo./$_9$ Cuando los niños entraron en la casa/$_{10}$ estaban muy sucios y cansados, pero muy contentos.

34. (Letter)

17 de junio de 1994

Querida Elena,

Este año ha sido maravilloso./$_1$ En todas las clases los profesores han preparado actividades interesantes./$_2$ A menudo visitamos exposiciones y museos./$_3$ Por ejemplo, en mi clase de arte fuimos a ver una exposición de Miró./$_4$ ¡Fue estupendo!/$_5$ Mis amigos y yo preparamos un proyecto/$_6$ sobre cómo el artista representaba la sociedad de su época./$_7$

Estoy contenta/$_8$ porque finalmente han llegado las vacaciones./$_9$ Me alegro de haber aprendido mucho/$_{10}$ y de haber salido bien en los exámenes.

Sinceramente,
Carmen

Examination January 1995

Comprehensive Examination in Spanish

PART 1

Your performance on Part 1, Speaking (24 credits), has been evaluated prior to the date of this written examination.

PART 2

Answer all questions in Part 2 according to the directions for *a* and *b*. [30]

a Directions (1–9): For each question, you will hear some background information in English once. Then you will hear a passage in Spanish *twice* and a question in English *once*. After you have heard the question, the teacher will pause while you read the question and the four suggested answers. Choose the best suggested answer and write its *number* in the space provided. Base your answer *on the content of the passage, only*. The passages that the teacher will read aloud to you are found in the ANSWERS section, Part 2, at the end of this examination. [18]

1 What is the tour guide talking about?

1 directions to points of interest
2 places to eat
3 some new attractions
4 rules to follow 1___

2 Who would be most interested in this information?

1 someone who wants to make a person-to-person call within Mexico
2 someone who wants to call Mexico from the United States
3 someone who wants to obtain information about Mexican telephone rates
4 someone who needs to have telephone repair service 2____

3 Why is Esteban unable to come to your home this evening?

1 He just learned that some company will be coming.
2 He has decided to go on a trip.
3 He has received some bad news from home.
4 He is expecting a call from his parents. 3____

4 What does your friend want you to do?

1 listen to a particular radio station
2 go to the movies with some friends
3 be a partner in a radio contest
4 work together this Saturday evening 4____

5 What is causing Asturias to become well known?

1 its distinctive architecture
2 the beauty of its countryside
3 its pleasant weather
4 the variety of its food 5____

6 What problem is being discussed?

1 preparing invitations
2 getting the right kind of cake
3 choosing a suitable gift
4 selecting the appropriate music 6____

7 What information was announced on the radio?

1 No electrical repairs will be made today.
2 Certain areas of the city will lose power today.
3 The entire city will have power interruptions all day long.
4 A recent electrical project was discontinued. 7____

8 Who would be most interested in this information?

1 people who want to decorate on a limited budget
2 people who need tutoring
3 people who want clothing that is color coordinated
4 people who need a quiet place to study 8____

9 How would you be able to get this camera?

1 by winning first prize in a photography contest
2 by sending in proofs of purchase of film
3 by purchasing a subscription to a magazine
4 by ordering through a catalog 9____

b Directions (10–15): For each question, you will hear some background information in English *once*. Then you will hear a passage in Spanish *twice* and a question in Spanish *once*. After you have heard the question, the teacher will pause while you read the question and the four suggested answers. Choose the best suggested answer and write its *number* in the space provided. Base your answer *on the content of the passage, only*. The passages that the teacher will read aloud to you are found in the ANSWERS section, Part 2, at the end of this examination. [12]

10 ¿Qué requisitos se necesitan para este trabajo?

1 tener experiencia
2 tener su propio automóvil
3 trabajar los sábados y domingos
4 trabajar con computadoras 10____

11 ¿Qué les dice el chófer del autobús al grupo?

1 El grupo no puede regresar en autobús.
2 Hay peligro en ciertos sectores en la ciudad por la noche.
3 No hay tiempo para ver toda la ciudad.
4 Las calles necesitan reparaciones. 11___

12 ¿Qué espera ser Miguel Gordillo Polidoro?

1 un piloto
2 un futbolista
3 un escritor
4 un torero 12___

13 ¿Por qué debes llamar a tu amigo?

1 Él quiere que tú le visites.
2 Él quiere darte información.
3 Él quiere cancelar sus planes.
4 Él quiere saber el tiempo que hace. 13___

14 ¿Para quiénes son estos consejos?

1 a los que quieren mantenerse en salud
2 a los que diseñan ropa para niños
3 a los que les interesan las vitaminas
4 a los que quieren hacerse médicos 14___

15 ¿Cuál es la atracción principal de la exhibición chilena?

1 fotos grandes del paisaje chileno
2 las bonitas canciones que cantaban
3 un enorme bloque de hielo
4 comida chilena bastante nutritiva 15___

PART 3

Answer all questions in Part 3 according to the directions for *a*, *b*, and *c*. [30 credits]

a Directions (16–20): After the following passage, there are five questions or incomplete statements. For *each*, choose the word or expression that best answers the question or completes the statement *according to the meaning of the passage*, and write its *number* in the space provided. [10]

Varios artistas hispanos con talento y carisma han usado sus carreras como trampolines para alcanzar su meta — ayudar a su gente. No buscan ni fama ni dinero. Lo que quieren estos artistas es servir a la sociedad, ser políticos, ya que se han preocupado por la realidad social de sus países.

Para llegar a ser político hay que demostrar ganas y méritos, y estar decidido a enfrentarse a lo que venga. Tal hombre es Rubén Blades, cantante, compositor y actor panameño. "Yo soy un artista que piensa, lee y tiene una opinión", afirma Rubén. "Desafortunadamente, cuando uno emite una opinión, ya sea en política o en religión, inmediatamente vamos a tener un punto de vista distinto, y eso a un artista no le conviene, porque trata de buscar la mayor cantidad de público, sin alienar a nadie". Su interés en la política lo tuvo antes que su carrera de músico y actor. Rubén era abogado en Panamá y después se dedicó a la vida artística. Tenía interés por las leyes, por la administración de la ciudad y del estado.

En 1972, el padre de Rubén tuvo problemas con el entonces Teniente Coronel Manuel Noriega. Él nunca tuvo ningún problema físico, sin embargo lo expulsaron del trabajo. Llegó el momento en que la familia ya no pudo sobrevivir económicamente y decidió trasladarse a Miami. Rubén permaneció todavía en su país como abogado del Banco Nacional. Dándose cuenta de la gravedad de la situación socio-política en su país, Rubén también decidió mudarse a los Estados Unidos. Se dedicó a las dos cosas que le gustaban: la música y la política. Siguió con sus estudios de abogado en la Universidad de Harvard.

Rubén Blades comenzó a realizar su ambición política. Hace unos años se trasladó a Panamá y formó el "Movimiento Papa Egoró" (MPE), nombre que proviene de un lenguaje indígena que significa "Madre Tierra". Con este nombre, Blades quería representar el concepto de patria. Los objetivos de esta agrupación eran la democracia real, la identidad nacional, los derechos humanos, la conservación natural y la acción social. El nombre de este panameño comenzó a aparecer en las encuestas como posible candidato a la presidencia de Panamá.

16 ¿Qué quieren hacer algunos artistas después de tener éxito?

1 escribir libros sobre su vida
2 trabajar con problemas sociales
3 ayudar a otros con sus carreras artísticas
4 presentar actuaciones gratis para los aficionados 16___

17 ¿Por qué se mudó la familia de Rubén Blades a los Estados Unidos?

1 El padre necesitó la ayuda de médicos norteamericanos.
2 Su mamá quería ser abogada en Miami.
3 Los parientes vivieron en la Florida.
4 Su padre tuvo un conflicto con un político. 17___

18 Rubén se fue a Miami con el propósito de estudiar la política y

1 ser profesor en una universidad
2 trabajar en un banco internacional
3 ayudar con los negocios de su padre
4 empezar una carrera musical 18____

19 ¿Qué hizo después de llegar a los Estados Unidos?

1 Ayudó a la administración de Noriega.
2 Continuó con sus estudios en la universidad.
3 Permaneció en la Florida.
4 Trabajó para el gobierno norteamericano. 19____

20 ¿Para qué regresó Rubén Blades a Panamá?

1 para grabar un nuevo disco
2 para hacer una gira artística
3 para fundar un partido político
4 para hacer una película 20____

b Directions (21–25): Below each of the following selections, there is either a question or an incomplete statement. For *each*, choose the word or expression that best answers the question or completes the statement *according to the meaning of the selection*, and write its *number* in the space provided. [10]

21

¡El color de su auto puede ser la diferencia entre la **VIDA** y la **MUERTE!**

Porque... ¿sabía usted que del color de su auto puede depender su seguridad personal ¡y hasta su vida!? Estudios recientes, llevados a cabo por una revista especializada, demuestran que los autos pintados de un solo color, claro, son menos propensos a verse envueltos en accidentes que los de cualquier otro color... Según dicho estudio, los autos de color verdoso-amarillo estuvieron envueltos en menos accidentes durante el período de estudio, siguiéndoles de cerca los pintados en tonos crema, amarillo claro y blanco. En cambio, los resultados del estudio indican que los autos pintados en tonos oscuros como el rojo o el negro, son considerados por los conductores más riesgosos, ya que son mucho más difíciles de ver bien en las carreteras, sobre todo por las noches.

What does this study indicate about the color of cars?

1 White cars are most likely to be in a collision.
2 Yellow cars are involved in fewer accidents.
3 Red cars are the safest at night.
4 Dark-colored cars suffer the least damage. 21___

22 **COMUNIDAD**

Uno de los acontecimientos más tristes en la vida de un joven puede ser la muerte de un animalito querido. Lógicamente que se trata de animales, pero muchas personas los consideran verdaderos amigos e incluso miembros de la familia.

El dolor de perder a un ser querido es algo que no se puede evitar, aun si éste tiene cuatro patas en vez de dos piernas. En el ejemplar de abril de 1992 de la revista The New Era, una publicación de La Iglesia de Jesucristo de los Santos de los Ultimos Días, dedicada especialmente a los jóvenes, aparecen las siguientes ideas que pueden ayudar a hacer frente a esta clase de dolor.

- No trates de ocultar tus sentimientos. Es normal y natural sentirse triste. Llora y trata de hablar con alguien al respecto.
- Haz algo especial en memoria de tu animalito muerto. Algo que puede ser muy útil para aliviar el dolor es llevar a cabo un servicio fúnebre, plantar algo en la sepultura, escribir un poema o reservar una página de tu libro de recuerdos especialmente para escribir sobre tu animalito.
- Recuerda los momentos divertidos que pasaron juntos; no trates de extinguir esos recuerdos. El pensar en los buenos ratos que pasaste con tu animalito te puede ayudar a aliviar los momentos de soledad.
- Presta servicio voluntario para trabajar con otros animales. Podrás ayudarle a tu vecino con el suyo u ofrecer tus servicios a la agencia local para la protección de los animales.
- Cuando estés listo para tener otro animalito, consíguelo; recuerda que hay muchos animales solitarios que necesitan que alguien los adopte. Y además, un nuevo compañero te hará olvidar el dolor de tu pérdida.

For whom is this article intended?

1 families with sick or injured pets
2 people allergic to pets
3 people dealing with the loss of a pet
4 families selecting a pet 22____

23 SANTIAGO
¿cómo vamos?

Si usted es habitante de la Región Metropolitana, le pedimos responder a esta encuesta y enviarla a: "ACCION CIUDADANA POR EL MEDIOAMBIENTE, Antonia Lope de Bello 024, Santiago".

1 A su juicio, ¿cuál es el problema ambiental más grave?
_____ Las aguas servidas
_____ La contaminación del aire
_____ Los basurales
_____ El ruido ambiente

2 A su juicio, ¿en cuál aspecto cree usted que se ha avanzado más?
_____ Descontaminación de aguas
_____ Descontaminación del aire
_____ Descontaminación de ruido
_____ Descontaminación de la basura
_____ Ninguno

3 ¿A quiénes considera usted los principales responsables de la contaminación de Santiago? (Marque dos que usted considera con mayor responsabilidad).
_____ La locomoción colectiva
_____ Las industrias
_____ Los hospitales
_____ Las calles de tierra
_____ Las autoridades de Gobierno
_____ Los automovilistas
_____ Los habitantes de Santiago

4 Y usted ¿cómo se porta? ¿Con qué frecuencia realiza usted estas acciones?:

	Siempre	A veces	Nunca
• Botar basura en sitios eriazos	_____	_____	_____
• Quemar basura	_____	_____	_____
• Separar la basura para que sea recirculada	_____	_____	_____
• Humedecer la vereda antes de barrer	_____	_____	_____
• Preferir el transporte colectivo al automóvil particular	_____	_____	_____
• Tomar el transporte colectivo sólo en los paraderos	_____	_____	_____
• Prender la chimenea u otra calefacción contaminante en invierno	_____	_____	_____
• Plantar árboles, cuidar áreas verdes	_____	_____	_____
• Hacer ruidos innecesarios, como tocar la bocina o prender la T.V. muy fuerte	_____	_____	_____
• Respetar la restricción vehicular	_____	_____	_____

ACCION CIUDADANA POR EL MEDIOAMBIENTE agradece a Adirmark Opinión Pública su colaboración en el diseño y procesamiento de esta encuesta.

What is the subject of this questionnaire?

1 the environment
2 health and physical fitness
3 consumer spending habits
4 leisure time

23____

24

Una Nota Personal de la Directora de Vanidades

Como madre que soy, he descubierto que una de las mejores maneras de ayudar a mis hijos a comprender y enorgullecerse de su herencia hispana, es exponerlos a los logros de otras gentes de habla hispana. Siempre me he preocupado por tener en mi hogar un constante surtido de revistas en español, pues he comprobado que ellas contribuyen a que mis hijos tengan una nueva perspectiva de los eventos mundiales.

Por eso, le aconsejo a cada familia preocupada por conservar su herencia hispana, que se suscriba a nuestras revistas en español. Estoy tan convencida de su importancia, que las estamos ofreciendo a precios sustancialmente reducidos, pero sólo por tiempo limitado. No pierda esta excelente oportunidad. Ordene su suscripción hoy mismo.

¡Ellas pueden significar para usted y su familia una enorme diferencia cultural!

Sara Castany

Sara Castany
Directora,
Vanidades y Harper's Bazaar en Español

This magazine would be of interest to parents because it

1 promotes a variety of charitable organizations that help children
2 provides information and advice about children at different ages
3 has many educational articles that will help children at school
4 encourages children to appreciate their cultural background

24____

25

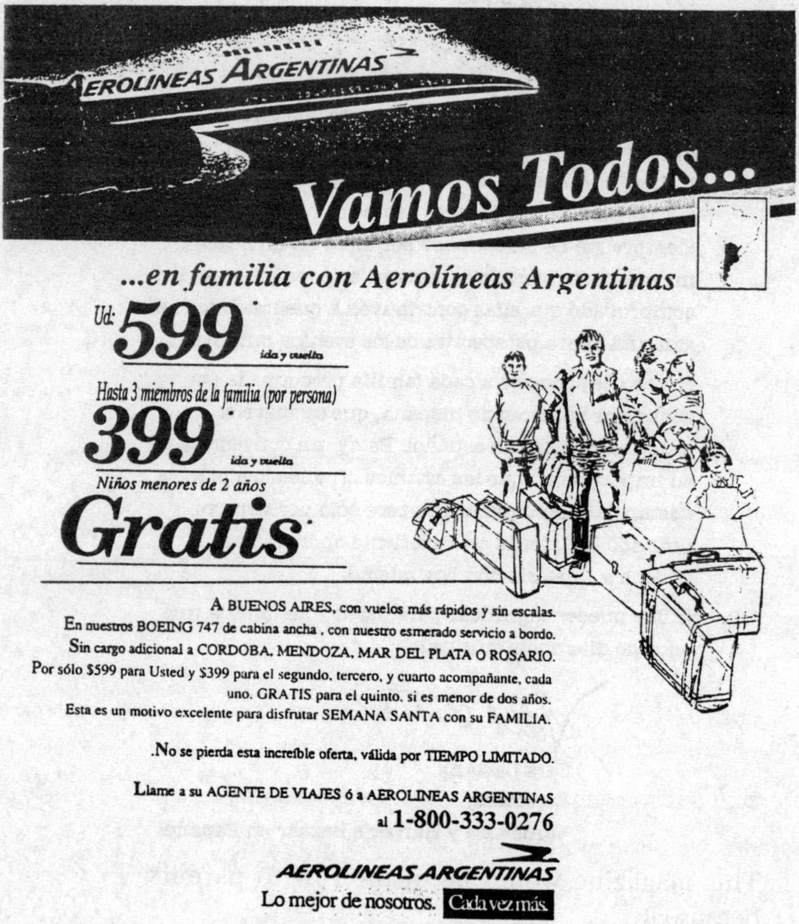
AEROLINEAS ARGENTINAS
Vamos Todos...
...en familia con Aerolíneas Argentinas
Ud: 599* ida y vuelta
Hasta 3 miembros de la familia (por persona)
399* ida y vuelta
Niños menores de 2 años
Gratis*
A BUENOS AIRES, con vuelos más rápidos y sin escalas.
En nuestros BOEING 747 de cabina ancha , con nuestro esmerado servicio a bordo.
Sin cargo adicional a CORDOBA, MENDOZA, MAR DEL PLATA O ROSARIO.
Por sólo $599 para Usted y $399 para el segundo, tercero, y cuarto acompañante, cada uno. GRATIS para el quinto, si es menor de dos años.
Esta es un motivo excelente para disfrutar SEMANA SANTA con su FAMILIA.
.No se pierda esta increíble oferta, válida por TIEMPO LIMITADO.
Llame a su AGENTE DE VIAJES ó a AEROLINEAS ARGENTINAS
al 1-800-333-0276
AEROLINEAS ARGENTINAS
Lo mejor de nosotros. Cada vez más.

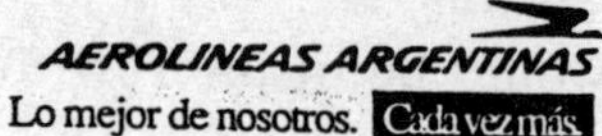

What does this company offer?

1 discounts for business travelers
2 inexpensive one-way fares
3 good value for large families
4 special services for children

25____

c *Directions* (26–30): In the following passage, there are five blank spaces numbered 26 through 30. Each blank space represents a missing word or expression. For each blank space, four possible completions are provided. Only one of them makes sense *in the context of the passage*.

First, read the passage in its entirety to determine its general meaning. Then read it a second time. For each blank space, choose the completion that makes the best sense and write its *number* in the space provided. [10]

Eurodisney abre sus puertas

Mickey Mouse y sus compañeros del "universo Disney" ya han conquistado el corazón de Europa. Durante el primer año el parque de la fantasía espera ___(26)___ a más de 11 millones de personas de Francia y del resto de los países europeos. Encontrarán un parque temático, genuinamente norteamericano, con un poco de pimienta francesa. Se ha intentado asegurar un mínimo de contribución europea en los cuentos que están representados y en las comidas que se ___(27)___ en sus restaurantes.

El castillo emblemático de todos los complejos Disney está dedicado a la Bella Durmiente del Bosque. Esta primera fase de Eurodisney se completa con una auténtica ciudad, donde hay seis hoteles con un total de 5.200 habitaciones, un camping, un campo de golf y el centro de diversiones "Festival Disney."

Debido al interés que los europeos han demostrado en todo lo relacionado con Disney, la compañía comunicó su ___(28)___ de construir un parque en Europa. A España le interesó mucho el plan. La posición geográfica de París y su importancia como red de comunicaciones fueron la base decisiva para la elección.

Los planes para el ___(29)___ son todavía más ambiciosos. En el año 2017 el proyecto se habrá completado con el Disney MGM Estudios-Europa, donde se podrán producir películas y programas televisivos. El Eurodisney del siglo 21 ocupará 1.943 hectáreas, que es igual a una quinta parte de la ciudad de París. El proyecto incluirá un parque acuático, un nuevo campo de golf, sitios para acampar, varias canchas de tenis y otros lugares ___(30)___

(26) 1 olvidar 3 controlar
2 devolver 4 atraer 26___

(27) 1 añaden 3 queman
2 sirven 4 envuelven 27___

(28) 1 deseo 3 miedo
2 duda 4 oposición 28___

(29) 1 viaje 3 futuro
2 transporte 4 zoológico 29___

(30) 1 recreativos 3 religiosos
2 cinematográficos 4 sedentarios 30___

PART 4

Write your answers to Part 4 according to the directions for *a* and *b*. [16 credits]

a Directions: Write **one** well-organized note in Spanish as directed below. [6]

Choose **either** question 31 **or** 32. Write a well-organized note, following the specific instructions given in the question you have chosen. Your note must consist of **at least six clauses.** To qualify for credit, a clause must contain a verb, a stated or implied subject, and additional words necessary to convey meaning. The six clauses may be contained in fewer than six sentences if some of the sentences have more than one clause.

31 You have been invited to a party by a Spanish-speaking friend, but you are unable to go. Write a note in Spanish to your friend explaining why you cannot attend.

In the note, you may wish to express your appreciation for the invitation and your disappointment at not being able to attend. Explain why you cannot attend. (You may want to mention a reason such as a family obligation, previous plans, or lack of transportation.) You may also want to include your best wishes for a successful party. **Be sure you accomplish the purpose of the note, which is *to inform your friend why you cannot attend the party.***

Use the following:

Salutation: Querido/Querida (name)
Closing: Tu amigo/Tu amiga

The salutation and closing will *not* be counted as part of the six required clauses.

32 You have borrowed something from your Spanish-speaking friend and are now returning it. Write a note in Spanish to your friend thanking him or her for letting you use it.

In the note, you should express your gratitude and you may wish to explain why you needed the item and how it was helpful to you. You may also want to offer to return the favor. **Be sure you accomplish the purpose of the note, which is *to thank your friend for lending you the item.***

Use the following:

Salutation: Querido/Querida (name)
Closing: Carinosamente

The salutation and closing will *not* be counted as part of the six required clauses.

b Directions: Write **one** well-organized composition in Spanish as directed below. [10]

Choose **either** question 33 **or** 34. Write a well-organized composition, following the specific instructions given in the question you have chosen. Your composition must consist of **at least 10 clauses**. To qualify for credit, a clause must contain a verb, a stated or implied subject, and additional words necessary to convey meaning. The 10 clauses may be contained in fewer than 10 sentences if some of the sentences have more than one clause.

33 In Spanish, write a story about the situation shown in the picture below. It must be a story relating to the picture, **not** a description of the picture. Do *not* write a dialogue.

34 An exchange student from Spain will be staying at your home for the next few months. In Spanish, write a letter to the exchange student telling him or her the plans you are making for the visit.

You must accomplish the purpose of the letter, which is *to tell the exchange student what plans you are making for the visit.*

In your letter, you may wish to explain why you are writing. You may also want to introduce yourself, tell about planned activities, places to be visited, accommodations that will be provided, household routines, your personal feelings about the exchange, and items the student should bring.

You may use any or all of the ideas suggested above *or* you may use your own ideas. **Either way, you must tell the exchange student what plans you are making for the visit.**

Use the following:

Dateline:	el 26 de enero de 1995
Salutation:	Querido/Querida (name)
Closing:	Espero verte pronto,

The dateline, salutation, and closing will *not* be counted as part of the 10 required clauses.

Answers January 1995

Comprehensive Examination in Spanish

PART 1

This part of the examination was evaluated prior to the date of this written examination. [24 credits]

PART 2

The following passages are to be read aloud to the students according to the directions given for this part at the beginning of this examination. The correct answers are given after number 15. [30 credits]

1. You are on a guided tour of a theme park and hear the guide say to the group:

Para disfrutar su visita les sugerimos que consulten los anuncios a las entradas de las atracciones para saber las reglas. No se permite tomar fotografías, ni consumir comidas o bebidas en los estudios de sonido, espectáculos o atracciones. Se prohibe fumar en las áreas de espera de las atracciones y en las tiendas.

What is the tour guide talking about?

2. You are listening to the radio and hear this announcement:

Por medio de cualquier aparato telefónico en los Estados Unidos, marque uno de los números que aparecen en este anuncio y hable a México Directo. Una operadora de Telmex le contestará en español y le comunicará con quien usted quiera. Llame a México desde los Estados Unidos en su idioma, con México Directo.

Who would be most interested in this information?

3. You are listening to your telephone answering machine and hear this message from Esteban, an exchange student:

Hola, habla Esteban. Lo siento, pero no puedo ir a tu casa para estudiar juntos esta noche como habíamos decidido. Es que vienen a visitarme unos amigos de mi familia que están viajando por los Estados Unidos. Acabo de saberlo. Quiero verlos y oír noticias de mis padres. Llámame cuando regreses y te explicaré más.

Why is Esteban unable to come to your home this evening?

4. Your friend calls you on the telephone and says to you:

Oye. ¡Te llamo porque tengo noticias sorprendentes! Es que acabo de ganar un sorteo que tuvo la estación WADO. Me regalaron dos entradas para la película *Noches Peligrosas* en el cine Apolo. La exhiben a las siete y media y también a las nueve y media. ¿Quieres acompañarme el sábado? Cristina y Lupe van a asistir también. Tal vez podamos ir juntos. ¿Qué te parece?

What does your friend want you to do?

5. You are listening to a radio program in Spain. The announcer says this about the region of Asturias:

La Fabada ha traspasado primero las fronteras regionales y luego las nacionales para convertirse en un plato representativo de Asturias. Este plato no es la única especialidad de la rica gastronomía asturiana. La cebolla rellena de carne, el queso de Cabrales y la excelente sidra son igualmente representativos.

What is causing Asturias to become well known?

6. You overhear two people discussing a problem. One of them says:

Ya no te rompas la cabeza pensando en qué regalar a tu amiga. Me has dicho que a ella le encanta mandar notitas simpáticas a sus amistades, y no sólo cuando se trata de un cumpleaños o celebración especial. Aquí tengo la solución perfecta . . . compra tarjetas bonitas sin ninguna leyenda en especial. Puedes ponerlas en una linda cesta decorada de modo atractivo y enviársela con una notita que diga: Para mi escritora favorita.

What problem is being discussed?

7. You are in Santo Domingo and hear this announcement on the radio:

La Corporación Dominicana de Electricidad realizará hoy trabajos de remodelación de las redes de distribución de la ciudad. Será necesario interrumpir el servicio energético que afectará a las siguientes zonas: San Juan de la Maguana, Avenida Bolívar, y Villa Juana. Pedimos perdón por las molestias que puedan ocasionarles estas interrupciones que son imprescindibles para mejorar el servicio.

What information was announced on the radio?

8. You are watching a Spanish-language cable television program and hear this advice:

Para renovar el aspecto de tu habitación, compra unos nuevos accesorios de colores que reflejen tu personalidad . . . lápices, plumas, reglas, tijeras, cinta adhesiva. En fin, todos estos materiales de uso diario sirven perfectamente para decorar tu refugio sin gastar mucho dinero. Deben ser simplemente seleccionados con formas modernas y colores vibrantes. Recuerda que con sólo un poco de imaginación las cosas más simples pueden convertirse en objetos decorativos.

Who would be most interested in this information?

9. You are listening to the radio and hear this commercial:

Suscríbase a nuestra revista y le regalaremos una magnífica cámara fotográfica. Queremos que recuerden sus vacaciones con imágenes de un tiempo feliz junto al mar o la montaña. Para conseguir esta cámara fotográfica, lo único que tiene que hacer es suscribirse por un año a nuestra revista. Envíe el sobre, dirigido a VIAJES Y VACACIONES. General Moscardó, Madrid, con el importe de 4.800 pesetas, y le enviaremos el regalo.

How would you be able to get this camera?

10. You are an exchange student in San José, Costa Rica. Your friend tells you about an announcement he read. He says:

Se solicitan distribuidores de periódicos en áreas de la capital, con o sin experiencia. Debe estar disponible para trabajar los fines de semana. Si desea una entrevista llame al 265-2979 para concertar una cita. Le agradeceremos no llamar si no puede trabajar los fines de semana.

¿Qué requisitos se necesitan para este trabajo?

11. You are with a school group on a tour bus in Seville. The bus driver is making an announcement to the group. The bus driver says:

Bueno, ahora vamos a salir para el hotel para que se den una ducha y se cambien. Una vez que estén listos, vamos a salir a ver la feria por la noche. Al regresar, no sé si vamos a poder pasar por la calle del hotel porque con esto de la feria, están todas las calles cerradas y hay demasiada gente para que los coches pasen. Así que, es mejor que los estudiantes se vayan a pie hasta el hotel.

¿Qué les dice el chófer del autobús al grupo?

12. You are in Spain and hear this news item on the radio:

Miguel Gordillo Polidoro ha adoptado el apodo de "Miguelín" para su entrada en el mundo taurino. Miguel nació en Sevilla el 26 de marzo de 1977. Los que reconocen su valentía y destreza opinan que son sorprendentes. Predicen que tendrá mucho éxito en las corridas. Habrá que esperar seis o siete años para ver si todo lo que promete se hace realidad.

¿Qué espera ser Miguel Gordillo Polidoro?

13. You are staying with a host family in Ecuador. You arrive at their home and hear this message on the telephone answering machine:

Oye, ¿dónde has estado? Hace dos días que intento llamarte y nunca estás. Por favor, llámame pronto porque ya tengo el itinerario de mi viaje y quiero que lo sepas lo más pronto posible para que puedas hacer los planes necesarios para acompañarme.

¿Por qué debes llamar a tu amigo?

14. You are listening to a guest speaker on a television talk show. The guest speaker says:

Les doy estos consejos: Les recomiendo hacer ejercicio regularmente y en dosis reducidas. Nunca hagan tanto ejercicio que pongan los músculos en peligro. Antes de cualquier sesión de entrenamiento, hay que calentar los músculos. No deben terminar de golpe los ejercicios. Es mejor enfriar el cuerpo poco a poco. Y por último, cuiden muy bien un detalle: el calzado. Debe ser de calidad y adecuado para el ejercicio que se va a realizar. Se puede dañar todo el cuerpo si no se utilizan zapatos diseñados para la actividad indicada.

¿Para quiénes son estos consejos?

15. You are watching television and hear this report about the World's Fair in Seville:

La exhibición de Chile en la Feria de Sevilla era un inmenso témpano de hielo traído de la Antártica. Representa para Chile un símbolo de la belleza y variedad de este diverso país. La compañía chilena "Ternofrío" tuvo que diseñar un sistema nuevo de refrigeración para mantenerlo durante su estancia.

¿Cuál es la atracción principal de la exhibición chilena?

PART 2

(1) 4	**(4)** 2	**(7)** 2	**(10)** 3	**(13)** 2
(2) 2	**(5)** 4	**(8)** 1	**(11)** 1	**(14)** 1
(3) 1	**(6)** 3	**(9)** 3	**(12)** 4	**(15)** 3

PART 3

(a)	**(16)** 2	**(b)**	**(21)** 2	**(c)**	**(26)** 4
	(17) 4		**(22)** 3		**(27)** 2
	(18) 4		**(23)** 1		**(28)** 1
	(19) 2		**(24)** 4		**(29)** 3
	(20) 3		**(25)** 3		**(30)** 1

PART 4

(a) Notes in writing

For each note, an example of a response worth six credits follows. The slash marks indicate how each sample note has been divided into clauses.

31. Querido Roberto,

Quisiera darte las gracias/$_1$ por invitarme a tu cumpleaños./$_2$ No podré venir/$_3$ porque tengo otros planes./$_4$ Es el aniversario de boda de mis padres/$_5$ y vamos a celebrarlo con mis abuelos./$_6$ Espero que tú y tus amigos se diviertan mucho.

Tu amigo,
Mariano

32. Querida Rosita,

Gracias por prestarme el disco compacto de mi cantante favorito, Luis Miguel./$_1$ El pasado fin de semana me pasé todo el día/$_2$ escuchando su música./$_3$ Para mi cumpleaños mi amiga me va a regalar la cinta de Ednita Nazario./$_4$ ¿Te gusta la música de Ednita?/$_5$ Te puedo prestar la cinta/$_6$ si la deseas escuchar.

Cariñosamente,
Carolina

(b) Narrative based on picture/letter

For each narrative/letter, an example of a response worth 10 credits follows. The slash marks indicate how each sample narrative/letter has been divided into clauses.

33. (Picture)

Es un día soleado de verano./$_1$ Carmen y Felipe son buenos amigos/$_2$ y les gusta ir a la playa./$_3$ Su deporte favorito es el vólibol./$_4$ Mañana hay una competencia/$_5$ y necesitan practicar./$_6$ Los muchachos se divierten/$_7$ y son buenos atletas./$_8$ Están seguros/$_9$ que van a ganar el campeonato./$_{10}$ ¡Qué manera ideal de pasar las vacaciones!

34. (Letter)

el 26 de enero de 1995

Querido Ricardo,

Deseo comunicarte todos nuestros preparativos para tu visita./$_1$ Vas a vivir con mi familia en un pueblo pequeño./$_2$ Tenemos un festival local con comidas típicas y competencias deportivas./$_3$ Visitaremos museos y restaurantes en una ciudad cercana./$_4$ Mi familia se levanta temprano/$_5$ y les encanta pasear./$_6$ Durante el invierno hace frío/$_7$ y necesitas un buen abrigo./$_8$ Trae fotografías de tu familia y de tu país./$_9$ Cuando llegues te recibiremos con una fiesta./$_{10}$

Espero verte pronto,
Carlos

Examination June 1995

Comprehensive Examination in Spanish

PART 1

Your performance on Part 1, Speaking (24 credits), has been evaluated prior to the date of this written examination.

PART 2

Answer all questions in Part 2 according to the directions for *a* and *b*. [30]

a *Directions* (1–9): For each question, you will hear some background information in English once. Then you will hear a passage in Spanish *twice* and a question in English *once*. After you have heard the question, the teacher will pause while you read the question and the four suggested answers. Choose the best suggested answer and write its *number* in the space provided. Base your answer *on the content of the passage, only.* The passages that the teacher will read aloud to you are found in the ANSWERS section, Part 2, at the end of this examination. [18]

1 What is this announcement urging workers to do?

1 use workplace equipment properly
2 vote during the next election
3 work more efficiently
4 strike if certain conditions are not met 1___

2 What is the main rule students in this program must follow?

1 arrive on time
2 attend all classes
3 go on all field trips
4 speak only Spanish

2____

3 What is the topic of conversation?

1 enjoying a hobby
2 making future plans
3 getting spending money
4 buying a gift

3____

4 What is the purpose of this message?

1 to advise drivers about traffic problems
2 to announce train arrival and departure times
3 to publicize the purpose of a new labor law
4 to advertise a sales promotion in the city

4____

5 What is this television program about?

1 home buying
2 home decorating
3 home security
4 home repair

5____

6 What does this student say concerning the Basque region of Spain?

1 Men play an active role in food preparation.
2 Women get together to share cooking experiences.
3 Both men and women increasingly prefer eating fast foods.
4 Families continue to prefer traditional regional dishes.

6____

7 What does the acquaintance explain?

1 Only telephones of certain colors can be used to call outside the airport.
2 You have to dial for the operator.
3 You need to know the local area code.
4 You must use a special coin from the telephone company. 7___

8 What does this technology allow the user to do?

1 automatically dial frequently called international telephone numbers
2 conduct multiple experiments in different countries simultaneously
3 purchase a more powerful computer at a lower cost
4 converse with speakers of different languages 8___

9 Why would someone use this service?

1 to have an appliance repaired
2 to find listings of employment opportunities
3 to mail a package
4 to purchase merchandise through a catalog 9___

b Directions (10–15): For each question, you will hear some background information in English *once*. Then you will hear a passage in Spanish *twice* and a question in Spanish *once*. After you have heard the question, the teacher will pause while you read the question and the four suggested answers. Choose the best suggested answer and write its *number* in the space provided. Base your answer *on the content of the passage, only.* The passages that the teacher will read aloud to you are found in the ANSWERS section, Part 2, at the end of this examination. [12]

10 ¿Por qué el guardia no les permite entrar?

1 Los salvavidas están en huelga.
2 No hay espacio para el carro.
3 Las olas están muy fuertes.
4 Van a cerrar la playa a las dos. 10___

11 ¿En qué consiste el plan?

1 de construir nuevos monumentos a los héroes coloniales
2 de mejorar cierta área de la capital dominicana
3 de alquilar carros a los turistas
4 de transformar el gobierno a una república 11___

12 ¿Por qué entrevistaron a Ellen Ochoa?

1 Es la primera mujer latina en hacer órbita a nuestro planeta.
2 Presentó un concierto de música clásica para la flauta en Los Angeles.
3 Estableció un programa de becas para estudiantes mexicoamericanos.
4 Publicó sus investigaciones médicas en una revista internacional. 12___

13 ¿Qué servicio nuevo ofrece la compañía Iberia?

1 vuelos entre Miami y Madrid
2 descuentos en vuelos a Centroamérica
3 servicio de España al resto de Europa
4 vuelos directos de Europa a Honduras y El Salvador 13___

14 ¿Qué hay que hacer para recibir el descuento?

1 ir directamente a la caja
2 hablar con el gerente
3 pagar con una tarjeta de crédito
4 esperar media hora 14___

15 ¿Qué ocurrió en esta ceremonia?

1 Se inauguró un libro sobre el monarca.
2 El Rey felicitó a unos niños que recibieron un premio.
3 El Rey participó en una reunión diplomática.
4 Un museo presentó una importante exposición. 15___

PART 3

Answer all questions in Part 3 according to the directions for *a*, *b*, and *c*. [30 credits]

a Directions (16–20): After the following passage, there are five questions or incomplete statements. For *each*, choose the word or expression that best answers the question or completes the statement *according to the meaning of the passage*, and write its *number* in the space provided. [10]

Cantinflas: el hombre y el actor

Cantinflas, famoso actor mexicano, murió en 1993 en su país natal. Fue un personaje extremadamente popular y querido no solamente en México sino también en el resto de América Latina y España. La televisión mexicana interrumpió sus programas para darle la noticia de la muerte de Cantinflas a la nación. Cantinflas era una de las grandes leyendas del mundo artístico mexicano del siglo XX. Para honrar su memoria el gobierno le ha preparado un gran reconocimiento póstumo.

Mario Moreno, conocido como Cantinflas, era un hombre de comportamiento sencillo. Diariamente iba a sus oficinas, almorzaba siempre en el mismo restaurante y dedicaba muchas horas del día a su familia.

El famoso actor nació en la Ciudad de México el 12 de agosto de 1911 en una familia de siete hermanos. La familia vivía del modesto sueldo del padre, funcionario de correos. El actor cursó su escuela en México y aunque obtuvo el bachillerato, pronto abandonó sus estudios. Fue limpiabotas, maletero, cartero, taxista y boxeador. Un día conoció a unos personajes del circo, y se quedó con ellos. Comenzó así una vida de cómico, y más tarde encontró en el cine la fama y la gloria. Su primera película, *No te engañes corazón,* fue un fracaso. Sin embargo, poco después Mario Moreno inició una carrera de gran éxito que le mantuvo frente a una cámara prácticamente de forma permanente hasta 1977. Fue definido por Charlie Chaplin come "el mejor cómico del mundo". El mensaje de Cantinflas fue de crítica social. Capturó las clases populares que se identificaron con su persona y vieron en sus películas escenas muy reales de la vida difícil del México cotidiano. Cantinflas hizo reír e hizo llorar a la gente. Era el héroe del barrio, protector de las criadas, y humilde representante de los valores eternos del pobre.

Cuando un día le preguntaron a Mario Moreno cómo surgió el personaje de Cantinflas, él respondió: "Una vez, de repente, sentí pánico frente a las cámaras. En ese momento yo no supe qué decir y de pronto surgió mi personaje 'Cantinflas', que se encargó de la situación y comenzó a decir palabras y tonterías sin sentido. Desde ese momento yo dejé de ser Mario Moreno y me convertí en Cantinflas".

Mario Moreno ha muerto dejando una impresionante fortuna. Fue considerado como uno de los hombres más ricos de América Latina, y también uno de los más generosos. Son innumerables las entidades y personas que se han beneficiado por su generosidad. Desde muy joven, quería compartir con los demás lo que tenía y hoy deja una obra social digna de elogio.

Se dice que diez años antes de morirse, Mario Moreno seleccionó la siguiente frase para su epitafio: "Parece que se ha ido, pero no es cierto". Para nosotros es la verdad que Mario Moreno se ha ido, pero en realidad, sabemos que Cantinflas permanecerá con nosotros para siempre.

16 ¿Por qué es famoso Mario Moreno?

1 por los restaurantes típicos que abrió
2 por sus ideas políticas
3 por los libros que escribió
4 por su carrera como actor 16___

17 ¿Qué le gustaba mucho a Mario Moreno?

1 participar en el gobierno
2 la vida rutinaria y familiar
3 almorzar con los famosos actores
4 sus estudios en la universidad 17___

18 Además de hacer reír a la gente, las películas de Cantinflas mostraron

1 la importancia de obtener riquezas
2 las aventuras en el circo
3 las relaciones internacionales
4 los problemas sociales de su época 18___

19 ¿Qué hizo con su dinero Mario Moreno?

1 Ayudó mucho a su pueblo.
2 Empezó una escuela para artistas.
3 Dejó toda su fortuna a su familia.
4 Estableció una beca bajo su nombre. 19___

20 Según esta selección, ¿cómo podemos interpretar el epitafio de Mario Moreno?

1 que se dedicó a luchar por la independencia de su patria
2 que ha sido un buen padre
3 que el espíritu del actor quedará
4 que el actor tenía miedo de morir 20___

b Directions (21–25): Below each of the following selections, there is either a question or an incomplete statement. For *each*, choose the word or expression that best answers the question or completes the statement *according to the meaning of the selection*, and write its *number* in the space provided. [10]

21

Fotógrafo aficionado

"Soy una gran admiradora de BUENHOGAR y les estoy muy agradecida por la ayuda recibida con sus consejos. Ahora quisiera que me contestaran qué puedo hacer para ver publicada mi foto en su revista y también los poemas que escribo y fotos que yo saco de cosas interesantes. Como esa es una publicación de temas variados, yo creo que sería lindo, tanto para mí como para muchos jóvenes, que pusieran una sección donde nosotros pudiéramos manifestarnos y dar a conocer nuestros trabajos. Muchas gracias de todo corazón".

Ruth Ramos
629 Washington Avenue.
Bldg. 5. Apt. 523
Bridgeport, Connecticut. 06604

Las fotos que publicamos, tanto en portada como en páginas interiores, son sólo de modelos enviadas por agencias especializadas, artistas o personajes de la vida pública. En cuanto a poner una sección de poesías o de fotos, no está considerada por el momento en nuestra línea editorial. Gracias por sus palabras.

One reason that Ruth Ramos wrote to this magazine was to

1 get her work published
2 renew a subscription
3 complain about an article
4 register for a photography class

21____

22

Hace varias semanas quería escribirte para contarte lo que me está pasando con mis padres. Tengo once años y mi hermanito nueve. Me llamo Luisa María. Vivimos en una casa muy bonita con piscina y mi hermano y yo tenemos todos los juguetes que queremos.

El problema es que lo que más quisiéramos no lo tenemos. Yo diría que soy millonaria pero no soy feliz, pues mi papá tiene muchos negocios y debido a eso siempre está de viaje y mi mamá también, porque lo ayuda en su trabajo. Casi nunca estamos juntos, sólo en determinadas fechas, como las navidades, cumpleaños y otras. Ellos no saben lo que yo daría por estar en un parque montando bicicleta y disfrutando con mi hermano y mis padres. ¿Crees tú que se lo debiera contar a mis padres o no?

According to this letter, what would Luisa Maria like to do?

1 spend more time with her family
2 celebrate her birthday at the park
3 become wealthy in the future
4 swim during her vacation 22____

23

Del editor

Hemos cumplido

ESTE SERA EL ULTIMO NUMERO DE *MAS*. EXPLICAR A FONDO LAS razones de nuestra retirada equivaldría a una conferencia sobre la economía editorial. Pero en pocas palabras, las revistas son entidades comerciales y, a pesar de que la nuestra parece estar llena de anuncios, los ingresos son menos que los gastos. Desde el principio nos propusimos darles a nuestros lectores calidad. Esta cuesta, cuesta mucho, pero pensamos que abriría una fuente de ingresos publicitarios que la justificarían. Llegamos cerca, pero no lo suficiente para seguir adelante. De cualquier manera, tratamos y, sobre todo, ahora preferimos terminar como empezamos. Con clase.

What is the editor telling the readers?

1 Articles on the economy will appear in the next issue.
2 Discounts are offered to new subscribers.
3 The magazine will no longer be published.
4 An advertising supplement is being included. 23____

24

PIENSALO

"He trabajado muy duro toda mi vida, y me siento muy orgulloso de todos mis logros. En 1980, fui uno de los escogidos durante la primera ronda de selección, cuando estaba finalizando mis estudios en la Universidad de California Sur (*University of Southern California*). He jugado en dos Super Tazones con los *Cincinnati Bengals;* y mis compañeros de la *NFL* votaron por mí para que participara en los últimos 10 Tazones Profesionales.

"Pero los logros que más me enorgullecen son mis diplomas, uno es de la *Chaffey High School* de Ontario, California, y el otro de la *USC*. La escuela es difícil. Estudiar toma mucho tiempo y, en ocasiones, las clases no son tan divertidas. Sin embargo, gracias a esos diplomas, puedo hacer prácticamente lo que yo quiera en este mundo—excepto atrapar un pase de *touchdown* de 70 yardas! Eso, se los dejo a los laterales."

—ANTHONY MUÑOZ, CINCINNATI BENGALS

Which of his accomplishments makes Anthony Muñoz most proud?

1 appearing in two Super Bowls
2 receiving a good education
3 playing in 10 All Star Games
4 making a 70-yard touchdown 24____

25

sus niños

Por Clara Baum

Los niños mismos pueden aprender a cuidar del planeta en que vivimos, si sus padres se toman el trabajo de explicarles algunas cosas y tratan de desarrollar en ellos hábitos positivos. Aunque a los niños les resulta difícil concebir "el futuro", trate de hacerles imaginar que "cuando sean grandes", como sus padres, quizás no haya papel para hacer libros, la tierra se habrá vuelto un lugar lleno de enfermedades ¡ni siquiera habrá aire puro para respirar! Y que podemos evitar todo esto no derrochando: apagando las luces que no se usan, escribiendo en ambas caras de los papeles, y reuniendo materiales plásticos para reciclaje. ¡Vale la pena!

This article stresses the importance of

1 exploring outer space
2 preserving our world
3 living peacefully with other peoples
4 creating good health habits 25____

c *Directions* (26–30): In the following passage, there are five blank spaces numbered 26 through 30. Each blank space represents a missing word or expression. For each blank space, four possible completions are provided. Only one of them makes sense *in the context of the passage*.

First, read the passage in its entirety to determine its general meaning. Then read it a second time. For each blank space, choose the completion that makes the best sense and write its *number* in the space provided. [10]

Asturias, Vacaciones Verdes

Asturias, con 10.564 kilómetros caudrados de tierra y una población de 1.100.00 personas, ha orientado su oferta vacacional en los últimos años hacia el turismo ecológico. Esta región de España ofrece a todos una forma distinta de pasar las vacaciones.

Asturias tiene una variedad de actividades turísticas para los ___(26)___ . Se puede disfrutar de las vacaciones en un ambiente natural que le permite ocupar el tiempo libre con actividades como el montañismo. Las estaciones invernales de Valgrande o de San Isidro ofrecen a los amantes del deporte de invierno una permanente cantidad de nieve y pistas en buenas condiciones para ___(27)___ .

Para acomodar a todos los viajeros al Principado de Asturias, muchos edificios, casas, y palacios tradicionales han sido rehabilitados. Estos se han convertido en hoteles que ofrecen a los visitantes alojamiento y comodidades de la más alta calidad. Así se ofrece una variedad de ___(28)___ para satisfacer las necesidades del público.

Asturias refleja su lema "Asturias, un paraíso natural"; también muestra su oferta gastronómica del mar y la de la huerta. Del mar encontramos merluzas, chopas, pulpos, calamares, y salmonetes. De la huerta hay manzanas, uvas y otras frutas frescas y sabrosas. Además de los pescados, mariscos, y frutas, están las tradicionales carnes y quesos. Asturias cuenta con la tabla de quesos más completa de Europa. Como podemos ver aquí se puede encontrar una gran variedad de ___(29)___.

En 1980 se creó la Fundación Príncipe de Asturias que cada año concede sus premios a personalidades españolas o iberoamericanas que se hayan destacado en los ámbitos científicos, sociales, deportivos, técnicos, y humanos. El Festival Internacional de Cine de Gijón o el Festival Internacional de Jazz son dos de las actividades ___(30)___. Con entusiasmo los asturianos quieren que los turistas descubran y gocen todo lo que su país ofrece. Será, sin duda, un sitio que cumplirá su lema, "Asturias, un paraíso natural."

(26) 1 vecinos 3 visitantes
2 parientes 4 nativos 26___

(27) 1 esquiar 3 correr
2 montar a caballo 4 nadar 27___

(28) 1 equipos 3 servicios
2 trabajos 4 transportes 28___

(29) 1 paisajes 3 diseños
2 vestidos 4 comidas 29___

(30) 1 técnicas 3 deportivas
2 culturales 4 científicas 30___

PART 4

Write your answers to Part 4 according to the directions for *a* and *b*. [16]

a Directions: Write **one** well-organized note in Spanish as directed below. [6]

Choose **either** question 31 **or** 32. Write a well-organized note, following the specific instructions given in the question you have chosen. Your note must consist of **at least six clauses.** To qualify for credit, a clause must contain a verb, a stated or implied subject, and additional words necessary to convey meaning. The six clauses may be contained in fewer than six sentences if some of the sentences have more than one clause.

31 The exchange student from Spain you are hosting will be staying home alone for the day. Write a note in Spanish to the exchange student giving suggestions about what to do.

In the note, you may wish to explain the reason for your absence and provide information about possible eating arrangements, anticipated telephone calls, possible deliveries, and people to contact in case of an emergency. **Be sure you accomplish the purpose of the note, which is *to give the exchange student suggestions about what to do*.**

Use the following:

Salutation: exchange student's first name
Closing: your first name

The salutation and closing will *not* be counted as part of the six required clauses.

32. Your Spanish teacher took your class on a field trip. Write a note in Spanish thanking your teacher for taking your class on this trip.

In the note, you may wish to tell your teacher what you have learned, how much you enjoyed the trip, and what the highlights were for you. You may also want to make suggestions about future trips. **Be sure you accomplish the purpose of the note, which is *to thank your teacher for taking your class on this trip.***

Use the following:

Salutation: Estimado/Estimada__________,
Closing: Atentamente,

The salutation and closing will *not* be counted as part of the six required clauses.

b Directions: Write **one** well-organized composition in Spanish as directed below. [10]

Choose **either** question 33 **or** 34. Write a well-organized composition, following the specific instructions given in the question you have chosen. Your composition must consist of **at least 10 clauses**. To qualify for credit, a clause must contain a verb, a stated or implied subject, and additional words necessary to convey meaning. The 10 clauses may be contained in fewer than 10 sentences if some of the sentences have more than one clause.

33 In Spanish, write a story about the situation shown in the picture below. It must be a story relating to the picture, **not** a description of the picture. Do *not* write a dialogue.

34 You have just won an all-expense-paid trip to Spain. In Spanish, write a letter to your pen pal telling him or her about your anticipated trip to Spain.

You <u>must</u> accomplish the purpose of the letter, which is *to tell your pen pal about your anticipated trip.*

In your letter, you may wish to describe your reactions to winning the trip, your plans to visit your pen pal, and the value of this trip to you. Additionally, you may want to include details about the trip, such as departure and arrival dates, planned activities, and accommodations.

You may use any or all of the ideas suggested above *or* you may use your own ideas. **Either way, you must tell your pen pal about your anticipated trip.**

Use the following:

Dateline:	el 20 de junio de 1995
Salutation:	Querido/Querida, __________
Closing:	Un abrazo, ______________

The dateline, salutation, and closing will *not* be counted as part of the 10 required clauses.

Answers June 1995

Comprehensive Examination in Spanish

PART 1

This part of the examination was evaluated prior to the date of this written examination. [24 credits]

PART 2

The following passages are to be read aloud to the students according to the directions given for this part at the beginning of this examination. The correct answers are given after number 15. [30 credits]

1. While listening to a Spanish radio station, you hear this announcement:

Tu voto es muy importante. En las próximas Elecciones Sindicales que se convocan entre el 1 de octubre y el 31 de diciembre, miles de hombres y mujeres se presentarán como candidatos para representar a los trabajadores. Son personas que quieren dedicar parte de su tiempo y de su esfuerzo a defender los intereses de los obreros. Es un oficio noble que merece el reconocimiento y apoyo de todos los trabajadores.

What is this announcement urging workers to do?

2. You are at the orientation meeting for a summer-abroad program in Argentina. The director says:

Bienvenidos a la Universidad Autónoma de Buenos Aires. Soy el señor Héctor Villalobos, director del programa de los cursos de verano para extranjeros. Las clases comenzarán mañana a las ocho. El único requisito que tenemos es que a partir de este momento están obligados a hablar en español entre Uds. Quiero presentarles a Martín García Guzmán, profesor de arqueología. El está encargado de las excursiones que tendremos los martes y los jueves. El servirá de guía cuando visiten los museos y los lugares de interés.

What is the main rule students in this program must follow?

3. You are chatting with a new friend at a party in Barcelona. Your friend says:

Pues, en España en general, nosotros los jóvenes, no tenemos empleo durante el año escolar. Mis padres me dan quinientas pesetas a la semana. De vez en cuando, si hago varias tareas tales como sacar la basura, ayudar con la limpieza del apartamento me dan otras doscientas pesetas. Lo malo es que me gasto todo en discos, libros y sobretodo en la ropa porque a mí me gustan mucho los estilos nuevos. En mi ciudad hay tiendas nuevas donde hay una gran variedad de prendas de vestir y regalos.

What is the topic of conversation?

4. You are in Mexico City and hear this public service message on the radio:

A causa de la rehabilitación del pavimento, las calles Cuernavaca y Naranjo estarán cerradas a la circulación por este día. La calle Cuernavaca entre Veracruz y Gastón Madrid estará cerrada desde las 7:00 a las 14:00 horas y la calle Naranjo entre Veracruz y Fronteras, desde las 7:00 a las 18:00 horas.

Un vocero del Ayuntamiento señaló que se avisa a los vecinos de estas calles, para que no los tome por sorpresa y tomen las precauciones necesarias.

What is the purpose of this message?

5. You are watching a program on television and hear the speaker say:

Esta es la época en que se cometen más robos; no des oportunidades a los ladrones que circulan por la ciudad. Antes de partir hacia el lugar donde pasas las vacaciones toma medidas de seguridad. Pide a algún vecino de confianza que te recoja la correspondencia mientras te encuentres fuera. Para mayor tranquilidad, aplica las recomendaciones que te ofrecemos.

What is this television program about?

6. A student from the Basque region of Spain has come to your Spanish Club to speak about life in his hometown. He says:

La comida tiene mucha importancia en nuestra región. Por eso, tenemos sociedades gastronómicas. Hace años estas sociedades eran solamente para hombres, pero ahora pueden ir todos, hombres y mujeres. En cada pueblo hay por lo menos una sociedad donde grupos se reúnen para preparar la comida y comer allí. Los hombres en el País Vasco casi siempre preparan la comida.

What does this student say concerning the Basque region of Spain?

7. You are in the airport in Lima, Peru, trying to place a telephone call to your host family. An acquaintance explains the following to you:

Tienes que meter una moneda especial para usar el teléfono. Se llama un rin-rin y se usa solamente con los teléfonos peruanos. Se vende en el aeropuerto y también en las tiendas de la red telefónica. Aquí tienes una.

What does the acquaintance explain?

8. You are listening to a guest speaker who is talking about some new technology. She says:

Una traducción asistida por computadora fue realizada por Japón, Alemania y los Estados Unidos. El experimento le dará la oportunidad de comunicarse en tres idiomas por teléfono. Mediante este equipo, uno puede hablar inglés a través de un teléfono y la persona en el otro extremo escuchará las palabras traducidas automáticamente por la computadora al japonés o alemán. Pero, este sistema no será comercializado antes de diez años debido a los costos elevados.

What does this technology allow the user to do?

9. You are walking in a shopping mall and hear this announcement:

Nosotros en el Centro de Servicio Melek sabemos lo importante que es su tiempo. Por esta razón le ofrecemos muchos servicios. Mientras usted va de compras puede disfrutar de nuestra ayuda que incluye: apartados postales, servicio de paquetería, sobres, estampillas, y mensajería.

Why would someone use this service?

10. You and a friend want to go to Luquillo Beach in Puerto Rico. At the entrance gate you are met by a guard, who says to you:

Lo siento mucho. No pueden entrar porque todos los estacionamientos están llenos. No cabe ni un carro más. Si desean, pueden volver a eso de las dos de la tarde. Estoy seguro de que a esa hora habrá estacionamiento disponible.

¿Por qué el guardia no les permite entrar?

11. You are listening to the radio and hear this news report:

El gobierno de la República Dominicana y La Organización de Estados Americanos anunciaron un plan especial para renovar la parte colonial de la ciudad de Santo Domingo. El objeto de este proyecto es principalmente turístico. Se construirán 20 hoteles, 40 restaurantes y 15.000 metros cuadrados de espacios para alquilar. El plan también incluye la creación de nuevos servicios públicos, y la restauración de monumentos y lugares históricos.

¿En qué consiste el plan?

12. A television talk show host is introducing a guest. The talk show host says:

Ellen Ochoa, una méxicoamericana de 34 años, nacida en Los Angeles, es una mujer moderna y dinámica. Además de ser doctora en ingeniería eléctrica y una notable flautista clásica, Ellen es la primera mujer astronauta de origen hispano y la primera en orbitar la Tierra en la nave *Discovery*. Su misión fue la de dirigir unos experimentos científicos para NASA. Cuando ella habla de su vida profesional a grupos de estudiantes, su mensaje es claro: para tener éxito en la vida hay que trabajar y estudiar muy duro.

¿Por qué entrevistaron a Ellen Ochoa?

13. You are at a travel agency in Spain and the agent gives you this information. He says:

A través de su centro de operaciones en Miami, Estados Unidos, la compañía española Iberia inaugurará este mes dos vuelos nuevos, uno a Honduras y otro a El Salvador. Nuestra compañía es la primera línea europea en ofrecer un servicio directo entre Europa y ambos países centroamericanos.

¿Qué servicio nuevo ofrece la compañía Iberia?

14. While shopping at a department store in Venezuela, you hear this announcement:

Atención damas y caballeros, durante los próximos quince minutos en nuestro departamento de ropa de niños tendremos una fantástica venta. Recibirá un descuento del veinte por ciento en cualquier ropa que escoja. Lo único que tiene que hacer es llevar la mercancía a la caja y la cajera le hará el descuento. Recuerde, sólo tiene quince minutos.

¿Qué hay que hacer para recibir el descuento?

15. You are in Mallorca and hear this item on a news program:

En una simpática celebración en el Palacio Real de Madrid, Su Majestad el Rey Juan Carlos ha recibido a los niños ganadores del concurso de arte, "Qué es un Rey para ti?", de la Fundación Institucional Española. Todos los niños han expresado lo que para ellos significa la figura del monarca. El ganador del primer premio fue Daniel Bertucci con su dibujo titulado "Para mí un Rey es...".

¿Qué ocurrió en esta ceremonia?

PART 2

(1) 2	**(4)** 1	**(7)** 4	**(10)** 2	**(13)** 4
(2) 4	**(5)** 3	**(8)** 4	**(11)** 2	**(14)** 1
(3) 3	**(6)** 1	**(9)** 3	**(12)** 1	**(15)** 2

PART 3

(a)		(b)		(c)	
	(16) 4		**(21)** 1		**(26)** 3
	(17) 2		**(22)** 1		**(27)** 1
	(18) 4		**(23)** 3		**(28)** 3
	(19) 1		**(24)** 2		**(29)** 4
	(20) 3		**(25)** 2		**(30)** 2

PART 4

(a) Notes in writing

For each note, an example of a response worth six credits follows. The slash marks indicate how each sample note has been divided into clauses.

31. Paquito,

Salí para una cita/$_1$ que me tomará todo el día./$_2$ Llegaré a casa a las seis de la tarde./$_3$ Para el almuerzo prepara/$_4$ lo que desees/$_5$ o ve al restaurante de la esquina./$_6$ En la tarde si quieres, puedes jugar baloncesto con los niños del vecindario. En caso de emergencia llama a este número 555-6789.

32. Estimada Sra. Cortés,

Le escribo esta carta/$_1$ para expresar mi agradecimiento/$_2$ por organizar el viaje para la clase./$_3$ Cuando fuimos al museo/$_4$ yo aprendí mucho./$_5$ Me encantaron las pinturas./$_6$ También me gustó muchísimo la exposición de artesanías. ¡Ojalá podamos hacer otro viaje pronto!

Atentamente,

(b) Narrative based on picture/letter

For each narrative/letter, an example of a response worth 10 credits follows. The slash marks indicate how each sample narrative/letter has been divided into clauses.

33. (Picture)

El señor Lugo es el dueño de una agencia de viajes./$_1$ Su agencia es muy popular/$_2$ porque ofrece excursiones a muy buenos precios./$_3$ Un día, un grupo de gente se presentó a su oficina/$_4$ para quejarse de su servicio./$_5$ El había hecho reservaciones para un crucero/$_6$ y cuando el día llegó,/$_7$ los nombres de los pasajeros no aparecían en la computadora./$_8$ Estaban furiosos/$_9$ y decidieron ir a hablar con el señor Lugo./$_{10}$ Cuando él los vio, se asustó y salió de prisa.

34. (Letter)

el 20 de junio de 1995

Querida Mercedes,

Acabo de recibir la mejor noticia del año./$_1$ Estoy muy contenta./$_2$ Gané un concurso de mi escuela,/$_3$ y el premio es un viaje a España./$_4$ Siempre he deseado visitar tu país./$_5$ El vuelo sale el primero de julio a las seis de la tarde./$_6$ El número del vuelo es Iberia 525./$_7$ Pensamos alojarnos en el Hotel Madrid./$_8$ Me gustaría verte/$_9$ cuando llegue./$_{10}$

Un abrazo,

Examination January 1996

Comprehensive Examination in Spanish

PART 1

Your performance on Part 1, Speaking (24 credits), has been evaluated prior to the date of this written examination.

PART 2

Answer all questions in Part 2 according to the directions for *a* and *b*. [30]

a *Directions* (1–9): For each question, you will hear some background information in English once. Then you will hear a passage in Spanish *twice* and a question in English *once*. After you have heard the question, the teacher will pause while you read the question and the four suggested answers. Choose the best suggested answer and write its *number* in the space provided. Base your answer *on the content of the passage, only*. The passages that the teacher will read aloud to you are found in the ANSWERS section, Part 2, at the end of this examination. [18]

1 What advice does the salesperson offer?

1 how to help a dog adapt to a new family
2 how to housebreak a dog
3 how to teach a dog to do special tricks
4 how to feed a dog 1___

2 What will the hotel do if you are not completely satisfied?

1 furnish additional services
2 upgrade your room
3 offer you a free dinner
4 provide the room without charge 2___

3 What was discussed on the radio?

1 a new language
2 a new book
3 a new soap opera
4 a new movie 3___

4 What is the purpose of this announcement?

1 to give passengers information about stopping for lunch
2 to tell passengers that they will arrive in $1\frac{1}{2}$ hours
3 to advise passengers that there will be a 10-minute delay
4 to direct passengers' attention to several tourist attractions 4___

5 What did Estelle Getty do?

1 She hosted a talk show.
2 She celebrated her 69th birthday.
3 She starred in a new television comedy.
4 She produced exercise tapes. 5___

6 What type of program will be presented?

1 a farm report show
2 an awards ceremony
3 a performance of traditional music
4 a teen talent show 6___

7 What does this video emphasize?

1 the beaches
2 the mountains
3 traditional customs
4 historic landmarks 7____

8 What information do these pamphlets provide?

1 how to drive safely
2 how to obtain a license
3 how to buy a car
4 how to conserve gasoline 8____

9 What kind of show is being advertised?

1 a comedy
2 a cartoon
3 a movie
4 a news program 9____

b Directions (10–15): For each question you will hear some background information in English *once*. Then you will hear a passage in Spanish *twice* and a question in Spanish *once*. After you have heard the question, the teacher will pause while you read the question and the four suggested answers. Choose the best suggested answer and write its *number* in the space provided. Base your answer *on the content of the passage, only.* The passages that the teacher will read aloud to you are found in the ANSWERS section, Part 2, at the end of this examination. [12]

10 ¿Qué información nos da este anuncio?

1 ideas para alegrar la vida
2 tiendas elegantes para ir de compras
3 hoteles lujosos para pasar las vacaciones
4 restaurantes típicos para comer bien 10____

11 ¿Qué se discute en este programa?

1 temas de interés popular
2 eventos deportivos nacionales
3 asuntos políticos locales
4 consejos de moda y belleza 11___

12 ¿Qué se ofrece en este anuncio?

1 un trabajo en las oficinas de turismo
2 un nuevo medio de transporte aéreo
3 información para adolescentes que piensan viajar
4 viajes especiales para los ancianos 12___

13 ¿Cómo se conocieron estas dos familias?

1 durante una visita al médico
2 por medio de la embajada americana
3 en un viaje por el Caribe
4 a través de una carta 13___

14 ¿Qué importancia tiene la exposición?

1 Enseña las lenguas de la península ibérica.
2 Honra a una persona célebre.
3 Conmemora la influencia árabe en España.
4 Exhibe objetos científicos. 14___

15 ¿De qué trata el programa que se anuncia?

1 la cultivación de un jardín de vegetales
2 la construcción de una casa
3 la vida personal de una persona famosa
4 la preparación de comidas 15___

PART 3

Answer all questions in Part 3 according to the directions for *a*, *b*, and *c*. [30 credits]

a Directions (16–20): After the following passage, there are five questions or incomplete statements. For *each*, choose the word or expression that best answers the question or completes the statement *according to the meaning of the passage*, and write its *number* in the space provided. [10]

Elena Castedo es una de las figuras más interesantes del mundo literario de hoy. Recientemente, *El Paraíso/Paradise*, su primera novela, fue publicada en los países hispanohablantes y en los Estados Unidos.

Elena Castedo ha tenido que adaptarse a distintos ambientes y países. Nació en Barcelona, España; fue exiliada a Francia después de la Guerra Civil española, pero creció en Chile. Después de la muerte de su primer marido, quedó viuda joven con dos hijos. Ellos pasaron años terribles viviendo en sólo un cuarto o en casas condenadas a ser demolidas. Trabajó como vendedora de puerta a puerta, profesora privada de español, modelo, empleada en una guardería infantil, y demostradora de aparatos eléctricos.

Tuvo la suerte de encontrarse con personas e instituciones que tuvieron fé en su capacidad. Ellos le otorgaron becas y ella pudo estudiar. Mientras mantenía sola a sus hijos, ella logró sacar el título de profesora de castellano en una universidad chilena, una maestría en la Universidad de California, y un doctorado en la Universidad de Harvard. Desde entonces, ha sido consultora de asuntos culturales, ha enseñado literatura en varias universidades y fue directora de la revista *Interamericana*.

Escribir la novela en dos lenguas no fue fácil, según la autora. Ella dice que su intención fue de crear en cada lengua, no de traducir solamente. Muchas veces "la palabra perfecta" en inglés producía un problema en español. A veces pasaba un día entero tratando de arreglar sólo una frase. No fue en vano. La crítica ha sido positivísima en España, en Hispanoamérica, y en los Estados Unidos. *El Paraíso* fue nominada en España para el premio Cervantes y en Chile fue nombrada "libro del año." En los Estados Unidos, *Paradise* fue nominada para el National Book Award. *Publisher's Weekly* dice que Elena Castedo es la primera mujer de origen hispano considerada "mainstream," o sea dentro de la literatura importante del país. Y en Puerto Rico, *El San Juan Star* dice "Castedo mete gol en dos idiomas."

En este momento, muchas universidades incluyen el libro en sus departamentos de inglés y de español, convirtiendo a la autora en un puente entre culturas. Después de muchos años Elena Castedo finalmente logró su sueño de escribir ficción. Descrita por la prensa como "la escritora hoy en día más celebrada en los dos lados del Atlántico" y "el fenómeno literario de la década," ha logrado un triunfo que todos hubieran considerado imposible.

16 ¿Cuál es el país de origen de Elena Castedo?

1 Francia
2 España
3 Estados Unidos
4 Chile

16___

17 ¿Cuál fue un gran problema para Elena y sus hijos?

1 Los hijos fueron a vivir con parientes.
2 Los hijos tuvieron que trabajar.
3 La familia vivió en condiciones muy pobres.
4 La familia dependió de la ayuda de los abuelos.

17___

18 ¿En qué tuvo buena suerte la señora?

1 Heredó mucho dinero de su familia.
2 Se casó con un hombre rico.
3 Recibió ayuda en cuidar a sus hijos.
4 Se interesaron otros en su habilidad. 18___

19 ¿Qué aprendió la autora al escribir su libro en dos lenguas?

1 que muchas palabras no se pueden traducir literalmente
2 que necesitaba a una persona para traducirlo
3 que ella podía escribirlo rápidamente
4 que sus experiencias personales no eran importante 19___

20 ¿Cuál era la gran esperanza de Elena Castedo?

1 traducir documentos históricos
2 viajar por el mundo
3 dedicarse a los pobres
4 contribuir al mundo literario 20___

b Directions (21–25): Below each of the following selections, there is either a question or an incomplete statement. For *each*, choose the word or expression that best answers the question or completes the statement *according to the meaning of the selection*, and write its *number* in the space provided. [10]

21

PROPUESTAS

Rutas alrededor de Madrid.

Cada sábado desde el 5 de junio hasta el 30 de octubre, la Comunidad de Madrid organiza siete recorridos diferentes por ciudades de la región, como Alcalá de Henares, San Lorenzo del Escorial, Chinchón. Cada excursión cuesta 2.950 pesetas con viaje en autocar, almuerzo y guía. Mayores de 65 y menores de 14 pagan la mitad. Plazas limitadas. Más información, en el 91/429 49 51.

What is this announcement about?

1 sightseeing tours
2 road construction sites
3 restaurants around Madrid
4 public transportation schedule changes 21___

22

Desafortunadamente los avisos de peligro no crecen en los árboles. Si usted enciende una fogata en el bosque, usted es responsable de controlarla y evitar el peligro de incendio. Para ello, siga estas reglas:

- Encienda siempre sus fogatas lejos de las ramas bajas de los árboles, troncos secos y hojas.
- No tire los fósforos hasta que estén apagados y fríos.
- Nunca deje sola una fogata encendida.
- Apague las fogatas con tierra, arena o agua.
- Y si fuma, pise las colillas hasta que estén completamente apagadas.

Siga estas reglas porque en el bosque, nadie le avisará si está en peligro.

Sólo usted puede prevenir incendios en los bosques.

This announcement offers advice about

1 hiking on the trails
2 avoiding injuries
3 the dangers of smoking
4 the prevention of fires 22____

23

Area urbana

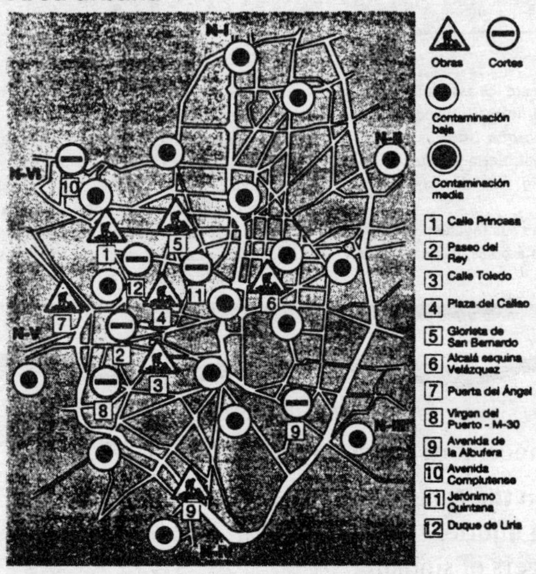

Cortada Ortega y Gasset

La calle de Ortega y Gasset quedará cortada hoy, curiosamente, para uso exclusivo de los coches, pero para vehículos antiguos que efectuarán una exhibición entre las cuatro de la tarde y las 9.30. El corte se efectuará entre las calles de Velázquez y Marqués de Salamanca.

Calles con obras. Princesa, Toledo, plaza del Callao, avenida de Entrevías a la altura de Timoteo Pérez Rubio, glorieta de Bilbao en la zona de la calle de Fuencarral y puerta del Ángel. En la autovía de Toledo, las obras de un paso elevado en Orcasitas ocupan dos carriles, uno en cada sentido.

Calles cortadas. Avenida de la Albufera y avenida de la Complutense, por la construcción de sendas bocas de metro; en ambos casos hay desvíos señalizados. Calle de Duque de Liria, por obras del intercambiador de Príncipe Pío. Paseo del Rey, por obras del Pasillo Verde.

According to this article, what will take place today on Ortega and Gasset streets?

1 an art exhibition
2 road construction
3 an antique car show
4 a visit by the Royal Family

23____

24

¿MUDANDOTE?

No te arriesgues a perder un solo número de

TU

internacional

Mi nueva dirección es (escribe con letra de molde):

Nombre________________________

____

Calle__________________________

Ciudad_________________________

Estado__________Zip Code_____

Por favor: Avísanos con 6 a 8 semanas de anticipación. Gracias.

Envía la etiqueta con tu nombre y nueva dirección a:

Editorial América S.A.
Subscription Service
P.O. Box 10990,
Des Moines, Iowa, 50340-0990

The magazine provides this form for people who are

1 purchasing a gift subscription
2 requesting a complimentary issue
3 looking for past issues
4 changing their address 24____

25

ROYAL GREEN CUP '95, EDICION VALENCIA

Se ha celebrado en el club de golf Escorpión de Valencia, la Royal Green Cup '95. Debido al mal tiempo reinante sólo pudieron competir 115 de los 200 participantes que se habían inscrito. Los ganadores de esta edición en la categoría hándicap inferior han sido Joaquín Monge Llinas, en caballeros, y Aurora García Comín, en damas, que aparece en la imagen con su trofeo conseguido.

Why did only 115 athletes participate in the Royal Green Cup?

1 The weather was bad.
2 Many of the invitations were lost.
3 The number of disqualifications was high.
4 The event was not well advertised. 25____

c *Directions* (26–30): In the following passage, there are five blank spaces numbered 26 through 30. Each blank space represents a missing word or expression. For each blank space, four possible completions are provided. Only one of them makes sense *in the context of the passage*.

First, read the passage in its entirety to determine its general meaning. Then read it a second time. For each blank space, choose the completion that makes the best sense and write its *number* in the space provided. [10]

Linda Ronstadt
El espejo de dos culturas

La historia de Linda Ronstadt refleja el encuentro de dos culturas: la rica tradición de México y la del suroeste de los Estados Unidos. Cuando su abuelo Fred Ronstadt atravesó la frontera entre México y los Estados Unidos y llegó a Tucson, Arizona, en 1882, comenzó la historia de una de las familias pioneras de Arizona. Sus sueños y aspiraciones, fracasos y realidades, no son muy diferentes a los de miles de inmigrantes que día a día han ___(26)___ la frontera. La familia siempre recuerda las palabras del abuelo: "Esta es la tierra de la oportunidad." Estas palabras hacen eco en las mentes de los que sueñan con una vida mejor.

Al llegar a los Estados Unidos los inmigrantes mexicanos trajeron su cultura, incluyendo la música del mariachi, parte integral de la vida mexicana.

Esta riqueza cultural fue transmitida de generación a generación. El 9 de mayo de 1986 en La Conferencia Internacional del Mariachi, Linda Ronstadt se convirtió en la embajadora del mariachi. Un conocido compositor mexicano dijo en esa ocasión, "Linda ___(27)___ la música del mariachi donde jamás ha llegado." Poco después Linda grabó los álbumes "Canciones de Mi Padre" y "Más Canciones", los cuales tuvieron mucho éxito durante una gira músical por todo el país. Linda, la cantante de rock, de pop, de jazz, de country y western así reafirmó la legitimidad de su rica herencia cultural.

A pesar de que Linda haya side parte integral de las diferentes expresiones de la cultura popular desde que tenía 18 años, para muchos hispanos era desconocida. Linda no cantó rock hasta que tenía 17 años aunque la música dominó toda su vida. Para ella la música es un rito, una experiencia mística y personal. Es un recuerdo mágico de su niñez, cuando ella cantaba las canciones tradicionales mexicanas y tocaba la guitarra con sus hermanos y su padre. Durante esta época de su vida ella ___(28)___ las canciones de su padre.

Linda admite que no habla español bien. Para ella, el español es la lengua en que la regañaban, la elogiaban, y en la que ella cantaba. Como siempre cantó en español, naturalmente le es más ___(29)___ cantarlo que hablarlo. Su experiencia no es diferente a la de miles de hispanos de segunda, tercera o cuarta generación. A causa de estas experiencias tiene más ___(30)___ en las comunidades mexicoamericanas. El idioma español seguirá siendo el denominador común entre Linda Ronstadt y los hispanos de este país.

(26) 1 dibujado 3 perdido
2 cruzado 4 olvidado 26___

(27) 1 llevará 3 leerá
2 negará 4 abandonará 27___

(28) 1 vendió 3 eliminó
2 aprendió 4 destruyó 28___

(29) 1 incómodo 3 extraño
2 fácil 4 aburrido 29___

(30) 1 documentos 3 problemas
2 humillación 4 aceptación 30___

PART 4

Write your answers to Part 4 according to the directions for *a* and *b*. [16]

a Directions: Write **one** well-organized note in Spanish as directed below. [6]

Choose **either** question 31 **or** 32. Write a well-organized note, following the specific instructions given in the question you have chosen. Your note must consist of **at least six clauses.** To qualify for credit, a clause must contain a verb, a stated or implied subject, and additional words necessary to convey meaning. The six clauses may be contained in fewer than six sentences if some of the sentences have more than one clause.

31 You are an exchange student in Spain. You have received an invitation from a Spanish friend to attend a special event. You are unable to attend. Write a note in Spanish to your friend declining the invitation.

In the note, you may wish to thank your friend for the invitation and explain why you cannot go, describe your feelings about being unable to attend, and suggest an alternate date for getting together. **Be sure you accomplish the purpose of the note, which is *to decline the invitation*.**

Use the following:

Salutation: your friend's first name
Closing: your first name

The salutation and closing will *not* be counted as part of the six required clauses.

32 You are an exchange student in Venezuela. You left an important item at school and must return to get it. Write a note in Spanish to your host family telling them why you are not at home.

In the note, you may wish to tell where you have gone, why you needed to go at this time, when you will return, and how you are getting there and back. **Be sure you accomplish the purpose of the note, which is *to explain to your host family why you are not at home*.**

Use the following:

Salutation: Señores Córdoba
Closing: your first name

The salutation and closing will *not* be counted as part of the six required clauses.

b Directions: Write **one** well-organized composition in Spanish as directed below. [10]

Choose **either** question 33 **or** 34. Write a well-organized composition, following the specific instructions given in the question you have chosen. Your composition must consist of **at least 10 clauses**. To qualify for credit, a clause must contain a verb, a stated or implied subject, and additional words necessary to convey meaning. The 10 clauses may be contained in fewer than 10 sentences if some of the sentences have more than one clause.

33 In Spanish, write a story about the situation shown in the picture below. It must be a story relating to the picture, **not** a description of the picture. Do *not* write a dialogue.

34 You and your family will be taking a trip by car throughout the United States next summer. In Spanish, write a letter to a friend from Spain inviting him/her to join your family on this trip.

You must accomplish the purpose of the letter, which is *to invite your friend to join you and your family on this trip.*

In the letter, you may wish to describe the length of the trip, places you will visit, probable weather conditions, accommodations, and things you will do. You may also wish to suggest what your friend should bring on the trip.

You may use any or all of the ideas suggested above *or* you may use your own ideas. **Either way, you must invite your friend to join you and your family on this trip.**

Use the following:

Dateline: el 25 de enero de 1996
Salutation: Querido ________/Querida ________,
Closing: Tu amigo,/Tu amiga,

The dateline, salutation, and closing will *not* be counted as part of the 10 required clauses.

Answers January 1996

Comprehensive Examination in Spanish

PART 1

This part of the examination was evaluated prior to the date of this written examination. [24 credits]

PART 2

The following passages are to be read aloud to the students according to the directions given for this part at the beginning of this examination. The correct answers are given after number 15. [30 credits]

1. You are in a pet store and hear the salesperson talking to another customer. The salesperson says:

Los recipientes de comida y bebida del perro siempre deben estar en el mismo sitio, preferiblemente en la cocina o en algún lugar en que el animal no sea molestado mientras come. Es importante ofrecerle la comida a la misma hora. El platón de agua siempre debe estar bien limpio y lleno. Así el perro comerá feliz.

What advice does the salesperson offer?

2. You call a hotel to obtain some information about its services. The employee says to you:

En nuestro hotel le ofrecemos grandes y cómodas habitaciones. Cada habitación tiene televisor a control remoto, teléfono, horno de microondas, cafetera y refrigerador. Hay cuartos disponibles para los que no fuman.

Tenemos una piscina y un gimnasio. El costo incluye desayuno y un periódico. Garantizamos comodidad y conveniencia durante su estadía. Si usted no está satisfecho, no pagará nada.

What will the hotel do if you are not completely satisfied?

3. You are listening to a radio announcement in Colombia. You hear:

Una casa editorial anuncia la última edición de la novela de Gabriel García Márquez titulada *El General en su laberinto*. En ella el autor se acerca a la figura de Simón Bolívar a través del lenguaje de la ficción. García Márquez nos relata aventuras de tragedia y magia del general que cambió la historia de Latinoamérica.

What was discussed on the radio?

4. You are on a bus tour in Puerto Rico. The tour guide announces:

Señores y señoras, vamos a llegar a Ponce en dos horas. Ya que se acerca la hora de almorzar, en diez minutos vamos a pararnos en un restaurante para comer. Continuaremos nuestro viaje después de una hora y media. Gracias por su atención.

What is the purpose of this announcement?

5. You are watching television in Mexico and hear the host say:

La actriz Estelle Getty no es ninguna jovencita pero mantiene muy bien sus 68 años. ¿Cuál es el secreto que la divertida Sofía del programa *Las chicas de oro* utiliza para mantener su buena apariencia? Ahora todos sus aficionados podrán ver en sus cintas de video los movimientos musculares que emplea para ponerse en forma. Se venden ahora los videos en su tienda local.

What did Estelle Getty do?

6. You are listening to the radio and hear this announcement:

El festival para la celebración del 5 de mayo se llevará a cabo en la Plaza Cívica este domingo desde las 10 de la mañana hasta las 8 de la noche. Este año el festival cultural contará con la presentación musical de tres cantantes famosos de la música ranchera. Les invitamos a pasar un día inolvidable en compañía de sus familiares y amistades.

What type of program will be presented?

7. You are listening to the radio and hear this announcement:

La Oficina de Turismo de Lleida ha preparado un video de promoción turística, celebrando su naturaleza. El video está traducido al inglés y francés. Refleja los atractivos turísticos de Lleida, con atención especial a las estaciones de esquí, al patinaje a hielo, y a otras actividades en la nieve. Han distribuido mil copias del video entre embajadas, consulados, y oficinas de turismo.

What does this video emphasize?

8. You are listening to the radio and hear this announcement:

Preocupada con que los chóferes conduzcan mejor en nuestras carreteras, para así evitar accidentes, la compañía gasolinera Shell tiene a su disposición una serie de sencillos folletos con información muy útil. Algunos de los títulos son: "Un guía de primeros auxilios en el camino" y "Cómo conducir en forma más segura en mal tiempo." Los folletos están disponibles en todas las estaciones Shell.

What information do these pamphlets provide?

9. You are watching television and hear this advertisement:

Todo es posible en el programa *Noticias y Más* . . . no importa la distancia o el peligro. Para traerle a usted las noticias más interesantes y eventos fuera de lo común, los reporteros de *Noticias y Más* siempre cumplen su misión. Vea *Noticias y Más* con Raúl Peimbert, lunes a viernes a las cinco en el canal Univisión.

What kind of show is being advertised?

10. You are listening to the radio and hear this advice:

¿Quién no tiene un "día gris" en su vida? Todos tenemos nuestros días malos. Si usted se despierta deprimida, trate de practicar alguna de estas tácticas para elevar su moral.

Estimule sus sentidos. Cómprese unas flores, una nueva bufanda o un perfume diferente.

Encuéntrese con su mejor amiga para tomarse un café o un té. Reúnase con ella en una cafetería íntima. Después de una hora de conversación, ¡se sentirá como nueva!

¿Qué información nos da este anuncio?

11. You are listening to the radio in Puerto Rico and hear this announcement:

Los acontecimientos más importantes de nuestra sociedad se discuten en *Mundo Social*. Entérese del último acontecimiento social en Puerto Rico a través de este dinámico programa radial. Cada semana distinguidos invitados comentan sobre interesantes temas de actualidad y contestan sus preguntas. Recuerde, *Mundo Social* se transmite los sábados de 9:00 a 10:00 de la mañana.

¿Qué se discute en este programa?

12. You are listening to the radio in Spain and hear this announcement:

¡Atención! Tenemos sugerencias de viajes a precios accesibles. Si usted es estudiante puede obtener billetes económicos para distintos medios de transporte como el Interrail. Por 41.700 pesetas puede recorrer en tren por Europa y Marruecos durante un mes. Vaya a una de las 38 oficinas de Turismo Joven repartidas por toda España.

¿Qué se ofrece en este anuncio?

13. You are watching television and hear about this unusual story:

En el 1989, el señor Bob Robinson de Texas viajaba en un barco con su esposa cuando decidió escribir una carta. La puso en una botella y la lanzó al mar. Seis meses más tarde, el señor José Cardoso de Cuba la encontró. El señor Cardoso le escribió al señor Robinson y pronto se hicieron amigos. Los Cardoso viajaron a Texas para conocer personalmente a los Robinson.

¿Cómo se conocieron estas dos familias?

14. You are listening to the radio in Spain and hear this news report:

Se inauguró recientemente en Córdoba una exhibición sobre la Civilización Islámica en España. La presencia islámica en la península ibérica fue factor determinante en la evolución de la vida y la cultura en España. La palabra árabe "Al-Andalus" es el título de la exhibición. La recolección de los objetos tomó cuatro años y muestra miles de objetos provenientes de todo el mundo.

¿Qué importancia tiene la exposición?

15. You are watching television with your host family in Madrid and you hear this commercial:

Carlos Arguiñano presenta los sábados un programa especial en el que ofrece recetas sencillas para los que no saben cocinar. Cada semana un personaje invitado se encarga de la preparación. De lunes a viernes, Arguiñano presenta *El menú de cada día*, a las 13.25, en el que explica recetas elaboradas pero fáciles.

¿De qué trata el programa que se anuncia?

PART 2

(1) 4	**(4)** 1	**(7)** 2	**(10)** 1	**(13)** 4
(2) 4	**(5)** 4	**(8)** 1	**(11)** 1	**(14)** 3
(3) 2	**(6)** 3	**(9)** 4	**(12)** 3	**(15)** 4

PART 3

(a)	**(16)** 2	**(b)**	**(21)** 1	**(c)**	**(26)** 2
	(17) 3		**(22)** 4		**(27)** 1
	(18) 4		**(23)** 3		**(28)** 2
	(19) 1		**(24)** 4		**(29)** 2
	(20) 4		**(25)** 1		**(30)** 4

PART 4

(a) **Notes in writing**

For each note, an example of a response worth six credits follows. The slash marks indicate how each sample note has been divided into clauses.

31. Mariano,

Quiero darte las gracias por tu invitación a la obra de teatro./$_1$ Lo siento/$_2$ pero no puedo ir./$_3$ Tengo que ir a la embajada americana/$_4$ porque perdí mi pasaporte./$_5$ Si quieres,/$_6$ podemos ir al cine mañana por la noche para ver la última película de Pedro Almodóvar.

32. Señores Córdoba,

Tuve que regresar al colegio/$_1$ porque dejé las llaves en el ropero./$_2$ Sin las llaves, no podré entrar en la casa./$_3$ Regresaré en media hora./$_4$ Mi amiga, Lucía, tiene su carro/$_5$ y me llevará a casa./$_6$ No se preocupen. Todo está bien.

(b) Narrative based on picture/letter

For each narrative/letter, an example of a response worth 10 credits follows. The slash marks indicate how each sample narrative/letter has been divided into clauses.

33. (Picture)

Es el primer día de clases./$_1$ Marisa va a ir a una escuela nueva./$_2$ Sus padres esperan con ella/$_3$ porque ella está un poco nerviosa./$_4$ Finalmente, llega el autobús./$_5$ Los padres saben/$_6$ que ella va a pasar un buen día./$_7$ Cuando Marisa ve a sus amigas/$_8$ se siente mucho mejor./$_9$ Dice adiós a sus padres/$_{10}$ y sube felizmente al autobús.

34. (Letter)

el 25 de enero de 1996

Querido Juan,

Este verano mi famila y yo pensamos hacer un viaje a través de los Estados Unidos./$_1$ El viaje durará un mes./$_2$ Vamos a salir el primero de julio/$_3$ y regresar en agosto./$_4$ Esperamos visitar sitios históricos./$_5$ Nos gustaría/$_6$ invitarte a pasar este mes con nosotros./$_7$ Necesitas traer ropa cómoda de verano,/$_8$ una cámara para sacar fotos/$_9$ y dinero para comprar recuerdos del viaje./$_{10}$ Escribe pronto.

Tu amigo,

Examination June 1996

Comprehensive Examination in Spanish

PART 1

Your performance on Part 1, Speaking (24 credits), has been evaluated prior to the date of this written examination.

PART 2

Answer all questions in Part 2 according to the directions for *a* and *b*. [30]

a Directions (1–9): For each question, you will hear some background information in English once. Then you will hear a passage in Spanish *twice* and a question in English *once*. After you have heard the question, the teacher will pause while you read the question and the four suggested answers. Choose the best suggested answer and write its *number* in the space provided. Base your answer *on the content of the passage, only.* The passages that the teacher will read aloud to you are found in the ANSWERS section, Part 2, at the end of this examination. [18]

1 What is this telephone designed to do?

1 change the tone of a person's voice
2 distinguish between the truth and a lie
3 provide a visual image in addition to sound
4 answer messages and act as a fax machine 1____

2 What do these students need?

1 summer jobs
2 a place to stay
3 a new high school
4 money for a summer camp 2____

3 What must be done in order to receive a special rate?

1 rent the car for a minimum of three days
2 rent the car in a specific city
3 return the car to the same location
4 return the car with a full tank of gas 3____

4 What is this helpful suggestion about?

1 planting a garden
2 selecting the best plants for your home
3 fertilizing flowers and plants
4 caring for plants while on vacation 4____

5 What is the problem?

1 There are only single seats left.
2 The seats have obstructed views of the stage.
3 Friday's performance is sold out.
4 The available seats are in the rear of the theater. 5____

6 What is the purpose of this announcement?

1 to notify customers about a raffle
2 to notify customers that a car is blocking the store's entrance
3 to notify customers about a special sale
4 to notify customers that someone's keys have been found 6____

7 What was reported on the news?

1 There is very little interest in speaking Spanish in Japan and Brazil.
2 There are 3 million people in the United States who speak Spanish.
3 The second most popular language in Europe is Spanish.
4 The number of Americans learning Spanish is increasing. 7___

8 What should you do next?

1 pay the extra fare
2 get a schedule
3 board the bus
4 wait for the next train 8___

9 According to this message, what does Iberia Airlines offer its passengers?

1 a Frequent Flyer Club
2 new youth and senior citizen fares
3 new air routes to the United States
4 a lower rate for travel in Europe 9___

b Directions (10–15): For each question, you will hear some background information in English *once*. Then you will hear a passage in Spanish *twice* and a question in Spanish *once*. After you have heard the question, the teacher will pause while you read the question and the four suggested answers. Choose the best suggested answer and write its *number* in the space provided. Base your answer *on the content of the passage, only*. The passages that the teacher will read aloud to you are found in the ANSWERS section, Part 2, at the end of this examination. [12]

10 ¿Cómo podrías contestar a tu amigo?

1 Lo siento. Espero que se mejore pronto.
2 ¡Pero es una película estupenda!
3 Está bien. Nos encontramos a las ocho.
4 Sí, voy ahora. Mi madre me espera. 10___

11 ¿Qué dice el guía sobre el arte de Frida?

1 que representa un paisaje mexicano
2 que se usa en comerciales para televisión
3 que se vende por mucho dinero
4 que unas obras desaparecieron del museo 11___

12 ¿Por qué presentaron este concierto Roberto Carlos y Julio Iglesias?

1 para inaugurar el Estadio Olímpico de Caracas
2 para dar dinero a los niños necesitados de Caracas
3 para tener la oportunidad de estar en la televisión juntos
4 para presentar el talento de unos niños de Caracas 12___

13 ¿Qué pasó con Juan Gabriel?

1 Volvió a cantar después de muchos años.
2 Escribió su autobiografía.
3 Hizo una gira musical en México.
4 Compró una compañía de discos. 13___

14 ¿Qué se estableció con esta nueva ley?

1 un nuevo partido político en Puerto Rico
2 una estampilla conmemorativa puertorriqueña
3 la lengua oficial de Puerto Rico
4 la fecha para las próximas elecciones 14___

15 ¿Qué problema tiene esta turista?

1 El empleado estaba ocupado.
2 El empleado estaba de mal humor.
3 La turista recibió la información incorrecta.
4 La turista recibió menos dinero del que esperaba. 15___

PART 3

Answer all questions in Part 3 according to the directions for *a*, *b*, and *c*. [30 credits]

a Directions (16–20): After the following passage, there are five questions or incomplete statements. For *each*, choose the word or expression that best answers the question or completes the statement *according to the meaning of the passage*, and write its *number* in the space provided. [10]

Bebeto a la Gloria

Su nombre completo es José Roberto Gama de Oliveira, pero para los aficionados del fútbol es simplemente "Be-be-to" — tres sílabas que se han convertido en el nuevo coro del público gallego. Es un hombre brasileño que cruzó el Océano Atlántico, con rumbo a España para perfeccionar su juego en el viejo mundo. Y fue en el Club Deportivo de La Coruña, en Galicia al norte de España, donde su talento y determinación lo convirtieron en una estrella del fútbol.

Lo más singular de este jugador de 29 años es su aspecto frágil y su rostro tan joven. Tiene dimensiones físicas más pequeñas de las de un típico jugador de fútbol — mide solo 5' 10" y pesa apenas 145 libras. Aunque parece débil, se ha convertido en el hombre fuerte del campeonato español capaz de meter 17 goles en las 17 primeras jornadas. Bebeto juega ritmo de samba, con una técnica sin igual, y puede desnivelar cualquier partido con sólo dos o tres toques del balón. Los españoles lo llaman el "matador con cara de ángel". Cada vez que le preguntan si su aspecto físico es un obstáculo, Bebeto replica "El fútbol se juega con cabeza, con inteligencia, y con velocidad". Es evidente que para Bebeto el éxito de un futbolista se debe a una combinación de factores.

Bebeto siempre ha jugado de una manera excepcional. Come ejemplo de esto son las victorias frente al Barcelona (3-2) y el Real Madrid (1-0), dos partidos en los cuales Bebeto marcó el gol decisivo. La mayor contribución de Bebeto es que, ha transformado a un Club Deportivo que tenía una larga y humilde tradición en un club que ahora ocupa las primeras filas del fútbol europeo.

En este momento, debido a su talento extraordinario, el gran jugador está ganando más de 10 millones de dólares. La Coruña le paga esta suma inmensa porque Bebeto ha contribuido tanto a su Club Deportivo.

Bebeto, uno de los ocho hijos de una modesta familia de San Salvador de Bahía, comenzó muy joven en el profesionalismo y las expectativas siempre fueron que llegará a ser otro Pelé u otro Zico. Ninguno de los entrenadores en los clubes deportivos del Brasil, el *Flamengo o* el *Vasco de Gama*, estuvo contento con la manera de ser de Bebeto: un matador con cara de ángel. "Era muy tranquilo, muy callado, muy introvertido", dice Carlos Alberto Perreira, director técnico de la selección nacional brasileña. "Por eso tuvo problemas con el público. La gente lo ha entendido mal. Bebeto es un hombre de mucha determinación y en el campo él es muy rápido, es un asesino, es un matador. Hay partidos en que toca la pelota sólo en dos ocasiones, pero ambas resultan en goles. Nunca falla. Para un jugador de fútbol no existe nada más importante".

16

E N B R E V E

Nombre: José Roberto Gama de Oliveira
Fecha de nacimiento: 2 de febrero de 1964 en San Salvador (Bahía)
Dimensiones: 5' 10" y 145 libras
Ciudad de residencia: Río de Janeiro
Partidos internacionales: 59 con 22 goles
Honores: Copa Libertadores, 1989; Jugador del año de Suramérica, 1989
Carrera profesional: Comenzó cuando apenas tenía 17 años, con el Vitoria de Bahía. En 1983, con 19 años, el poderoso Flamengo de Río de Janeiro lo compró por $500,000. En 1989 pasó al Vasco de Gama. En 1992 se une a la gran inmigración europea de las estrellas brasileñas y firma con el Deportivo de La Coruña de la Primera División española. Fue el máximo goleador de la liga en dos ocasiones con Flamengo y en otra con el Vasco de Gama.
Vida personal: Es tranquilo y casero. Proviene de una familia grande y tiene seis hermanos. Es casado y tiene dos hijos.

¿Por qué son el talento y la técnica de Bebeto sorprendentes?

1 El es demasiado viejo para ser jugador de fútbol.
2 El no tiene el físico asociado con un jugador de fútbol.
3 El sufrió un accidente en el Mundial de 1990.
4 El tiene poca experiencia profesional. 16___

17 Según Bebeto, lo necesario para jugar fútbol es

1 la capacidad mental y física
2 el ritmo desarrollado con lecciones de baile
3 la habilidad de los entrenadores
4 el soporte del público cuando gana 17___

18 ¿Por qué es apreciado Bebeto en Galicia?

1 Ha ofrecido la mayor parte de su sueldo a los desafortunados.
2 Ha inspirado el estudio de la lengua española.
3 Ha aumentado la fama del Club Deportivo de La Coruña.
4 Ha enseñado el fútbol a los jóvenes gallegos. 18___

19 ¿Cuál era la preocupación de uno de los entrenadores en el Brasil?

1 que Bebeto provenía de una familia modesta
2 que Bebeto no quería al público
3 que Bebeto no quería jugar con Pelé y Zico
4 que Bebeto era muy tímido 19___

20 ¿Qué ilustra la carrera de Bebeto?

1 que el talento no es siempre reconocido inmediatamente
2 que es difícil trabajar en otros países
3 que es mejor sobresalir en dos deportes
4 que la familia no es olvidada nunca 20___

b Directions (21–25): Below each of the following selections, there is either a question or an incomplete statement. For *each*, choose the word or expression that best answers the question or completes the statement *according to the meaning of the selection*, and write its *number* in the space provided. [10]

21

What does the letter writer want Snoopy to do?

1 contribute a story
2 return the magazine
3 stop submitting material
4 send money 21____

22

La lengua española

¿Ya lo oyó decir? La "ch" y la "ll" no viven más con existencia propia... Ahora están supeditadas a la "c" y a la "l". Hasta el presente, y principalmente en Latinoamérica, los diccionarios, ficheros, etc., catalogaban la "ch" y la "ll" como dos letras adicionales dentro del alfabeto. Pero como todo cambia, los pobres "llantos", "llamas", "llagas" y demás palabras que empiezan con "ll", habrá que buscarlas ahora dentro de la sección de la "l". Por otra parte, los "chinos", "chivos", "churros" y "charcos", pertenecen ahora a la letra "c". Esta nueva norma la determinó hace poco la Asociación de Academias de la Lengua Española, organismo que rige el buen uso del idioma. Por supuesto, el dictamen no es retroactivo. Es decir, que podemos seguir usando los viejos diccionarios, enciclopedias y glosarios, sin temor a ganarnos un regaño de los académicos.

What will occur in future dictionaries of the Spanish language?

1 The Academy of the Spanish Language will write a preface.
2 Several words will be omitted.
3 Two letters will be eliminated from the alphabet.
4 More meanings of words will be included. 22____

23

El Instituto Cervantes lamenta comunicar a sus amigos que el cantautor PACO IBAÑEZ sufre una lesión de las cuerdas vocales que le imposibilita estar con nosotros el miércoles 27 de abril, según se había anunciado en algunos boletines informativos. Esperamos que se recupere y podamos contar con su presencia en un futuro próximo.

Why will Paco Ibáñez be unable to appear?

1 He has another engagement.
2 He has a health problem.
3 He has canceled his performance as a protest.
4 He has agreed to support a strike against the Institute

23____

24

ChachAlaca

Ya está a la venta

INVITACION A CHACHALAQUEAR

Si te gustan los juegos, las aventuras y los animales... Si te encanta conocer nuevos cuates, hacer experimentos, enterarte de cómo viven otros niños y descubrir nuevos lugares... En fin, si te gusta ¡divertirte! Déjame que te invite a conocer una revista diferente:

ChaChAlaca

Sale el 15 de febrero y se vende en puestos de periódico y en casi todos los supermercados.
Ah, se me olvidaba presentarme, soy Chachalaca y quiero ser tu amiga.
Ésta es nuestra revista; sí, tuya y mía.
Si me escribes, podrás ver tus cuentos y dibujos publicados, también tus cartas, y sobre todo sabrás que aquí tu opinión cuenta.

P.D. Te pongo mis datos para que me conozcas:
Apariencia: Agradable
Carácter: Entre tímido y chachalaquero
Especie preferida: Niños
Comida favorita: Chilaquiles
Miedos: La mayor parte de los adultos, las jaulas y los sombreros con plumas.

Si quieres escríbeme a:
ChaChAlaca
EDITORIAL JILGUERO, S.A. DE C.V.:
Monte Pelvoux 110-planta jardín. México, D.F. 11000
Tels. 202 65 85 / 259 06 89 y 259 08 14 FAX: 540 17 71

What does Chachalaca invite readers to do?

1 buy a videotape of the characters from the magazine
2 enter a contest sponsored by the magazine
3 place an advertisement in the magazine
4 contribute original material to the magazine 24____

25

Tiene un fin de semana maravilloso
para viajar.
Conduzca estos días con cuidado,
a la ida y a la vuelta, y piense que
en la carretera, como en la vida,
sólo hay un sentido obligatorio:
su sentido común.
Cuando llegue la hora de partir,
siga nuestro consejo.

En los largos desplazamientos:

- Revise los puntos vitales de su vehículo.
- Abróchese siempre el cinturón.
- Respete los límites de velocidad.
- Mantenga la distancia de seguridad.
- No adelante sin visibilidad.
- Al mínimo síntoma de cansancio, no conduzca.
- Póngase el casco si viaja en moto o ciclomotor.
- **Siga estos consejos también en los trayectos cortos.**

LA VIDA ES EL VIAJE MAS HERMOSO

This announcement provides information about

1 driving safety
2 tourist attractions
3 activities to do during vacation
4 applying for a driver's license 25___

c *Directions* (26–30): In the following passage, there are five blank spaces numbered 26 through 30. Each blank space represents a missing word or expression. For each blank space, four possible completions are provided. Only one of them makes sense *in the context of the passage*.

First, read the passage in its entirety to determine its general meaning. Then read it a second time. For each blank space, choose the completion that makes the best sense and write its *number* in the space provided. [10]

Cartas al Director del Periódico ABC Bicicletas

Señor director: Quiero hacerle una pregunta muy importante que me molesta. La bicicleta está de moda por todas partes de Europa pero aquí en Sevilla la gente, en general, no monta en bicicleta. ¿Por qué la gente no monta en bici?

En los países europeos más desarrollados, la bici se utiliza como un medio de transporte sencillo y muy útil. Los usuarios son personas de todas las edades y estatus social y con objetivos más ___(26)___ : para ir a la Universidad, a la fábrica, a la oficina, de compras, a las casas de amigos, en fin, para todo. Y lo bueno es que la persona montando en bicicleta puede viajar a su propia velocidad, despacio o con mucha prisa.

En Sevilla, la imagen estereotipada del ciclista es la de un joven atlético-deportista o la de un desgraciado "hippy" que no tiene ___(27)___ para comprarse un coche. Si una persona utiliza la bici para ir a la oficina, lo primero que se piensa es en un pobre hombre, muerto de hambre, que no puede comprar nada.

Hay muchas ventajas de montar en bici. En nuestros tiempos de crisis económica cuando todo cuesta más, sería una buena manera de ahorrar gasolina y ayudar a eliminar la contaminación. También para perder peso y ponerse en muy buena condición, este tipo de ___(28)___ sería excelente. La buena salud siempre es algo en que piensan las personas. Es ideal para ___(29)___ los problemas de aparcamiento (el mismo espacio que ocupa un coche es el que ocupan doce bicicletas). También es ideal para aprovecharse del aire fresco con el clima agradable de Sevilla.

Con todos estos ___(30)___ que ofrece la bicicleta, la gente de nuestra bella ciudad de Sevilla debe considerar este medio de transporte. ¿Qué más se puede pedir?

Si la gente tiene el interés de ser ciclistas, el gobierno debe construir los caminos "carril-bici" y entonces ambos, los automovilistas y los ciclistas podrán viajar con seguridad.

(26)	1 complicados	3 variados	
	2 chistosos	4 aburridos	26___
(27)	1 interés	3 deseos	
	2 dinero	4 tiempo	27___
(28)	1 escuela	3 servicio	
	2 trabajo	4 ejercicio	28___
(29)	1 resolver	3 saber	
	2 entender	4 encontrar	29___
(30)	1 gastos	3 consejos	
	2 beneficios	4 colores	30___

PART 4

Write your answers to Part 4 according to the directions for *a* and *b*. [16]

a Directions: Write **one** well-organized note in Spanish as directed below. [6]

Choose **either** question 31 **or** 32. Write a well-organized note, following the specific instructions given in the question you have chosen. Your note must consist of **at least six clauses.** To qualify for credit, a clause must contain a verb, a stated or implied subject, and additional words necessary to convey meaning. The six clauses may be contained in fewer than six sentences if some of the sentences have more than one clause.

31 Your Spanish Club is trying to decide what to do with some extra money that it has at the end of the year. Write a note in Spanish to your club advisor suggesting what to do with that extra money.

In the note, you may wish to mention how much money you want to spend as well as ways to spend the money (such as to buy books, take the club to a restaurant, offer a scholarship, donate to a charity, have a club party, or go on a trip). You may also wish to ask for the advisor's opinion of your suggestions. **Be sure you accomplish the purpose of the note, which is *to suggest what to do with your club's extra money*.**

Use the following:

Salutation: Estimado (Estimada) __________,
Closing: Su estudiante, [your name]

The salutation and closing will *not* be counted as part of the six required clauses.

32 You attended a performance in which your friend Juan took part. Write a note in Spanish to Juan expressing your opinion about the performance.

In the note, you may wish to mention where and when you saw the performance, who went with you, and what your reaction to the performance was. You may also wish to mention what the other people thought about the performance. **Be sure you accomplish the purpose of the note, which is *to express your opinion about the performance*.**

Use the following:

Salutation: Querido Juan,
Closing: Un abrazo, [your name]

The salutation and closing will *not* be counted as part of the six required clauses.

b Directions: Write **one** well-organized composition in Spanish as directed below. [10]

Choose **either** question 33 **or** 34. Write a well-organized composition, following the specific instructions given in the question you have chosen. Your composition must consist of **at least 10 clauses**. To qualify for credit, a clause must contain a verb, a stated or implied subject, and additional words necessary to convey meaning. The 10 clauses may be contained in fewer than 10 sentences if some of the sentences have more than one clause.

33 In Spanish, write a story about the situation shown in the picture below. It must be a story relating to the picture, **not** a description of the picture. Do *not* write a dialogue.

34 You received a letter from your Spanish pen pal, who has told you about his or her plans for a future career. Your pen pal has asked you to respond by telling him or her about your plans for a future career. In Spanish, write a letter to your pen pal telling him or her about your career plans.

You must accomplish the purpose of the letter, which is *to tell your pen pal about your career plans.*

In your letter, you may wish to express your appreciation for your pen pal's last letter and explain why you are writing. In addition to telling your pen pal what plans you have in mind, you may wish to mention why you chose this career, who influenced you, and where you would like to work. You may also wish to discuss your feelings about this type of work and mention people you know who are already working in this field.

You may use any or all of the ideas suggested above or you may use your own ideas. **Either way, you must tell your pen pal about your career plans.**

Use the following:

Dateline: 18 de junio de 1996
Salutation: Querido (Querida) ________,
Closing: Abrazos,

The dateline, salutation, and closing will *not* be counted as part of the 10 required clauses.

Answers June 1996

Comprehensive Examination in Spanish

PART 1

This part of the examination was evaluated prior to the date of this written examination. [24 credits]

PART 2

The following passages are to be read aloud to the students according to the directions given for this part at the beginning of this examination. The correct answers are given after number 15. [30 credits]

1. You are listening to a guest speaker talk about a particular type of telephone. The speaker says:

    Se ha puesto a la venta un teléfono que sirve también como detector de mentiras. El aparato se llama "teléfono de la verdad". Según sus defensores, el teléfono detecta en la voz las verdades y las mentiras que se digan. Pero sus detractores no lo creen posible en absoluto. A pesar de esta controversia, este tele-verdad está teniendo éxito en las tiendas grandes de Nueva York.

    What is this telephone designed to do?

2. You are listening to the radio and hear this announcement:

Unos estudiantes de intercambio necesitan hogares donde quedarse en agosto. Ellos son de la escuela secundaria de diferentes países de Europa y América Latina. Si usted desea ofrecer su casa a uno de estos jóvenes, llame a nuestra oficina al teléfono 347-7575.

What do these students need?

3. You and your host family are at a car rental agency. You overhear the clerk giving your host parents the following information:

Este mes tenemos precios especiales. Estos precios son válidos para alquileres que se produzcan en cualquier lugar de España. Es necesario devolver el coche al punto de origen. Pero, si quiere devolverlo en un sitio diferente al de origen, tiene que pagar más.

What must be done in order to receive a special rate?

4. While shopping for souvenirs in Quito, Ecuador, you overhear this conversation:

Mañana me voy de viaje por unos días, y tengo el problema de siempre: el cuidado de las plantas. No me gusta contar con el vecino para cuidarlas en mi ausencia. Acabo de oír de una idea muy buena que voy a probar. Se sabe que la lana es muy absorbente. Voy a poner un recipiente grande lleno de agua en el medio del suelo. Entonces voy a poner un extremo de una cuerda de lana del recipiente a cada una de mis plantas. De esta manera no tendré que preocuparme de atender las plantas, y así estarán bien regadas.

What is this helpful suggestion about?

5. You and some friends are at the box office of a theater in Buenos Aires to purchase tickets to a play. The box office cashier tells you:

Sí, quedan boletos para la función del viernes por la noche. Lo único es que ninguno de los lugares que quedan están juntos. Están en el centro del teatro pero en filas diferentes. Usted y sus compañeros tendrán que sentarse separados si quieren asistir a esa función. Todos los boletos cuestan igual.

What is the problem?

6. You are shopping in Almacenes Rodríguez, a large store in Puerto Rico. You hear this announcement:

¡Atención clientes! Queremos recordarles que todavía hay tiempo para llenar el cupón y participar en nuestra rifa que conmemora el quinto aniversario de esta tienda. El gran premio es un carro de último modelo que está estacionado a la entrada principal. También hay otros premios de gran valor. Pidan su cupón a un dependiente para tener la oportunidad de llevarse las llaves del carro. Les deseamos buena suerte a todos.

What is the purpose of this announcement?

7. You are listening to the radio and hear this news item:

Según las cifras, en este momento hay trescientos millones de hispanohablantes en el mundo y este número está subiendo. "En los Estados Unidos hay mucho interés por aprender español", afirmó el director del Instituto Cervantes en Madrid. El número de estudiantes aprendiendo esta lengua en los Estados Unidos creció un setenta por ciento en los últimos cinco años. Además de los Estados Unidos, hay un fuerte aumento de interés en aprender el español en el Japón y el Brasil. Sin embargo, en los países de Europa, el español queda en cuarto lugar después del inglés, francés, y alemán.

What was reported on the news?

8. You are in the metro station in Mexico City and hear this announcement over the loudspeaker:

Señores y señoras, sentimos informarles que a causa de un accidente en las vías, el servicio será interrumpido en esta estación por unas dos horas. Al salir de la estación recibirán un pase que les permitirá transbordar un autobús hasta la próxima parada donde podrán abordar el metro de nuevo en la misma línea. Sentimos este pequeño inconveniente.

What should you do next?

9. You are in Barcelona and call Iberia Airlines for travel information. You hear this recording:

Iberia les ofrece tarifas especiales para aquellos jóvenes y mayores que deseen viajar al continente americano. Los menores de 26 años y los mayores de 60 años pueden viajar desde España a quince destinos diferentes en América a precios excepcionales. Por ejemplo, un billete de ida y vuelta a Nueva York cuesta 48.000 pesetas. Los billetes tienen una validez máxima de tres meses.

According to this message, what does Iberia Airlines offer its passengers?

10. Your friend Luis calls you on the telephone. You answer and he says:

¡Oye Raúl! Lo siento mucho, pero me resulta imposible asistir a la fiesta esta noche. El problema es que anoche mi hermanito se enfermó. No es cosa grave, pero mi mamá no quiere dejarlo solito, y ella había aceptado una invitación para cenar. Esta noche seré el niñero de Juanito y no tendré más remedio que quedarme en casa.

¿Cómo podrías contestar a tu amigo?

11. You are on a tour of an art museum. The tour guide says:

Durante la década pasada, la mexicana Frida Kahlo se fue convirtiendo en un fenómeno internacional. En 1990 una de sus obras fue la primera pieza de arte latinoamericano vendida por más de un millón de dólares. Los autorretratos de Kahlo aparecen en las publicaciones y en los lugares más raros del mundo. Hoy se habla de *Frida* con la misma familiaridad con que se habla de otros grandes artistas.

¿Qué dice el guía sobre el arte de Frida?

12. You are in Caracas, Venezuela, watching the news on television. The announcer reads this cultural news item:

Ayer, en el Estadio Olímpico de Caracas, los famosos cantantes Roberto Carlos y Julio Iglesias presentaron un recital conjunto que fue trasmitido para todos los países de América latina. Las ganancias del espectáculo fueron donadas a instituciones de caridad dedicadas a ayudar a los niños pobres de Caracas. El recital fue un gran éxito. Los dos artistas prometieron realizar otro recital a fines de este año con el mismo propósito, para dar ayuda financiera a los niños desafortunados de esta ciudad.

¿Por qué presentaron este concierto Roberto Carlos y Julio Iglesias?

13. You are listening to the radio and hear this broadcast:

Después de ocho años de ausencia, volvió al mundo de los discos el famoso cantante y compositor Juan Gabriel. Tras una serie de negociaciones, la compañía Ariola firmó un contrato con el conocido artista mexicano, autor de canciones como "Querida" y "Amor eterno". Igualmente, la empresa *Show Time* acaba de firmar un contrato para representar a este intérprete de la música popular. El público de Juan Gabriel está muy alegre con el regreso de su voz a la canción mexicana.

¿Qué pasó con Juan Gabriel?

14. While you are watching a television newscast, you hear this announcement:

El gobernador de Puerto Rico y presidente del Partido Popular Democrático, estampó su firma al pie de la ley de la Cámara de Representantes puertorriqueña. En ésta se establece que el idioma español será, de aquí en adelante, el idioma oficial del país.

¿Qué se estableció con esta nueva ley?

15. You are standing in a line at a bank in Spain. A visiting student is changing American dollars for Spanish pesetas. You hear the bank teller say to her:

Señorita, el problema es que usted me dio sólo 50 dólares americanos y se los devolví en pesetas. Como el cartel indica, el cambio de hoy en pesetas es menos del que usted anticipaba. Yo le dí la suma correcta. Lo siento, señorita, le aseguro que no hay error.

¿Qué problema tiene esta turista?

PART 2

(1) 2
(2) 2
(3) 3
(4) 4
(5) 1
(6) 1
(7) 4
(8) 3
(9) 2
(10) 1
(11) 3
(12) 2
(13) 1
(14) 3
(15) 4

PART 3

(a) **(16)** 2
(17) 1
(18) 3
(19) 4
(20) 1

(b) **(21)** 3
(22) 3
(23) 2
(24) 4
(25) 1

(c) **(26)** 3
(27) 2
(28) 4
(29) 1
(30) 2

PART 4

(a) Notes in writing

For each note, an example of a response worth six credits follows. The slash marks indicate how each sample note has been divided into clauses.

31. Estimada Sra. Fernández:

Le escribo esta nota/$_1$ para sugerirle/$_2$ cómo podemos gastar el dinero extra de nuestro club de español./$_3$ Nos gustaría usar una parte en una fiesta/$_4$ y otra parte comprando libros para la biblioteca./$_5$ ¿Tiene Ud. otra idea?/$_6$ Dedicaremos la próxima reunión a este asunto.

Su estudiante,

32. Querido Juan,

El sábado pasado mi prima y yo asistimos al programa de variedades/$_1$ en el cual participaste tú./$_2$ ¡El programa fue estupendo!/$_3$ Tu participación ayudó mucho al éxito de la función./$_4$ Como siempre, cantaste a las mil maravillas./$_5$ Oímos muchos comentarios favorables./$_6$ ¡Felicitaciones!

Un abrazo,

(b) Narrative based on picture/letter

For each narrative/letter, an example of a response worth 10 credits follows. The slash marks indicate how each sample narrative/letter has been divided into clauses.

33. (Picture)

Miguel acaba de entregarle a la profesora su tarea./$_1$ Pero no es la de anoche sino la de hace dos días./$_2$ La profesora está un poco enojada/$_3$ y quiere saber por qué/$_4$ no se dedica a sus estudios./$_5$ Miguel empieza a darle unas explicaciones./$_6$ Miguel no pone atención en la clase./$_7$ Ahora el probrecito tiene miedo de/$_8$ lo que vaya a pasar esta noche en casa./$_9$ Tendrá que pasar la noche estudiando./$_{10}$

34. (Letter)

18 de junio de 1996

Querida Isabel,

Tu carta me ha llegado hace una semana./$_1$ ¡Qué sorpresa! Las dos hemos decidido estudiar para doctora./$_2$ Por eso, te escribo en seguida./$_3$ Siempre he querido ser médico./$_4$ No es para ganar dinero./$_5$ Quiero hacer un papel muy importante en el mundo entero./$_6$ Pienso viajar a muchos países/$_7$ donde los habitantes necesiten ayuda./$_8$ Ojalá pasemos tiempo juntas/$_9$ discutiendo nuestros planes para el futuro./$_{10}$

Abrazos,
Lola

Examination January 1997

Comprehensive Examination in Spanish

PART 1

Your performance on Part 1, Speaking (24 credits), has been evaluated prior to the date of this written examination.

PART 2

Answer all questions in Part 2 according to the directions for *a* and *b*. [30]

a *Directions* (1–9): For each question, you will hear some background information in English once. Then you will hear a passage in Spanish *twice* and a question in English *once*. After you have heard the question, the teacher will pause while you read the question and the four suggested answers. Choose the best suggested answer and write its *number* in the space provided. Base your answer *on the content of the passage, only*. The passages that the teacher will read aloud to you are found in the ANSWERS section, Part 2, at the end of this examination. [18]

1 Who is encouraged to enter this contest?

1 poets
2 short story writers
3 amateur photographers
4 sculptors

1___

2 What is being offered in this announcement?

1 part-time summer employment
2 a vacation package promoted for the summer
3 adult education classes held at night
4 a school for high school students that emphasizes job training 2____

3 What did the tour guide announce?

1 The day's schedule may change.
2 The cathedral is closed today.
3 The evening program has been canceled.
4 There may not be enough room for everyone. 3____

4 What type of book is this?

1 a collection of science fiction stories
2 a study of fashion trends
3 a history of Spanish literature
4 a reference for proper writing 4____

5 What is the purpose of this exhibit?

1 to observe the birthday of Léon Gaumont
2 to recognize young artists
3 to honor the founders of a museum
4 to celebrate a century of filmmaking 5____

6 Who would be most interested in this establishment?

1 someone who needs to have repairs made to a car engine
2 someone who needs to rent a new or used car
3 someone who wants to buy the latest technology
4 someone who has a computer game that is not working properly 6____

7 Why is *Gaby's Club* so popular?

1 Children can win prizes.
2 Children can play the role of the teacher.
3 Children learn while they have fun.
4 Children can stay all day on Saturday. 7____

8 According to the message, what is your friend supposed to do?

1 return the key to her friend's parents
2 help a friend with some homework
3 join her parents at the restaurant
4 finish several chores before the end of the evening 8____

9 What did this person become?

1 the director of Hispanic Affairs
2 the co-owner of a baseball team
3 the assistant to the Governor of Colorado
4 the chief executive officer of an airline 9____

b Directions (10–15): For each question, you will hear some background information in English *once*. Then you will hear a passage in Spanish *twice* and a question in Spanish *once*. After you have heard the question, the teacher will pause while you read the question and the four suggested answers. Choose the best suggested answer and write its *number* in the space provided. Base your answer *on the content of the passage, only.* The passages that the teacher will read aloud to you are found in the ANSWERS section, Part 2, at the end of this examination. [12]

10 ¿Cuándo toca esta banda?

1 de lunes a viernes
2 solamente los sábados
3 cada noche de la semana
4 dos noches por semana 10____

11 Según la información, ¿cuándo se debe seguir estos consejos?

1 cuando sale con amigos
2 cuando solicita empleo
3 cuando asiste a la escuela
4 cuando va de compras 11____

12 ¿Qué puede hacer este aparato electrónico?

1 Puede hablar varios idiomas.
2 Puede comprender unas órdenes.
3 Puede limpiar la cocina.
4 Puede preparar comidas rápidas. 12____

13 ¿Quién es Concha García?

1 una bibliotecaria
2 una periodista
3 una cantante
4 una escritora 13____

14 Según este reportaje, ¿cómo pasa los ratos libres la mayoría de españoles?

1 mirando la televisión
2 disfrutando del teatro
3 charlando con los amigos
4 viajando por Europa 14____

15 ¿Qué se ofrece a los estudiantes?

1 una subscripción a un periódico español
2 una oportunidad de estudiar en el extranjero
3 un viaje a una isla tropical
4 un curso para aprender a usar computadoras 15____

PART 3

Answer all questions in Part 3 according to the directions for *a*, *b*, and *c*. [30 credits]

a Directions (16–20): After the following passage, there are five questions or incomplete statements. For *each*, choose the word or expression that best answers the question or completes the statement *according to the meaning of the passage*, and write its *number* in the space provided. [10]

Los Conciertos de Miguel Bosé

Después de muchísimo tiempo de no hacer presentaciones masivas en la Ciudad de México, Miguel Bosé se presentó durante tres noches en el Auditorio Nacional, ganando un triunfo absoluto según todos los diarios principales de la capital.

Gracias a su extraordinaria banda y al espectacular y sofisticado juego de luces que se montó para la ocasión, Bosé tuvo un espectáculo fantástico. Su actuación demostró que es uno de los artistas más completos y talentosos de habla hispana. En el escenario, Bosé es un ser sensual, gracioso, entusiasta, chistoso y dramático. Aunque es cierto que ya no baila como antes, sigue conservando bastante gracia en sus movimientos. Entre el público todo fue gritos y emoción. Cada vez que Bosé trataba de hablar, los piropos que echaban sus admiradores con un entusiasmo ruidoso se lo impedían. La atmósfera del concierto iba cambiando constantemente, dependiendo de las canciones. Se transformaba de lenta, romántica y oscura a un ambiente alegre y festivo en pocos minutos.

Su dominio sobre el público es impresionante. Vimos el mejor ejemplo de esto durante su interpretación de *Sol forastero*. Esta canción tan popular puso a 10.000 personas presentes a moverse como si estuvieran en una clase de aeróbicos. Esta reacción del público no sorprendió nada a su familia porque está acostumbrada a presenciar el gran entusiasmo de la gente.

Bosé cerró el concierto con *Amante bandido*, pero su público le pidió que no se fuera. Así lo hizo. Volvió al escenario para interpretar *Los chicos no lloran*. Se despidió otra vez, pero de nuevo regresó a los pocos minutos. Entonces solamente acompañado de su guitarrista, con quien interpretó versiones acústicas de sus primeros éxitos, cantó *Amiga, Mi libertad y Te amaré*. Para acabar este segmento, regresó con su banda al escenario y cantó una hermosísima versión de *Linda*. Se despidió por tercera vez, pero de nuevo su público le pidió que continuara cantando y, sorprendiendo a muchos, cumplió la petición. Finalmente cerró el concierto con *Sevilla*, la canción predilecta.

No hay muchos artistas que tienen su carisma. Esto es lo que lo hace único. Ya que tuvo tan gran éxito con este concierto, su público desea que Bosé continúe dando conciertos con más frecuencia. Sus admiradores siguen comprando sus álbumes y esperan los nuevos con anticipación.

16 Esta presentación de Miguel Bosé fue importante porque

1 se repitió en tres países
2 marcó su regreso al escenario mexicano
3 el auditorio quedó casi vacío
4 compartió el escenario con su familia 16___

17 ¿Por qué no podía Bosé hablarle al público?

1 Malfuncionaban los micrófonos durante el concierto.
2 Tenía prisa para terminar.
3 Le dolía la garganta.
4 Los gritos de sus aficionados eran demasiado fuertes. 17___

18 ¿Cómo fue el concierto?

1 Tuvo un tono político.
2 Fue solemne y triste.
3 Estuvo lleno de emoción.
4 Aburrió a muchos. 18___

19 ¿Qué característica sigue demostrando Miguel Bosé?

1 la habilidad de captar y conmover al público
2 su facilidad de recitar hechos históricos
3 su costumbre de vestirse exageradamente
4 la capacidad de tocar varios instrumentos 19___

20 ¿Qué les sorprendió a muchos que asistieron al concierto?

1 que Bosé tuvo un accidente
2 que se apagaron las luces
3 que fue muy breve el espectáculo
4 que Bosé volvió al escenario varias veces 20___

b Directions (21–25): Below each of the following selections, there is either a question or an incomplete statement. For *each*, choose the word or expression that best answers the question or completes the statement *according to the meaning of the selection*, and write its *number* in the space provided. [10]

21

CARTAS

Después de leer su revista por espacio de muchos años, mi fascinación por Centro y Sudamérica me lleva a sugerir que *Américas* inicie una nueva rama de actividades—excursiones guiadas a los numerosos lugares interesantes que ustedes fotografían y sobre los cuales escriben—y que la misma esté vinculada con museos de distintas partes del mundo. Muchas veces he deseado visitar los lugares descritos, pero como las agencias de excursiones generalmente se concentran en los lugares más conocidos, no me ha sido posible. ¿Les parece factible esta sugerencia?

Agradecemos sus comentarios, pero en estos momentos Américas *no cuenta con los recursos ni con el mandato para expandirse a otras actividades. El propósito de la revista no es necesariamente promover el turismo, sino ampliar la comprensión del público en general acerca de las diversas culturas de las Américas.*

Why did this person write to the magazine *Américas*?

1 to make a suggestion
2 to submit an article
3 to inquire about a museum
4 to get information about a subscription 21____

22

La Voz de la Escuela es un suplemento de La Voz de Galicia que se publica todos los miércoles del curso escolar, con el patrocinio del Banco Bilbao Vizcaya. El suplemento cumple dos funciones básicas: es, en primer lugar, un instrumento de trabajo para la escuela y un ejemplo de cómo organizar el aprendizaje partiendo de las noticias que publican diariamente los periódicos; en segundo lugar, sirve de soporte para informar sobre algunas estrategias diseñadas con el fin de animar a profesores y alumnos a utilizar regularmente el periódico en la escuela.

Cada semana, en colaboración con el BBV, La Voz de la Escuela invita a viajar a La Coruña a 49 escolares de centros públicos o privados de Galicia y a dos profesores y dos padres de alumnos del centro, con el fin de conocer el periódico, el Banco Bilbao Vizcaya y la Casa de las Ciencias.

Toda la correspondencia relacionada con el suplemento deberá dirigirse a la Escuela de Medios de Comunicación de La Voz de Galicia. c/ Concepción Arenal, 11 y 13. Teléfono 18 03 04. 15006 La Coruña.

Why is this supplement to *La Voz de Galicia* being offered?

1 to provide an opportunity for students to study in other countries
2 to encourage the use of the newspaper in the classroom
3 to focus on Galicia as a tourist attraction
4 to attract foreign students to Galicia

22____

23

LOS NIÑOS Y LAS COMPUTADORAS

A medida que las computadoras se generalizan y cuestan menos, surgen nuevos programas educacionales llenos de colorido, gráficos, voces, cantos y hasta de lecturas para los niños. Los padres y maestros de muchos alumnos preescolares, aseguran que sus hijos se encantan con los juegos instructivos de las computadoras. Kandie Demarest, dueña de un círculo infantil en Hayward, California, enseña a los chicos menores de tres años a leer mediante el uso de programas del alfabeto que traen dibujos animados y efectos de sonido. Jina Howell, de Seattle, inició a su hija en la computadora a los 14 meses y ahora, a los 19 meses, la chica sabe manejar y mover los muñecos y colores en la pantalla y reconoce las letras, divirtiéndose de lo lindo al mismo tiempo. "Hoy en día hay que saber usar las computadoras desde antes de los cuatro años", dice Donna Stoker, de Virginia. Su hijo Steven, de 4 años, tiene una en su hogar y otra en la escuela.

What does this article suggest about the use of computers?

1 Computers can be used to help diagnose the educational needs of teenagers.
2 Children should learn to use computers at an early age.
3 Better software and computer programs need to be developed for children.
4 Spending too much time at the computer can be harmful to children.

23____

24

La oficina

¡ Es muy fácil! Siguiendo estos sencillos consejos que, además, harán que su área de trabajo se vea más recogida y linda:

• Coloque los recipientes para el reciclaje de periódicos, cajas de cartón, botellas y latas, en un solo lugar.

• Para poner notas y otros anuncios importantes, ubique una pizarra en un lugar que todos vean, y no mande copias innecesarias de sus cartas a sus compañeros. De ese modo, no desperdiciará papel y, además, protegerá el medio ambiente.

• Si le mandan un paquete en una caja o sobre, vuélvalos a usar para otras cosas.

• Apague las computadoras, máquinas de escribir eléctricas y luces, cuando termine su trabajo.

• Compre los artículos para la oficina, al por mayor, pues si lo hace en pocas cantidades le saldrá más caro y, además, después tendrá muchas cajas que desechar.

• Ahorre energía no manteniendo encendidas luces innecesarias.

This article offers advice on

1 communicating quickly with many offices
2 hiring competent office help
3 renting office space at competitive rates
4 maintaining an environmentally efficient and clean office

24____

25

MUJERES ORIGINALES

Annie Smith Peck, quien fuera la primera mujer en ascender la cima del Matterhorn y del Monte Huascarán en el Perú, escandalizó a todo el mundo cuando en su primera expedición, en 1895, decidió usar tan sólo un par de "pantalones", en vez de las usuales faldas largas, que—por decencia—se llevaban. ¡Y la noticia de su "atrevimiento" fue ampliamente cubierta en la prensa! Y la inglesa Lady Hester Stanhope casi creó una crisis mundial cuando en 1810 se fue de Inglaterra a visitar Turquía . . . ¡y se vistió como un hombre turco, con enormes pantalones, una blusa abierta de seda y un turbante! Al llegar a los países musulmanes—donde las mujeres llevaban velos y la sociedad era muy cerrada—el "encanto" de Lady Stanhope era tal, que venció todos los obstáculos y terminó viviendo hasta su muerte en el Medio Oriente, en medio del desierto y rodeada de todo lo que le gustaba.

What did these women do?

1 They wrote newspaper articles about their travels.
2 They organized natural-disaster relief efforts.
3 They wore clothing that was different from what was acceptable.
4 They published children's stories that were popular in other countries. 25___

c *Directions* (26–30): In the following passage, there are five blank spaces numbered 26 through 30. Each blank space represents a missing word or expression. For each blank space, four possible completions are provided. Only one of them makes sense *in the context of the passage*.

First, read the passage in its entirety to determine its general meaning. Then read it a second time. For each blank space, choose the completion that makes the best sense and write its *number* in the space provided. [10]

Surf de Invierno

El *surf de nieve* es como una forma de esquiar pero se usa una tabla por la pista de nieve en vez de esquís. Esta actividad tiene gran aceptación en la mayoría de las estaciones de esquí en España. Hasta hace poco tiempo este deporte se conocía muy poco en España, pero su popularidad ha aumentado tanto que se puede ver practicado en muchas pistas de nieve.

En este ___(26)___ las diferentes condiciones de nieve están obligando a los fabricantes a crear distintos modelos y longitudes de tablas. Se construyen tablas diseñadas especialmente para varios propósitos. Hay tablas clásicas para usarse fuera de pista, y otras tablas de mayor rigidez que son especialmente ___(27)___ para nieves duras. También hay otras de diferentes modelos para las personas que quieren tomar esta actividad como diversión y no con objetivo de competencia.

La forma de bajar la pista sobre una tabla es en una postura lateral, semejante a los *surfistas* de agua, usando los brazos y el cuerpo para mantener el equilibrio; las piernas dirigen el movimiento. La simplicidad de esta técnica sorprende a todo el mundo. Se dice que los primeros descensos deben ser por suaves bajadas. Así se puede captar la forma de conducir. Hay que deslizar la tabla y encontrar la posición de equilibrio. Los que ___(28)___ deportes acuáticos podrán hacer *el surf de nieve* con mucha facilidad, ya que se usa la misma técnica en estos dos deportes. La mayor diferencia es que el uno se hace en la nieve y el otro en el ___(29)___.

Para aprender o perfeccionar el manejo de la tabla, se han organizado escuelas de esquí en España con profesores especializados en esta disciplina.

Para la persona que desee iniciarse al *surf de nieve* hay dos maneras de adquirir el equipo necesario: se puede alquilar una tabla en las tiendas que normalmente existen en las pistas, o recomendamos a aquellos que decidan ___(30)___ su propia tabla que vayan a tiendas especializadas en equipamiento para la nieve. Necesitarán aproximadamente entre 45.000 y 60.000 pesetas, dependiendo de los modelos y las marcas.

(26) 1 club 3 deporte
2 oficio 4 edificio 26___

(27) 1 lavadas 3 dañadas
2 construídas 4 corridas 27___

(28) 1 rechazan 3 apoyan
2 graban 4 practican 28___

(29) 1 aire 3 hielo
2 agua 4 campo 29___

(30) 1 comprar 3 lavar
2 prestar 4 compartir 30___

PART 4

Write your answers to Part 4 according to the directions for *a* and *b*. [16]

a *Directions*: Write **one** well-organized note in Spanish as directed below. [6]

Choose **either** question 31 **or** 32. Write a well-organized note, following the specific instructions given in the question you have chosen. Your note must consist of **at least six clauses.** To qualify for credit, a clause must contain a verb, a stated or implied subject, and additional words necessary to convey meaning. The six clauses may be contained in fewer than six sentences if some of the sentences have more than one clause.

31 You have been given a class assignment that involves doing a project with another student. You would prefer to work on the project with a certain classmate. Write a note in Spanish to that classmate, asking that he or she work with you on the assignment.

In the note, you may wish to explain the purpose of the note and suggest a topic for the class project. You may want to explain why you want him or her to work with you and how you could help each other. **Be sure you accomplish the purpose of the note, which is *to ask a classmate to work with you on a class project*.**

Use the following:

Salutation: (First name of classmate)
Closing: Tu amigo,

The salutation and closing will *not* be counted as part of the six required clauses.

32 You just found out that your friend received the highest grade on an important test. Write a note in Spanish to your friend expressing your congratulations on receiving the highest grade.

In the note, you may wish to mention how you found out that he or she received the highest grade, in addition to expressing your congratulations. You may also wish to identify the test and express how you feel about your friend's accomplishment. **Be sure you accomplish the purpose of the note, which is *to express your congratulations on receiving the highest grade.***

Use the following:

Salutation: Querido/Querida (Name)
Closing: (Your first name)

The salutation and closing will *not* be counted as part of the six required clauses.

b Directions: Write **one** well-organized composition in Spanish as directed below. [10]

Choose **either** question 33 **or** 34. Write a well-organized composition, following the specific instructions given in the question you have chosen. Your composition must consist of **at least 10 clauses**. To qualify for credit, a clause must contain a verb, a stated or implied subject, and additional words necessary to convey meaning. The 10 clauses may be contained in fewer than 10 sentences if some of the sentences have more than one clause.

33 In Spanish, write a story about the situation shown in the picture below. It must be a story relating to the picture, **not** a description of the picture. Do *not* write a dialogue.

34 Your pen pal has just told you about his or her favorite holiday. In Spanish, write a letter to your pen pal telling him or her about one of your favorite holidays.

You must accomplish the purpose of the letter, which is *to tell your pen pal about one of your favorite holidays.*

In your letter, you may wish to mention the name of the holiday, the date when it usually falls, the purpose of the holiday, why you like it, how people celebrate it, what the weather is usually like that time of year, and whether you or those you know travel on or around that holiday. You may also wish to ask your pen pal if he or she also celebrates this holiday.

You may use any or all of the ideas suggested above *or* you may use your own ideas. **Either way, you must tell your pen pal about one of your favorite holidays**.

Use the following:

Dateline: el 29 de enero de 1997
Salutation: Querido(a)__________,
Closing: Con carino,

The dateline, salutation, and closing will *not* be counted as part of the 10 required clauses.

Answers January 1997

Comprehensive Examination in Spanish

PART 1

This part of the examination was evaluated prior to the date of this written examination. [24 credits]

PART 2

The following passages are to be read aloud to the students according to the directions given for this part at the beginning of this examination. The correct answers are given after number 15. [30 credits]

1. Your friend has just received a Spanish magazine and is calling to tell you about something she thinks will interest you. She says:

Si te gusta la fotografía creativa puedes participar en este concurso enviando tus mejores fotos a la redacción de esta revista en Valladolid. Las imágenes ganadoras serán publicadas y el premio será 3.000 pesetas. Las originales no serán devueltas en ningún caso.

Who is encouraged to enter this contest?

2. You are in Spain. You are watching television and hear this announcement:

Ofrecemos un programa de empleo de verano para jóvenes que les ayudará a aprovechar su verano, ganando experiencia y dinero. Se trata de un programa de empleo parcial de siete semanas de duración para jóvenes de 14 a 21 años de edad, que comienza el cinco de julio.

What is being offered in this announcement?

3. You are on a tour in Madrid with a student group. The tour guide is explaining the events planned for today and says:

Van a hacer una excursión en autocar a Toledo al mediodía con guía. Visitarán la Catedral, Casa Museo de El Greco, la Sinagoga, y la Iglesia de Santo Tomé. A veces, debido a razones ajenas a nuestra voluntad, existe la necesidad de modificar el plan de visitas en Toledo. Si hay cambios en el programa los anunciaremos.

What did the tour guide announce?

4. You are in a classroom in Madrid and hear the teacher make this recommendation:

Este es un libro con todas las fórmulas y todos los secretos para no cometer errores al escribir. Por tres años un equipo de académicos e intelectuales universitarios y periodistas ha trabajado para hacer el mejor "Libro de estilo" del periodismo en lengua española, con un solo objetivo: la perfección del periodismo escrito. Es una referencia útil y clara para todas las personas preocupadas por el idioma.

What type of book is this?

5. You are listening to the radio and hear an announcer say:

Para celebrar los cien años de la cinematografía, el Museo de Arte Moderno de Nueva York inaugura la primera de varias exposiciones que rinden homenaje a un siglo de cine. Los creadores de las primeras compañías cinematográficas del mundo fueron Charles Pathé y Léon Gaumont.

En esta exhibición se podrán descubrir las películas que han marcado el siglo y todo tipo de género: desde las primeras cintas del cine mudo, hasta la evolución del cine sonoro, culminando con el color y las nuevas técnicas de sonido. La exposición viajará a 50 ciudades norteamericanas.

What is the purpose of this exhibit?

6. You are listening to the radio and hear this announcement:

¡Ahora en Chetumal! Se ofrece un servicio para darle la solución al problema del motor de su auto o camión. Tenemos servicio y mantenimiento con equipo computarizado. Usamos la más avanzada tecnología para todo tipo de motor. No competimos con precio, sino con calidad y servicio.

Who would be most interested in this establishment?

7. You are in Mexico and you hear this advertisement for a program for children:

Con dos horas llenas de diversión y aprendizaje, la "maestra" Gabriela Rivero capta la atención de los niños del país. Es que en su club, *el Club de Gaby*, aprenden, de manera divertida, pintura, escultura, música, cocina y ecología. El programa incluye un taller de arte, el personaje de la semana, una aventura ecológica, el noticiero, los sueños de los niños, la cocina de Gaby, juegos y cuentos. El programa es muy popular. Míralo los sábados de las 8:00 a las 10:00 en el Canal de las Estrellas.

Why is *Gaby's Club* so popular?

8. You are with your friend while she is listening to a message on her answering machine. The message says:

Tu padre y yo tuvimos que salir a una cena. Vamos a volver tarde. No nos esperes. Estaremos en el restaurante "Parrón". Andrea te llamó por teléfono y quiere que la llames. Por favor, lava los platos. Tu papá pide que busques la llave del garaje porque no puede encontrarla. Haz tus tareas y acuéstate temprano. Besitos, mamá.

According to the message, what is your friend supposed to do?

9. You are watching television and hear this introduction to an interview about to be broadcast:

Últimamente Linda Alvareda es una mujer ocupadísima. Hoy está en el aeropuerto de Dallas. Mañana estará en Nueva York. Y el lunes, estará de vuelta en Denver. Alvareda, que lleva años dirigiendo su propia empresa de construcción, aceptó una nueva posición el año pasado. Se hizo la primera mujer hispana copropietaria de un equipo de béisbol, los Rockies de Colorado. Alvareda siempre ha sido aficionada al béisbol. Fue una oportunidad sin igual cuando el gobernador de Colorado la invitó a comprar un porcentaje de los nuevos Rockies de Colorado. Ninguna mujer, y por cierto ninguna hispana, había recibido semejante invitación.

What did this person become?

10. You are listening to the radio and hear this advertisement about a travel promotion:

El Hotel y Club Boca Ratón anuncia un fin de semana inolvidable. Los viernes y sábados por la noche presentarán el melancólico sonido de la banda de León Kelner. Le ofrecemos un atractivo paquete turístico que incluye dos días y noches con desayuno y cena. Además incluimos lecciones de baile, demostraciones culinarias, golf y mucho más. Estas dos noches por sólo $135. Decídase y llámenos pronto al 1-800-327-0101.

¿Cuándo toca esta banda?

11. You are listening to the radio and hear this advice:

Para triunfar en las entrevistas de trabajo, siga estas recomendaciones. Llegue temprano. Vaya vestido de forma profesional. Péinese bien. Para dar una buena impresión, sea muy amable con todas las personas que usted encuentre en la oficina. Si se demoran en atenderle, espere y no diga que tiene prisa. Deje que sea el jefe quien hable, y responda usted directamente. Muestre confianza.

Según la información, ¿cuándo se debe seguir estos consejos?

12. You are listening to a guest speaker who is talking about a new invention. The speaker says:

La firma electrónica Toshiba del Japón ha creado un robot destinado a vender hamburguesas tras un mostrador. El robot está equipado con 49 palabras japonesas para entender órdenes como: "Déme dos hamburguesas". Pero ¡no hay motivo para alarmarse! El robot es hasta ahora sólo un prototipo. De momento, no es la función del robot de estar en la cocina. Las personas siguen cocinando.

¿Qué puede hacer este aparato electrónico?

13. You are in Buenos Aires and hear this announcement on the radio:

Queremos informarles que Concha García leerá algunos de sus poemas esta tarde en la Biblioteca Nacional. Presentará poemas de su último libro, *Ayer y calles*. También firmará ejemplares. Esta obra acaba de ser premiada con el premio *Jaime Gil de Biedma* de poesía. A causa de la celebración en honor a la ganadora, se venderán sus libros a un descuento de treinta por ciento.

¿Quién es Concha García?

14. You are in a Spanish culture class in Barcelona, Spain, and the teacher tells you about a recent survey. She says:

Los españoles usan su tiempo libre sobre todo viendo televisión o haciendo deporte. Casi no van al teatro, leen pocos diarios y su participación en asociaciones es de las más bajas en Europa. De cada cuatro españoles, tres comparten su tiempo libre con los familiares, y solo un 15% con los amigos, según el reciente informe del Centro Estudios del Cambio Social.

Según este reportaje, ¿cómo pasa los ratos libres la mayoría de españoles?

15. While you are visiting Mexico, you hear this announcement on the radio:

La Universidad de Madrid y el Diario ABC ofrecen cuatro becas para estudiantes mexicanos interesados en periodismo. Aquellas personas que estén interesadas, deben enviar el formulario oficial y una composición donde muestren sus habilidades para el periodismo. Cada beca incluye la matrícula, el viaje de ida y vuelta de México a Madrid, y los gastos de residencia durante los nueve meses que dura el curso. ¡Buena suerte!

¿Qué se ofrece a los estudiantes?

PART 2

(1) 3	**(4)** 4	**(7)** 3	**(10)** 4	**(13)** 4
(2) 1	**(5)** 4	**(8)** 4	**(11)** 2	**(14)** 1
(3) 1	**(6)** 1	**(9)** 2	**(12)** 2	**(15)** 2

PART 3

(a)	**(16)** 2	**(b)**	**(21)** 1	**(c)**	**(26)** 3
	(17) 4		**(22)** 2		**(27)** 2
	(18) 3		**(23)** 2		**(28)** 4
	(19) 1		**(24)** 4		**(29)** 2
	(20) 4		**(25)** 3		**(30)** 1

PART 4

(a) Notes in writing

For each note, an example of a response worth six credits follows. The slash marks indicate how each sample note has been divided into clauses.

31. Roberto,

¿Quieres trabajar conmigo en el proyecto de la clase de español?/$_1$ Podemos escribir sobre el país de España./$_2$ Después de la escuela, vamos a la biblioteca cerca de tu casa./$_3$ Tenemos dos semanas/$_4$ para terminar este trabajo./$_5$ Si quieres/$_6$ podemos usar la computadora de mis padres. Llámame a mi casa después de las tres.

Tu amigo,
Julio

32. Querida María,

Me dijeron/$_1$ que tú sacaste la nota más alta en el examen de matemáticas./$_2$ ¡Felicitaciones! Ese fue el examen más difícil del año./$_3$ No sé/$_4$ cómo pudiste hacer esos problemas./$_5$ Toda la clase quiere felicitarte./$_6$ y darte una fiesta de celebración.

(Your first name)

(b) Narrative based on picture/letter

For each narrative/letter, an example of a response worth 10 credits follows. The slash marks indicate how each sample narrative/letter has been divided into clauses.

33. (Picture)

Bob está muy ocupado./$_1$ Está escribiendo en la computadora./$_2$ La mamá de Bob espera/$_3$ porque tiene la cena preparada/$_4$ y quiere comer./$_5$ El padre de Bob quiere jugar al básquetbol/$_6$ y también espera con paciencia./$_7$ Lo interesante de todo es/$_8$ que Bob no hace su propio trabajo./$_9$ De momento está terminando un reportaje para su madre/$_{10}$ y más tarde tiene que ayudarle al padre con un problema estadístico. Pobre Bob, será muy tarde cuando él empiece su tarea.

34. (Letter)

el 29 de enero de 1997

Querido José,

Mi favorito día festivo es el 4 de julio./$_1$ Es el día de la independencia de los Estados Unidos./$_2$ Me gusta/$_3$ porque estamos de vacaciones./$_4$ No tengo clases./$_5$ Hace buen tiempo./$_6$ Muchas veces mi familia va de camping en las montañas/$_7$ y puedo nadar y tomar el sol./$_8$ ¿Cuándo es el día de independencia en tu país?/$_9$ ¿Cómo se celebra ese día allá?/$_{10}$ Escríbeme pronto y cuéntame de eso y otras cosas más.

Con cariño,

Examination June 1997

Comprehensive Examination in Spanish

PART 1

Your performance on Part 1, Speaking (24 credits), has been evaluated prior to the date of this written examination.

PART 2

Answer all questions in Part 2 according to the directions for *a* and *b*. [30]

a *Directions* (1–9): For each question, you will hear some background information in English once. Then you will hear a passage in Spanish *twice* and a question in English *once*. After you have heard the question, the teacher will pause while you read the question and the four suggested answers. Choose the best suggested answer and write its *number* in the space provided. Base your answer *on the content of the passage, only*. The passages that the teacher will read aloud to you are found in the ANSWERS section, Part 2, at the end of this examination. [18]

1 What problem did your friend have while in Spain?

1 The Spanish people were not friendly.
2 He did not have much fun.
3 It was difficult to find time to sleep.
4 He was not able to go out at night. 1____

2 According to the talk show host, how do many young people spend their free time?

1 They earn money working in stores.
2 They play a variety of sports.
3 They go to town and meet friends.
4 They read a variety of teen magazines. 2____

3 What does this business establishment offer?

1 home decorations
2 children's books
3 art lessons
4 stylish clothing 3____

4 What is an advantage of traveling with Iberia?

1 You will be offered a guided tour.
2 You will arrive more quickly at your destination.
3 You will pay less for the trip.
4 You will travel in more comfort. 4____

5 Who would be most interested in this publication?

1 people who enjoy classical music
2 people who love the outdoors
3 people who have trouble sleeping
4 people who want to play video games 5____

6 What does the speaker predict?

1 Burned forest land will be replanted.
2 Some parks will be closed this summer.
3 Wildlife will thrive in the forest this summer.
4 Fires will continue to threaten the Spanish countryside. 6____

7 What is the purpose of "el Centro de Vida Nueva?"

1 to improve people's quality of life
2 to campaign for conservation and recycling
3 to offer classes on prenatal care
4 to teach new cooking techniques 7___

8 What does the flight attendant tell you to do?

1 take all personal belongings
2 fasten your seat belt
3 fill out a form
4 leave the plane by the rear exit 8___

9 What instructions does your host mother give you?

1 to always leave a note telling where you are going
2 to return home by midnight
3 not to talk to strangers when no one is home
4 not to go out without permission 9___

b Directions (10–15): For each question you will hear some background information in English *once*. Then you will hear a passage in Spanish *twice* and a question in Spanish *once*. After you have heard the question, the teacher will pause while you read the question and the four suggested answers. Choose the best suggested answer and write its *number* in the space provided. Base your answer *on the content of the passage, only.* The passages that the teacher will read aloud to you are found in the ANSWERS section, Part 2, at the end of this examination. [12]

10 ¿Qué celebró la joven Natalia Conchita Sanz?

1 su boda en la Iglesia de Santa María
2 su cumpleaños de quinceañera
3 la inauguración de un nuevo restaurante
4 la graduación de su amiga 10___

11 ¿Por qué viajó Pedro Pacheco a Nueva York?

1 porque quería participar en un maratón
2 porque quería hacer un intercambio económico
3 porque quería saber más sobre la ciudad
4 porque quería participar en un suceso político 11____

12 ¿Para qué sirve el Programa de Verano?

1 para estudiar la historia de la ciudad
2 para enseñar dependencia en el trabajo
3 para nadar en la playa
4 para divertirse con los amigos 12____

13 Según este recado, ¿qué ha hecho tu amiga?

1 Ha cambiado la fecha de su vuelo.
2 No ha ido a su trabajo hoy.
3 Ha perdido su billete de avión.
4 Ha encontrado un nuevo trabajo. 13____

14 ¿Qué discute el agente de viajes?

1 dónde comprar pasaje a Bolivia
2 el miedo de volar
3 las consecuencias físicas de la altura
4 cuánto equipaje llevar 14____

15 ¿Por qué no sale este vuelo a tiempo?

1 El avión no puede despegar debido al mal tiempo.
2 Los pasajeros tienen que almorzar antes de embarcar.
3 El piloto insiste en saludar a todos los pasajeros.
4 Hay que arreglar un problema en el avión. 15____

PART 3

Answer all questions in Part 3 according to the directions for *a*, *b*, and *c*. [30 credits]

a Directions (16–20): After the following passage, there are five questions or incomplete statements. For *each*, choose the word or expression that best answers the question or completes the statement *according to the meaning of the passage*, and write its *number* in the space provided. [10]

Costa Rica: Paraíso Centroamericano

Costa Rica es una república que se encuentra en Centroamérica. El turismo internacional está descubriendo cada día esta belleza natural. Costa Rica es el país ideal cuando el turista quiere viajar con el propósito de salir del concreto y acero de las ciudades y tiene la necesidad de escaparse para disfrutar del verdor del campo y gozar de la naturaleza. Allí se pueden encontrar parques nacionales, ríos, montañas, una fauna increíble, bosques y hasta volcanes. Todo lo necesario se encuentra en Costa Rica para unas vacaciones ideales disfrutando de la naturaleza.

La cantidad de tiempo ideal para disfrutar de las maravillas que este país ofrece es de por lo menos una semana. En esta semana visite San José y haga un viaje a Limón donde encontrará el famoso Parque Nacional de Tortuguero, en la Costa del Caribe. En este parque se crían tortugas marinas. También encontrará que el parque se compone de zonas de playa y de zonas de campo. En la ciudad de San José existen varias excursiones para diferentes lugares interesantes, las cuales tienen una duración de medio día o un día completo.

Si le gusta la naturaleza y le gusta descubrir sitios interesantes, encontrará estas excursiones muy agradables. Tome el paseo en el Tren Histórico por la selva para conocer la flora y la fauna de este bello país. Visite el Valle Orosí, el Lago Arenal y los volcanes. Visite el Parque Nacional del Volcán Irazú o tome el paseo en bote por el Río Reventazón. Si le gusta pescar, pase unos días a la orilla del mar o en una playa. En estos viajes encontrará preciosa artesanía y también encontrará que la gente costarricense es muy simpática.

Costa Rica cuenta con hoteles localizados en medio de la naturaleza y algunos como el hotel Casa Turire, de tipo hacienda colonial que está sólo a hora y media de San José. Está situado en lo alto de una montaña y el Río Reventazón pasa al pie de la misma. Una excursión en bote por el río le costará sesenta y cinco dólares por persona. Si opta quedarse en este hotel hay otras actividades, como por ejemplo, montar a caballo, nadar en la piscina o ir al Parque Nacional de Guayabo. Pero si desea un día de plena tranquilidad, siéntese en el jardín y escuche el calmante sonido de las aguas del río y el cantar de los exóticos pájaros de este paraíso tropical.

Existen otros hoteles campestres como Villablanca en las montañas, San José Palacio en una colina con vista a la ciudad, o el Hotel Tara, inspirado por la película "Lo que el viento se llevó".

Costa Rica es un país pacífico y democrático con bellas playas y exquisita naturaleza. Tiene uno de los más interesantes eco-sistemas en Latinoamérica. Además es uno de los países más amistosos de la América Latina. Cuando se sienta que necesita escaparse de las presiones de la vida diaria, haga una cita con este paraíso.

16 Costa Rica le ofrece al visitante la oportunidad de

1 divertirse en una variedad de sitios
2 disfrutar de las estaciones del año
3 ganar bastante dinero
4 participar en un proyecto internacional 16___

17 Para visitar Costa Rica, según el autor un viajero necesita un mínimo de

1 un mes
2 un fin de semana
3 siete días
4 un año escolar 17___

18 El autor aconseja que el turista

1 vaya sólo a la ciudad de Limón
2 visite solamente los parques nacionales
3 visite sólo la ciudad de San José
4 haga varias excursiones cortas 18___

19 ¿Qué dice el autor de la gente de Costa Rica?

1 Es muy amable.
2 Trabaja en la artesanía.
3 Viaja frecuentemente a otro país.
4 Disfruta de películas americanas. 19___

20 ¿Cuál es el tema principal de este artículo?

1 la economía
2 el gobierno
3 la historia
4 el ambiente 20___

b Directions (21–25): Below each of the following selections, there is either a question or an incomplete statement. For *each*, choose the word or expression that best answers the question or completes the statement *according to the meaning of the selection*, and write its *number* in the space provided. [10]

21

NUEVO MAPA OFICIAL DE ESPAÑA

ESPAÑA cuenta con un nuevo mapa oficial, presentado a primeros de mayo por el ministro de Administraciones Públicas, Jerónimo Saavedra. La principal novedad radica en que se disipan las dudas acerca de la ubicación del archipiélago canario: las islas aparecen, por primera vez, en el Atlántico, más cerca de donde realmente se encuentran, al suroeste de la península y sobre el norte de África.

Otra de las novedades es que la elaboración del mapa se ha hecho mediante información digital, que posibilitará las posibles actualizaciones. En la representación cartográfica hay un recuadro en el que se incluyen superficie, población y banderas de todas las autonomías españolas.

What is new about this map of Spain?

1 The geographic accuracy is improved.
2 Roads under construction are shown.
3 The official languages of Spain are included.
4 Popular tourist sites are marked. 21____

22

ESPAÑA ES EL TERCER PAÍS DEL MUNDO DONDE MEJOR SE VIVE

El semanario británico "The Economist" ha vuelto a realizar, en su último número, un estudio comparativo sobre la calidad de la vida en veintidós países de todo el mundo. España ha quedado situada en tercer lugar, sólo por detrás de Suiza y Alemania.

En el análisis, factores como la temperatura, las lluvias, la esperanza de vida al nacer, el paro, la inflación, el número de médicos por habitante, la situación de la mujer, el porcentaje de divorcios y los niveles de educación han probado que la vida en España se ha mejorado desde 1983.

Los editores de "The Economist" advierten, no obstante, que la elección del mejor país del mundo para vivir es puramente subjectiva y que cada uno puede tomar los resultados del estudio según sus preferencias personales, sin embargo, una vez sentada esta subjetividad, destacan también el rigor del estudio.

Which statement is best supported by this article?

1 The income of most Spaniards has dramatically increased.
2 Spain has had serious economic and social setbacks.
3 Spain has greatly elevated its quality of living.
4 The Spanish population has increased slightly. 22____

23

DEPORTES

Jugar al golf en el desierto

Si el golf ya es un deporte que requiere enormes dosis de precisión y habilidad cuando se juega en inmaculados céspedes, hacerlo en un desierto parecía imposible. Sin embargo, ya se puede hacer en el club de golf más insólito del mundo, el Woomera Gold, situado en pleno desierto australiano. En sus áridas instalaciones, los *green* ya no son verdes y los jugadores deben llevar, además de palos y bolas, un pequeño trozo de césped para que el golpe resulte más cómodo. Este campo, de 5.316 metros cuadrados, tiene, evidentemente, los *bunkers* –zonas de arena– más grandes del mundo. Además, los jugadores tienen que contar con dos invitados insólitos: las tormentas de arena y las hormigas. En cualquier caso, ya se ha celebrado el primer trofeo en pleno desierto. Su vencedor, el australiano Paul Nieckel, comentó tras su último recorrido que jugar en el desierto puede ser un buen aprendizaje para ganar en precisión ante los torneos tradicionales.

RADIAL PRESS

Cien golfistas participaron en el primer torneo jugado en pleno desierto australiano.

What is the advantage of playing on this golf course?

1 One does not have to be a member nor pay much money to play.

2 It is a small course and easy to play if one is a good golfer.

3 There are experienced players to assist beginning golfers.

4 It is a challenge and prepares one well for the traditional competitions. 23____

24

MARIO VARGAS LLOSA

El premio Miguel de Cervantes de Literatura le fue concedido al escritor peruano Mario Vargas Llosa en reconocimiento a su extensa obra literaria. Vargas Llosa es autor de "La ciudad y los perros," "La tía Julia y el escribidor," "Conversación en la Catedral," "La guerra del fin del mundo" y otras obras. El premio Cervantes, instituido por el Ministerio de Cultura español, ha sido concedido a otros escritores latinoamericanos, como Jorge Luis Borges, Ernesto Sábato y Carlos Fuentes.

Why is Mario Vargas Llosa receiving an award?

1 for his help in saving abandoned dogs
2 for his Latin American research
3 for his numerous literary publications
4 for his dedication to the study of Cervantes 24___

25

La compañía Iberia ha tenido el placer de atender a su llegada al aeropuerto de San Pablo de Sevilla a cerca de 500 invitados a la boda de la Infanta Elena con don Jaime de Marichalar.

Del 15 al 20 de marzo, Iberia reforzó su servicio de protocolo y relaciones públicas para atender a los representantes de las casas reales y personalidades del Gobierno que asistieron al enlace de la primogénita de S.S. M.M. los Reyes de España.

Desde estas páginas, Iberia felicita a S.S. M.M. don Juan Carlos y doña Sofía por el matrimonio de su hija mayor.

Why did Iberia provide special services in Seville?

1 There was a meeting of the parliament.
2 There was a royal wedding.
3 There was an international summit.
4 There was a world conference on children. 25___

c Directions (26–30): In the following passage, there are five blank spaces numbered 26 through 30. Each blank space represents a missing word or expression. For each blank space, four possible completions are provided. Only one of them makes sense *in the context of the passage*.

First, read the passage in its entirety to determine its general meaning. Then read it a second time. For each blank space, choose the completion that makes the best sense and write its *number* in the space provided. [10]

Disney se anotó otro triunfo con la leyenda de "Pocahontas"

El número 33 es un número mágico. Es el número total de películas de dibujos animados de los Estudios Disney. La película número 33 se llama "Pocahontas". Se ha creado una verdadera fiebre en los Estados Unidos con esta película. En Latino América y los Estados Unidos los cines se han llenado a capacidad. Por ejemplo, en Chile "Pocahontas" se programó en forma simultánea para el 29 de junio en las ciudades de Santiago, Valparaíso, Viña del Mar, Concepción, y Antofagasta. La distribuidora de la película en Chile, "Conate", mandó hacer diez y seis copias de la cinta. Lo normal es hacer cuatro copias de la película para __(26)__ los principales cines del país.

La historia captura el interés desde el comienzo. Todos los elementos característicos de los Estudios de Disney—animales amorosos, consejeros sabios, villanos malos de verdad y vistas naturales dejan al ___(27)___ impresionado y sin respiración. Sin duda los aficionados al cine gozan de esta fantasía.

"Pocahontas" es una preciosa historia de dibujos animados que relata la amistad que nace entre la princesa "Pocahontas" y el capitán inglés "John Smith". El jefe de la tribu india quiere que su hija, Pocahontas, se case con el guerrero más valiente de la tribu. Sin embargo, ella se enamora del capitán.

Alan Menken, compositor, trabajó con el letrista Stephen Schwartz en siete canciones, una de las cuales—"Colors of the Wind"— se está ___(28)___ en la radio. La voz de "John Smith" corresponde a Mel Gibson. Judy Kuhn es la ___(29)___ que interpreta las canciones de Pocahontas. Irene Bedard, sin embargo, hace la voz de Pocahontas en los diálogos.

La espectacular campaña de propaganda que los ejecutivos de Walt Disney organizaron para promoverla, hizo posible que se ___(30)___ noventa mil entradas en tres semanas. En otras palabras "Pocahontas" ganó más dinero para la compañía que la película "El Rey León". La película es una atracción para personas de todas las edades. Su éxito tiene que ver con una mezcla de belleza, inspiración, imaginación, esperanzas y sueños.

(26) 1 destruirlas en 3 devolverlas a
2 conservarlas en 4 distribuirlas a 26____

(27) 1 conductor 3 dueño
2 espectador 4 vendedor 27____

(28) 1 tocando 3 clasificando
2 creando 4 pensando 28____

(29) 1 estudiante 3 investigadora
2 historiadora 4 cantante 29____

(30) 1 escribieran 3 vendieran
2 perdieran 4 regalaran 30____

PART 4

Write your answers to Part 4 according to the directions for *a* and *b*. [16]

a Directions: Write **one** well-organized note in Spanish as directed below. [6]

Choose **either** question 31 **or** 32. Write a well-organized note, following the specific instructions given in the question you have chosen. Your note must consist of **at least six clauses.** To qualify for credit, a clause must contain a verb, a stated or implied subject, and additional words necessary to convey meaning. The six clauses may be contained in fewer than six sentences if some of the sentences have more than one clause.

31 One of your Spanish friends has been out of school for a few days due to illness. Write a note in Spanish to your friend expressing your concern and your hope that he or she will feel better soon.

In the note, you may wish to tell your friend that you missed him or her at school, to express your concern that he or she is ill, and to offer to visit him or her. **Be sure you accomplish the purpose of the note, which is *to express your concern and your hope that your friend will feel better soon.***

Use the following:

Salutation: Querido/Querida (name)
Closing: [your name]

The salutation and closing will *not* be counted as part of the six required clauses.

32 You are an exchange student in Spain. One day while you are alone in your host family's home, someone calls and asks you to leave a message for one of your host parents. Write a note in Spanish to your host parent to tell him or her about the message.

In the note, you may wish to include who called, when the person called, what the person wanted, and what you told the person. You may also wish to mention whether the person will call back. **Be sure you accomplish the purpose of the note, which is *to tell your host parent about the message*.**

Use the following:

Salutation: Querido/Querida (name)
Closing: [your name]

The salutation and closing will *not* be counted as part of the six required clauses.

b Directions: Write **one** well-organized composition in Spanish as directed below. [10]

Choose **either** question 33 **or** 34. Write a well-organized composition, following the specific instructions given in the question you have chosen. Your composition must consist of **at least 10 clauses**. To qualify for credit, a clause must contain a verb, a stated or implied subject, and additional words necessary to convey meaning. The 10 clauses may be contained in fewer than 10 sentences if some of the sentences have more than one clause.

33 In Spanish, write a story about the situation shown in the picture below. It must be a story relating to the picture, **not** a description of the picture. Do *not* write a dialogue.

34 Your pen pal recently described a vacation he or she had taken and has asked you where you would like to take a vacation or visit. In Spanish, write a letter to your pen pal identifying one place where you would like to take a vacation or visit.

You must accomplish the purpose of the letter, which is *to identify one place where you would like to take a vacation or visit.*

In your letter, you may wish to state the name of the place (continent, country, state, park, tourist area, etc.) that you would like to see and mention why you would like to go there, what you would expect to see or do there, who might go with you, and how long you would like to stay there. You might also like to mention another area where you would like to go and explain why that area is also of interest to you.

You may use any or all of the ideas suggested above or you may use your own ideas. **Either way, you must identify one place where you would like to take a vacation or visit.**

Use the following:

Dateline: el 18 de junio de 1997
Salutation: Querido/Querida (name)
Closing: [your name]

The dateline, salutation, and closing will *not* be counted as part of the 10 required clauses.

Answers June 1997

Comprehensive Examination in Spanish

PART 1

This part of the examination was evaluated prior to the date of this written examination. [24 credits]

PART 2

The following passages are to be read aloud to the students according to the directions given for this part at the beginning of this examination. The correct answers are given after number 15. [30 credits]

1. A friend who just returned from Spain is telling you about his trip. He says:

¡Me encantó España! Pasé las mejores seis semanas de mi vida. Fíjate, los jóvenes españoles salen con sus amigos todas las noches. Su pasatiempo favorito es pasear y hablar pero también van a restaurantes, bares y discotecas. Se divierten mucho. Son muy simpáticos y se interesan en los extranjeros. Me hubiera gustado quedarme más tiempo en España pero no sé si hubiera aguantado, pues el problema era ¡encontrar tiempo para dormir!

What problem did your friend have while in Spain?

2. You are watching a television talk show program and hear the host say:

La mayoría de los adultos ven a los jóvenes como personas que se preocupan únicamente por su ropa, por las últimas tendencias de la moda, o por la pronta llegada de sus vacaciones. Consideran que les gusta perder el tiempo y pasar el día sin hacer nada. Sin embargo, al recorrer las tiendas de la capital en estos días, uno se da cuenta de la gran cantidad de adolescentes que utilizan su tiempo trabajando en tiendas de ropa, zapaterías y todo tipo de comercio. Con sus labores, estos jóvenes se mantienen activos y, a la vez, sienten autoestima al recibir su propio salario, que ganan gracias a su trabajo, y no a la buena voluntad de los padres.

According to the talk show host, how do many young people spend their free time?

3. You are watching television and hear this advertisement:

Descubra más de cien estilos maravillosos de cortinas y maneras de adornar sus ventanas en una variedad de colores agradables y una gran selección de telas y modelos. Muchos diseños son exclusivos de nuestra tienda. Todos están listos para colgarlos en sus ventanas. Llámenos hoy día por un catálogo gratis. ¡Satisfacción garantizada!

What does this business establishment offer?

4. You are listening to this commercial on the radio:

Iberia introduce una nueva clase de servicio: la Gran Clase. En esta clase todo está pensado y planificado para que usted descubra el placer de volar. Disfrute de un servicio exquisito en todo momento. Puede elegir entre varias comidas elegantes, servidas en vajilla de porcelana y refrescos de todas clases, en fino cristal. En la Gran Clase usted hace el viaje en las nuevas butacas-siesta; son más amplias y ofrecen la posibilidad de convertirse prácticamente en una cama. Queremos que llegue totalmente descansado a su destino. Además tendrá regalos de bienvenida y salas de espera especiales en algunos aeropuertos. La Gran Clase de Iberia es generosa con el espacio y exquisita en el servicio.

What is an advantage of traveling with Iberia?

5. While you are shopping in Spain, a salesclerk tells you about a new publication. She says:

Hay apasionados de la naturaleza que sufren cuando no se encuentran rodeados de plantas y animales. También hay gente urbana que nunca tiene tiempo de abandonar la ciudad para respirar el aire puro, aunque de vez en cuando sueñan con hacerlo. Para ambos, la editorial Trea ha publicado *Bosques de Asturias —En el reino del Busgosu*, un libro con fotografías que incluye, además, un disco compacto con sonidos grabados en los bosques asturianos: desde el canto de los pájaros hasta el sonido de los ciervos en el otoño. Este disco compacto es una escapada a la naturaleza.

Who would be most interested in this publication?

6. You are an exchange student in Valencia. In a current events class, you hear the speaker say:

España se prepara para un verano de fuego. Este verano, más que ningún otro, será recordado trágicamente como la peor época de fuegos. Las estadísticas dejan pocas dudas. Durante los seis primeros meses de este año, han ardido ya sesenta mil hectáreas de superficie forestal en nuestro país. Esto es un treinta y tres por ciento más que en el año anterior, considerado por los expertos como un año bastante terrible en la lucha contra los incendios.

What does the speaker predict?

7. You hear this announcement on a Caracas radio station:

Cada día más personas buscan desesperadamente la tranquilidad. Desean unas vacaciones o alejarse por un tiempo del estrés y la contaminación de la ciudad. Es por eso que el Centro de Vida Nueva ofrece una serie de terapias y técnicas que solucionan los problemas de fatiga crónica, nutrición, y falta de ejercicio. Entonces, se han programado varios seminarios, talleres y conferencias sobre el desarrollo humano. Para más información visite la Calle 28 Número 91 o llame por teléfono al 6-10-49-01.

What is the purpose of "el Centro de Vida Nueva"?

8. You are on a flight returning from Spain to the United States. You hear the flight attendant make this announcement:

A su llegada a los Estados Unidos es necesario entregar el formulario de aduana. Todos los pasajeros deben presentar la declaración de aduana totalmente completa. Esta declaración será recogida por las autoridades de aduana. Les pedimos que, a su llegada, tengan el formulario preparado correctamente. Así usted evitará un retraso al entrar a los Estados Unidos.

What does the flight attendant tell you to do?

9. You are an exchange student in Alajuela, Costa Rica. Your host mother tells you:

Me alegro mucho que estés con nosotros y quiero que te diviertas y que te sientas cómodo. Hasta que nos conozcas mejor, es importante que cuando quieras salir a la calle, que nos pidas permiso antes. Si no estamos en casa, tienes que esperar para pedírnoslo. Por favor, no nos dejes ningún recado y no salgas sin permiso.

What instructions does your host mother give you?

10. You are an exchange student in Colombia and are talking to a friend about a special event she attended recently. Your friend says:

El sábado pasado tuve la oportunidad de asistir a una fiesta muy acogedora. Natalia Conchita Sanz debutó en sociedad el 16 de diciembre, con motivo de sus 15 años. Primeramente fuimos a una misa en su honor en la Iglesia de Santa María. Luego celebramos su día de nacimiento con una gran fiesta en el elegante restaurante, Las Palmas, un restaurante de sus encantadores padres, Rocío y Eduardo Sanz.

¿Qué celebró la joven Natalia Conchita Sanz?

11. You are watching the news in Spain and you hear this report:

Pedro Pacheco, alcalde de Jerez de la Frontera de España, viajó a la ciudad de Nueva York para correr los 42 kilómetros de carreteras, puentes y calles. La carrera empezó cuando sonó la pistola de salida a las 10:50 y Pedro llegó a la meta cuatro horas más tarde.

¿Por qué viajó Pedro Pacheco a Nueva York?

12. You are listening to the radio in Puerto Rico and hear this announcement:

El Alcalde Rafael Cordero Santiago anunció que el Municipio Autónomo de Ponce será el primero en implementar el Programa de Verano con la participación activa de las compañías privadas. En el Programa de Verano los jóvenes participantes trabajarán con los comerciantes de la Zona Histórica de Ponce y los comercios tradicionales de La Cantera y La Playa de Ponce. El programa espera crear en el joven la responsabilidad que requiere el estar empleado, es decir, despertar en ellos las características de buen empleado.

¿Para qué sirve el Programa de Verano?

13. When you arrive home, you hear this message on your telephone answering machine:

Hola, habla Juana. Estoy llamando para decirte que no puedo ir a los Estados Unidos en julio. Hay ciertas obligaciones con mi trabajo. Así que he cambiado mi billete para el mes de agosto. Por favor, llámame cuando puedas para que hablemos de la fecha de mi visita.

Según este recado, ¿qué ha hecho tu amiga?

14. You are listening to a travel agent tell a group:

A las personas que próximamente van a viajar a una población de gran altitud, como el caso de La Paz, Bolivia, a 4.300 metros sobre el nivel del mar, les conviene conocer los efectos que pueden presentarse. El síntoma más común es insuficiencia respiratoria; también puede haber mareo o náusea, dolor de cabeza o problemas de dormir. Lo mejor es experimentar cambios de altitud gradualmente. Si su programa de viaje es flexible, considere detenerse en un lugar con un incremento de altitud moderado.

¿Qué discute el agente de viajes?

15. You are at the airport in Mexico City, ready to take a flight for New York, when you hear this announcement:

El vuelo de Mexicana de Aviación ha sido retrasado hasta las seis de la tarde, debido a un mal funcionamiento eléctrico en la cabina del avión. Los pasajeros de este vuelo podrán pasar al restaurante y almorzar. El piloto les avisará cuando todo esté arreglado.

¿Por qué no sale este vuelo a tiempo?

PART 2

(1) 3	**(4)** 4	**(7)** 1	**(10)** 2	**(13)** 1
(2) 1	**(5)** 2	**(8)** 3	**(11)** 1	**(14)** 3
(3) 1	**(6)** 4	**(9)** 4	**(12)** 2	**(15)** 4

PART 3

(a) **(16)** 1	**(b)** **(21)** 1	**(c)** **(26)** 4
(17) 3	**(22)** 3	**(27)** 2
(18) 4	**(23)** 4	**(28)** 1
(19) 1	**(24)** 3	**(29)** 4
(20) 4	**(25)** 2	**(30)** 3

PART 4

(a) Notes in writing

For each note, an example of a response worth six credits follows. The slash marks indicate how each sample note has been divided into clauses.

31. Querido Carlos,

Ana me ha contado/$_1$ que estás enfermo./$_2$ Lo siento mucho./$_3$ Espero que te mejores pronto./$_4$ Si necesitas algo/$_5$ sólo tienes que avisarme./$_6$ Hasta pronto.

Fernando

32. Querida mamá,

Te llamó la Sra Torres./$_1$ Quería invitarnos a cenar el sábado por la noche./$_2$ Podemos ir a su casa/$_3$ o podemos salir juntos al restaurante "Villa Bonita"./$_4$ Tienes que llamarla esta noche./$_5$ Estará en casa después de las ocho./$_6$

Miguel

(b) Narrative based on picture/letter

For each narrative/letter, an example of a response worth 10 credits follows. The slash marks indicate how each sample narrative/letter has been divided into clauses.

33. (Picture)

La hermana de Juan sale para la universidad hoy./$_1$ Ella va a ir en coche/$_2$ y lleva muchísimas cosas./$_3$ Sus hermanos le ayudan/$_4$ a meter todas las cajas en el coche./$_5$ No saben si todo va a caber./$_6$ Ya tiene las cosas necesarias como la ropa y la computadora/$_7$ pero quiere llevar una caja de comestibles/$_8$ y parece que no hay espacio./$_9$ Es posible que tengan que enviarla por correo./$_{10}$ ¡Qué lío!

34. (Letter)

el 18 de junio de 1997

Querido Pepe,

Me gustaría muchísimo visitar la ciudad de Madrid/$_1$ porque es la capital de España/$_2$ y porque tiene tanta cultura y grandes edificios./$_3$ Allí quisiera ver el Prado/$_4$ donde hay tantas obras de arte./$_5$ Me interesa también/$_6$ visitar el Palacio Real/$_7$ y el domingo asistir a una corrida./$_8$ Me encanta cuando la gente grita "¡Olé!"/$_9$

Mi hermano mayor quiere venir conmigo./$_{10}$ Él habla español muy bien y ya tiene muchos amigos en España. El viaje duraría una semana o diez días.

Tu amigo,
Carlos

Examination January 1998

Comprehensive Examination in Spanish

PART 1

Your performance on Part 1, Speaking (24 credits), has been evaluated prior to the date of this written examination.

PART 2

Answer all questions in Part 2 according to the directions for *a* and *b*. [30]

a Directions (1–9): For each question, you will hear some background information in English *once.* Then you will hear a passage in Spanish *twice* and a question in English *once.* After you have heard the question, the teacher will pause while you read the question and the four suggested answers. Choose the best suggested answer and write its *number* in the space provided. Base your answer *on the content of the passage, only. The passages that the teacher will read aloud to you are found in the ANSWERS section, Part 2, at the end of this examination.* [18]

1 What is this news about?

1 a marriage
2 a reunion
3 a death
4 a birthday

1_____

2 What is the message of this notice?

1 Walking every day can be an important health benefit.
2 Certain foods are necessary for good health.
3 People who laugh are healthier and happier.
4 Open and direct communication is necessary for good relationships. 2____

3 What is being announced?

1 the summer plans for two teachers
2 a contest to win a computer
3 the students who made the honor roll
4 the accomplishments of former students 3____

4 According to this commentary, what has been a change for Bianca Jagger?

1 She has hosted a lot of parties.
2 She has joined a new band.
3 She has had another baby.
4 She has become interested in politics. 4____

5 What was the purpose of Ramón's message?

1 to tell you about his future plans
2 to invite you on a trip
3 to thank you for your hospitality
4 to give you his new address 5____

6 Which suggestion should you follow?

1 take the subway
2 take the bus
3 walk to the corner and turn left
4 call a taxi 6____

7 What observation does the veterinarian make?

1 People are looking for different breeds of dogs to buy.
2 Owning a dog can be beneficial to a person's health.
3 Older people have more time for pets.
4 Pet owners must have their animals receive certain inoculations. 7____

8 What should you do next?

1 board the plane
2 check your luggage
3 go to the information booth
4 wait for further announcements 8____

9 What does this parent suggest about parties?

1 tell the child what to bring to the party
2 teach the child how to plan the party
3 make sure that there are adults at the party
4 use an upcoming party as a reason to teach table manners 9____

b Directions (10–15): For each question, you will hear some background information in English *once.* Then you will hear a passage in Spanish *twice* and a question in Spanish *once.* After you have heard the question, the teacher will pause while you read the question and the four suggested answers. Choose the best suggested answer and write its *number* in the space provided. Base your answer *on the content of the passage, only.* The passages that the teacher will read aloud to you are found in the ANSWERS section, Part 2, at the end of this examination. [12]

10 ¿Por qué se necesita llevar diferentes tipos de ropa en este viaje?

1 Hay que estar a la moda.
2 Hay variación de clima.
3 Hay viajes en barco.
4 Hay que salir con frecuencia. 10____

11 ¿Por qué fue éste un programa memorable?

1 La bailarina recitaba poemas mientras bailaba.
2 Hay muchas bailarinas en la escena.
3 Los trajes eran muy elegantes.
4 El movimiento de la bailarina fue poético y apasionado. 11_____

12 ¿De qué está hablando?

1 de las personas que buscan riquezas
2 de un viaje que hará en unos meses
3 de su participación en competiciones deportivas
4 de la situación política en su país 12_____

13 ¿De qué nos informa esta noticia?

1 Es difícil aprender las lenguas extranjeras.
2 El español tiene una importancia grande en el mundo.
3 Se enseña el idioma inglés en Madrid.
4 El francés es un idioma muy fácil a aprender. 13_____

14 ¿Qué se está anunciando?

1 un viaje a algunos pueblos mexicanos
2 un programa de música folklórica mexicana
3 una exposición de arte de México
4 una oferta de trabajo en México 14_____

15 ¿Qué sucederá en cuanto al nuevo plan escolar?

1 Los estudiantes tomarán más clases.
2 Los profesores darán más tarea.
3 El día escolar será más largo.
4 Se construirá otra escuela secundaria. 15_____

PART 3

Answer all questions in Part 3 according to the directions for *a*, *b*, and *c*. [30]

a Directions (16–20): After the following passage, there are five questions or incomplete statements. For *each,* choose the word or expression that best answers the question or completes the statement *according to the meaning of the passage,* and write its *number* in the space provided. [10]

Ecuador—Un País Lleno De Tesoros

Para el turista que busca aventura, una visita al Ecuador es viajar a un lugar distinto, un cien por ciento lleno de sorpresas y también de muchos e inesperados tesoros. Es conocer una tierra de exóticas junglas, playas y palmeras, majestuosos volcanes y el Bosque de Lluvia, del que tanto se habla ahora en círculos ecológicos; además de encontrarse con una antiquísima herencia colonial española y una cultura indígena variada e impresionante. Viajando al Ecuador, el visitante curioso puede viajar en canoa por el río, escalar los picos de los Andes, conocer la extraña belleza de las Islas Galápagos, observar fascinantes mercados indígenas y ver, de primera mano, el Bosque de Lluvia.

La gente piensa que el Ecuador es un país tropical. Sin embargo, el turista que va a Quito, la capital, debe estar preparado llevando ropa apropiada para las mañanas frescas de primavera, el mediodía cálido y a veces lluvioso del verano, el atardecer ligeramente frío del otoño y el frío invernal de las noches. La altísima ciudad de Quito, donde el aire es más fino y casi transparente, está a 2,827 metros de altura. Es importante saber que, debido a su altura, en un mismo día Quito experimenta "las cuatro estaciones".

Los famosos mercados cerca de la ciudad están abiertos los lunes, miércoles, viernes, sábados y domingos. El Mercado de Otavalo, el más famoso, está a 75 kilómetros al norte de Quito. Allí venden textiles de todo tipo, artículos de cuero, cerámicas y hasta animales. Parte del encanto de la visita es observer a los indígenas de la zona y su forma de peinar y vestir.

Un viaje muy interesante, de un par de días, es al Río Aguarico, en la región Amazónica donde se puede tomar un crucero en un barco-hotel flotante llamado el Flotel Orellana. En este viaje se puede conocer la jungla, pueblecitos, bosques y aprender muchísimo de la cultura indígena y plantas medicinales. En este viaje se puede hasta viajar en ríos y lagos por canoas hechas de troncos de árboles huecos y rústicos.

Para conocer bien el paisaje, la flora y fauna del Ecuador, existe un encantador viaje al interior de 2 días en el Quito-Riobamba Expreso. Durante la excursión, se atraviesan montañas y valles en tren. El tren pasa cerca de volcanes incluyendo la silueta simétrica del célebre Cotopaxi. Cotopaxi es uno de los volcanes activos más altos del mundo (si no el más alto). Durante el viaje se puede desembarcar en lugares donde hay pequeños mercados de artesanía, almorzar al pasar cerca del lago Yambo y pasar la noche en Riobamba (la que tiene un maravilloso Museo de Arte Religioso).

La comida ecuatoriana es muy interesante. Incluye bacalao y filetes de pescado usados en el famoso "ceviche", y mariscos como los langostinos y camarones. También hay empanadas muy sabrosas, tamales, pastelillos de yuca, sopas como "locro", o sopa de patatas, la Sopa Quiteña, el Chupe con Camarones, el Ají de Pollo, el Seco de Chivo y varios platos de arroces como el Arroz de Cebada a la Criolla.

Aquí hay una nota curiosa. ¡Es en Ecuador—y no en Panamá—donde se fabrican los muy populares sombreros de Panamá y allí los puede comprar a muy buen precio! Es otra razón por la cual se conoce Ecuador como un país lleno de tesoros.

16 ¿Qué tipo de clima se espera en Quito?

1 variado y cambiable
2 caluroso y seco
3 húmedo y nevoso
4 constante y soleado

16____

17 ¿Cuándo están cerrados los mercados fuera de Quito?

1 los domingos
2 los días de trabajo
3 tres días a la semana
4 los martes y jueves

17____

18 Según este artículo, ¿qué debe hacer el turista en la región Amazónica?

1 cultivar plantas y árboles
2 hacer excursión en bote
3 estudiar la contaminación del agua
4 cazar animales exóticos

18____

19 ¿Por qué es famoso Cotopaxi?

1 su mercado
2 su lago
3 su altura
4 su ciudad indígena

19____

20 Uno debe probar el ceviche si le gusta

1 la fruta del mar
2 el postre
3 la carne
4 las legumbres frescas

20____

b Directions (21–25): Below each of the following selections, there is either a question or an incomplete statement. For *each,* choose the word or expression that best answers the question or completes the statement *according to the meaning of the selection,* and write its *number* in the space provided. [10]

21

¿Sabías que tu cabecita produce de 30 a 50 mil pensamientos durante el día, y que no descansa ni aun cuando duermes? ¡PLOP! Despierta y entérate. El ser humano está creando pensamientos constantemente. Estos nos sirven de guía y de fuente de información. Para lograr una vida sana y saludable es indispensable que estés bien por dentro y por fuera, tener paz interior y mirar hacia adelante con optimismo. La clave es: dejar atrás el pasado, vivir el presente sin amargura y no adelantar lo que aún es incierto: el futuro. Es de vital importancia que alimentes a diario tu mente con una gran dosis de pensamientos positivos; incluye en ellos valores como el amor y la paz, la alegría y el entusiasmo, el respeto y la armonía, la sinceridad y la honradez, la paciencia y la tolerancia. Son éstos los que nos permiten resolver nuestros problemas y vencer los obstáculos. El lema es: "Mente sana en cuerpo sano". ¿Te apuntas en esta onda?

What is the topic of this article?

1 the importance of positive thinking
2 new ways to make friends
3 a cure for insomnia
4 the need for daily exercise 21_____

22

Defiende tus derechos como consumidora

Existen instituciones gubernamentales encargadas de proteger al consumidor, como la Procuraduría Federal del Consumidor (Profeco). Así que dirígete a ellas si:

- Te sientes estafada porque los precios de los productos básicos están alterados caprichosamente.
- Te niegan la venta de un producto o te exigen condiciones inaceptables para comprarlo, o marcan un precio que crees no es razonable.
- Observas que las medidas de peso son inexactas.
- Compruebas que eres víctima de discriminación.
- No se cumplen las garantías prometidas que te ofrecieron al hacer la compra de un producto.
- Violan los términos acordados cuando alquilas una casa o la acondicionas, porque no son los que te habían prometido al realizar el pago.

Ahora bien, debes recordar que hay artículos (comestibles, ropa, etc.), que varían su precio según la temporada, como ocurre con las ventas de fin de año.

This article indicates that some government agencies

1 provide health care for citizens
2 help protect the interests of consumers
3 promote competition in business
4 react favorably to special-interest groups 22_____

23

¿QUÉ HACER SI SURGE UN COMPROMISO?

Hace muchos años, para cubrir las necesidades que podían surgir a cada momento, era preciso llevar una buena suma de dinero a todas partes.

Hoy día, usted dispone de un práctico sistema de pago: la Tarjeta Bancómer, que le permite administrar eficazmente su dinero sin llevarlo a todos lados; y efectuar compras en miles de negocios afiliados.

Y para su seguridad, si se llegara a extraviar su tarjeta, usted queda protegido del uso indebido que se le pudiera dar. Nos debe notificar la pérdida de la misma inmediatamente.

Usted no paga intereses si liquida mensualmente la totalidad de su cuenta.

What is being promoted?

1 savings accounts
2 a trip to Spain
3 a credit card
4 traveler's checks 23____

24

Ni amarilla, ni roja, ni gris, ni opaca.

La Verdad es Transparente.

Porque hay una gran diferencia entre el chisme, el rumor y la verdadera noticia, escuche El Noticiario por las estaciones del Grupo IMER.
Los acontecimientos más importantes en 3 emisiones diarias. Y cada hora, los resúmenes noticiosos.
Información clara, objetiva, seria y oportuna, porque para nosotros Usted es Líder de su propia opinión.

EL NOTICIARIO

Porque Usted es el Líder de su Propia Opinión.

Diariamente a las 7:00 AM, 2:00 PM y 7:00 PM.

XEB la B grande 1220 AM, Radio 660 AM, Opus 94 94.5 FM, Estéreo Joven 105.7 FM, Radio 710 AM y 12 estaciones de provincia.

This station is proud of its

1 musical variety
2 children's programs
3 unbiased reporting
4 popular hosts

24____

25

CASA DE S. M. EL REY
SECRETARIA GENERAL
RELACIONES CON LOS MEDIOS DE COMUNICACION

Con motivo de la boda de Su Alteza Real la Infanta Doña Elena con Don Jaime de Marichalar el próximo 18 de marzo en Sevilla, la Familia Real asistirá la víspera, día 17, a las 5 de la tarde, a un espectáculo benéfico de la Escuela Española de Arte Ecuestre en la Plaza de la Real Maestranza que organizará el acto conjuntamente con el Ayuntamiento de Sevilla.

Por la noche, Sus Majestades los Reyes ofrecerán una cena para sus familiares e invitados más allegados en el Palacio de Villamanrique de la Condesa, residencia de Sus Altezas Reales Don Pedro y Doña Esperanza de Orleans-Braganza, antigua casa de los abuelos maternos de Su Majestad el Rey.

CASA DE S. M. EL REY
SECRETARIA GENERAL
RELACIONES CON LOS MEDIOS DE COMUNICACION

Al día siguiente, a las 12,30 se celebrará el enlace matrimonial ante el Altar Mayor de la Catedral de Sevilla. Tras la ceremonia, los contrayentes se trasladarán a la Iglesia del Salvador donde Doña Elena hará entrega de su ramo de flores. En esta Iglesia reposan los restos mortales de sus bisabuelos paternos, SS.AA.RR. el Infante Don Carlos de Borbón-Dos Sicilias y la Infanta doña Luisa de Orleans.

A continuación el nuevo matrimonio se dirigirá al Real Alcázar donde Sus Majestades ofrecerán un almuerzo a sus invitados.

LA ZARZUELA, 15 de Enero de 1995

What kind of event is discussed in this announcement?

1 a visit by a foreign head of state
2 a royal wedding ceremony
3 an important exhibit by an artist
4 a funeral for the king 25____

c *Directions* (26–30): In the following passage, there are five blank spaces numbered 26 through 30. Each blank space represents a missing word or expression. For each blank space, four possible completions are provided. Only one of them makes sense *in the context of the passage.*

First, read the passage in its entirety to determine its general meaning. Then read it a second time. For each blank space, choose the completion that makes the best sense and write its *number* in the space provided. [10]

Para hacer el esquí nórdico no hay que ir a Escandinavia. España puede ser una alternativa.

La cita era a las diez de la mañana en un pueblo de Soria, a los pies de las montañas de Urbión. La razón era un curso básico de esquí organizado por la compañía Ociotur, dedicada a la promoción de turismo activo y de naturaleza en la provincia de Soria. Según la publicidad, se ofrecían dos días de actividad por 12.000 pesetas, con habitación en un (26)____, comidas y alquiler de material necesario. El lugar elegido fue el pueblo de Santa Inés, en plena sierra de las montañas entre Soria y La Rioja.

Aunque parece extraño, Soria es una zona muy frecuentada por los amantes del esquí nórdico, que encuentran entre sus árboles y suaves montes un lugar apropriado para practicar el esquí. Además, la nieve cae en abundancia en diciembre y dura hasta abril.

Arriba, en las montañas de Santa Inés, hacía un tiempo muy frío. Las nubes bajas hacían la mañana gris y el viento cortaba el aliento. Pero el bosque se mostraba precioso. Los árboles parecían vestidos de blanco para alguna ocasión especial y un lindo manto de ___(27)___ lo cubría todo.

Las clases de esquí comenzaban en un claro protegido del viento por los árboles. Primero, deslizar sin los bastones; segundo elevar los brazos para coordinarlos con el movimiento de las piernas; finalmente unos pasos sobre unas pistas de ___(28)___. La clase, vista desde lejos, parecía fácil, pero el simple hecho de mantener paralelos los esquís resultaba muy ___(29)___; evitar que los esquís se cruzaran y te tiraran al suelo, imposible.

Este tipo de curso trata de que en un día el estudiante aprenda las nociones básicas del esquí nórdico. Se dedican cuatro horas a ___(30)___ el movimiento de los brazos y las piernas, y el uso correcto de los bastones. Al segundo día el estudiante puede recorrer varios kilómetros de pista sin caídas ni sobresaltos.

La recompensa llega a la mañana siguiente: un par de horas permiten disfrutar de la paz y la soledad del bosque nevado, descubriendo rincones hermosos a los que sería difícil ver de otra manera.

26 1 valle 3 hotel
2 periódico 4 precio 26____

27 1 nieve 3 viento
2 lluvia 4 calor 27____

28 1 nadar 3 correr
2 esquiar 4 patinar 28____

29 1 sencillo 3 suave
2 aburrido 4 difícil 29____

30 1 olvidar 3 caer
2 coordinar 4 saltar 30____

PART 4

Write your answers to Part 4 according to the directions for *a* and *b*. [16]

a Directions: Write **one** well-organized note in Spanish as directed below. [6]

Choose **either** question 31 **or** 32. Write a well-organized note, following the specific instructions given in the question you have chosen. Your note must consist of **at least six clauses.** To qualify for credit, a clause must contain a verb, a stated or implied subject, and additional words necessary to convey meaning. The six clauses may be contained in fewer than six sentences if some of the sentences have more than one clause.

31 You are an exchange student in Peru and you have a train ticket to visit Lima, the capital, on the next day. You find out that the train is not running. Write a note in Spanish to your Peruvian friend asking about other ways to get to Lima.

In your note, you may wish to include why you are going to Lima and when and how you will return. You may wish to thank him or her in advance. **Be sure you accomplish the purpose of the note, which is *to ask about other ways to get to Lima.***

Use the following:

Salutation: Querido/Querida (name)
Closing: (your name)

The salutation and closing will *not* be counted as part of the six required clauses.

32 You are supposed to go shopping with a Spanish-speaking friend today, but your plans have changed. Write a note in Spanish to your friend telling him or her that you are not going shopping today.

In the note, you may wish to explain why you cannot go and why your plans have changed, or include an apology for the change in plans and a suggestion of another day and time. **Be sure you accomplish the purpose of the note, which is *to tell your friend that you are not going shopping today.***

Use the following:

Salutation: Querido/Querida (name)
Closing: (your name)

The salutation and closing will *not* be counted as part of the six required clauses.

b Directions: Write **one** well-organized composition in Spanish as directed below. [10]

Choose **either** question 33 **or** 34. Write a well-organized composition, following the specific instructions given in the question you have chosen. Your composition must consist of **at least 10 clauses.** To qualify for credit, a clause must contain a verb, a stated or implied subject, and additional words necessary to convey meaning. The 10 clauses may be contained in fewer than 10 sentences if some of the sentences have more than one clause.

33 In Spanish, write a story about the situation shown in the picture below. It must be a story relating to the picture, **not** a description of the picture. Do *not* write a dialogue.

34 You are writing to an organization that is looking for student volunteers for a 2-week period in the summer to help with a project in Paraguay. In Spanish, write a letter to the Program Director to offer your participation in the project.

You must accomplish the purpose of the letter, which is *to offer your participation in the project.*

In your letter, you may wish to include information about yourself; tell where you found out about this opportunity; describe your qualifications, your interests, your ability to speak Spanish, and your desire to help; and mention why you want to participate and when you are able to go.

You may use any or all of the ideas suggested above *or* you may use your own ideas. **Either way, you must write a letter to the Program Director to offer your participation in the project.**

Use the following:

Dateline:	el 28 de enero de 1998
Salutation:	Estimado Director/Estimada Directora
Closing:	Atentamente, (your name)

The dateline, salutation, and closing will *not* be counted as part of the 10 required clauses.

Answers January 1998

Comprehensive Examination in Spanish

PART 1

This part of the examination was evaluated prior to the date of this written examination. [24 credits]

PART 2

The following passages are to be read aloud to the students according to the directions given for this part at the beginning of this examination. The correct answers are given after number 15. [30 credits]

1. You are staying with a host family as an exchange student. One day you overhear a neighbor talking to your host mother. The neighbor says:

¿Has oído lo que ha pasado? Marcos David Cuello ha pedido la mano de la hija de los Señores Rafael Cánoras. Dicen que la boda se celebrará en el mes de septiembre. La recepción tendrá lugar en la casa de los padres de la novia.

What is this news about?

2. You are listening to the radio and hear the announcer read this report:

Para mantener buena salud y mantener entusiasmo en la vida, las personas tienen que reír. La risa es capaz de eliminar ansiedad, angustia, y nerviosidad. Veinte segundos de pura y dura risa y carcajada pueden producir un efecto inmediato de optimismo y alegría. La risa es una buena razón para estar contento y tener una gran dosis de felicidad y energía vital.

What is the message of this notice?

3. At a school in Costa Rica you hear this morning announcement:

El colegio está planeando una gran sorpresa para los alumnos. El último día de clases van a tener la oportunidad de ganarse un equipo nuevo de computadoras. Esta oportunidad fue posible debido a la generosidad de los antiguos alumnos del colegio. Para participar en el concurso los participantes tienen que haber pasado todas las asignaturas y seleccionar un número a suerte.

What is being announced?

4. You are listening to a commentary about the recent activity of Bianca Jagger. You hear:

Siempre se ha asociado el nombre de Bianca Jagger con el de Mick Jagger del grupo The Rolling Stones, y con la vida frívola de Nueva York. Pero en estos últimos años participó en la política de Nicaragua, su país natal. Ella quiere crear un partido que se preocupe por los más necesitados, y quiere presentarse para presidente en las futuras elecciones. "Mi filosofía es que, con perseverancia y paciencia, la gente se va a dar cuenta de quien soy realmente", afirma Bianca.

According to this commentary, what has been a change for Bianca Jagger?

5. Your Mexican friend Ramón left this message on your answering machine:

Habla Ramón. Te llamo para decirte cuánto nos divertimos durante las últimas vacaciones que pasamos en tu casa. Hace tres semanas que volvimos y todos seguimos hablando de esos días maravillosos. Esperamos no haberte causado demasiadas molestias. Estamos muy agradecidos por todo. Recuerda que siempre tienes una casa aquí con nosotros.

What was the purpose of Ramón's message?

6. In Barcelona, Spain, you are late for an appointment and are trying to find the department store El Corte Inglés. You ask someone for directions. The person says:

El Corte Inglés está en la Plaza Cataluña. Está un poco lejos de aquí. Si vas a pie necesitarás unos cuarenta minutos más o menos. Si tomas el metro llegarás en cinco minutos. Toma la línea roja. Existe también un autobús pero no es muy rápido y realmente no te ahorrarás mucho tiempo. La parada está en la esquina. Recuerda que si tomas el metro tendrás que bajarte en la Plaza Cataluña.

Which suggestion should you follow?

7. You are listening to a veterinarian on a local talk show in Caracas, Venezuela. The veterinarian says:

De todas las formas de vida que nos rodean, sólo el perro ha establecido una alianza con nosotros. Los gatos se limitan a tolerarnos, los caballos sólo obedecen nuestras órdenes, pero los perros se han convertido verdaderamente en nuestros mejores amigos. Ellos son benéficos para la salud humana en muchos sentidos. Los investigadores de la Universidad de Cambridge descubrieron que hay una reducción de estrés cuando los mayores tienen estos animales fieles.

What observation does the veterinarian make?

8. You are at the airport in Mexico City and hear this announcement on the public address system about your flight:

Anunciamos a los señores pasajeros que a causa del mal tiempo el vuelo número 230 de Aereoméxico con salida a las diez y media con destino a Yucatán ha sido cancelado. El vuelo saldrá mañana a la misma hora. Rogamos a estos pasajeros que pasen por la oficina de información que está localizada en el centro del aeropuerto Benito Juárez para recoger un cupón que les permitirá permanecer en un hotel esta noche a cuenta nuestra.

What should you do next?

9. You overhear two parents talking about children's parties. One of them says:

La preparación para la fiesta de cumpleaños es una buena oportunidad para enseñar al niño la forma de comportarse a la mesa. Se le puede indicar la manera correcta de usar la servilleta, de comer con moderación, a no lanzarse sobre el plato y a no hablar con la boca llena. A los niños pequeños les fascina imitar a los adultos. Antes de la fiesta también es ideal enseñarles cómo colocar los cubiertos sobre el plato y cómo coger el tenedor o la cuchara.

What does this parent suggest about parties?

10. You are an exchange student living with a family in the Dominican Republic. You come home for lunch and your host parent says to you:

Pedro, mañana salimos para Puerto Plata. Espero que tengas tu equipaje listo porque saldremos muy temprano. Tendrás que llevar ropa adecuada para que puedas disfrutar del mar y del campo. En la playa hará mucho calor pero en el campo estará muy fresco. Las temperaturas de la costa y de las montañas son muy diferentes, por lo tanto hay que ir bien preparado.

¿Por qué se necesita llevar diferentes tipos de ropa en este viaje?

11. You are listening to a review of a recent show. The announcer says:

Hay silencio y oscuridad total. De repente, en el escenario se ilumina la silueta inmóvil de Pilar Rioja, quien con un taconeo, las palmadas y el grito de su canción flamenca, empieza el tablado con el grito y el braceo del flamenco. La música enciende la flama de Rioja, quien mantiene constante en su espectáculo la pasión y la intensidad. Expresa en su baile lo más alto de lo poético y musical.

¿Por qué fue éste un programa memorable?

12. You are listening to a guest lecturer in class. He says:

Comencé a entrenar 6 o 7 meses antes. Participé en un maratón nacional y llegué tercero. Luego gané las eliminatorias para decidir quién iba a los Juegos Panamericanos. Allí me sentía bien relajado. Fue una gran emoción obtener la medalla de oro y la marca nacional en esa misma carrera, además establecer la marca del evento para Juegos Panamericanos. La medalla de oro me abrió las puertas para participar en el extranjero; me llovían las invitaciones. Me sentía bien, valió la pena el sacrificio que hice; hice lo que la gente esperaba de mí y eso me dio la satisfacción.

¿De qué está hablando?

13. You are listening to the news in Spanish and hear this report:

El Instituto Cervantes de Madrid nos informa que la enseñanza del español se ha duplicado en los últimos años. El español es la lengua extranjera que más se enseña en los Estados Unidos y en Europa.

El francés ocupa el segundo lugar como lengua internacional del mundo. Quizás en el futuro el español puede llegar a ocupar este lugar. Se dice que la población de habla española llega a trescientos cincuenta y seis millones. Esto incluye España, la América Latina, los Estados Unidos, las Filipinas y Guinea. El informe reporta que para el año 2000, habrá 35 millones de personas de origen hispano en los Estados Unidos.

¿De qué nos informa esta noticia?

Examination June 1998

Comprehensive Examination in Spanish

PART 1

Your performance on Part 1, Speaking (24 credits), has been evaluated prior to the date of this written examination.

PART 2

Answer all questions in Part 2 according to the directions for *a* and *b*. [30]

a *Directions* (1–9): For each question, you will hear some background information in English *once*. Then you will hear a passage in Spanish *twice* and a question in English *once*. After you have heard the question, the teacher will pause while you read the question and the four suggested answers. Choose the best suggested answer and write its *number* in the space provided. Base your answer *on the content of the passage, only*. The passages that the teacher will read aloud to you are found in the ANSWERS section, Part 2, at the end of this examination. [18]

1 Who would be most interested in this contest?

1 the parent of a young child
2 someone who wants to be an actor
3 an elementary school teacher
4 a professional photographer 1 2

2 Who would benefit most from this service offered by El Corte Inglés?

1 a city resident who has no car
2 a visitor from outside Spain
3 a person who needs a credit card
4 a person looking for a job

2 2·3

3 What does your host mother want you to do?

1 go shopping for the family
2 start to prepare dinner for the family
3 get ready to go out in 45 minutes
4 help José when he arrives

3 2

4 What is a unique feature of this activity?

1 A tour of the park will be given.
2 The community will host a sports competition.
3 No admission fee is charged for children.
4 People can watch a movie while they enjoy the water.

4 4

5 What opportunity is being offered to students?

1 to improve their reading skills
2 to attend summer camp at no cost
3 to go sightseeing in Boston
4 to get a summer job

5 ✓

6 What is this product designed to do?

1 allow rapid dialing of numbers
2 permit unlimited calls to be made at special rates
3 lower telephone bills by limiting long-distance calls
4 keep a record of each call received

6 1

7 What is the purpose of this message?

1 to accept an invitation
2 to cancel an appointment
3 to request a favor
4 to express appreciation 7 _____

8 What does this announcement describe?

1 a vacation trip
2 a special sale
3 a course of study
4 a job opportunity 8 _____

9 What is the subject of this exhibition?

1 modern art
2 ancient cultures
3 urban life
4 famous artists 9 _____

b *Directions* (10–15): For each question you will hear some background information in English *once*. Then you will hear a passage in Spanish *twice* and a question in Spanish *once*. After you have heard the question, the teacher will pause while you read the question and the four suggested answers. Choose the best suggested answer and write its *number* in the space provided. Base your answer *on the content of the passage, only*. The passages that the teacher will read aloud to you are found in the ANSWERS section, Part 2, at the end of this examination. [12]

10 ¿Cómo era el nuevo restaurante?

1 Todo era desagradable.
2 Todo era muy bueno.
3 La comida era deliciosa.
4 Era barato. 10 _____

11 ¿Qué les dijo el cantante Sting a los estudiantes universitarios?

1 que a pesar de ser rico, comprende que la gente tiene problemas
2 que regalará su castillo a los pobres
3 que necesita escribir más canciones para los jóvenes
4 que su música no le gusta a la gente 11 ____

12 ¿Por qué no se debe tomar la Avenida Juárez?

1 Hay mucho tráfico a esa hora.
2 Es fácil perderse en el túnel del metro.
3 Es imposible encontrar la parada del tren.
4 No se puede pasar por esa calle. 12 ____

13 ¿Qué recomienda esta persona?

1 ponerse en dieta ahora
2 levantar peso en el verano
3 hacer ejercicios acuáticos
4 dormir más para aliviar los dolores 13 ____

14 ¿Por qué es popular este hotel?

1 Es el más barato de la isla.
2 Ofrece tranquilidad a los visitantes.
3 Está situado en el centro.
4 Tiene habitaciones muy lujosas. 14 ____

15 ¿Qué recomienda el guía?

1 no entrar en los templos sin guía
2 traer dinero para un refresco y una comida
3 cubrirse la cabeza y llevar zapatos adecuados
4 recoger artefactos antiguos 15 ____

PART 3

Answer all questions in Part 3 according to the directions for *a*, *b*, and *c*. [30 credits]

a *Directions* (16–20): After the following passage, there are five questions or incomplete statements. For *each*, choose the word or expression that best answers the question or completes the statement *according to the meaning of the passage,* and write its *number* in the space provided. [10]

Conozca a Enrique Iglesias—hijo de un famoso cantante

Enrique Iglesias Preysler nació el 8 de mayo de 1975. Él es hijo del ultrafamoso cantante Julio Iglesias y de Isabel Preysler, una de las mujeres más guapas y queridas de España. Enrique tiene dos hermanos, Julio José y Chabeli, y dos medias hermanas chiquititas llamadas Tamara y Ana que, según dice, son su adoración. El cantante es de 1.88 metros de altura, y bastante delgado. Tiene ojos cafés, piel bronceada y cabello castaño. Enrique ha pasado casi toda su vida en Miami. Aunque ha estado separado de su papá y de su mamá, llevan una relación muy buena y son muy buenos amigos. Sus principales pasatiempos desde niño son los deportes acuáticos, la escritura—escribe canciones y poemas—y la música. Le gusta escuchar desde un aria de ópera hasta un buen mariachi.

Desde pequeño, Enrique sintió la necesidad de expresarse con la música y formó un grupo con varios amigos de la escuela. Pero ellos siempre practicaban en secreto. No quería lanzarse al mundo musical hasta estar completamente seguro de sus habilidades artísticas. Esa seguridad precisamente le llegó hace poco menos de un año cuando, juntando sus ahorros, grabó su primer disco.

Hablando un poquito de su infancia Enrique nos dijo: "Yo fui un niño muy normal dentro de la normalidad que se puede tener cuando se viaja por todo el mundo desde muy chico. Siempre me sentí muy querido y apoyado por mis padres. En los grandes recuerdos que tengo de mi niñez nunca puedo olvidar a 'la Seño'. Es la mujer que nos ha dado a mis hermanos y a mí más tiempo, cuidados, y cariño. En la escuela yo era un muchacho muy inquieto, pero tan común y corriente como los demás. Quizás la única diferencia era que yo viajaba mucho, que conocía a mucha gente, que me tomaban fotos en la calle y que tenía unos padres que salían en las portadas de todas las revistas.

Ahora siento que mi vida ha sufrido un cambio radical. Soy reconocido por mis talentos artísticos por todo el mundo y por esto estoy más presionado. Vivo en un constante estado de estrés, pero puedo decir que he sido y soy muy feliz."

Por si te queda alguna duda, hoy por hoy en cuanto a cantantes juveniles se refiere, Enrique es el número uno. Hasta la fecha ha superado a otros cantantes como Ricky Martin y Luis Miguel en países como España, donde ha vendido casi 200 mil discos; en Portugal donde ha vendido 50 mil; en México con más de 400 mil, y en Argentina y Chile donde ha superado las ventas anticipadas. Hoy día se encuentra promoviendo sus canciones en italiano y portugués, y dentro de poco, las grabará en inglés.

Para el futuro, Enrique piensa incluir canciones más expresivas, más realistas, más vividas porque ya tiene experiencia para hablar de muchas cosas. Quiere conocer a todo el mundo y desea ser respetado como músico, algo que le agradará muchísimo a su padre—el famoso cantante español—Julio Iglesias.

16 ¿Dónde ha vivido Enrique Iglesias por la mayor parte de su vida?

1 en los Estados Unidos
2 en España
3 en México
4 en Portugal 16 _____

17 ¿Por qué tocaba Enrique la música en secreto con sus amigos?

1 Sus padres le prohibían tocar.
2 Sus hermanos se reían de él.
3 No quería ofender a nadie.
4 No estaba seguro de su talento. 17 _____

18 ¿Cómo era Enrique como niño?

1 Era un chico serio y callado.
2 Era un chico solitario.
3 Era un chico parecido a los otros.
4 Era un chico perezoso. 18 _____

19 ¿Quién era "la Seño"?

1 una aficionada que siempre le escribía
2 una señora que cuidaba a Enrique y a sus hermanos
3 una tía a quien quería Enrique
4 una cantante que lo influía mucho 19 _____

20 ¿Qué está causando el estrés en la vida de Enrique?

1 su gran fama
2 sus problemas familiares
3 el descontento con las ventas
4 la pérdida de la voz 20 _____

b Directions (21–25): Below each of the following selections, there is either a question or an incomplete statement. For *each,* choose the word or expression that best answers the question or completes the statement *according to the meaning of the selection,* and write its *number* in the space provided. [10]

21

Desde increíbles desiertos hasta bosques tropicales. Desde paisajes lunares hasta ricos fondos marinos. Todo existe en Canarias. Vívelo. Podrás contar que el mar te ha descubierto sus secretos. Que has entrado en parajes inexplorados y has llegado al centro de la tierra. Todo eso y mucho más es posible en Canarias. Cada una de sus siete islas te ofrece un mundo fascinante y distinto. Tan excitante como tú quieras. Vive unas vacaciones intensas, sorprendentes e imaginativas.

This advertisement would be most interesting to people who

1 need a job
2 like to travel
3 want to shop
4 enjoy museums

21 _____

22

Muy señores míos:

Desearía que tomaran en consideración mi solicitud para el puesto de Secretaria Bilingüe con MTL S.A. anunciado en "La Opinión" el lunes 27 de mayo de 1996.

Adjunto mi currículum dando detalles de mi carrera y títulos hasta este momento. En líneas generales es como sigue:

Después de finalizar mis estudios universitarios en 1992 estudié a tiempo parcial el español, el francés y el alemán.

Durante los últimos dos años he trabajado como secretaria en el Departamento de Ventas Extranjeras de Selby, donde tengo la responsabilidad de toda la correspondencia extranjera. En este tiempo he introducido un sistema nuevo de archivo y he modernizado los métodos de trabajo de toda la oficina.

Habiendo trabajado a este nivel durante algún tiempo, me gustaría tener mayor responsabilidad en este campo y quisiera tener la oportunidad de hacer frente a las exigencias de un nuevo puesto.

Les agradecería que me concedieran una entrevista a fin de decidir si este puesto es adecuado para mí.

Les saludo atentamente

María González

Why did María González write this letter?

1 to apply for a job
2 to find a secretary
3 to enroll in a language course
4 to file a complaint

22 _____

23

Bicicletas gratis en Copenhague

Los turistas y habitantes de la ciudad de Copenhague (Dinamarca) pueden utilizar gratuitamente bicicletas puestas a su disposición con el fin de combatir el ruido y la polución. Desde fines del mes de mayo, el Ministerio de Cultura, la comuna (Ayuntamiento) de la ciudad y la dirección de Turismo ha puesto mil bicicletas en la calle que pueden ser usadas y devueltas después en cincuenta puntos repartidos por toda la ciudad.

What problem is the city of Copenhagen trying to resolve?

1 a lack of public transportation
2 an excess of old bicycles
3 contamination of the air
4 insufficient parking for cars

23 _____

24

LA TRIVIA DE "CILANTRO Y PEREJIL"

¿Te gustaría cenar con los actores **JUAN MANUEL BERNAL** y **ALPHA ACOSTA?** Pues esta vez ERES e IMCINE (Instituto Mexicano de Cinematografía) te invitan a concursar. La cuestión es muy fácil. Se trata de que te conviertas en reportero y nos mandes las lo mejores preguntas que se te ocurriría hacerle a ambos artistas. ERES elegirá los lo cuestionarios más padres, que ganarán una cena en el restaurante TecamaCharlie's con la pareja joven de la película "Cilantro y perejil". Está fácil, ¿verdad?

Manda tus cuestionarios cuanto antes a:
REVISTA ERES
APARTADO POSTAL
5-733 Y 5-750
C.P. 06500, MEXICO, D.F.

La fecha límite para entregar tus cuestionarios es el 16 de junio de 1996.

This advertisement offers readers the chance to

1 be interviewed by a reporter for a magazine
2 take a photography course at no cost
3 obtain information about well-known restaurants
4 meet some people who are famous 24 ____

25

• YA LLEGO EL VERANO •

"Ya se aplica el aumento en los cargos de electricidad. Actúe ahora para controlar su consumo."

- Limpie la basura alrededor de su unidad exterior de aire acondicionado para asegurar que haya un flujo normal.
- Apague el aire acondicionado cuando sale de casa por más de cuatro horas.
- Fije la temperatura del tanque de calentar agua a 120 grados o menos.
- Fije el aire acondicionado a 78 grados o más.
- Use abanicos para aumentar la comodidad aún cuando fije el termostato a una temperatura alta.
- Mantenga la ventanilla de aire de regreso libre de muebles y otras obstrucciones. La ventanilla de regreso es la ventanilla grande que saca el aire fuera del cuarto.
- Cubra las ventanas por donde entra más el sol.
- Si tiene problemas con su aire acondicionado llame a un profesional, y asegúrese que tenga licencia.
- Cambie o limpie el filtro del aire acondicionado una vez al mes. El filtro se encuentra normalmente detrás de la ventanilla de aire de regreso, o en la unidad del aire acondicionado.

This information is intended to help people to

1 find employment
2 heat their homes
3 prevent fires
4 save energy

25 _____

c *Directions* (26–30): In the following passage, there are five blank spaces numbered 26 through 30. Each blank space represents a missing word or expression. For each blank space, four possible completions are provided. Only one of them makes sense *in the context of the passage.*

First, read the passage in its entirety to determine its general meaning. Then read it a second time. For each blank space, choose the completion that makes the best sense and write its *number* in the space provided. [10]

Sensacional método de guitarra

¿Tiene su propia guitarra pero no sabe tocarla? ¿Siempre quería aprender a tocar la guitarra? Esta es su gran oportunidad. Hay un método muy sencillo, agradable y en video. Úselo en su propio hogar, sin tener que ir a una escuela, sin ejercicios aburridos y sobre todo con canciones hermosas y de moda. Las canciones que aprenderá son muy conocidas, por ejemplo: "El Reloj", "Tu Cárcel", "Amor Eterno", "La Puerta Negra".

GUITARRA FACILISIMA es la sensación del momento. Desde la publicación de este método para aprender a tocar la guitarra, la reacción del público ha sido explosiva. Hay miles y miles de personas, que están (26) con este método. La aceptación de este método por tantas personas ha hecho que varias bibliotecas de los Estados Unidos lo tengan para prestar al público.

Ud. aprende con canciones de (27) famosos como Roberto Carlos, Juan Gabriel, Los

Bukis y muchos más. Además, en video es donde el maestro no se cansa de repetir hasta que Ud. aprenda. Su costo es sumamente módico...sólo $24.95. Incluye un libro con instrucciones, un (28) de larga duración y se está regalando un juego de cuerdas de nilón para su guitarra con valor de $12.00, completamente gratis.

Se han hecho varios años de estudio e investigación para (29) el método que hace que tocar la guitarra sea fácil...facilísimo. Además, es super económico, ya que no tiene que pagar grandes cantidades por clases particulares, las cuales pueden ser costosas. El video es equivalente a muchísimas horas de estudio por lo que el costo es mínimo.

Es posible ordenar su método hoy mismo o pedirlo en su librería o tienda de discos favorita.

Y tiene una super garantía. Si en 60 días no aprende, puede devolver su método para una vuelta de su (30) y por supuesto, se puede quedar con las cuerdas. Pregunte a sus amigos. Estamos seguros que ya han oído hablar de GUITARRA FACILISIMA. Tanta gente satisfecha no se puede equivocar. Ordene su curso hoy mismo y empiece a ser feliz.

(26) 1 satisfechas
2 enojados
3 aburridas
4 casadas

26 ____

(27) 1 abogados 3 aduaneros
2 artistas 4 arquitectos 27 ____

(28) 1 reloj 3 video
2 vuelo 4 recuerdo 28 ____

(29) 1 perfeccionar 3 comprar
2 parar 4 cantar 29 ____

(30) 1 tarjeta 3 diccionario
2 guitarra 4 dinero 30 ____

PART 4

Write your answers to Part 4 according to the directions for *a* and *b*. [16]

a Directions: Write **one** well-organized note in Spanish as directed below. [6]

Choose **either** question 31 **or** 32. Write a well-organized note, following the specific instructions given in the question you have chosen. Your note must consist of **at least six clauses.** To qualify for credit, a clause must contain a verb, a stated or implied subject, and additional words necessary to convey meaning. The six clauses may be contained in fewer than six sentences if some of the sentences have more than one clause.

31 You just found something that belongs to your friend. You stop by to return it, but your friend is not at home. Write a note in Spanish to your friend to explain that you have found something that belongs to him or her.

In the note, you may wish to tell your friend what you found, where you found it, and when it was found. You may also wish to suggest how your friend can get it back from you. **Be sure you accomplish the purpose of the note, which is *to tell your friend that you have found something that belongs to him or her.***

Use the following:

Salutation: Hola [your friend's first name],
Closing: Un abrazo, [your first name]

The salutation and closing will *not* be counted as part of the six required clauses.

32 You and a friend had made plans to get together this weekend for outside activities. However, bad weather is expected all weekend. Write a note in Spanish to your friend suggesting other activities that you could do.

In the note, you may wish to explain that bad weather is expected and tell how you learned about it. You may then want to suggest inside activities that you could do together. **Be sure you accomplish the purpose of the note, which is *to suggest activities that you could do.***

Use the following:

Salutation: [your friend's first name],
Closing: [your first name]

The salutation and closing will *not* be counted as part of the six required clauses.

b Directions: Write **one** well-organized composition in Spanish as directed below. [10]

Choose **either** question 33 **or** 34. Write a well-organized composition, following the specific instructions given in the question you have chosen. Your composition must consist of **at least 10 clauses.** To qualify for credit, a clause must contain a verb, a stated or implied subject, and additional words necessary to convey meaning. The 10 clauses may be contained in fewer than 10 sentences if some of the sentences have more than one clause.

33 In Spanish, write a story about the situation shown in the picture below. It must be a story relating to the picture, **not** a description of the picture. Do *not* write a dialogue.

34 You recently participated in a community service activity. In Spanish, write a letter to your pen pal telling him or her about this activity.

You must accomplish the purpose of the letter, which is *to tell your pen pal about the community service activity.*

In your letter, you may wish to identify the activity (helping out in a hospital, cleaning local parks, working with young children, etc.). You may want to mention how often you participate, tell where you go and who else is involved with you in this activity, and tell why you like to participate in this activity. You may also want to ask if your pen pal has participated in a similar activity.

You may use any or all of the ideas suggested above *or* you may use your own ideas. **Either way, you must tell your pen pal about the community service activity.**

Use the following:

Dateline: el 18 de junio de 1998
Salutation: Querido/Querida [your pen pal's first name],
Closing: [your first name]

The dateline, salutation, and closing will *not* be counted as part of the 10 required clauses.

Answers June 1998

Comprehensive Examination in Spanish

PART 1

This part of the examination was evaluated prior to the date of this written examination. [24 credits]

PART 2

The following passages are to be read aloud to the students according to the directions given for this part at the beginning of this examination. The correct answers are given after number 15. [30 credits]

1. You are listening to a radio program in Puerto Rico. You hear this announcement about an upcoming contest:

   ¡Convierta a su bebé en video-estrella! ¡Envíenos un video con alguna escena cómica de su bebé! Gane diez mil dólares para la educación de su hijo u otros premios fabulosos. Hágalo pronto porque también hay regalos especiales para los primeros cien videos que se reciban.

   Envíe su cinta con su nombre, dirección, y el nombre y la edad del pequeño a *TeleMujer,* Apartado 600, San Juan, Puerto Rico. Los mejores concursantes saldrán en el programa *TeleMujer*.

   Who would be most interested in this contest?

2. You are shopping at El Corte Inglés, a major department store in Madrid. You hear this announcement:

   ¡Atención, viajero! Hemos creado un servicio único: el "servicio pasaporte", que le ofrece exclusiva atención al turista. Entre las ventajas increíbles hay un diez por ciento de descuento, envío de mercancía a su hotel o al extranjero, y dos horas de estacionamiento gratis. Solicite la tarjeta de compras "servicio pasaporte". ¡Con nosotros, su pasaporte de otro país vale dinero y la máxima comodidad en sus compras!

Who would benefit most from this service offered by El Corte Inglés?

3. You are living with a family in Mexico. While your host mother is away from home, she calls and says:

Hola. Vamos a llegar tarde a casa hoy. Necesito que empiece a preparar la cena. En la nevera hay cebollas, tomates y pescado fresco. Corte las cebollas y los tomates. Póngalos en una cacerola y añada el pescado. Cocínelo todo junto durante 45 minutos. José y yo llegaremos aproximadamente a las nueve. Muchas gracias por su ayuda.

What does your host mother want you to do?

4. You are listening to a Spanish-language program and hear this announcement:

El Departamento de Parques y Recreación de Austin invita a toda la comunidad a las fiestas acuáticas todos los sábados en diferentes piscinas municipales. Todos los invitados pueden traer sus flotadores. Mientras ellos flotan en el agua fresca, pueden ver sus películas favoritas que comienzan a las nueve. La entrada es de dos dólares por adulto; los menores de dieciocho años pagan cincuenta centavos. Se proveen refrescos.

What is a unique feature of this activity?

5. You are listening to a Spanish radio program from Boston and you hear this announcement:

La compañía Kraft anuncia que va a apoyar el programa "Lectores Jóvenes" de los centros educativos nacionales Lulac. Kraft va a donar dinero y premios a este programa de verano en Boston. El objetivo principal de este proyecto es ayudar a los estudiantes a mejorar su capacidad para leer. Al mismo tiempo se quiere entusiasmarlos para que lean por toda la vida.

What opportunity is being offered to students?

6. You hear this advertisement about a new product:

Una compañía española acaba de anunciar un nuevo sistema telefónico que ayuda a limitar la duración de las llamadas y a hacer un uso racional del teléfono. Según sus creadores, este sistema puede ahorrar entre el 30 y el 40 por ciento de la cuenta normal. Otra ventaja para los padres de familia es que este aparato puede limitar las llamadas de larga distancia de sus niños. Así, en general, las llamadas serán más cortas. Para más información, llame a NETTEL, 314–49–13.

What is this product designed to do?

7. Your Spanish friend has left you this message on your answering machine:

Oye, ¿dónde estás cuando te necesito? Hace tres horas que trato de llamarte. No entiendo nada de la lección de historia. Tú eres el único que saca buenas notas en este curso. No voy a salir bien sin tu ayuda. Llámame o ven a mi casa. Hasta pronto.

What is the purpose of this message?

8. You hear this announcement on a Mexican radio station:

¿Hablas inglés? Si tienes excelente presentación, estudios de bachillerato o equivalente y tu edad es entre los 20 y 30 años, te invitamos a integrarte a nuestro equipo de trabajo. Solicitamos vendedores para trabajar en nuestras tiendas del aeropuerto de Vallarta. Ofrecemos buen sueldo y posibilidad de avance.

What does this announcement describe?

9. You are watching a Mexican channel on television and hear this news item:

Aprovechando la celebración de su Quinto Centenario, el Instituto de Arte de Chicago organizó una gran exposición sobre el arte y la cultura precolombinos. Esta exposición llamada "La América Antigua" representa una colaboración entre los museos nacionales de países centro y sudamericanos y también de los Estados Unidos y Europa. La exhibición contiene unas 300 piezas procedentes de diez y siete culturas diferentes como las culturas maya, inca, y azteca. Muchas de estas obras se exhiben por primera vez en este país. La exposición también se trasladará a Houston y a Los Angeles.

What is the subject of this exhibition?

10. Your Argentinian friend is telling you about a new restaurant. She says:

Entré en el nuevo restaurante de la ciudad y pedí de comer. Noté que el mantel de la mesa no estaba muy limpio. También se olvidaron de ponerme una cuchara y una servilleta. Me sirvieron la sopa fría y la carne dura. Todo lo que me dieron era malo y caro.

¿Cómo era el nuevo restaurante?

11. You are listening to the radio and you hear this news item:

El cantante británico Sting ha participado en un coloquio en la Universidad Complutense de Madrid. Sting, uno de los cantantes más ocupados del momento, confesó: "Vivo en un castillo maravilloso, pero estoy conectado con los problemas de la gente". También reafirmó su decisión de participar en causas nobles. Sting comentó: "No he hecho el dinero explotando a nadie ni robando, y pienso que con mis canciones doy felicidad a la gente".

¿Qué les dijo el cantante Sting a los estudiantes universitarios?

12. While staying with a family in Mexico City, you hear your host brother talking on the telephone. He is giving someone directions:

Cuando vengas a visitarme no tomes la Avenida Juárez. Sé que el viaje va a ser más largo, pero ya hace tres semanas que tienen cerradas varias calles a causa de la construcción del nuevo túnel para el tren subterráneo. Es mejor si cruzas por el puente y en veinte minutos estarás en mi casa.

¿Por qué no se debe tomar la Avenida Juárez?

13. You are watching television and hear this information:

La natación es perfecta para mejorar el tono muscular de todo el cuerpo, aliviar dolores de espalda y cuello, y tranquilizar los nervios. Nadando se realiza un buen ejercicio sin riesgo de lesiones. Se mueven casi todos los músculos del cuerpo y se gastan un montón de calorías. Aprovecha tus vacaciones para iniciarte en este deporte con la promesa de seguir todo el año. Las personas que lo hacen dicen sentirse eufóricas después de nadar. A ti puede ocurrirte lo mismo.

¿Qué recomienda esta persona?

14. You are visiting Puerto Rico and a travel agent is explaining about a place to stay:

La Hacienda Miramar es uno de los dieciséis hoteles estilo paradores de Puerto Rico. Este parador está ganando popularidad entre los visitantes cansados de grandes hoteles. Muchos viajeros buscan escapar de la multitud de turistas para explorar los lugares históricos de la isla y al mismo tiempo disfrutar de la paz que el ambiente rural les ofrece.

¿Por qué es popular este hotel?

15. While you are touring Mérida, Mexico, your guide says:

Hay que visitar los templos arqueológicos de Yucatán. Para disfrutar mejor de su viaje a los templos arqueológicos, le recomendamos lo siguiente: Utilice sombrero. Lleve una loción bloqueadora de sol. Utilice zapatos cómodos. Recuerde que es ilegal llevarse objetos o materiales encontrados en los sitios arqueológicos.

¿Qué recomienda el guía?

PART 2

(1) 1	**(4)** 4	**(7)** 3	**(10)** 1	**(13)** 3
(2) 2	**(5)** 1	**(8)** 4	**(11)** 1	**(14)** 2
(3) 2	**(6)** 3	**(9)** 2	**(12)** 4	**(15)** 3

PART 3

(a) (16) 1	**(b) (21)** 2	**(c) (26)** 1
(17) 4	**(22)** 1	**(27)** 2
(18) 3	**(23)** 3	**(28)** 3
(19) 2	**(24)** 4	**(29)** 1
(20) 1	**(25)** 4	**(30)** 4

PART 4

(a) Notes in writing

For each note, an example of a response worth six credits follows. The slash marks indicate how each sample note has been divided into clauses.

31. Hola Miguel,

Encontré tus llaves esta mañana./$_1$ Estaban en la sala de mi casa./$_2$ Pasé por tu casa/$_3$ y no estabas./$_4$ Puedes llamarme esta noche/$_5$ para recogerlas./$_6$ Sé que las necesitas para entrar en tu casa.

Un abrazo,
Ricardo

32. Pepita,

Tenemos que cambiar nuestros planes para este fin de semana./$_1$ Si quieres/$_2$ vamos a ver una película a las dos de la tarde./$_3$ Después nos vamos de compras./$_4$ También podemos comer una hamburguesa./$_5$ Por la noche escuchamos música en mi casa./$_6$

Lucía

(b) Narrative based on picture/letter

For each narrative/letter, an example of a response worth 10 credits follows. The slash marks indicate how each sample narrative/letter has been divided into clauses.

33. (Picture)

Los señores Gómez caminaban por la tarde,/$_1$ y vieron a la señora Hernández./$_2$ Ella salió a pasearse con su hijita./$_3$ La señora Gómez miró a la niñita/$_4$ y empezó a sonreír a la bebé./$_5$ Habló de la belleza de la pequeña./$_6$ La mamá les contó las grandes cosas/$_7$ que hacía su niña/$_8$ y que era una bebé muy buena./$_9$ Después de varios minutos, la pareja, muy alegre, continuó su paseo/$_{10}$ y la señora, con su hija, volvió a casa.

34. (Letter)

el 18 de junio de 1998

Querido Diego,

Recientemente yo participé en una actividad muy interesante./$_1$ Mi clase y yo decidimos/$_2$ que ayudaríamos a limpiar nuestro pueblo./$_3$ Primero, fuimos al parque/$_4$ donde recogimos la basura/$_5$ que estaba por todas partes./$_6$ Después fuimos al río/$_7$ para coleccionar botellas y latas./$_8$ Las llevamos al centro de reciclaje./$_9$ Trabajamos cada fin de semana por tres meses./$_{10}$ Me gustó mucho esta actividad. ¿Tiene tu escuela un programa como éste?

Felipe

Examination January 1999

Comprehensive Examination in Spanish

PART 1

Your performance on Part 1, Speaking (24 credits), has been evaluated prior to the date of this written examination.

PART 2

Answer all questions in Part 2 according to the directions for *a* and *b*. [30]

a Directions (1–9): For each question, you will hear some background information in English *once.* Then you will hear a passage in Spanish *twice* and a question in English *once.* After you have heard the question, the teacher will pause while you read the question and the four suggested answers. Choose the best suggested answer and write its *number* in the space provided. Base your answer *on the content of the passage, only.* The passages that the teacher will read aloud to you are found in the ANSWERS section, Part 2, at the end of this examination. [18]

1 As a child, what did this celebrity always want to do?

1 become an artist
2 visit other countries
3 perform in the theater
4 learn several languages 1 _____

2 What information does this announcement give to tourists?

1 There will be a short delay due to problems at Customs.
2 Food and beverages will be served during the flight.
3 Travelers bringing produce into the United States will be fined.
4 Passengers traveling with young children will board first. 2 _____

3 Why is a new price being advertised?

1 as a result of an increase in mailing costs
2 as a result of a delay in the production schedule
3 as a result of a temporary labor problem
4 as a result of a special supplement 3 _____

4 What message did Alicia leave on the answering machine?

1 She forgot to buy the watch.
2 The jeweler did not have the gift ready.
3 Her father borrowed her car for the day.
4 She was unable to do the favor you wanted. 4 _____

5 Where did this traveler spend most of her time?

1 relaxing on the beach in Belize
2 visiting ruins from an ancient civilization
3 shopping in a large historical city
4 visiting historical museums in Belize 5 _____

6 How did Angélica Rivera achieve international fame?

1 She was a model with several foreign agencies.
2 Her soap opera was televised in other countries.
3 She was a conductor of a Mexican orchestra.
4 Her appearance in Mexican commercials made her popular. 6 _____

7 What does this message concern?

1 disconnecting telephone service
2 a new answering machine
3 additional telephone numbers
4 changes in telephone rates 7 _____

8 How would visitors to this small village in Spain participate in its festival?

1 by throwing ripe tomatoes
2 by marching in a parade
3 by tasting a variety of regional dishes
4 by dancing in the streets 8 _____

9 What new type of product is being made available to consumers?

1 vegetables that are grown in water rather than soil
2 vitamins that can replace many foods
3 products that are natural and healthy
4 foods that are easy to prepare 9 _____

b Directions (10–15): For each question, you will hear some background information in English *once.* Then you will hear a passage in Spanish *twice* and a question in Spanish *once.* After you have heard the question, the teacher will pause while you read the question and the four suggested answers. Choose the best suggested answer and write its *number* in the space provided. Base your answer *on the content of the passage, only.* The passages that the teacher will read aloud to you are found in the ANSWERS section, Part 2, at the end of this examination. [12]

10 ¿De qué trata este anuncio?

1 el precio de billetes para un juego de béisbol profesional
2 la falta de respeto de los aficionados
3 la fabricación de bates de aluminio
4 el aumento en popularidad de un artículo de ropa de béisbol 10 _____

11 ¿Cómo se escapa tu amiga de su rutina en el trabajo?

1 Habla por teléfono con su novio.
2 Lee su revista favorita.
3 Contesta su correo personal.
4 Escucha su música predilecta. 11 _____

12 ¿Qué beneficio ofrece el sistema Clarión?

1 Mejora su habilidad como conductor.
2 Disminuye el número de accidentes.
3 Hace los viajes menos aburridos.
4 Reduce la contaminación del ambiente. 12 _____

13 ¿Por qué no pudo disfrutar la película Geraldo?

1 porque no podía ver la película
2 porque no se sentó con sus amigos
3 porque no era violenta
4 porque no podía oír bien 13 _____

14 ¿Cuál es una ventaja de este producto?

1 que alivia el dolor dental al rellenar las caries
2 que blanquea los dientes sin sustancias químicas fuertes
3 que reduce el mal aliento
4 que elimina la necesidad de cepillarse los dientes 14 _____

15 ¿Qué problema tienen Graciela y Rosa?

1 Dejaron el dinero en casa.
2 Se perdieron en la ciudad.
3 Llegaron temprano al restaurante.
4 Tomaron el autobús equivocado. 15 _____

PART 3

Answer all questions in Part 3 according to the directions for *a*, *b*, and *c*. [30]

a Directions (16–20): After the following passage, there are five questions or incomplete statements. For *each,* choose the word or expression that best answers the question or completes the statement *according to the meaning of the passage,* and write its *number* in the space provided. [10]

Miguel de Cervantes Saavedra

Me llamo Miguel de Cervantes Saavedra. Mis padres eran nobles pero muy pobres. Mi vida está llena de aventuras de todas clases. Yo creo que nací en Alcalá de Henares en 1547, pero nadie puede asegurarlo. Estudié en la Universidad de Alcalá y en la de Salamanca.

Recuerdo que cuando era niño me gustaba mucho leer. Siempre estaba leyendo. Cuando iba por la calle recogía los papeles de la calle para leerlos.

A los veintiún años me marché de España para probar mi fortuna. Trabajé al servicio del Cardenal Aquaviva cuando llegué a Roma. Italia me gustó mucho y allí pude leer muchos libros de los escritores clásicos italianos. Pero yo no había nacido para ser criado y dos años después me enlisté como soldado en el ejército, y me fui a pelear contra los piratas turcos.

Nuestro jefe era Don Juan de Austria, un príncipe valiente, que era hijo de Carlos V. Peleamos contra los piratas en las ciudades de Corfú, Túnez y Navarino. En 1571 luchamos en el Golfo de Lepanto contra los turcos. En esta batalla yo fui herido en el pecho y en la mano. Perdí el uso de la mano izquierda y por eso me llaman el Manco de Lepanto. Estoy orgulloso de ese apodo.

Pero con una sola mano no podía pelear. Entonces decidí volver a Italia donde pasé el tiempo necesario para curarme y aprender el italiano.

Muchos años después volví a España. ¡Qué triste! Mi padre había muerto, y mi familia estaba en la pobreza. En este punto de mi vida decidí cambiar de carrera. Yo dejé de ser soldado y empecé a escribir. Desde niño siempre tuve interés en la literatura y en escribir.

Estaba yo entonces enamorado de Catalina Salazar y Palacios. Me casé con ella, y ella fue la inspiración para mi primera obra, titulada *La Galatea.* Pero esta novela no tuvo éxito. Entonces decidí escribir para el teatro y por cuatro años escribí muchas obras breves y unas treinta comedias. De las numerosas obras que yo escribí solamente la *Numancia* y los *Tratos de Argel* tuvieron éxito. Confieso que me dejó muy triste que solamente dos de mis obras tuvieron éxito. Decidí buscar otro trabajo. Encontré un empleo de administración en Sevilla. Pero aún allí me persiguió la mala fortuna. Por hacer un error financiero con el dinero de la compañía me pusieron en la cárcel.

¡Qué días más tristes pasé en la cárcel! Pero, allí empecé a escribir mi primera novela, *El ingenioso hidalgo don Quijote de La Mancha,* también conocido como *Don Quijote.* Por fin lo terminé. Se publicó. Fue un éxito. En un año se publicaron dos ediciones que fueron traducidas a varios idiomas.

Continué escribiendo. Publiqué una colección de *Novelas Ejemplares;* éstas son cuentos cortos sobre costumbres españolas de esta época. También escribí la segunda parte de *Don Quijote.* Muchos críticos creen que la segunda parte de *Don Quijote* es mejor que la primera parte. La última obra que escribí fue *Los Trabajos de Persiles y Segismunda.*

Es verdad que mi vida fue muy difícil, pero mis dificultades me hicieron filósofo. Mis aventuras fueron la materia que les dio vida a mis narraciones. Mis viajes me dieron nuevas ideas y material que puedo usar por muchos años. ¡Estoy orgulloso de haber escrito el libro divertido, *Don Quijote*, y de que me llamen *el Manco de Lepanto!*

16 ¿Cuáles son algunos de los trabajos de Miguel de Cervantes?

1 músico y vendedor
2 soldado y escritor
3 carpintero y profesor
4 bibliotecario y médico 16 _____

17 ¿Qué otro nombre tiene Miguel de Cervantes Saavedra?

1 Catalina Salazar y Palacios
2 Don Juan de Austria
3 Manco de Lepanto
4 Carlos V 17 _____

18 ¿Con quién contrae matrimonio Miguel de Cervantes?

1 doña Juana
2 Catalina Salazar y Palacios
3 una mujer italiana
4 una estudiante de la Universidad de Salamanca 18 _____

19 ¿Dónde comenzó a escribir *Don Quijote?*

1 en la cárcel
2 en la universidad
3 en un teatro
4 en una biblioteca italiana 19 _____

20 ¿Cuál es el resultado de sus dificultades?

1 Decide abandonar sus sueños.
2 Se casó varias veces cuando era joven.
3 Nunca puede viajar al extranjero.
4 Tiene mucha información para seguir escribiendo. 20 _____

b Directions (21–25): Below each of the following selections, there is either a question or an incomplete statement. For *each*, choose the word or expression that best answers the question or completes the statement *according to the meaning of the selection*, and write its *number* in the space provided. [10]

21

Ahora siempre hay algo bueno en la TV. Gracias a Inglés Sin Barreras, el curso de inglés americano con explicaciones en español.

Nuestros videocassettes hacen su aprendizaje tan fácil como ver su programa favorito de TV.

Nuestros audiocassettes mejoran su inglés en su automóvil, en su hogar, o en el trabajo.

Nuestros libros ilustrados le permiten aprender a leer, escribir y practicar lo aprendido.

Lo mejor de todo es que aprenderá inglés en forma natural, mirando, escuchando y repitiendo, tal como aprendió español cuando niño, con la misma escritura, pronunciación y acentos usados en EE.UU.

Su videocasetera se habrá convertido en su mejor maestro.

Empiece a aprender inglés ahora mismo. Llámenos hoy mismo al teléfono **1-800-473-1111.**

This advertisement provides information about

1 a way to learn English
2 a course in television repair
3 the benefits of using videos in the classroom
4 a collection of cassettes of popular music 21 _____

22 **¡Alerta!**

Según la División de Agencias de Modelaje nada como una agencia reconocida para descubrir el talento de su niño modelo. Las siguientes son algunas precauciones que debe tomar antes de acurdir a una agencia de modelaje:

• Asegúrese de que la agencia tenga licencia del estado.

• Conozca cuanto sea posible sobre la industria del modelaje.

• Esté alerta ante agencias que tratan de presionarla para que invierta dinero en ofertas de fotografía para el portafolio de su niño

• Revise el portafolio de la agencia.

• Solicite una lista de clientes satisfechos. Llámelos y pídales su opinión.

• Desconfíe de los anuncios en la prensa que solicitan modelos infantiles.

What advice does this notice give?

1 Children should be dressed in practical clothing.
2 Children should be encouraged to develop artistic talents.
3 A legal contract should be understood before it is signed.
4 The credentials of modeling agencies should be investigated.

22 ______

23

Nuevas tarifas de la Edición Internacional de EL PAÍS

A partir de este número, y en coincidencia con el inicio del año 1996, la Edición Internacional de EL PAÍS va a aumentar sus tarifas generales, tanto de suscripción como del precio de portada. Dichas tarifas no habían sufrido variación alguna desde enero de 1991, salvo un pequeño ajuste introducido en abril de 1994 en las correspondientes a los países del norte de América, Asia Oriental y Oceanía. El aumento de los costes, sobre todo en lo referente al papel y a la distribución, hacen obligatoria esta revisión tarifaria, que contempla un incremento del 11,1% en los precios que han permanecido sin cambios durante más tiempo y menor en las tarifas que fueron modificadas en abril de 1994. El precio del ejemplar suelto de venta al número pasa a ser de $2,25. El nuevo cadro de tarifas de suscripción queda fijado como sigue:

NUEVAS TARIFAS DE LA EDICIÓN INTERNACI

Destino	US $ 1 año (52 números)	US $ 9 meses (39 números)	US $ 6 meses (26 números)	US $ 3 meses (13 númerc
EE UU y Canadá	105	80	55	30
Asia oriental y Oceanía	125	95	65	35
Resto de países	100	75	50	25

This announcement informs readers that

1 subscribers will receive additional copies at no cost
2 an international edition will soon be available
3 subscription prices will be raised
4 more copies will be printed each day

23 ______

24

▶ POR AMERICO ESPINAL HUED

A los santiagueros sólo les resta llorar por su ciudad. Han resultado inútiles todos los esfuerzos que ha hecho la prensa y las amas de casas para mantener limpia la ciudad de Santiago.

Santiago se ha convertido en una ciudad altamente contaminada, con una fea imagen por la basura que anda por dondequiera.

Los escasos camiones recolectores de basura que le quedan al Ayuntamiento de la ciudad están deteriorados.

En las zonas céntricas de la ciudad pasan cada diez o quince días a recoger la basura y los desperdicios que se amontonan en la ciudad. En los barrios periféricos la ausencia es mayor.

La ciudadanía aprende a no lanzar desperdicios a las calles. Pero hace falta el rigor de la ley para disciplinar a los insensatos que todavía echan basura en la ciudad.

A los santiagueros sólo les resta llorar por el abandono de su otrora ciudad limpia y organizada.

El autor es abogado

According to this editorial, the city of Santiago has a problem with

1 repairing public streets
2 inadequate garbage removal
3 deterioration of the city hall
4 excessive automobile traffic

24 ______

25

UNO DE LOS ALIMENTOS QUE MEJOR RESPONDE A LAS NECESIDADES DE LOS HOGARES DE HOY

Cada vez somos más los que tendemos a llevar una alimentación sana y equilibrada. Y cada vez es menos el tiempo del que disponemos para preparar platos realmente sanos, nutritivos y atractivos para todo la familia.

Con los seis sabores de Gelatina Royal-Naranja, Limón, Fresa, Piña, Frambuesa y Tutti Frutti- o en su variedad de Gelatina Neutra Royal, se pueden hacer deliciosas y espectaculares recetas, preparándolas en un momento y dejándolas en el frigorífico (mínimo dos horas) antes de sorprender a grandes y pequeños con un desayuno, postre, merienda o cena excepcionales a la vista, suaves y frescos al paladar, y muy saludables.

This advertisement is intended to appeal to

1 teachers of health courses
2 families who want to buy a refrigerator
3 people interested in fast ways of cooking
4 families with health problems 25 _____

c Directions (26–30): In the following passage, there are five blank spaces numbered 26 through 30. Each blank space represents a missing word or expression. For each blank space, four possible completions are provided. Only one of them makes sense *in the context of the passage.*

First, read the passage in its entirety to determine its general meaning. Then read it a second time. For each blank space, choose the completion that makes the best sense and write its *number* in the space provided. [10]

Puerto Rico: Isla Turística

Al ponerse el sol sobre las altas montañas de la Cordillera Central de Puerto Rico, los techos rojos de Hacienda Juanita brillan en medio de la vegetación tropical. El patio central de la Hacienda Juanita es un refugio tranquilo con una plaza, una fuente y flores vibrantes. El aire fresco y los colores pastel le dan al comedor un ambiente agradable.

La Hacienda Juanita fue establecida hace más de 150 años por un aristócrata español. La tierra era fértil para establecer una plantación de café. Hoy día la Hacienda Juanita es uno de los destinos turísticos más especiales de la isla. La Hacienda es parte del sistema de paradores de Puerto Rico. Los paradores, o posadas, son hoteles pequeños con un espíritu particular. Los paradores se encuentran en los lugares menos visitados de la isla por los turistas. La Hacienda Juanita y los otros ___(26)___ están ganando popularidad con los turistas que están cansados de los grandes hoteles. Estos ___(27)___ están ansiosos de escapar de la multitud para explorar los variados encantos del campo puertorriqueño.

Según María Alicia Laird, una turista que viajó allí de Nueva York, la Hacienda Juanita provee una experiencia típica de esta bella isla. En la Hacienda "hay un verdadero deseo de preservar lo que es auténticamente ___(28)___. El menú es muy típico. La piscina es una maravilla. La librería y la tienda de regalos tienen cosas auténticas. ¡Nos encantó!"

En otros lugares de la isla, el sistema de paradores que son administrados por el gobierno ofrece experiencias similares. Otra posada llamada Villa Parguera, al sudoeste de la isla, combina las comodidades de un gran hotel con la atmósfera de informalidad de un parador. "Hay gente que viene cada año desde hace 25 años", dice el gerente, Nelson Ortega. "Tenemos un ___(29)___ familiar que se adapta perfectamente para cualquiera, desde parejas de Luna de Miel hasta ancianos".

Una de las atracciones del lugar es el maravilloso espectáculo nocturno en la Bahía Fosforescente. Otro lugar para visitar está a apenas 20 minutos. Se trata del pueblo de Cabo Rojo, con sus acantilados lisos, sus olas fuertes y un faro construido en estilo español.

Cerca de la ciudad de Coamo, el Parador Baños de Coamo refleja la elegancia que cultivaba décadas atrás, con los baños termales más exclusivos de la isla. Las aguas termales y el ambiente rural con aspectos coloniales hace del Parador Baños de Coamo uno de los paradores más __(30)__.

A la sombra de la montaña más alta de Puerto Rico en la ciudad de Jayuya, la Hacienda Gripiñas es otro de los paradores históricos. La vieja finca de café de la Hacienda Gripiñas está rodeada de palmeras. El terreno cuidadosamente mantenido da la imagen de elegancia ganada con esfuerzo.

Luis Rivera, dueño de la Hacienda Juanita dice que "En España, los paradores usualmente están en viejos castillos. Pero en Puerto Rico no usamos los castillos como paradores, pero sí tenemos un encanto que es únicamente nuestro".

(26) 1 comedores 3 lagos
2 paradores 4 terrenos 26____

(27) 1 visitantes 3 trabajadores
2 nativos 4 estudiantes 27____

(28) 1 puertorriqueño 3 americano
2 neoyorquino 4 internacional 28 ____

(29) 1 número 3 ambiente
2 país 4 mercado 29 ____

(30) 1 complicados 3 aburridos
2 baratos 4 atractivos 30 ____

PART 4

Write your answers to Part 4 according to the directions for *a* and *b*. [16]

a Directions: Write **one** well-organized note in Spanish as directed below. [6]

Choose **either** question 31 **or** 32. Write a well-organized note, following the specific instructions given in the question you have chosen. Your note must consist of **at least six clauses.** To qualify for credit, a clause must contain a verb, a stated or implied subject, and additional words necessary to convey meaning. The six clauses may be contained in fewer than six sentences if some of the sentences have more than one clause.

31 You are an exchange student in Venezuela and have been asked by a teacher at your host school to talk to students about your own school in New York State. Write a note in Spanish to that teacher responding to the teacher's request.

In the note, you may want to thank the teacher for the opportunity to talk about your school and indicate whether you will be able to carry out the teacher's request. If you are unable to talk to students, you may wish to express your regret and tell why you cannot do what was requested. You may also want to make an alternate suggestion. If you are able to talk to students, you may wish to mention what topics you would like to talk about (e.g., use of time, food, music, school activities), ask your teacher any questions you have about the request, and indicate how much time you need to prepare. You may also wish to suggest a time and place for this activity. **Be sure to accomplish the purpose of the note, which is *to respond to the teacher's request.***

Use the following:

Salutation: Estimado Profesor/Estimada Profesora,
Closing: [your name]

The salutation and closing will *not* be counted as part of the six required clauses.

32 Your teacher gave everyone in your class a different assignment to complete. You do not like your topic and want to change it. Write a note in Spanish to your teacher to request a change in the topic.

In the note, you may wish to explain why you do not like the topic that was assigned and what topic you want to be assigned and why (e.g., availability of sources for references, familiarity with the topic, interest in the topic). You may also want to express your appreciation for considering your request to change the topic. **Be sure to accomplish the purpose of the note, which is *to request a change in the topic.***

Use the following:

Salutation: Estimado/Estimada [teacher's name],
Closing: Su estudiante, [your name]

The salutation and closing will *not* be counted as part of the six required clauses.

b Directions: Write **one** well-organized composition in Spanish as directed below. [10]

Choose **either** question 33 **or** 34. Write a well-organized composition, following the specific instructions given in the question you have chosen. Your composition must consist of **at least 10 clauses.** To qualify for credit, a clause must contain a verb, a stated or implied subject, and additional words necessary to convey meaning. The 10 clauses may be contained in fewer than 10 sentences if some of the sentences have more than one clause.

33 In Spanish, write a story about the situation shown in the picture below. It must be a story relating to the picture, **not** a description of the picture. Do *not* write a dialogue.

34 Your Spanish Club is planning a trip to Mexico during summer vacation. You are responsible for getting information in order to help plan the trip. In Spanish, write a letter to the Mexican Embassy requesting information.

You <u>must</u> accomplish the purpose of the letter, which is *to request information about Mexico*.

In your letter, you may want to ask about places and sites to visit, accommodations, weather, appropriate dress, public transportation, special events, and festivals. You may also wish to mention when you will take the trip and how you feel about going.

You may use any or all of the ideas suggested above *or* you may use your own ideas. **Either way, you must request information about Mexico.**

Use the following:

Dateline: el 27 de enero de 1999
Salutation: Estimado Director/Estimada Directora,
Closing: Atentamente, [your name]

The dateline, salutation, and closing will *not* be counted as part of the 10 required clauses.

Answers January 1999

Comprehensive Examination in Spanish

PART 1

This part of the examination was evaluated prior to the date of this written examination. [24 credits]

PART 2

The following passages are to be read aloud to the students according to the directions given for this part at the beginning of this examination. The correct answers are given after number 15. [30 credits]

1. A Spanish-speaking celebrity is being interviewed on television. She says:

Yo era una niña como todas, con mucha fantasía y tenía el gran sueño de ser pintora. Hija de padre chino y madre cubana, yo contemplaba con deleite mi mundo lleno de color que deseaba con fuerza en imágenes.

As a child, what did this celebrity always want to do?

2. You are at the airport in Cancun, Mexico, and hear this announcement:

Señores y Señoras. Es prohibido llevar frutas o vegetales de México a los Estados Unidos. Todos los pasajeros deben abordar el avión sin productos cultivados en México. La aduana en los Estados Unidos va a confiscar alimèntos de este país traídos por los turistas y también les pondrá una multa.

What information does this announcement give to tourists?

3. You are at a shopping mall and hear this announcement over the public address system:

Cambio 16, fiel a su cita, ofrece a los hombres todo lo que necesitan saber para estar a la última moda esta primavera-verano en el extra *Moda 16.* En esta edición especial hablamos de las tendencias en la moda de baño; los colores blancos, crudos y tostados, protagonistas de la temporada; la nueva ropa interior; los cuidados personales o los movimientos que marcan el estilo nuevo en la decoración. Por eso, *Cambio 16* cuesta esta semana 475 pesetas.

Why is a new price being advertised?

4. When you arrive home from school, you hear your Spanish friend's message on your telephone answering machine:

Te habla, Alicia. Lo siento, pero no fui a recoger el reloj como te prometí. Escucha. Es que esta mañana mi coche no funcionó y pasé todo el día con mi papá y el mecánico. ¡Qué horror! Ya llamé al joyero para decirle que no podía ir. Lo siento mucho. ¡Llámame cuando regreses!

What message did Alicia leave on the answering machine?

5. A visitor has come to your Spanish class to speak about her recent trip to Belize, Central America. She says:

Este verano visité un lugar histórico maravilloso. Escondido en las junglas, existe un auténtico tesoro de ciudades mayas. Este sitio data de miles de años y empieza ahora a ser apreciado por los arqueólogos. Al visitar este lugar histórico, se hace evidente que Belice fue una vez un gran centro del Imperio Maya. Allí, pasé la mayor parte de mis vacaciones, y yo lo recomiendo a quien tenga interés en las civilizaciones antiguas.

Where did this traveler spend most of her time?

6. You are listening to a television program about famous Latin Americans and hear this information:

La actriz mexicana Angélica Rivera actúa en la telenovela "La Dueña". La telenovela que recientemente terminó ahora se transmite en otros países. Es un éxito en Chile, Puerto Rico, Perú y los Estados Unidos. Las transmisiones a estos países le han dado a esta estrella mexicana fama internacional. Ahora Angélica Rivera iniciará su carrera como modelo y conductora de programas de videos.

How did Angélica Rivera achieve international fame?

7. You are an exchange student in Spain. During your hosts' absence, you answer this call from a telephone company representative:

Hola. Soy representante de la telefónica y quisiera ofrecerles un servicio nuevo, *Teletimbres*. Este servicio les permite tener hasta dos números telefónicos adicionales en su línea. Los números, aunque usan sólo una línea, tienen sonidos distintos. Así, el sonido del teléfono indicará para quién es la llamada antes de descolgar.

What does this message concern?

8. Your Spanish teacher is telling the class about an unusual "festival" in Spain. She says:

En Buñol, un pequeño pueblo en el este de España, se celebra "la tomatina" el último miércoles de agosto. No es una fiesta religiosa, sino un corto tiempo de gozo en tirarse tomates. Camiones llenos de tomates bien maduros pasan por la calle y reparten tomates a la gente, especialmente entre los chicos jóvenes. Con mucha risa, todos se tiran los tomates que vuelan por todas partes. "La tomatina" comienza y termina según un horario estricto y con reglas de cuidado. Dos horas después de tirarse el último tomate, la calle está tan limpia como si nunca hubiera ocurrido esta diversión.

How would visitors to this small village in Spain participate in its festival?

9. While shopping in a supermarket in Mexico, you hear this advertisement:

"Comebien", una marca líder en Europa, garantiza que sus productos son sanos y mantienen el sabor original y la riqueza en nutrientes. Estos productos son naturales y, además, protegen y cuidan el medio ambiente. Se nota que no utilizan los elementos químicos que contaminan los alimentos y que destruyen la riqueza de la tierra.

What new type of product is being made available to consumers?

10. While in Madrid, you hear a sports commentator on television. He says:

El origen de las gorras de béisbol fue muy práctico: para proteger a los jugadores de los rayos del sol. Pero pronto se han hecho populares las gorras en otros deportes. Hoy día la fabricación y comercialización de gorras deportivas es un negocio de primera magnitud. Ahora cuestan entre 1.850 pesetas y 15.000 pesetas. Las gorras más deseables son las de los Yankees de Nueva York y las de los White Sox de Chicago.

¿De qué trata este anuncio?

11. Your friend is telling you about a way to relax. Your friend says:

Yo trabajo como secretaria bilingüe en una agencia internacional. Como pueden imaginarse siempre tengo mucho que hacer. A veces quiero dejarlo todo y salir corriendo. Los únicos momentos en que me siento aliviada, son cuando leo mi nueva edición de VANIDADES. Cada página de esta revista es una sorpresa agradable para mí; siempre la leo toda, incluyendo la sección de correspondencia y sé que reciben miles de felicitaciones, las cuales apoyo sinceramente.

¿Cómo se escapa tu amiga de su rutina en el trabajo?

12. You are listening to the radio and hear this advertisement:

Los largos viajes por carretera serán más agradables gracias al sistema multimedia Clarión para el automóvil. Detrás del asiento del conductor se instala un televisor a color de 15 centímetros, con vídeo, para que los viajeros del coche disfruten de los largos viajes. Por sólo 250.000 pesetas los viajeros pueden disfrutar de juegos en la televisión o ver sus películas favoritas.

¿Qué beneficio ofrece el sistema Clarión?

13. You are talking to your friend Geraldo from Bolivia. He tells you about what happened to him last night at the movies. He says:

Le pedí a una señora que estaba sentada delante de mí si sería tan amable de quitarse el sombrero. Ella me dijo en tono violento que si no podía ver que me sentara en otro lugar. Como el cine estaba bastante lleno decidí quedarme donde estaba porque no íbamos a conseguir otros asientos para sentarnos todos juntos. Así que no pude disfrutar mucho la película.

¿Por qué no pudo disfrutar la película Geraldo?

14. You are listening to the radio in Lima, Peru, and you hear this advertisement:

Si tus dientes no están blancos es porque tú no quieres. Blanx, el nuevo producto dentífrico, reúne dos conceptos en un solo producto: salud y belleza para tus dientes. Blanx es el primer dentífrico cosmético protector que blanquea tus dientes naturalmente. Contiene una sustancia natural, y previene la formación de las caries. El blanco natural de tus dientes volverá. Es hora de que regrese el blanco de tus dientes. Blanx, dientes blancos, dientes sanos y de forma natural.

¿Cuál es una ventaja de este producto?

15. You are walking on a street in Barcelona and you hear Graciela and Rosa talking. Rosa says:

Oye, estoy harta de caminar. No conozco esta ciudad para nada. Hace media hora que caminamos y no encontramos el restaurante. Dices que estaba en esta esquina, pero ya le hemos dado la vuelta a la manzana varias veces y no lo vimos. Vamos a preguntarle a alguien porque si no, vamos a llegar tarde a la cita.

¿Qué problema tienen Graciela y Rosa?

PART 2

(1) 1	**(4)** 4	**(7)** 3	**(10)** 4	**(13)** 1
(2) 3	**(5)** 2	**(8)** 1	**(11)** 2	**(14)** 2
(3) 4	**(6)** 2	**(9)** 3	**(12)** 3	**(15)** 2

PART 3

(a) **(16)** 2	**(b)** **(21)** 1	**(c)** **(26)** 2
(17) 3	**(22)** 4	**(27)** 1
(18) 2	**(23)** 3	**(28)** 1
(19) 1	**(24)** 2	**(29)** 3
(20) 4	**(25)** 3	**(30)** 4

PART 4

(a) Notes in writing

For each note, an example of a response worth six credits follows. The slash marks indicate how each sample note has been divided into clauses.

31 Estimada Profesora,

En mi opinión, es una buena idea hablar a sus clases./$_1$ Puedo darles mucha información sobre mi escuela en Nueva York./$_2$ Si quiere,/$_3$ puedo compartir información sobre las clases, el horario, y también sobre los profesores./$_4$ Tengo muchas fotos y un vídeo también./$_5$ No tengo clases los martes./$_6$ ¿Es posible que venga la semana próxima?

Joseph Smith

32 Estimado Señor López,

Tengo un problema grande con el tópico/$_1$ que me dio./$_2$ Es que/$_3$ no sé mucho de la comida típica de España/$_4$ y, sería imposible preparar una receta enfrente de la clase./$_5$ ¡No sé cocinar!/$_6$ ¿Puede darme otro tópico? Me gustan los deportes. Pero me encanta la música. Aún puedo tocar la guitarra. ¡Por favor, señor López!

Su estudiante,
Carmen

(b) Narrative based on picture/letter

For each narrative/letter, an example of a response worth 10 credits follows. The slash marks indicate how each sample narrative/letter has been divided into clauses.

33 **(Picture)**

La madre de Javier está muy enojada con él./$_1$ Javier sabe/$_2$ que es prohibido jugar con la pelota en la casa./$_3$ Javier también sabe/$_4$ que esa lámpara era un regalo especial de sus abuelos./$_5$ Normalmente, Javier sale de la casa/$_6$ para jugar con sus amigos./$_7$ Pero hoy llueve mucho/$_8$ y decidió quedarse en casa./$_9$ Javier se aburrió/$_{10}$ y encontró la pelota para divertirse. Ahora, tiene que ahorrar dinero para reembolsar a su mamá.

34 **(Letter)**

el 27 de enero de 1999

Estimado Director,

Le escribo esta carta de la parte de mi clase de español./$_1$ Queremos visitar su país/$_2$ y por eso le pido el favor de mandarme alguna información./$_3$ ¿Qué tiempo hará en agosto en la capital?/$_4$ ¿Se puede usar los dólares americanos?/$_5$ ¿Hay hoteles buenos a precios razonables para estudiantes?/$_6$ También, quiero saber/$_7$ si es mejor usar el metro o los autobuses./$_8$ Nuestro profesor no quiere/$_9$ que comamos en los restaurantes de servicio rápido./$_{10}$ ¿Me puede recomendar unos restaurantes buenos con la comida típica de México? Espero recibir su respuesta pronto para prepararnos para el viaje.

Atentamente,
Ana Gómez

Examination June 1999

Comprehensive Examination in Spanish

PART 1

Your performance on Part 1, Speaking (24 credits), has been evaluated prior to the date of this written examination.

PART 2

Answer all questions in Part 2 according to the directions for *a* and *b*. [30]

a Directions (1–9): For each question, you will hear some background information in English *once.* Then you will hear a passage in Spanish *twice* and a question in English *once.* After you have heard the question, the teacher will pause while you read the question and the four suggested answers. Choose the best suggested answer and write its *number* in the space provided. Base your answer *on the content of the passage, only.* The passages that the teacher will read aloud to you are found in the ANSWERS section, Part 2, at the end of this examination. [18]

1 What will take place this afternoon?

1 a field trip to a local theater
2 tryouts for the basketball team
3 a presentation by the principal
4 a meeting about a school play 1 ______

2 What is required to purchase one of these dolls?

1 a toy that can be recycled
2 a photograph of the child
3 a pediatrician's prescription
4 a monetary contribution to charity 2 _____

3 What did Steven Fisher discover?

1 the purpose of the wooden tablets
2 the importance of languages
3 the meaning of some writings
4 the first person to inhabit Easter Island 3 _____

4 What does this advertisement offer?

1 an opportunity to change careers
2 an opportunity to spend a vacation helping others
3 special rates for traveling around the country
4 special classes to improve your Spanish 4 _____

5 What information does the news report give?

1 the latest plan to reduce smog
2 the personal health dangers of smog
3 the daily smog level advisory
4 the rise in the level of contamination of crops by smog 5 _____

6 What kind of work are these volunteers expected to do?

1 provide food for the children's programs
2 work in the gift shop
3 provide transportation to the office
4 help with the cleanup 6 _____

7 What does the desk clerk explain to the tourist?

1 the itinerary for the trip
2 the hours of departure from the hotel
3 information about exchanging money
4 the price of 4- and 5-star hotels in Madrid 7 _____

8 What is unusual about this restaurant?

1 It never closes.
2 It is covered with exotic flowers.
3 It serves tapas.
4 It serves meals in the pool. 8 _____

9 According to this lecturer, where did the game of chess originate?

1 Spain
2 Persia
3 Arabia
4 India 9 _____

b Directions (10–15): For each question, you will hear some background information in English *once.* Then you will hear a passage in Spanish *twice* and a question in Spanish *once.* After you have heard the question, the teacher will pause while you read the question and the four suggested answers. Choose the best suggested answer and write its *number* in the space provided. Base your answer *on the content of the passage, only.* The passages that the teacher will read aloud to you are found in the ANSWERS section, Part 2, at the end of this examination. [12]

10 ¿De qué se trata este anuncio?

1 una fiesta en el restaurante "El gato negro"
2 dos famosas orquestas de música salsa
3 un disco compacto nuevo del cantante Gilberto Santarosa
4 un menú especial de la región 10 _____

11 ¿Qué es la Puerta del Sol?

1 una obra teatral madrileña
2 un museo famoso
3 un centro de mucha actividad
4 una época histórica 11 _____

12 ¿Qué dice el guía de la ciudad de San Juan?

1 Allí se encuentran varios tipos de arquitectura.
2 Ponce de León destruyó la vieja ciudad.
3 La playa está muy lejos de la ciudad.
4 Todos los edificios son modernísimos. 12 _____

13 ¿Qué se le ofrece al pasajero?

1 revistas internacionales para leer
2 programación para todos los gustos de música
3 unos ejercicios para hacer durante el vuelo
4 unas películas para niños 13 _____

14 ¿Qué es Nueva Dermis?

1 un programa que cambia lo que va a comer
2 un tratamiento para mantener sano el pelo
3 unas clínicas famosas que acaban de abrir en España
4 un plan para mejorar el aspecto de la piel de la cara 14 _____

15 ¿Qué información da este anuncio?

1 Quiere comentarios sobre el servicio ofrecido.
2 Informa donde recoger el equipaje.
3 Anuncia nuevas rutas y mejores precios.
4 Aconseja a los pasajeros que siempre vuelen por Avianca. 15 _____

PART 3

Answer all questions in Part 3 according to the directions for *a*, *b*, and *c*. [30]

a Directions (16–20): After the following passage, there are five questions or incomplete statements. For *each*, choose the word or expression that best answers the question or completes the statement *according to the meaning of the passage*, and write its *number* in the space provided. [10]

Alcanzando las Estrellas

Como muchos niños que se criaron en los años 50 y 60, Franklin Chang Díaz soñaba con ser astronauta. La guerra fría había hecho de la conquista del espacio una carrera en la que parecía que todo el mundo tenía algo que ganar, o perder. Cuando miraba hacia el cielo desde San José, Costa Rica, Franklin Chang Díaz no se imaginaba que sería uno de los primeros hispanoamericanos en viajar al espacio.

Cuando tenía 9 años, Franklin Chang Díaz construyó su propia nave espacial usando una silla de la cocina y una caja de cartón. A los 15 años, el ingenioso joven diseñó un cohete mecánico y lo disparó hacia el cielo con un pobre ratoncito amarrado a la cabina delantera. "Parecía que había subido muchísimo, llegando a la estratosfera, pero seguramente no llegó a más de 100 pies." (No se preocupen, el ratón regresó a la tierra sano y salvo gracias a un paracaídas.)

Hoy día, los cohetes y el espacio no son juegos de niños para este astronauta de la NASA. Chang Díaz, de 49 años, es el astronauta hispanoamericano más destacado de la NASA y el primer director latino del Laboratorio de Propulsión Avanzada de la NASA en Houston. En 1986, Chang Díaz se convirtió en el primer hispanoamericano en viajar en el transbordador espacial y ahora está trabajando en el proyecto más importante de su vida: el motor de una nave espacial que llevará a personas al planeta Marte. "El espacio siempre me fascinó", recuerda. 'Fue mi sueño".

Luchar por sus sueños es parte de la tradición familiar de Chang Díaz. A principios del siglo XX, su abuelo paterno, José Chang, emigró de la China en busca de una vida mejor en Costa Rica. Su abuelo materno, Roberto Díaz, vivió en los Estados Unidos durante 20 años trabajando con la marina mercante, antes de regresar a su país natal, Costa Rica. "Mi familia es una familia de inmigrantes", dice Franklin, cuyo nombre de pila fue inspirado por el presidente estadounidense Franklin Delano Roosevelt, a quién su abuelo Díaz admiraba mucho. "Mi abuelo siempre me dijo que si quería lograr mis sueños tenía que ir a los Estados Unidos".

Pero sus sueños no se iban a realizar tan fácilmente. Hijo de Ramón, un jefe de construcción, y María Eugenia, una ama de casa, Franklin se crió junto a sus cinco hermanos en una modesta casa colonial. A los 18 años, viajó a los Estados Unidos con sólo $50 en el bolsillo y, como muchos latinos, fue a quedarse en casa de un primo lejano que vivía con sus nueve hijos en un pequeño apartamento en Hartford, Connecticut. "Sé que yo era una carga para ellos, pero no tenía más remedio".

Aunque ya se había graduado de la escuela secundaria en Costa Rica, Franklin se matriculó en una escuela pública de Hartford para aprender inglés. Tan buenas fueron sus notas al hacer la secundaria en inglés, que se ganó una beca de un año para empezar sus estudios en la Universidad de Connecticut. "Esa ayuda económica era lo que yo necesitaba y de allí, mi carrera se encaminó".

Hoy, Franklin ayuda a encaminar a otros, aconsejando a jóvenes estudiantes sobre oportunidades en la NASA. Y tampoco quiere que sus hijos se olviden de sus raíces. "Él no habla conmigo si no es en español", dice su hija Lidia.

Aunque Franklin tiene una gran colección de trofeos y títulos, su orgullo es la Medalla de la Libertad que le fue otorgada por el ex presidente Ronald Reagan en 1986. "Ésa es la más importante porque reconoce las contribuciones de un inmigrante a los Estados Unidos", dice Franklin.

16 Desde su juventud se podía notar que Franklin Chang Díaz

1 se interesaba por el espacio
2 no tenía habilidad mecánica
3 quería trabajar con su familia
4 tenía muchos juguetes 16 _____

17 ¿Por qué es conocido Franklin Chang Díaz?

1 Viene de una familia con influencia política.
2 Tiene una larga tradición de científicos en su familia.
3 Llegó a dirigir un programa espacial norteamericano.
4 Era una autor célebre de ciencia ficción en Costa Rica. 17 _____

18 ¿Qué tiene en común Franklin Chang Díaz con sus abuelos?

1 Todos asistieron a la misma universidad.
2 Ellos eran de Hartford, Connecticut.
3 Comenzaron por trabajar en construcción.
4 Tuvieron que trabajar mucho para realizar sus sueños. 18 _____

19 Según Franklin, ¿qué le ayudó a comenzar su carrera?

1 Vio un programa de televisión sobre el espacio.
2 Ganó un concurso científico.
3 Recibió asistencia financiera para ir a la universidad.
4 Trabajó para una compañía de construcción. 19 _____

20 Según Franklin, ¿por qué es importante la Medalla de la Libertad?

1 Es necesario para luchar por la libertad de expresión.
2 Es la evidencia que los inmigrantes ofrecen mucho al país adoptado.
3 Simboliza el fin de la guerra fría.
4 Pone énfasis en la cooperación internacional. 20 _____

b Directions (21–25): Below each of the following selections, there is either a question or an incomplete statement. For *each,* choose the word or expression that best answers the question or completes the statement *according to the meaning of the selection,* and write its *number* in the space provided. [10]

21

Llevará su 'Amor' a Caracas

CARACAS (NTX).—El internacional cantante mexicano Emmanuel llegará el próximo 9 de octubre a la capital venezolana para promocionar su más reciente producción discográfica, informaron hoy fuentes locales del espectáculo.

Emmanuel promocionará en la radio, televisión y medios impresos de Venezuela su nuevo álbum **Amor Total,** del sello PolyGram, al que pertenece.

En **Amor Total,** que cuenta con la dirección del conocido productor, Manuel Alejandro, Emmanuel interpreta temas del género musical ranchero y baladas románticas como "Mi Mujer".

El artista mexicano también tiene previsto presentarse el próximo 12 de octubre en el programa **Sábado Sensacional,** uno de los más sintonizados por los televidentes venezolanos.

Which statement is best supported by this newspaper article?

1 Emmanuel will show his paintings in Venezuela in the fall.
2 Emmanuel will promote his new release in another country.
3 Emmanuel will begin his world tour in South America.
4 Emmanuel will play rock music in an outdoor theater.

21 ______

22

NOTICIAS

Una de las grandes cocinas de Barcelona

En el corazón del Puerto Marítimo barcelonés, esa zona admirablemente recuperada por la ciudad con motivo de los Juegos Olímpicos del 92, el restaurante Talaia Mar (Marina, 16. ☎ 93-2219090), participado y supervisado por El Bulli de Rosas, ofrece una de las mejores cocinas de Barcelona. Carlos Abellán, como jefe de cocina, y sus colaboradores Oriol Balaguer y Sergio Arola, junto con Artur Saques, como director de sala, están dando de comer con calidad y esmero asombrosos, en una zona de ocio y esparcimiento. Detrás está, sin duda, la «mano alagada» de Ferrán Adriá y Juli Soler, jefe de cocina y director de sala, respectivamente, de El Bulli.

Arola consiguió el premio en el último concurso de cocineros jóvenes celebrado en Vitoria. Oriol Balaguer es, por su parte, uno de los mejores reposteros de España. Tuvimos la oportunidad de disfrutar recientemente de un menú preparado por ambos. Desde unos mejillones de Cala Montjoi en escabeche ligero y unas sardinas marineras al vinagre de frambuesa, hasta unos admirables *calçots* rebozados en tempura al estilo japonés. Luego, la menestra de verduras y legumbres en ensalada (exquisita, diez sobre diez) y el consomé frío de Jabugo, flan de *ceps, gelée* de frutas y ensalada de oreja de cerdo y alcachofas, todo un prodigio. A continuación, el plato que obtuvo el triunfo en Vitoria: *espardonyes* con un *rissotto* de queso Idiázabal, espárragos y vinagreta.

Para terminar, la terrina caliente de foie-gras y ave con salsa de *periguex,* quizás lo menos conseguido del menú. De postre, raviolis de mango rellenos de tomate a la vainilla con sorbete de yogur y su puré de albahaca, también premio en Vitoria 96.

What is the topic of this article?

1 a cruise ship
2 the Olympic Games
3 a cooking class
4 a restaurant

22 ______

23

Estimado Sr. Woodard:

Deseo expresarle mi agradecimiento por su ayuda para que mi hijo Javier pueda estudiar el grado 12 en su escuela el próximo año escolar.

Estoy seguro que Javier se adaptará perfectamente a la escuela y creo que será un buen embajador español lo cual será demostrado por los resultados de sus estudios, a pesar del problema del idioma que tendrá al principio, —pero que lo superará con buena calificación.

Me comunica la Embajada de los Estados Unidos que necesitamos la aplicación FY-20 del Estado firmada y autorizada por el Colegio para poder realizar los trámites de visado y permanencia allí durante un año.

Con mi reconocimiento por todo ello, le saluda atentamente,

Javier Montoya

According to this letter, what is Mr. Montoya's son going to do?

1 work for the Spanish Embassy in the United States
2 study in the United States for one year
3 improve his English before coming to the United States
4 move permanently to the United States 23 ____

24

> Gracias por esta linda revista, e informativa, ya que tiene de todo un poco y para todos los gustos. El motivo por el que les estoy escribiendo es que la revista No. 14 no me ha llegado. Como podrán saber, mi correspondencia llega a una caja en el correo y yo no tengo problemas de que se me pierda. Por favor, ¿pudieran enviarme ese ejemplar No. 14, ya que nunca lo recibí? También quiero pedirles que escriban algo del cantante argentino Sandro. ¿Qué ha sido de él en estos años?
>
> —Alicia E. Mastrangelo
> Los Angeles, CA, EE.UU.

Why did Alicia write to this magazine?

1 to contact a pen pal
2 to request a back issue
3 to answer an advertisement
4 to renew a subscription 24______

25

ANUNCIOS

SOY UNA FRANCESA de 19 años y después de las vacaciones vendré a estudiar en la universidad de Cádiz. Ya que no conozco a nadie en esta provincia, busco amigos y amigas con quienes cartearme. Si eres de Cádíz o incluso de otra región, escríbeme. Te contestaré. Y luego, nos podremos encontrar personalmente y hacernos grandes amigos. Sigrid Beaupain. 149 rue du Fort. 59330 Hautmont, Francia.

What is this person looking for?

1 people with whom she could study Spanish
2 information about foreign study
3 someone with whom to correspond
4 a friend with whom she has lost contact 25 ____

c *Directions* (26–30): In the following passage, there are five blank spaces numbered 26 through 30. Each blank space represents a missing word or expression. For each blank space, four possible completions are provided. Only one of them makes sense *in the context of the passage.*

First, read the passage in its entirety to determine its general meaning. Then read it a second time. For each blank space, choose the completion that makes the best sense and write its *number* in the space provided. [10]

Antonio Banderas

Antonio Banderas nació en Málaga, España, en 1960, y se interesó por la actuación desde muy pequeño. Pero al ver en un escenario el musical *Hair,* Banderas decidió seguir una carrera artística. "Quiero hacer lo mismo que esta gente", se dijo. Era tal la energía que demostraban los ___(26)___ de la obra musical, tan moderno el espectáculo y los colores, que Banderas dio el paso. Al día siguiente creó su propio grupo dramático.

Durante cinco años hizo teatro clásico, estudió en la escuela de arte dramático, hizo teatro experimental hasta que se fue a Madrid porque estaba aburrido. Allí tenía un amigo argentino que le ofreció el sofá para que durmiera. Pasó seis meses en aquella casa, durmiendo en el sofá. Luego consiguió un trabajo y se mudó. En dos años en Madrid, Antonio ___(27)___ en once casas. Hubo ocasiones en que ni siquiera deshizo la maleta.

Un amigo de Antonio le dijo que él conocía a un director de cine que tal vez lo podía ayudar. Fue entonces cuando conoció a Pedro Almodóvar. Almodóvar fue a ver una función en la que trabajaba Antonio y le dijo: "¡Oye! ¿Quieres hacer una ___(28)___ conmigo? Es un papelito corto que te puede interesar". Antonio dijo que sí, y así comenzó una relación de trabajo que duró por siete años.

Antonio hace el "crossover" al cine norteamericano con la película "The Mambo Kings", que es la historia de dos hermanos cubanos que vienen en busca del sueño americano. Con esta película Banderas despertó mucho entusiasmo y se le consideró un amante latino. "Me imagino que eso ocurrió porque tengo el cabello oscuro y están buscando a un nuevo actor romántico como Rodolfo Valentino", dijo él.

En la actualidad, Hollywood mantiene a Banderas muy ___(29)___. Y por eso él trabaja mucho. Una de sus películas, "Desperado", tiene lugar en una población mexicana. Antonio se muestra capaz de ingresar a la liga de los héroes de acción y con un toque latino.

El actor asumió el dasafío más grande de su carrera al participar en la famosa película "Evita". Esta película es la versión cinematográfica del musical del mismo ___(30)___ creado por el compositor Andrew Lloyd Webber. La película, a un costo de 40 millones de dólares, fue dirigida por Alan Parker. Madonna interpretó a Eva Perón y Banderas a Ché Guevara. A Antonio Banderas le gustaría seguir trabajando en los Estados Unidos, un país que según él facilita el crecimiento de los artistas que tienen talento. "Esto está clarísimo. Es una lección que ya me aprendí".

(26) 1 jugadores　　3 productores
2 actores　　4 traductores　　26 ______

(27) 1 cantó 3 vivió
2 actuó 4 estudió 27 _____

(28) 1 película 3 escuela
2 canción 4 investigación 28 _____

(29) 1 desilusionado 3 triste
2 aburrido 4 ocupado 29 _____

(30) 1 título 3 horario
2 estado 4 concurso 30 _____

PART 4

Write your answers to Part 4 according to the directions for *a* and *b*. [16]

a Directions: Write **one** well-organized note in Spanish as directed below. [6]

Choose **either** question 31 **or** 32. Write a well-organized note, following the specific instructions given in the question you have chosen. Your note must consist of **at least six clauses.** To qualify for credit, a clause must contain a verb, a stated or implied subject, and additional words necessary to convey meaning. The six clauses may be contained in fewer than six sentences if some of the sentences have more than one clause.

31 The host mother of a Spanish exchange student in your school is having a birthday. The student does not know what to buy for her and is looking for suggestions. Write a note in Spanish to the exchange student suggesting an appropriate present.

In your note, you may wish to mention why the present you suggest is appropriate, where the student can buy the present, approximately how much it will cost, and your willingness to help the student shop. **Be sure to accomplish the purpose of the note, which is *to suggest an appropriate present.***

Use the following:

Salutation: [exchange student's first name]
Closing: [your name]

The salutation and closing will *not* be counted as part of the six required clauses.

32 Your Spanish teacher has given your class a homework assignment that is due tomorrow. However, you will be unable to complete it by then and want to request a time extension. In Spanish, write a note to your Spanish teacher requesting a time extension on this homework assignment.

In the note, you may wish to include the reason for the request (e.g., what you have to do tonight, why completing the homework is not possible), the amount of time you need, and what you are going to do to complete the assignment (e.g., work in the library, read more books, rewrite material). You may also wish to express your appreciation to your teacher for considering your request. **Be sure to accomplish the purpose of the note, which is *to request a time extension on the homework assignment.***

Use the following:

Salutation: Sr./Sra. [your teacher's name]
Closing: [your name]

The salutation and closing will not be counted as part of the six required clauses.

b Directions: Write **one** well-organized composition in Spanish as directed below. [10]

Choose **either** question 33 **or** 34. Write a well-organized composition, following the specific instructions given in the question you have chosen. Your composition must consist of **at least 10 clauses.** To qualify for credit, a clause must contain a verb, a stated or implied subject, and additional words necessary to convey meaning. The 10 clauses may be contained in fewer than 10 sentences if some of the sentences have more than one clause.

33 In Spanish, write a story about the situation shown in the picture below. It must be a story relating to the picture, **not** a description of the picture. Do *not* write a dialogue.

34 You have just returned from a trip to Spain and have discovered that you left something in your host family's home. In Spanish, write a letter to your host family to request the return of the item.

You <u>must</u> accomplish the purpose of the letter, which is *to request the return of the item.*

In your letter, you may wish to mention how much you enjoyed your trip to Spain and staying at your host family's home. You may then want to mention that you left something at their home, describe the item, and explain why the item is important to you. You may want to suggest how the item should be returned to you and offer to pay for the expense. You may also wish to thank the family for their help in retuming the item.

You may use any or all of the ideas suggested above *or* you may use your own ideas. **Either way, you must request the return of the item.**

Use the following:

Dateline: el 22 de junio de 1999
Salutation: Querida Familia
Closing: Con cariño

The dateline, salutation, and closing will *not* be counted as part of the 10 required clauses.

Answers June 1999

Comprehensive Examination in Spanish

PART 1

This part of the examination was evaluated prior to the date of this written examination. [24 credits]

PART 2

The following passages are to be read aloud to the students according to the directions given for this part at the beginning of this examination. The correct answers are given after number 15. [30 credits]

1. You are an exchange student in a school in Chile. On the morning announcements, you hear:

Hay una reunión esta tarde a las tres y media para todos los que quieran participar en la primera producción dramática de la escuela. No es necesario tener experiencia. Lo más importante es tener interés en el teatro y el deseo de trabajar con nosotros.

What will take place this afternoon?

2. You hear this advertisement on a television program:

En épocas pasadas todas las niñas recibían una muñeca de regalo. Y era el juguete favorito de la niña. Hoy, sin embargo, los promovedores de muñecas tienen algo nuevo para las niñas, la muñeca clónica. Los padres mandan una foto de su hija a la compañía que fabrica las muñecas clónicas. Entonces, las muñecas son hechas a mano y las hacen parecidas a la persona en la foto. Algunos pediatras norteamericanos dicen que estas muñecas pueden ayudar a los niños.

What is required to purchase one of these dolls?

3. You are listening to the radio and hear this report:

Steven Fisher de los EEUU es especialista en lenguas del Pacífico. Es la primera persona que ha podido interpretar la misteriosa escritura jeroglífica de la isla chilena de Pascua. El señor Fisher mostró el texto escrito sobre tabla de madera. Esta escritura se basa en 120 pictogramas de criaturas y objetos. Cuando los pictogramas y los objetos se combinan, forman glifos o inscripciones. El señor Fisher pasó seis años visitando museos que poseen las tablas y descubrió la llave de los glifos en el Museo de Historia Natural de Santiago de Chile.

What did Steven Fisher discover?

4. While traveling in Costa Rica, you hear this announcement on the radio:

¡Viaja, hermano, para echar una mano! Cambiar las clásicas vacaciones en la playa por un viaje para ayudar a otros es una buena alternativa para este verano. Nuestra organización ofrece la posibilidad de cuidar a enfermos, participar en programas de educación, de sanidad, de agricultura o limpieza medioambiental. Los participantes tendrán que tomar cursos para prepararse para todos los aspectos del viaje.

What does this advertisement offer?

5. You are in Santiago, Chile, and hear this news item:

En la ciudad, el señor Esmog está cada día más grande y poderoso. Señor Esmog crece con el humo negro y denso de los autos. Para combatir el esmog, las autoridades tienen una restricción de vehículos. De lunes a viernes, el último dígito de la matrícula determina cuando se puede usar un auto. Por ejemplo, si es martes y el número termina en 6 o 0, hay que esperar hasta mañana para conducir su coche, o tiene que usar transporte público. Todos los días hay dos números diferentes y menos contaminación. ¡Pobre Esmog!

What information does the news report give?

6. After viewing a program at the planetarium, you hear this request:

Los voluntarios hacen muchos trabajos vitales en el Museo y el Planetario. Se emplean voluntarios en la tienda de regalos. También dan programas para estudiantes, ayudan con exhibiciones y eventos, o proveen seguridad para las funciones de laser y mucho más. Por favor, infórmese en la oficina si usted está interesado. ¡Nosotros lo necesitamos!

What kind of work are these volunteers expected to do?

7. You are at a hotel in Madrid, Spain, and you overhear the desk clerk talking to a newly arrived tourist. The desk clerk says:

Si Ud. desea cambiar sus dólares en pesetas lo puede realizar en muchos lugares. Los bancos están abiertos los días laborales de 8,30 a 14h., y los sábados de 9 a 13h. Casi todos los hoteles de 4 y 5 estrellas pueden cambiar su dinero igualmente que las agencias de viajes y los grandes almacenes. Si Ud. lo desea, nuestra caja aquí le puede ayudar con ese servicio. Estamos a sus órdenes.

What does the desk clerk explain to the tourist?

8. You hear this advertisement about a restaurant:

El restaurante "Mesónde Oro" debe ser el único en la ciudad que ofrece comidas en la piscina. Durante el invierno, tapan la piscina con una alfombra y se convierte en comedor. El resto del año, la descubren sólo con propósitos decorativos.

What is unusual about this restaurant?

9. You are an exchange student in Spain. You hear a lecturer discuss the origin of chess. He says:

El juego de ajedrez nació en India en el siglo VI. Los jugadores usaban cuatro peones, un rey, un barco y un elefante. El juego tenía las mismas reglas que una verdadera batalla. El objetivo de esta competencia era capturar al rey. De la India el juego pasó a Persia y después a Arabia. Los árabes introdujeron el juego en África del Norte y en España. Desde España, pasó a Europa, donde el barco y el elefante fueron sustituidos por la torre y el caballo.

According to this lecturer, where did the game of chess originate?

10. You are listening to a radio station in Puerto Rico and you hear this announcement:

"El gato negro" en Joyudas, Cabo Rojo, anuncia su apertura y lo celebra este sábado, primero de agosto, con una gran fiesta de inauguración. Para ayudar a celebrar el estreno de este restaurante se presentarán al gran cantante de música salsa, Gilberto Santarosa y el grupo "Zona Roja". Tendremos disponible nuestro sabroso pollo asado, mariscos, empanadas de camarones, pescado y carne. ¡Les esperamos!

¿De qué se trata este anuncio?

11. You are with a tour group in Madrid and the tour guide says:

La Puerta del Sol, o solamente Sol, como la llaman los madrileños, es desde hace siglos el centro del Madrid popular. Es lugar de encuentro y de paso de muchos de los turistas y otros extranjeros que viajan a Madrid: unos se citan a la entrada del Metro, otros pasean, van de compras o simplemente, toman un refresco y observan a la gente desde un café.

¿Qué es la Puerta del Sol?

12. While touring Puerto Rico you hear this commentary by a tour guide:

En todas las Antillas, pocas ciudades muestran las etapas de su historia tan claramente como San Juan. A principios del siglo XVI, Juan Ponce de León estableció un pueblo que, en 1521, se convirtió en el Viejo San Juan. Hoy es uno de los mejores museos vivientes de arquitectura colonial, repleto de balcones de hierro y de calles de piedras. El fuerte de El Morro, al lado del mar, es un recuerdo del pasado militar.

A pocos pasos de la parte antigua de la ciudad brillan los hoteles modernos de la Playa del Condado. Hay numerosos casinos y espectáculos, y más allá, existen rascacielos y grandísimos centros comerciales en la parte nueva de la ciudad.

¿Qué dice el guía de la ciudad de San Juan?

13. While on a flight to Spain, you hear this announcement:

Con la confianza de ofrecerle lo mejor, Iberia ha seleccionado para usted 10 canales de audio donde podrá escoger desde los grandes músicos clásicos, hasta los últimos éxitos de las listas internacionales, así como música iberoamericana, japonesa...y mucho más. Para nuestros amigos más pequeños hemos dedicado un canal especial. Los auriculares para música le serán facilitados gratuitamente.

¿Qué se le ofrece al pasajero?

14. You are watching television in Barcelona, Spain, and you hear this announcement:

Pruebe Nueva Dermis, para rejuvenecer su piel sin cirugía. Nueva Dermis es un tratamiento moderno que renueva la piel, eliminando gradualmente las arrugas y las manchas de la vejez dando a la piel un nuevo tono joven y fresco. Además, Nueva Dermis es también un extraordinario tratamiento contra el acné y sus cicatrices, devolviendo al rostro un aspecto limpio y normal.

¿Qué es Nueva Dermis?

15. You are on an airplane that is landing at the airport in Mexico City and you hear this announcement:

El capitán y toda la tripulación espera que usted haya gozado de este vuelo con destino a la Ciudad de México. Y queremos recordarles que sus sugerencias y opiniones acerca de nuestro servicio son agradecidas. Queremos poder servirle mejor en el futuro.

En estos momentos nuestras asistentes de vuelo les entregarán un corto cuestionario para que usted haga sus comentarios. Antes de desembarcar, deje el cuestionario en el asiento. Gracias por su cooperación.

En nombre de todo el personal de aviación les damos las gracias por volar con nosotros. Esperamos poder servirles pronto.

¿Qué información da este anuncio?

PART 2

(1) 4	**(4)** 2	**(7)** 3	**(10)** 1	**(13)** 2
(2) 2	**(5)** 1	**(8)** 4	**(11)** 3	**(14)** 4
(3) 3	**(6)** 2	**(9)** 4	**(12)** 1	**(15)** 1

PART 3

(a)	**(16)** 1	**(b)**	**(21)** 2	**(c)**	**(26)** 2
	(17) 3		**(22)** 4		**(27)** 3
	(18) 4		**(23)** 2		**(28)** 1
	(19) 3		**(24)** 2		**(29)** 4
	(20) 2		**(25)** 3		**(30)** 1

PART 4

(a) Notes in writing

For each note, an example of a response worth six credits follows. The slash marks indicate how each sample note has been divided into clauses.

31 Angela,

¡Mira!/$_1$ Sé/$_2$ que a tu madre le gusta mucho navegar por la red./$_3$ ¿Por qué no le regalas un libro/$_4$ que le ayudará en las búsquedas?/$_5$ Hay una librería buena en la esquina de las calles José Ortega y Joan Miró./$_6$

Rosa

32 Sra. Rivera,

Lo siento./$_1$ No puedo terminar el proyecto para mañana./$_2$ Necesito dos días más/$_3$ porque los libros que pedí/$_4$ no han llegado todavía a la biblioteca./$_5$ ¿Podría entregarle el informe el lunes?/$_6$ Muchísimas gracias.

José Ángel

(b) Narrative based on picture/letter

For each narrative/letter, an example of a response worth 10 credits follows. The slash marks indicate how each sample narrative/letter has been divided into clauses.

33 **(Picture)**

Hoy es el aniversario de matrimonio de los Señores Rodríguez./$_1$ El Sr. Rodríguez tenía la idea/$_2$ de regalarle a su mujer una cena elegante./$_3$ Están en un restaurante de tres estrellas,/$_4$ donde el servicio es mejor de lo acostumbrado./$_5$ El camarero les pregunta/$_6$ qué vino quieren/$_7$ pero el señor no sabe/$_8$ qué escoger./$_9$ Cuando el otro camarero les describe las especialidades del menú,/$_{10}$ a la señora no le gustan. La noche especial será un fracaso.

34 **(Letter)**

el 22 de junio de 1999

Querida familia,

Ya llegué a casa/$_1$ y al deshacer mis maletas/$_2$ descubrí/$_3$ que se me había olvidado el collar de oro/$_4$ que Uds. me regalaron./$_5$ Me da mucha vergüenza/$_6$ tener que pedirles/$_7$ que me lo envíen./$_8$ Sé exactamente/$_9$ donde lo dejé./$_{10}$ Está en el tercer cajón del tocador cerca de la puerta. ¿Me lo podrían enviar por correo certificado, por favor? Les agradeceré mucho el favor.

Con cariño,

Examination January 2000

Comprehensive Examination in Spanish

PART 1

Your performance on Part 1, Speaking (24 credits), has been evaluated prior to the date of this written examination.

PART 2

Answer all questions in Part 2 according to the directions for *a* and *b*. [30]

a Directions (1–9): For each question, you will hear some background information in English *once*. Then you will hear a passage in Spanish *twice* and a question in English *once*. After you have heard the question, the teacher will pause while you read the question and the four suggested answers. Choose the best suggested answer and write its *number* in the space provided. Base your answer *on the content of the passage, only*. The passages that the teacher will read aloud to you are found in the ANSWERS section, Part 2, at the end of this examination. [18]

1 What does this announcement describe?

1 a job opportunity
2 a sale on leather goods
3 a lost item
4 a child looking for his parent

1 2

2 For whom is this advice most useful?

1 people who are tired after traveling
2 people who want to become more physically fit
3 people who want to book direct flights to their destinations
4 people who are afraid of flying 2 1

3 According to this program, what is now available for tourists?

1 a new vacation and travel guide
2 a free tour of Galicia
3 a video on regional cooking in Spain
4 a magazine about architecture in Galicia 3 1

4 What information tells you which bus to take?

1 the color of the ticket
2 the number of the bus
3 the city name on the front of the bus
4 the letter of the gate 4 2

5 What does this announcement describe?

1 a series of newspaper articles
2 an international art exhibit
3 a sale of recently issued stamps
4 a political demonstration 5 3

6 What are students expected to do?

1 stay after school for extra help
2 complete each lesson before learning new material
3 converse in the language as much as possible
4 read short stories and write short essays 6 3

7 What is a unique feature of this theater?

1 It shows films that appear 10 times larger on the screen.
2 It is built in a special location.
3 It only shows Spanish movies.
4 It is the oldest movie theater in Spain. 7 ____

8 What do you need to do to take advantage of this offer?

1 buy a magazine
2 make a telephone call
3 go to the place of business
4 send a letter 8 ____

9 What are passengers advised to do?

1 board the plane now
2 pick up their suitcases and go to customs
3 remove their carry-on luggage
4 get off the plane and enjoy a free lunch 9 ____

b Directions (10–15): For each question, you will hear some background information in English *once*. Then you will hear a passage in Spanish *twice* and a question in Spanish *once*. After you have heard the question, the teacher will pause while you read the question and the four suggested answers. Choose the best suggested answer and write its *number* in the space provided. Base your answer *on the content of the passage, only*. The passages that the teacher will read aloud to you are found in the ANSWERS section, Part 2, at the end of this examination. [12]

10 ¿De qué se trata en esta exposición de arte?

1 la vida de los conquistadores de Sudamérica
2 la cultura y la vida de la gente
3 la celebración de la independencia de estos países
4 el descubrimiento del nuevo mundo 10 ____

11 ¿Qué se ofrece aquí?

1 un postre
2 un cereal
3 una bebida
4 una comida 11 _____

12 ¿Por qué se les da estos consejos a los padres?

1 para que los niños duerman mejor
2 para que los niños aprendan a cocinar
3 para que los niños hagan más ejercicio
4 para que los niños se levanten temprano 12 _____

13 ¿Por qué recibieron una medalla estos animales?

1 porque eran animales que han desaparecido
2 porque eran animales que volaron al espacio
3 porque eran animales que ayudaron a muchas personas
4 porque eran animales que vivían sin contacto humano 13 _____

14 ¿Por qué fue importante el descubrimiento del dragón?

1 Fue un regalo del oriente.
2 Tomó más de cien años para construir.
3 Fue un juguete de la familia real.
4 Formó parte de un monumento famoso de Madrid. 14 _____

15 ¿Cuál es el mensaje principal de este anuncio?

1 Aconseja al pasajero qué medicinas puede llevar.
2 Informa dónde comprar los boletos.
3 Informa el número de asiento a cada pasajero.
4 Aconseja a los pasajeros qué hacer con las maletas. 15 _____

PART 3

Answer all questions in Part 3 according to the directions for *a*, *b*, and *c*. [30]

a Directions (16–20): After the following passage, there are five questions or incomplete statements. For *each*, choose the word or expression that best answers the question or completes the statement *according to the meaning of the passage* and write its *number* in the space provided [10]

Papel de la Tierra

No hay duda, la tierra todo lo da. Y un claro ejemplo es el papel que se fabrica en las montañas chiapanecas (una región de México) utilizando pétalos de flores, hojas de árbol, y otras partes de la vegetación como del maíz, bejucos, cepa de plátano, bambú, hasta se usa ropa reciclada.

Continuando la tradición del pueblo maya, un grupo de artesanos que se compone de mujeres y hombres mayas y mestizos, produce desde hace veinte años papel hecho a mano. También hacen libros impresos, pinturas e ilustraciones en madera. Estos artesanos son los miembros del Taller de Leñateros en Chiapas.

En este establecimiento, además de fabricar papel con fibras naturales y material reciclado, enseñan, por medio de sus publicaciones, el arte popular y la tradición maya de cerámica y manuscritos. Este grupo ha ganado tres premios por el papel hecho a mano, dos veces el Premio Nacional de Artesanía de México y también el premio Manos de México.

Las mujeres indígenas son las responsables de darle forma, color y vida a los diferentes tipos de papel. En el patio de una casa humilde se repite una escena sacada del año 800 de nuestra era. Una mujer maya, vestida a la manera tradicional, seca al sol pedazos de papel. Ella nos transporta a la elaboración tradicional de los manuscritos mayas que fueron destruidos por los conquistadores para eliminar su historia. El material con que se hacían los antiguos manuscritos era la piel de venado y la corteza de árboles. El papel era importante en la decoración de la ropa de los dioses y sacerdotes en los ritos sagrados. Para algunos este papel representa el espíritu indio, un espíritu profundo y sabio, lo esencial de la tierra.

En 1978 el taller editó su primer libro dedicado a los niños con un tema ecológico y para 1992 editaron "La Jícara", una revista-objeto de arte que representa lo mejor de la literatura maya actual.

Así es Chiapas, una tierra llena de milagros. El papel de los viejos mayas, que hoy llega a nuestras manos para escribir la historia de un amor o de una guerra, tiene origen en esta tierra.

16 El papel del que se habla en este artículo se produce exactamente en

1 una región de indios aztecas
2 la capital de México
3 la región de Chiapas en México
4 un museo nacional de México 16 3

17 La tradición de hacer papel a mano fue originada por

1 los indios maya
2 una familia con influencia
3 los artesanos europeos
4 un grupo de escritores 17 1

18 ¿Para qué se usaba este papel en esa civilización antigua?

1 para decorar las casas
2 para hacer juguetes de niños
3 para utilizar como moneda
4 para adornar ropa ceremonial 18 ____

19 ¿De qué trataba el primer libro editado por esta organización?

1 de un tema de ecología para niños
2 de cantos rituales
3 de las aventuras de los conquistadores
4 de la autobiografía de un jefe indio 19 ____

20 Además de hacer papel ¿a qué se dedican los miembros del Taller de Leñateros?

1 a vender premios hechos de oro
2 a preservar la cultura indígena maya a través de libros
3 a escribir poesías y canciones indígenas
4 a enseñar bailes típicos regionales 20 ____

b Directions (21–25): Below each of the following selections, there is either a question or an incomplete statement. For *each,* choose the word or expression that best answers the question or completes the statement *according to the meaning of the selection,* and write its *number* in the space provided. [10]

21

Colección Privada Nicoló Maria Albrizzi

Conviértase en uno de los coleccionistas de arte más importantes del mundo. Suscríbase a FMR. El verdadero valor de FMR, no se mide por su sensibilidad a la hora de mostrarnos las obras de los museos más importantes del mundo, sino por su capacidad de abrirnos las puertas de las colecciones privadas más notables, hasta hoy inaccesibles para los amantes del arte. Creada por el prestigioso editor Franco Maria Ricci, los reportajes de FMR ponen en sus manos arte en estado puro y en sus más variadas expresiones, y cuentan con la narración de escritores como Jorge Luis Borges, Octavio Paz o Umberto Eco. En FMR encontrará además, todas las exposiciones que se celebrarán en museos y galerías en los próximos meses.

FMR: LA REVISTA DE ARTE MÁS BELLA DEL MUNDO.

What is being offered in this advertisement?

1 a series of tickets to several museums
2 a series of art videos
3 a magazine about world art
4 a course about art appreciation 21 3

22

¡Somos los mejores del mundo!

¡Y todo el mundo lo reconoce!

Con su juego de excelencia, calidad, gallardía y entrega demostraron su superioridad...Nos colocaron en ¡el primer lugar del mundo!

La Asociación de Jugadores de Baloncesto de Puerto Rico y su Capítulo de Ex-Jugadores felicita a los integrantes del Equipo Nacional de Baloncesto Sub-22 por su gran gesta de ganar la Medalla de Plata en el Torneo Mundial de Baloncesto Sub-22 celebrado en Australia. Unete al recibimiento de nuestros héroes HOY a las 10:57 a.m. en el Aeropuerto Internacional Luis Muñoz Marín.

¡Contra todo y con todo, nos quedamos con la plata!

What is the purpose of this notice?

1 to honor a team for winning a worldwide event
2 to announce new economic ties with Australia
3 to publish the schedule of the basketball season
4 to dedicate a statue in the airport

22 1

23

Ha llegado un perrito de uno o dos meses a su hogar y usted no sabe cómo tratarlo. ¡Es tan delicado que hasta se asusta cuando le hablan alto! Sin embargo, éste es el momento ideal para imponer una cariñosa disciplina y enseñarle las buenas costumbres que mantendrá durante toda su vida adulta:

- Cuando usted no esté en casa, manténgalo dentro de una perrera o casita de la cual no pueda salir (a menos que usted lo mantenga en un patio grande con yerba y tierra abundante). Como los perros no ensucian el sitio donde descansan y duermen, aguantará sus necesidades hasta que usted llegue o lo saque al patio.
- Cuando ya tenga tres o cuatro meses, no le deje agua y comida puesta todo el día. Déle su comida por las mañanas y por las noches, y retírela cuando la termine de comer. La comida seca es la mejor para todos los perros. Si a él le resulta un poco dura, la puede ablandar con un poco de agua tibia.
- Si lo va a regañar, no le pegue. Tan sólo háblele con firmeza (un "¡No!" con tono enojado es suficiente) y golpee con un periódico enrollado el sitio donde hizo la "gracia".

What is discussed in this article?

1 how to teach a dog to "speak"
2 what to do with a stray animal
3 how to train a pet
4 when to vaccinate a puppy

23 3

24

Libros que ayudan a conservar la naturaleza

En 1947 el Dr. Herbert R. Axelrod fundó T.F.H. Publications, la más prestigiosa editorial de libros sobre animales domésticos del mundo. En 1991, el Dr. Axelrod creó una fundación que lleva su nombre. Es una institución sin fines lucrativos cuyos objetivos son conservar la naturaleza y promover el interés hacia ella. Los fondos de esta fundación son destinados a adquirir y proteger las tierras en la selva del Amazonas. Esta colección «Salvemos la naturaleza» que incluye 10 títulos, todos ellos de gran interés, contribuye a salvar la naturaleza en virtud de los acuerdos entre T.F.H. Publications y Editorial Hispano Europea, ya que más de un 20 por ciento de los beneficios de su venta se destinarán a la adquisición de tierras amazónicas para evitar su explotación y conservar su flora y fauna. Editorial Hispano Europea.
Precio aprox: 1.580 ptas.

How will part of the funds raised from the sale of these books be used?

1 to open pet shelters in large cities
2 to purchase land in the jungle
3 to plant new trees in Europe
4 to promote new industry

24 ___2___

25

Querida amiga

En este número de Mía te queremos proponer un plan diferente y verdaderamente original para que disfrutes las próximas vacaciones de Semana Santa. En las páginas del ESPECIAL VIAJAR, además de conocer nuevos y atractivos destinos, te ofrecemos un sinfín de opciones que invitan a practicar un deporte: montar a caballo, senderismo, parapente, submarinismo, paracaidismo, esquí, ciclismo. . . . Aprovecha esta oportunidad para aficionarte y practicar una actividad que hasta ahora no habías probado. Ya sabes, hacer ejercicio no solamente está de moda, sino que es bueno para el cuerpo y la mente. ¡Anímate y regálate unos días de ocio y descanso!

What information will the reader find in this issue of the magazine?

1 how to subscribe to the magazine
2 how to lose weight quickly
3 how to spend a healthy vacation
4 how to travel for less money

25 ____ 

c *Directions* (26–30): In the following passage, there are five blank spaces numbered 26 through 30. Each blank space represents a missing word or expression. For each blank space, four possible completions are provided. Only one of them makes sense *in the context of the passage.*

First, read the passage in its entirety to determine its general meaning. Then read it a second time. For each blank space, choose the completion that makes the best sense and write its *number* in the space provided. [10]

Cartagena, Colombia, el 30 de junio

Querido Kevin,

Tú no puedes imaginarte qué país tan lindo es Colombia. Es un país rico en cultura. La gente, la música y la comida me fascinan muchísimo. Sería difícil darte una descripción completa de este país en el espacio limitado de una carta. ¡Para hacerlo tendría que escribir un libro entero!

La semana pasada hicimos un viaje interesante. Fuimos a Barranquilla. No tuvimos tiempo para ir a Santa Marta. Yo quería visitar Santa Marta porque tiene ___(26)___ maravillosas para nadar. Y además allá podría tomar el sol, esquiar en el agua, e ir de pesca. Me encanta Colombia y mis padres me prometieron que en nuestro próximo viaje a este bello ___(27)___ pasaríamos varios días en Santa Marta.

En las dos semanas que hemos estado aquí, he visitado muchos lugares importantes. Ayer tuve la oportunidad de ver varias exposiciones de arte colombiano. Cuando entré en ___(28)___ vi una enorme figura de oro impresionante que llevaba un collar de esmeraldas enormes. Era un objeto increíble. Te mandaré una tarjeta postal con una fotografía de esta figura.

Antes de volver a los Estados Unidos me gustaría ver una corrida de toros. A mis hermanas no les gustan las corridas. Ellas prefieren ir de compras a las tiendas. Ellas siempre ___(29)___ muchos recuerdos para regalar a sus amigos. Durante estas vacaciones no sólo he visto muchos lugares interesantes. Sino que al mismo tiempo he aprendido muchas palabras nuevas. Me gusta mucho hablar español con mis amigos colombianos. Al volver al colegio voy a estudiar el español con más interés.

¡Qué carta tan larga! En unos pocos minutos salimos para cenar en el restaurante del hotel.

Bueno, Kevin, te veré en septiembre y te contaré más de nuestro viaje ___(30)___ a Colombia.

Tu amigo,
Juan

(26) 1 plazas 3 canchas
2 montañas 4 playas 26 4

(27) 1 castillo 3 país
2 camino 4 rascacielos 27 3

(28) 1 la corrida 3 el banco
2 el museo 4 la estación 28 2

(29) 1 compran 3 venden
2 pierden 4 prestan 29 1

(30) 1 fascinante 3 problemático
2 triste 4 aburrido 30 1

PART 4

Write your answers to Part 4 according to the directions for *a* and *b*. [16]

a Directions: Write **one** well-organized note in Spanish as directed below. [6]

Choose **either** question 31 **or** 32. Write a well-organized note, following the specific instructions given in the question you have chosen. Your note must consist of **at least six clauses.** To qualify for credit, a clause must contain a verb, a stated or implied subject, and additional words necessary to convey meaning. The six clauses may be contained in fewer than six sentences if some of the sentences have more than one clause.

31 A group of Spanish-speaking exchange students is coming to your school for two weeks. Write a note in Spanish to your Spanish teacher suggesting activities this group could do.

In your note, you may wish to include places to visit, afterschool activities, costs of certain events, things not to do, arrangements for transportation, and/or ways your Spanish Club could help. **Be sure to accomplish the purpose of the note, which is *to suggest activities this group could do.***

Use the following:

Salutation: [your teacher's name]
Closing: [your name]

The salutation and closing will *not* be counted as part of the six required clauses.

32 You recently heard that a friend's feelings were hurt as a result of something that you said or did. You did not intend to hurt his or her feelings. Write a note in Spanish to apologize to this friend.

In your note, you may wish to explain how you found out that your friend was upset or that his or her feelings were hurt. You may wish to explain that you are sorry for how your friend feels and that you want to continue to be friends. **Be sure to accomplish the purpose of the note, which is *to apologize to your friend.***

Use the following:

Salutation: [your friend's name]
Closing: [your name]

The salutation and closing will *not* be counted as part of the six required clauses.

b Directions: Write **one** well-organized composition in Spanish as directed below. [10]

Choose **either** question 33 **or** 34. Write a well-organized composition, following the specific instructions given in the question you have chosen. Your composition must consist of **at least 10 clauses.** To qualify for credit, a clause must contain a verb, a stated or implied subject, and additional words necessary to convey meaning. The 10 clauses may be contained in fewer than 10 sentences if some of the sentences have more than one clause.

33 In Spanish, write a story about the situation shown in the picture below. It must be a story relating to the picture, **not** a description of the picture. Do *not* write a dialogue.

34 A local television station is sponsoring a contest to identify a teacher in your school for special recognition. In Spanish, write a letter to the television station manager, nominating a teacher you know for this award.

You <u>must</u> accomplish the purpose of the letter, which is *to nominate a teacher for this award.*

In your letter, you may wish to identify this teacher, tell what he or she teaches, explain what this person does in classes, state how long you have known this teacher, state where this person teaches, and/or explain how this person contributes to your community.

You may use any or all of the ideas suggested above *or* you may use your own ideas. **Either way, you must nominate a teacher for this award.**

Use the following:

Dateline:	el 27 de enero de 2000
Salutation:	Estimados señores,
Closing:	[your name]

The dateline, salutation, and closing will *not* be counted as part of the 10 required clauses.

Answers January 2000
Comprehensive Examination in Spanish

PART I

This part of the examination was evaluated prior to the date of this written examination. [24 credits]

PART 2

The following passages are to be read aloud to the students according to the directions given for this part at the beginning of this examination. The correct answers are given after number 15. [30 credits]

1. You are in a department store in Spain and you hear this announcement:

   Apreciados clientes, en estos momentos deseamos informarles que en pocos minutos empezará una venta muy especial. La sección de accesorios en la planta tres pone a la venta todos los artículos de piel. Usted puede comprar zapatos, bolsos, carteras, billeteras y cinturones a mitad de precio solamente durante la próxima hora. ¡Apresúrense! ¡Apresúrense! ¡Ésta es una oportunidad única para nuestros clientes!

   What does this announcement describe?

2. You hear this advice being given by a radio announcer in San Juan:

   ¿Está muy cansado después de viajar por avión? ¿Quiere combatir esta fatiga pasajera? Pues, hay una manera muy simple de aliviar esta molestia. Frótese con mucha fuerza y energía la palma de la mano derecha durante unos segundos. Así estimula unos nervios directamente y dentro de poco tiempo se está combatiendo este problema de estar cansado.

   For whom is this advice most useful?

3. You are listening to a radio program about tourism in Spain and hear this information:

Ya está a la venta en kioscos por toda España. El libro de bolsillo más completo sobre establecimientos de las cuatro provincias gallegas: restaurantes, mesones, bodegones, casas tradicionales de comidas, hoteles, cafeterías, campings y alojamientos rurales. Contiene más de 1.000 fotografías a color. Además encontrará Ud. planos de las poblaciones más importantes. Hay una sección dedicada a informaciones complementarias: por ejemplo fiestas y ferias gastronómicas, vinos gallegos, etc. Busque Ud. la guía de la hostelería de Galicia.

According to this program, what is now available for tourists?

4. You are in the bus station in Mexico City and ask how to get the bus to Cuernavaca. This is what you are told:

Bueno, para comprar un boleto de autobús, tiene que ir a la oficina de información. Allí verá el horario de todos los autobuses. Es necesario averiguar el número del autobús porque no anuncian las destinaciones. Sólo se anuncia el número. Este número está escrito cerca de la puerta del autobús. No se olvide de recordarlo porque a esa hora siempre hay muchos autobuses esperando en la calle enfrente de la estación. Entonces, vaya a la taquilla y pida el boleto. Apresúrese porque para Cuernavaca no hay muchos. El último sale a las nueve.

What information tells you which bus to take?

5. While listening to the radio in Venezuela, you hear this announcement:

La Administración Postal de las Naciones Unidas anuncia la circulación de una serie de sellos muy especiales. El conjunto de noventa estampillas constituye una galería en miniatura de arte famoso dedicado a los derechos del hombre. Estos papelitos hermosos, con su texto e ilustraciones, han llamado la atención del público por su valor artístico y político.

What does this announcement describe?

6. On the first day in your Spanish class, your teacher says:

Bueno, saben que lo más importante en esta clase es hablar español. Cada día ustedes van a hablar conmigo y en parejas. Algunas veces van a trabajar en grupos pequeños. Quiero que todos se hagan responsables de contribuir a la conversación. Después de unas lecciones, ustedes van a crear proyectos orginales. Más tarde discutiremos algunas ideas para estos proyectos. Entonces, ¡empecemos a charlar!

What are students expected to do?

7. A friend is telling you about a new movie theater that has opened in Barcelona. Your friend says:

Ayer se inauguró en Barcelona un cine con una pantalla gigantesca. La sala de cine, situada en el puerto de Barcelona, ha costado 2.000 millones de pesetas. La sala proyectará películas OMNIMAX. En estas películas el tamaño de la imagen ha sido alterado. Ahora la pantalla de este cine es diez veces más grande que la de un cine convencional.

What is a unique feature of this theater?

8. While listening to the music channel on television, you hear this advertisement:

¿Te gusta la música para bailar? ¿Vas a menudo a las discotecas? ¿Quieres conocer más? Bueno, a continuación te vamos a hacer una oferta que no podrás resistir. Las primeras cien personas que manden una carta a ERES van a recibir el estupendo álbum "Música para bailar: volumen número uno", en el que incluyen temas de los mejores artistas de hoy. Y, ¡todo es música bailable como en las discotecas! Ya sabes, si quieres tener la mejor música de hoy, escribe ya a Editorial ERES, Apartado Postal 5-733, México D.F.

What do you need to do to take advantage of this offer?

9. Before takeoff at the Juan Santamaria Airport in Costa Rica, the pilot makes this announcement:

¡Señores pasajeros! Tengo que informarles que debido a un problema con el transportador de equipaje, tenemos que desembarcar del avión en seguida. Un autobús les llevará a la terminal. Allá recibirán un cupón para el almuerzo gratis en la cafetería de la terminal. Esperamos embarcar el avión dentro de una hora y media. Sentimos mucho la demora y las molestias.

What are passengers advised to do?

10. You are visiting an exhibit of Latin American art. The museum guide says:

Los artistas representados en esta exposición son del Perú, de la Argentina, del Ecuador y de Colombia. Ustedes van a ver fotografías, muebles, ropa y artículos de cerámica. El arte refleja la vida y la cultura del presente y del pasado de la gente en estos países. Lo más interesante de esta exposición es que representa la vida diaria de la gente.

¿De qué se trata en esta exposición de arte?

11. You are listening to the radio in Colombia and hear this advertisement:

Postobón lanzó al mercado de refrescos en Colombia su nueva línea de jugos, llamado "Chispa".

El producto, que estará disponible en todo el país, inicialmente tendrá cinco sabores: mora, mango, guayaba, tropical y naranja.

Durante su proceso de elaboración, Postobón emplea técnicas que lo convierten en un producto de óptima calidad, que conserva las propiedades de la fruta.

¿Qué se ofrece aquí?

12. You are listening to a Spanish talk show and hear this advice for parents:

De usted depende darle o no al niño algún dulce antes de irse a la cama para que duerma mejor. Científicamente no se ha probado que esto ayude al niño a dormir. Pero si desea hacerlo de todos modos, tenga presente las siguientes recomendaciones:

Primero, no le sirva al niño nada que contenga cafeína, por ejemplo chocolates, galletitas de chocolate, té caliente o té frío, ni gaseosas. Segundo, no le dé demasiado líquido antes de dormir.

¿Por qué se les da estos consejos a los padres?

13. You are listening to a documentary in Chile and you hear the narrator say:

Dieciocho perros, treinta pájaros mensajeros y cuatro caballos han sido condecorados por el Museo Imperial de la Guerra. La frase militar "Ellos también sirven" ha sido el motivo principal por esta extraña ceremonia. Estos animales recibieron la medalla de oro, que reconoce el trabajo de estos animales por ser muy útiles al servicio de la humanidad durante la Segunda Guerra Mundial. Estos animales buscaban y encontraban a las víctimas de este conflicto. Los periódicos cuentan de una paloma mensajera que voló 250 kilómetros con el mensaje de un accidente, y las personas fueron salvadas.

¿Por qué recibieron una medalla estos animales?

14. You are listening to the news in Spain and hear:

Una figura de un dragón se ha encontrado recientemente en la Casa de Cisneros, un taller de restauración en Madrid. Este dragón, antiguo símbolo de la ciudad, era parte de la famosa fuente de Cibeles, un gran monumento madrileño. Pero en 1864 se llevaron la estatua del dragón para restaurarla, y fue olvidada por muchos años. Ahora se planea devolver esta figura a su lugar original al lado de la diosa Cibeles.

¿Por qué fue importante el descubrimiento del dragón?

Examination June 2000

Comprehensive Examination in Spanish

PART 1

Your performance on Part 1, Speaking (24 credits), has been evaluated prior to the date of this written examination.

PART 2

Answer all questions in Part 2 according to the directions for *a* and *b*. [30]

a Directions (1-9): For each question, you will hear some background information in English *once.* Then you will hear a passage in Spanish *twice* and a question in English *once.* After you have heard the question, the teacher will pause while you read the question and the four suggested answers. Choose the best suggested answer and write its *number* in the space provided. Base your answer *on the content of the passage, only.* The passages that the teacher will read aloud to you are found in the ANSWERS section, Part 2, at the end of this examination. [18]

1 What does the airline offer?

1 better in-flight service
2 a free flight to Japan
3 more flights to Japan
4 more modern airplanes 1 _____

2 What is the purpose of this announcement?

1 to promote a new children's game
2 to warn parents of the danger of a toy
3 to advertise a new health clinic
4 to introduce faster mail service 2 _____

3 What did the message say?

1 The item you ordered is no longer made.
2 Your rebate is in the mail.
3 The company has changed its address.
4 The product you wanted is now on sale. 3 _____

4 What is being advertised?

1 health foods
2 a set of cookware
3 kitchen cabinets
4 a new heating system 4 _____

5 What kind of television program begins soon?

1 musical show 3 historical drama
2 game show 4 soap opera 5 _____

6 What is being offered to the public?

1 a new Latin dance club
2 a new chain of music stores
3 an easier way to purchase music
4 a chance to meet a Latin star 6 _____

7 Who would be most interested in this announcement?

1 those planning to take adult education courses
2 those wishing to visit their child's school
3 those seeking information about college
4 those hoping to work with schoolchildren 7 _____

8 What service has been initiated?

1 a safe way of sending credit information
2 a special new charge card for Spanish-speaking countries
3 a computer program for managing clients' financial records
4 a guarantee of the lowest interest rates available 8 _____

9 Who would be most interested in this announcement?

1 someone wanting a driver's license
2 someone with a medical problem
3 someone going on a field trip
4 someone looking for employment 9 _____

b Directions (10-15): For each question you will hear some background information in English *once.* Then you will hear a passage in Spanish *twice* and a question in Spanish *once.* After you have heard the question, the teacher will pause while you read the question and the four suggested answers. Choose the best suggested answer and write its *number* in the space provided. Base your answer *on the content of the passage, only.* The passages that the teacher will read aloud to you are found in the ANSWERS section, Part 2, at the end of this examination. [12]

10 ¿De quién se habla en este pasaje?

1 una autora
2 una deportista
3 una cantante
4 una ilustradora 10 _____

11 Según este anuncio, ¿qué hará el cantante Carlos Vives?

1 Va a cambiar su estilo.
2 Va a cantar en otras lenguas.
3 Va a dar más dinero a su comunidad.
4 Va a actuar en una película. 11 _____

12 ¿Qué discute el médico?

1 dónde hacer ejercicios
2 cómo seleccionar zapatos
3 la práctica del atletismo
4 el cuidado de los pies 12 _____

13 Según el agente, ¿qué puedes hacer si vas de vacaciones a Veracruz?

1 viajar a las ruinas prehistóricas
2 visitar muchos museos y monumentos
3 competir en un consurso de geografía
4 gozar de mucha acción en la naturaleza 13 _____

14 ¿Qué ventaja tiene este hotel?

1 Está en un buen sitio para negocios.
2 Está cerca del supermercado.
3 Está en un lugar tranquilo.
4 Está cerca de la estación de trenes. 14 _____

15 ¿Para quiénes es este anuncio?

1 para estudiantes interesados en ir a un concierto
2 para estudiantes que quieren visitar museos
3 para estudiantes interesados en participar en una obra teatral
4 para estudiantes que quieren aprender a dibujar 15 _____

PART 3

Answer all questions in Part 3 according to the directions for *a*, *b*, and *c*. [30]

a Directions (16-20): After the following passage, there are five questions or incomplete statements. For *each,* choose the word or expression that best answers the question or completes the statement *according to the meaning of the passage,* and write its *number* in the space provided. [10]

La carrera artística de Miriam Colón se puede describir en tres palabras: Teatro Rodante Puertorriqueño. Este teatro fundado por ella hace más de treinta años, es motivo de orgullo y es su destino, aunque algunas veces es un dolor de cabeza. El Teatro Rodante Puertorriqueño es para Miriam Colón, el drama de su vida.

A principios de los años 50, ella era una adolescente que estudiaba en la escuela Baldorioty del Viejo San Juan, en Puerto Rico. "La noche de la última función de la producción escolar donde debuté como actriz, me di cuenta de que me había enamorado del teatro", recuerda ella. Hoy, casi cincuenta años después, su entusiasmo es el mismo. Se le ilumina la cara cuando habla de sus grandes pasiones: la producción de teatro latino y el descubrir y estimular el talento joven.

Comenzó sus estudios en la Universidad de Puerto Rico. Poco después, el profesorado de esta universidad se dio cuenta de su gran talento y le dio una beca para que Miriam continuara sus estudios en Nueva York. Entonces Miriam tenía solamente 17 años. Más tarde estudió en el famoso Actors Studio. "Fui la primera puertorriqueña que estudió allí", dice con un brillo en sus ojos oscuros.

A principios de los años 60, Colón comenzó su carrera cinematográfica en Hollywood. "Imagínate cómo sería para mí, una jibarita de Ponce, el poder actuar junto con Marlon Brando: ¡Lo máximo!", dice. Luego se desilusionó con los papeles pequeños que le ofrecían a las actrices hispanas y decidió buscar otras maneras de satisfacer su ambición.

En 1967, organizó en Nueva York un teatro rodante similar al de la Universidad de Puerto Rico, que daba representaciones gratis a los pueblos de la isla. Ahora, todos los veranos el Teatro Rodante Puertorriqueño lleva funciones al aire libre y gratuitas a los vecindarios de Nueva York. Además de las presentaciones en inglés y español aquí se ofrecen también talleres para actores y Miriam Colón participa en todo.

Pero a pesar de los títulos honorarios, de los premios recibidos como actriz y como líder en la comunidad, Miriam Colón piensa que no ha tenido un éxito completo. "Producimos producciones de primera clase en el Teatro Rodante, la crítica es excelente, pero nos faltan miles de dólares para llevar al público una obra. Ojalá que en el futuro haya latinos que quieran producir teatro, en vez de esperar sombrero en mano, que ocurra un milagro", dice la célebre puertorriqueña.

El Teatro Rodante acaba de celebrar sus 30 años. Colón se siente satisfecha, y en cuanto al futuro dice, "Me gustaría encontrar una persona a quien le apasione el teatro y que tenga la voluntad necesaria para dirigir una organización artística hispana. Cuando la encuentre, me haré a un lado y le diré, 'Aquí está, mi hijo. Qué Dios te bendiga'."

16 ¿Cuándo descubrió Miriam su gran pasión?

1 cuando era muy joven
2 cuando tenía 50 años
3 cuando viajó a Nueva York
4 cuando terminó la universidad

16 _____

17 ¿Qué le entusiasma a ella todavía?

1 trabajar como profesora de lengua española
2 dar becas a los jóvenes con talento excepcional
3 actuar con el grupo de la escuela Baldorioty
4 crear teatro latino y animar a jóvenes actores 17 _____

18 ¿Qué empezó Miriam en el año 1967?

1 un teatro para los estudiantes de la Universidad de Puerto Rico
2 un teatro rodante que no cobra dinero por sus presentaciones
3 una escuela de música para niños
4 una compañía para construir nuevos teatros 18 _____

19 ¿Cuál es uno de los problemas que tiene que enfrentar Miriam Colón?

1 la falta de dinero
2 la crítica negativa
3 la falta de buenos actores
4 la gente que no habla español 19 _____

20 ¿Qué espera Miriam Colón en el futuro?

1 encontrar un edificio nuevo para su teatro
2 encontrar un nuevo líder para la organización
3 producir otro tipo de teatro en Nueva York
4 obtener más títulos honorarios de la comunidad 20 _____

b Directions (21-25): Below each of the following selections, there is either a question or an incomplete statement. For *each,* choose the word or expression that best answers the question or completes the statement *according to the meaning of the selection,* and write its *number* in the space provided. [10]

21

LA HIGIENE EN LA COCINA

■ Conviene tener dos termómetros: uno en el congelador (la temperatura debe ser inferior a los 32 grados Fahrenheit y otro en la nevera donde debe haber 40 grados para que los alimentos se mantengan frescos.

■ Utiliza las sobras refrigeradas al cabo de uno o dos días. Al congelar las carnes, no las coloques encima de las cubeteras de hielo porque los líquidos en el paquete podrían escurrirse y contaminar los cubitos.

■ Guarda los restos de comida que no contengan carne y los de las salsas durante menos de una semana.

■ Guíate con la fecha sellada en los paquetes que dice "úsese antes del día..." para los productos que se echan a perder como la leche. Estas fechas están determinadas por la agencia que regula la sanidad de los alimentos— para asegurar que el público los consuma frescos y sanos.

What is this article about?

1 the importance of balanced, nutritious meals
2 the need to wash frequently
3 the importance of handling and storing food safely
4 the need to keep an activities calendar in the kitchen

21 _____

22

¿Sabía usted...?

A esta fecha ya se han invertido más de $12 millones en restaurar la preciosa joya verde de Nueva York, el Parque Central, incluyendo un nuevo lago para pescar, el Discovery Center, donde usted puede alquilar la caña de pescar y comprar carnada, para pescar en el lago. Igualmente, finalizaron las obras de renovación del New York Botanical Garden, en el Bronx, a un costo de $165 millones. Este Jardín Botánico tiene una extensión de 250 acres.

Tompkin Square Park, que incluye canchas de "handball" y baloncesto, así como una elegante fuente, se ha reabierto, a un costo de $5.5 millones. En la zona de Queens, el área de Flushing Meadows - Corona State Park, ya está en pleno disfrute de una restauración que costó $5 millones. Ahí se encuentra el Unisphere.

Después de dos años de reparación, ya abrió el Aquarium Wildlife Conservation, donde se pueden ver delfines y leones marinos. Lo que antes fue el Brooklyn's Floyd Bennet Field, se ha convertido en un complejo municipal para educación y recreo. Este fue el primer aeropuerto municipal de Nueva York.

Desde este año, Brooklyn disfruta ya de una arena deportiva y un estadio, construidos a un costo de $70 millones, donde acaban de celebrarse los Juegos de Buena Voluntad.

What is this article about?

1 information for tourists on how to travel to important places
2 the lack of money for renovations in recreational sites
3 improvements made to recreational sites in New York City
4 the closing of various places of interest in New York City

22 ______

23

LIBROS

Por Elizabeth Subercaseaux

"HUMO DE TRENES"

Poli Délano. Editorial Andrés Bello. Cada día se escuchan más y más voces de padres preocupados por la escasa literatura para sus hijos adolescentes que se está escribiendo hoy día. Los chiquillos de 12, 13, y 14 años no leen y muchas veces no lo hacen no porque no les guste leer, sino porque no tienen qué leer. Pasan medio día pegados a la televisión y de libros, poco o nada.

Pero ahora tenemos una buena noticia. "Humo de trenes", novela para adolescentes, escrita por el reconocido escritor chileno Poli Délano, autor de novelas y libros de cuentos ("En este Lugar Sagrado", "Dos lagartos en una botella", "Sin morir del todo", "La misma esquina del mundo" y "Cuentos mexicanos", entre otros). Premio Casa de las Américas en 1973. Premio Nacional de Cuento en México en 1975. Ha publicado esta deliciosa novela para sacar a los adolescentes del hipnotismo de la televisión e invitarlos, en cambio, a la literatura.

Why did Poli Délano write this novel?

1 to show how a television series is produced
2 to encourage adolescents to read novels written for them
3 to inform teenagers about the pleasures of traveling by train
4 to provide parents with advice on raising adolescents.

23 _____

24

Señora Directora:

Nosotros los ciudadanos de Medellín, Colombia, nos sentimos muy halagados por el excelente artículo que su revista "Geomundo" de septiembre ha publicado sobre nuestra bella ciudad. Créanos que ha sido un honor el sentirnos incluidos en una de las revistas más importantes del mundo de habla hispana.

Por su intermedio deseo agradecerle a la periodista Olga Lucía Jaramillo y al fotógrafo Jorge Ernesto Bautista por su magnífico artículo y bellas fotografías.

Medellín siempre será su casa, cuente con nuestra permanente colaboración; no podemos olvidar a los amigos que entienden bien esta ciudad y realzan sus bondades.

Reciba un cordial y afectuoso saludo.

Atentamente,
Luis Bernardo Duque Osorio
Director de Fomento y Turismo
de Medellín.

Why did Luis Bernardo write to the magazine?

1 to compliment them for an article they printed
2 to find out how to contact the photographer
3 to renew his subscription for another year
4 to complain about inaccurate statements 24 ____

25

PARA OBTENER INFORMACIÓN CON FACILIDAD...llame directamente a las oficinas siguientes marcando el número 808 seguido de los números que aparecen al lado de los nombres a continuación:

Plan de estudios de música y arte	2333
Director atlético, y salud	2420
Presupuesto	2016
Programas comunitarios	2071
Plan de estudios para estudiantes de comercio	2236
Curso de estudios de inglés	2060
Curso de estudios de lenguas extranjeras	2073
Servicios de consejería	2035
Programa sobre estrategias de aprendizaje	2232
Servicios alimenticios	2040
Curso de estudios de matemáticas	2180
Servicios médicos	2050
Programa para estudiantes superdotados	2230
Centro de información para padres	2174
Programa de Pre-escolar	2039
Servicios estudiantiles, trabajo social, servicios psicológicos, habla, asistencia	2425
Departamento de investigaciones, pruebas y evaluación	2248
Curso de estudios de ciencias	2172
Curso de estudios sociales	2037
Oficina de información estudiantil	2438
Transporte, autobuses escolares	2057
Voluntarios	2013

These telephone listings are all related to

1 a hotel
2 an employment agency
3 a hospital
4 a school

25 ______

c *Directions* (26-30): In the following passage, there are five blank spaces numbered 26 through 30. Each blank space represents a missing word or expression. For each blank space, four possible completions are provided. Only one of them makes sense *in the context of the passage.*

First, read the passage in its entirety to determine its general meaning. Then read it a second time. For each blank space, choose the completion that makes the best sense and write its *number* in the space provided. [10]

La fiesta:
herencia cultural española

España está siempre de fiesta, más de 25.000 al año. Cada veinte minutos se celebra una fiesta en cualquier parte del país. Algunas fiestas se originaron hace muchos siglos; otras empezaron en los recientes __(26)__. Para los españoles cualquier razón es buena para tener una fiesta.

Ningún país del mundo tiene tantas fiestas, celebraciones, carnavales, corridas, desfiles, procesiones, y alegría en general para gritar, bailar, comer, __(27)__ y disfrutar de la vida. Los historiadores y autores clásicos son muy aficionados a estudiar este carácter de alegría nacional. "Descansemos hoy, necesitamos la energía para celebrar mañana. ¡Qué buena vida es ésta!" dicen los españoles.

Hay fiestas de origen histórico, pero la mayoría son religiosas, como las procesiones, y las ofrendas navideñas. Al mismo tiempo existen fiestas como la Tomatina, donde los participantes se tiran tomates como manera de divertirse. De hecho, España es una fiesta constante que empezó hace ya muchos siglos, y que no va a __(28)__ muy pronto.

Hay más fiestas que ciudades. Hay fiestas donde el motivo es expresar __(29)__ con música, risas, gritos, y ruidos tan altos que podrían dañar los oídos.

El antropólogo Enrique Gil Calvo escribió en su libro *Estado de Fiesta* que los pueblos mediterráneos presentan unas de las manifestaciones más coloridas del continente europeo. Para Gil Calvo, la fiesta es una expresión más de la capacidad humana de demostrar sus sentimientos.

Esplendor, alegría e imaginación popular son características básicas de las fiestas españolas. Las grandes celebraciones festivas que tienen lugar cada año tienen al pueblo como protagonista y como espectador. Las fiestas son parte de la herencia cultural, fenómeno propio de la vitalidad española. Hay celebraciones en diferentes lugares y en todas las estaciones del año sin ninguna interrupción. El viajero encontrará siempre el momento apropiado para asistir a algunos de estos eventos mágicos y espectaculares que alteran el ritmo cotidiano de la ___(30)___.

(26) 1 clubes 3 tiempos
2 puertos 4 pensamientos 26 _____

(27) 1 callar 3 seguir
2 criticar 4 jugar 27 _____

(28) 1 terminar 3 animar
2 interesar 4 nacer 28 _____

(29) 1 la alegría 3 la ayuda
2 la información 4 el miedo 29 _____

(30) 1 edad 3 sociedad
2 enfermedad 4 verdad 30 _____

PART 4

Write your answers to Part 4 according to the directions for *a* and *b*. [16]

a Directions: Write **one** well-organized note in Spanish as directed below. [6]

Choose **either** question 31 **or** 32. Write a well-organized note, following the specific instructions given in the question you have chosen. Your note must consist of **at least six clauses.** To qualify for credit, a clause must contain a verb, a stated or implied subject, and additional words necessary to convey meaning. The six clauses may be contained in fewer than six sentences if some of the sentences have more than one clause.

31 A Spanish-speaking classmate is recovering from an illness and will not be at school for several days. Write a note in Spanish to your classmate offering your help to him or her.

In your note, you may wish to include an expression of sympathy and/or hope for a quick recovery. You may wish to make a general offer to help or you may wish to suggest something specific, such as taking notes in class, providing homework assignments, or performing some errands that he or she needs to have done. **Be sure to accomplish the purpose of the note, which is *to offer to help your classmate*.**

Use the following:

Salutation: Querido/Querida [classmate's name],
Closing: [your name]

The salutation and closing will *not* be counted as part of the six required clauses.

32 Your pen pal is visiting from Spain. You would like to bring him or her to your Spanish class. Write a note in Spanish to your Spanish teacher about bringing your pen pal to class.

In your note, you may wish to include where your pen pal is from, when he or she is coming, and what he or she can contribute to the class. You may also wish to tell your teacher other details about your pen pal. **Be sure to accomplish the purpose of the note, which is *to write about bringing your Spanish pen pal to Spanish class.***

Use the following:

Salutation: Estimado Profesor/Estimada Profesora,
Closing: [your name]

The salutation and closing will *not* be counted as part of the six required clauses.

b Directions: Write **one** well-organized composition in Spanish as directed below. [10]

Choose **either** question 33 **or** 34. Write a well-organized composition, following the specific instructions given in the question you have chosen. Your composition must consist of **at least 10 clauses.** To qualify for credit, a clause must contain a verb, a stated or implied subject, and additional words necessary to convey meaning. The 10 clauses may be contained in fewer than 10 sentences if some of the sentences have more than one clause.

33 In Spanish, write a story about the situation shown in the picture below. It must be a story relating to the picture, **not** a description of the picture. Do **not** write a dialogue.

34 Schools are sometimes the subject of criticism. Your Spanish teacher would like to know your ideas about what is positive and/or good about your school. In Spanish, write a letter to your Spanish teacher discussing what is positive and/or good about your school.

You must accomplish the purpose of the letter, which is *to discuss what is positive and/or good about your school.*

In your letter, you may wish to mention and give some examples of how certain teachers, friends, classes, sports, art, music, drama, clubs, and/or afterschool activities make attending your school a good and positive experience.

You may use any or all of the ideas suggested above *or* you may use your own ideas. **Either way, you must discuss what is positive and/or good about your school.**

Use the following:

Dateline: el 20 de junio de 2000
Salutation: Sr./Sra. [your teacher's name],
Closing: [your name]

The dateline, salutation, and closing will *not* be counted as part of the 10 required clauses.

Answers June 2000

Comprehensive Examination in Spanish

PART 1

This part of the examination was evaluated prior to the date of this written examination. [24 credits]

PART 2

The following passages are to be read aloud to the students according to the directions given for this part at the beginning of this examination. The correct answers are given after number 15. [30 credits]

1 You hear a representative of an airline make this announcement:

Los gobiernos de los Estados Unidos y el Japón firmaron un tratado de aviación que nos permite ofrecer más vuelos competitivos y accesibles entre los dos países. Me complace anunciar que con este nuevo servicio extendido al Japón, ahora tendrá la oportunidad de llegar a su destino más fácil—y más rápidamente que antes. Este es el resultado de muchos años de negociaciones con el gobierno japonés para un servicio más rápido y más frecuente.

What does the airline offer?

2 While watching television in Spain, you hear this announcement:

Ayúdenos a retirar este producto del mercado. El juguete se llama "Osito Meloso". Hemos detectado que si un bebé se lo pone en la boca, podría obstruirle la respiración. Por esto, hemos decidido quitarlo del mercado inmediatamente. Si su hijo tiene este juguete, por favor, envíelo por correo certificado. Incluya una carta donde nos indique su nombre y apellidos, dirección completa con código postal y teléfono. Para nosotros la seguridad de su bebé es lo primero.

What is the purpose of this announcement?

3 You hear this message on your answering machine:

Lo sentimos mucho, pero la bicicleta que usted pidió la semana pasada ya no se fabrica. La compañía interrumpió la fabricación de ese modelo hace seis meses. Si quiere le podemos enviar una de otro modelo más moderno, pero tiene un costo adicional. O si prefiere le devolveremos su dinero sin ningún problema. En todo caso, por favor llame nuestra oficina para indicarnos su decisión.

What did the message say?

4 While watching a Spanish television station, you hear this commercial announcement:

Por más de 50 años, nuestra compañía ha traído a la cocina una línea completa de sartenes, ollas, y cacerolas de alta calidad, diseñada para un estilo de vida saludable. Nuestro exclusivo equipo de cocina se distingue por su bella construcción y por su rápida distribución de calor. Es fácil de limpiar. Cocina con un mínimo de energía. Es tan durable, que nosotros ofrecemos una garantía de por vida.

What is being advertised?

5 You are in Mexico watching television. You hear an announcer say:

El actor brasileño Guy Ecker será el protagonista central de "La mentira", la telenovela que se empieza a transmitir el próximo lunes.

"La mentira" es muy diferente. Tiene características interesantes, distintas a la telenovela tradicional; el tema es el drama de la vida moderna y los personajes tienen actitudes muy dramáticas.

What kind of television program begins soon?

6 While you are listening to some music on the radio, you hear the announcer say:

Apreciado aficionado a la música latina: ¿Recuerda cuando la pasión por la música latina crecía en todas partes ... pero la selección disponible era escasa y difícil de conseguir?

Nosotros mismos hemos sentido esa falta. En 1991 nosotros, los aficionados a la música latina decidimos formar el Club Música Latina, un club con una misión: ofrecer el mejor servicio a nuestra comunidad con la facilidad de comprar desde su casa la mejor selección de música latina.

What is being offered to the public?

7 The principal of a school is being interviewed on a local television channel in Spain. The principal says:

Se les invita a todos los padres a visitar la escuela de sus hijos. Todos los visitantes deben ir primero a la oficina. Todos los que deseen reunirse con un maestro o con el director de la escuela, deben llamar primero para hacer una cita. Si desea entrar en el salón de clase de su hijo, debe hablar con el director para que le indique la fecha y la hora en que lo puede hacer.

Who would be most interested in this announcement?

8 You are listening to the radio and hear this commercial:

El Banco de Santander ha iniciado en Colombia un programa de comercio electrónico seguro que permitirá a los consumidores comprar con seguridad en la red mundial. Esta nueva tecnología garantiza la integridad de la información de crédito que se envía por la Internet. Este servicio fue creado para la división de América Latina y el Caribe del Banco de Santander.

What service has been initiated?

9 While you are visiting a school in Puerto Rico, you hear this announcement:

Todos los jóvenes entre las edades de 14 y 18 años necesitan un permiso para trabajar. Los estudiantes de la escuela pueden obtener los formularios en la oficina de la enfermera o en la oficina del sub-director. El solicitante necesita que uno de sus padres o su tutor firme la solicitud. También necesita un documento que pruebe su edad y un certificado de salud de su médico o del médico de la escuela. Los permisos para trabajar serán procesados y otorgados en las oficinas indicadas.

Who would be most interested in this announcement?

10 You are listening to a program and hear this information:

Es joven, hermosa y bilingüe. María del Carmen Romero es una poetisa chilena que acaba de publicar su tercera antología de poemas, *Recuerdos,* en la que resaltan su simplicidad, su preocupación social y sus sentimientos románticos. Según lo confiesa al iniciar su colección de poemas, cada palabra que escribe es un escape. Se mueve entre el pasado y el presente, e intenta tocar la esencia de la vida. El libro está ilustrado con dibujos en negro y rojo. El negro simboliza lo concreto en su vida y el rojo sus sentimientos o los sentimientos del arte en relación a lo que escribe.

¿De quién se habla en este pasaje?

11 You are listening to the radio and hear this report:

"Tengo fe", el nuevo álbum del artista Carlos Vives que hizo popular por todo el mundo el vallenato, una música típica colombiana, ha batido records de venta en su país. El disco tiene temas escritos por él, con una mezcla de ritmos que mantienen la esencia de la música vallenata. Aunque todo el álbum es en español, el primer día vendió 300.000 copias en su país, lo que le valió seis discos de platino. Carlos Vives piensa grabar en otros idiomas para dar a conocer mejor su música por el mundo entero.

Según este anuncio, ¿qué hará el cantante Carlos Vives?

12 You are listening to the radio and hear this commentary from a doctor:

Probablemente, todos tenemos o hemos tenido algún problema con los pies, pero casi siempre limitamos su cuidado a cortar las uñas. El primer paso en el cuidado de los pies es la prevención, y realmente, es muy simple. Lavar y secar escrupulosamente los pies sólo requiere unos instantes. ¿Cuántos de nosotros tenemos esta rutina?

¿Qué discute el médico?

13 While you are at a travel agency in Mexico, the agent tells you about Veracruz:

Caer de una cascada de agua de 30 metros de altura, arrojarse desde un globo en pleno vuelo, navegar contra la fuerza del agua mar abierto o de los ríos, escalar montañas, andar en bicicleta, ¡todo es adrenalina pura! Gracias a su favorable geografía, Veracruz es reconocido por la Secretaría de Turismo como el estado de mayor actividad ecoturística.

Según el agente, ¿qué puedes hacer si vas de vacaciones a Veracruz?

14 A travel agent in Mexico City tells you about a hotel. The travel agent says:

Por encontrarse en un lugar céntrico, el hotel Bristol satisface las necesidades de los ejecutivos más exigentes. Situado a sólo dos calles del Paseo de la Reforma, detrás de la embajada de Estados Unidos y a un paso de la Zona Rosa—con sus tiendas, restaurantes y boutiques—usted encontrará los bancos y comercios más importantes para resolver todos sus asuntos.

¿Qué ventaja tiene este hotel?

15 You are an exchange student in Valencia, Spain. While visiting your host's school, you hear this announcement:

¿Tienes talentos artísticos? ¿Te gustaría actuar? Si respondiste que sí a estas dos preguntas, ven a nuestra reunión esta tarde. Este año vamos a presentar una obra del escritor español Alejandro Casona. Necesitamos todo tipo de ayuda ... y si no quieres actuar, puedes ayudar con el diseño del escenario o del programa, la venta de boletos y muchas otras actividades.

¿Para quiénes es este anuncio?

PART 2

(1) 3	**(4)** 2	**(7)** 2	**(10)** 1	**(13)** 4
(2) 2	**(5)** 4	**(8)** 1	**(11)** 2	**(14)** 1
(3) 1	**(6)** 3	**(9)** 4	**(12)** 4	**(15)** 3

PART 3

(a)	(b)	(c)
(16) 1	**(21)** 3	**(26)** 3
(17) 4	**(22)** 3	**(27)** 4
(18) 2	**(23)** 2	**(28)** 1
(19) 1	**(24)** 1	**(29)** 1
(20) 2	**(25)** 4	**(30)** 3

PART 4

(a) Notes in writing

For each note, an example of a response worth six credits follows. The slash marks indicate how each sample note has been divided into clauses.

31 Querido Carlos,

Oí/$_1$ que estás enfermo./$_2$ ¡Lo siento!/$_3$ ¿Te puedo ayudar con algo?/$_4$ Si quieres,/$_5$ te traigo la tarea y los apuntes./$_6$ Dime cuando puedo ir a tu casa.

José

32 Estimada Profesora,

Mi amiga Carolina acaba de llegar de Aravaca./$_1$ Quiere visitar nuestra clase./$_2$ Ella puede hablar de su país y de las costumbres españolas./$_3$ ¿Cuándo le parece mejor/$_4$ que venga a la clase?/$_5$ Estará acá por dos semanas./$_6$ Le hablaré a Ud. más tarde.

Teresa

(b) Narrative based on picture/letter

For each narrative/letter, an example of a response worth 10 credits follows. The slash marks indicate how each sample narrative/letter has been divided into clauses.

33. (Picture)

Fernando e Isabel están muy preocupados./$_1$ Acaban de tomar un examen muy difícil en la clase de ciencias./$_2$ Fernando se queja/$_3$ porque no tuvo bastante tiempo/$_4$ para terminar el examen./$_5$ Pero Isabel estudió mucho/$_6$ y no le pareció tan difícil./$_7$ El siempre ha tenido más problemas con las ciencias./$_8$ Ellos saben/$_9$ que van a recibir sus notas mañana./$_{10}$ Isabel dormirá muy tranquila.

34. (Letter)

el 20 de junio de 2000

Sra. Soto,

Aunque existen muchos problemas en nuestro colegio,/$_1$ en mi opinión hay muchas cosas buenas también./$_2$ Por ejemplo, aunque hay mucha construcción,/$_3$ vamos a tener muchas clases nuevas y una nueva biblioteca./$_4$ Además, nuestra escuela hoy día ofrece muchas actividades,/$_5$ y con las renovaciones podríamos tener más conciertos, partidos y bailes./$_6$ Hay muchos estudiantes aquí/$_7$ que pueden tomar cursos para crédito universitario./$_8$ Tenemos también un buen equipo de baloncesto/$_9$ que es conocido en todo el estado./$_{10}$ Me gusta asistir a este colegio.

Sinceramente,

Miguel

Notes

Notes

Notes